T0180808

Communications
in Computer and Information Science 2117

Rationale

The CCIS series is devoted to the publication of proceedings of computer science conferences. Its aim is to efficiently disseminate original research results in informatics in printed and electronic form. While the focus is on publication of peer-reviewed full papers presenting mature work, inclusion of reviewed short papers reporting on work in progress is welcome, too. Besides globally relevant meetings with internationally representative program committees guaranteeing a strict peer-reviewing and paper selection process, conferences run by societies or of high regional or national relevance are also considered for publication.

Topics

The topical scope of CCIS spans the entire spectrum of informatics ranging from foundational topics in the theory of computing to information and communications science and technology and a broad variety of interdisciplinary application fields.

Information for Volume Editors and Authors

Publication in CCIS is free of charge. No royalties are paid, however, we offer registered conference participants temporary free access to the online version of the conference proceedings on SpringerLink (http://link.springer.com) by means of an http referrer from the conference website and/or a number of complimentary printed copies, as specified in the official acceptance email of the event.

CCIS proceedings can be published in time for distribution at conferences or as postproceedings, and delivered in the form of printed books and/or electronically as USBs and/or e-content licenses for accessing proceedings at SpringerLink. Furthermore, CCIS proceedings are included in the CCIS electronic book series hosted in the SpringerLink digital library at http://link.springer.com/bookseries/7899. Conferences publishing in CCIS are allowed to use Online Conference Service (OCS) for managing the whole proceedings lifecycle (from submission and reviewing to preparing for publication) free of charge.

Publication process

The language of publication is exclusively English. Authors publishing in CCIS have to sign the Springer CCIS copyright transfer form, however, they are free to use their material published in CCIS for substantially changed, more elaborate subsequent publications elsewhere. For the preparation of the camera-ready papers/files, authors have to strictly adhere to the Springer CCIS Authors' Instructions and are strongly encouraged to use the CCIS LaTeX style files or templates.

Abstracting/Indexing

CCIS is abstracted/indexed in DBLP, Google Scholar, EI-Compendex, Mathematical Reviews, SCImago, Scopus. CCIS volumes are also submitted for the inclusion in ISI Proceedings.

How to start

To start the evaluation of your proposal for inclusion in the CCIS series, please send an e-mail to ccis@springer.com.

Constantine Stephanidis · Margherita Antona ·
Stavroula Ntoa · Gavriel Salvendy
Editors

HCI International 2024 Posters

26th International Conference
on Human-Computer Interaction, HCII 2024
Washington, DC, USA, June 29 – July 4, 2024
Proceedings, Part IV

 Springer

Editors
Constantine Stephanidis
University of Crete and Foundation for
Research and Technology - Hellas (FORTH)
Heraklion, Crete, Greece

Margherita Antona
Foundation for Research and Technology -
Hellas (FORTH)
Heraklion, Crete, Greece

Stavroula Ntoa
Foundation for Research
and Technology - Hellas (FORTH)
Heraklion, Crete, Greece

Gavriel Salvendy
University of Central Florida
Orlando, FL, USA

ISSN 1865-0929   ISSN 1865-0937 (electronic)
Communications in Computer and Information Science
ISBN 978-3-031-61952-6   ISBN 978-3-031-61953-3 (eBook)
https://doi.org/10.1007/978-3-031-61953-3

This Springer imprint is published by the registered company Springer Nature Switzerland AG
The registered company address is: Gewerbestrasse 11, 6330 Cham, Switzerland

If disposing of this product, please recycle the paper.

Foreword

This year we celebrate 40 years since the establishment of the HCI International (HCII) Conference, which has been a hub for presenting groundbreaking research and novel ideas and collaboration for people from all over the world.

The HCII conference was founded in 1984 by Prof. Gavriel Salvendy (Purdue University, USA, Tsinghua University, P.R. China, and University of Central Florida, USA) and the first event of the series, "1st USA-Japan Conference on Human-Computer Interaction", was held in Honolulu, Hawaii, USA, 18–20 August. Since then, HCI International is held jointly with several Thematic Areas and Affiliated Conferences, with each one under the auspices of a distinguished international Program Board and under one management and one registration. Twenty-six HCI International Conferences have been organized so far (every two years until 2013, and annually thereafter).

Over the years, this conference has served as a platform for scholars, researchers, industry experts and students to exchange ideas, connect, and address challenges in the ever-evolving HCI field. Throughout these 40 years, the conference has evolved itself, adapting to new technologies and emerging trends, while staying committed to its core mission of advancing knowledge and driving change.

As we celebrate this milestone anniversary, we reflect on the contributions of its founding members and appreciate the commitment of its current and past Affiliated Conference Program Board Chairs and members. We are also thankful to all past conference attendees who have shaped this community into what it is today.

The 26th International Conference on Human-Computer Interaction, HCI International 2024 (HCII 2024), was held as a 'hybrid' event at the Washington Hilton Hotel, Washington, DC, USA, during 29 June – 4 July 2024. It incorporated the 21 thematic areas and affiliated conferences listed below.

A total of 5108 individuals from academia, research institutes, industry, and government agencies from 85 countries submitted contributions, and 1271 papers and 309 posters were included in the volumes of the proceedings that were published just before the start of the conference, these are listed below. The contributions thoroughly cover the entire field of human-computer interaction, addressing major advances in knowledge and effective use of computers in a variety of application areas. These papers provide academics, researchers, engineers, scientists, practitioners and students with state-of-the-art information on the most recent advances in HCI.

The HCI International (HCII) conference also offers the option of presenting 'Late Breaking Work', and this applies both for papers and posters, with corresponding volumes of proceedings that will be published after the conference. Full papers will be included in the 'HCII 2024 - Late Breaking Papers' volumes of the proceedings to be published in the Springer LNCS series, while 'Poster Extended Abstracts' will be included as short research papers in the 'HCII 2024 - Late Breaking Posters' volumes to be published in the Springer CCIS series.

I would like to thank the Program Board Chairs and the members of the Program Boards of all thematic areas and affiliated conferences for their contribution towards the high scientific quality and overall success of the HCI International 2024 conference. Their manifold support in terms of paper reviewing (single-blind review process, with a minimum of two reviews per submission), session organization and their willingness to act as goodwill ambassadors for the conference is most highly appreciated.

This conference would not have been possible without the continuous and unwavering support and advice of Gavriel Salvendy, founder, General Chair Emeritus, and Scientific Advisor. For his outstanding efforts, I would like to express my sincere appreciation to Abbas Moallem, Communications Chair and Editor of HCI International News.

July 2024   Constantine Stephanidis

HCI International 2024 Thematic Areas
and Affiliated Conferences

- HCI: Human-Computer Interaction Thematic Area
- HIMI: Human Interface and the Management of Information Thematic Area
- EPCE: 21st International Conference on Engineering Psychology and Cognitive Ergonomics
- AC: 18th International Conference on Augmented Cognition
- UAHCI: 18th International Conference on Universal Access in Human-Computer Interaction
- CCD: 16th International Conference on Cross-Cultural Design
- SCSM: 16th International Conference on Social Computing and Social Media
- VAMR: 16th International Conference on Virtual, Augmented and Mixed Reality
- DHM: 15th International Conference on Digital Human Modeling & Applications in Health, Safety, Ergonomics & Risk Management
- DUXU: 13th International Conference on Design, User Experience and Usability
- C&C: 12th International Conference on Culture and Computing
- DAPI: 12th International Conference on Distributed, Ambient and Pervasive Interactions
- HCIBGO: 11th International Conference on HCI in Business, Government and Organizations
- LCT: 11th International Conference on Learning and Collaboration Technologies
- ITAP: 10th International Conference on Human Aspects of IT for the Aged Population
- AIS: 6th International Conference on Adaptive Instructional Systems
- HCI-CPT: 6th International Conference on HCI for Cybersecurity, Privacy and Trust
- HCI-Games: 6th International Conference on HCI in Games
- MobiTAS: 6th International Conference on HCI in Mobility, Transport and Automotive Systems
- AI-HCI: 5th International Conference on Artificial Intelligence in HCI
- MOBILE: 5th International Conference on Human-Centered Design, Operation and Evaluation of Mobile Communications

List of Conference Proceedings Volumes Appearing Before the Conference

1. LNCS 14684, Human-Computer Interaction: Part I, edited by Masaaki Kurosu and Ayako Hashizume
2. LNCS 14685, Human-Computer Interaction: Part II, edited by Masaaki Kurosu and Ayako Hashizume
3. LNCS 14686, Human-Computer Interaction: Part III, edited by Masaaki Kurosu and Ayako Hashizume
4. LNCS 14687, Human-Computer Interaction: Part IV, edited by Masaaki Kurosu and Ayako Hashizume
5. LNCS 14688, Human-Computer Interaction: Part V, edited by Masaaki Kurosu and Ayako Hashizume
6. LNCS 14689, Human Interface and the Management of Information: Part I, edited by Hirohiko Mori and Yumi Asahi
7. LNCS 14690, Human Interface and the Management of Information: Part II, edited by Hirohiko Mori and Yumi Asahi
8. LNCS 14691, Human Interface and the Management of Information: Part III, edited by Hirohiko Mori and Yumi Asahi
9. LNAI 14692, Engineering Psychology and Cognitive Ergonomics: Part I, edited by Don Harris and Wen-Chin Li
10. LNAI 14693, Engineering Psychology and Cognitive Ergonomics: Part II, edited by Don Harris and Wen-Chin Li
11. LNAI 14694, Augmented Cognition, Part I, edited by Dylan D. Schmorrow and Cali M. Fidopiastis
12. LNAI 14695, Augmented Cognition, Part II, edited by Dylan D. Schmorrow and Cali M. Fidopiastis
13. LNCS 14696, Universal Access in Human-Computer Interaction: Part I, edited by Margherita Antona and Constantine Stephanidis
14. LNCS 14697, Universal Access in Human-Computer Interaction: Part II, edited by Margherita Antona and Constantine Stephanidis
15. LNCS 14698, Universal Access in Human-Computer Interaction: Part III, edited by Margherita Antona and Constantine Stephanidis
16. LNCS 14699, Cross-Cultural Design: Part I, edited by Pei-Luen Patrick Rau
17. LNCS 14700, Cross-Cultural Design: Part II, edited by Pei-Luen Patrick Rau
18. LNCS 14701, Cross-Cultural Design: Part III, edited by Pei-Luen Patrick Rau
19. LNCS 14702, Cross-Cultural Design: Part IV, edited by Pei-Luen Patrick Rau
20. LNCS 14703, Social Computing and Social Media: Part I, edited by Adela Coman and Simona Vasilache
21. LNCS 14704, Social Computing and Social Media: Part II, edited by Adela Coman and Simona Vasilache
22. LNCS 14705, Social Computing and Social Media: Part III, edited by Adela Coman and Simona Vasilache

23. LNCS 14706, Virtual, Augmented and Mixed Reality: Part I, edited by Jessie Y. C. Chen and Gino Fragomeni

24. LNCS 14707, Virtual, Augmented and Mixed Reality: Part II, edited by Jessie Y. C. Chen and Gino Fragomeni

25. LNCS 14708, Virtual, Augmented and Mixed Reality: Part III, edited by Jessie Y. C. Chen and Gino Fragomeni

26. LNCS 14709, Digital Human Modeling and Applications in Health, Safety, Ergonomics and Risk Management: Part I, edited by Vincent G. Duffy

27. LNCS 14710, Digital Human Modeling and Applications in Health, Safety, Ergonomics and Risk Management: Part II, edited by Vincent G. Duffy

28. LNCS 14711, Digital Human Modeling and Applications in Health, Safety, Ergonomics and Risk Management: Part III, edited by Vincent G. Duffy

29. LNCS 14712, Design, User Experience, and Usability: Part I, edited by Aaron Marcus, Elizabeth Rosenzweig and Marcelo M. Soares

30. LNCS 14713, Design, User Experience, and Usability: Part II, edited by Aaron Marcus, Elizabeth Rosenzweig and Marcelo M. Soares

31. LNCS 14714, Design, User Experience, and Usability: Part III, edited by Aaron Marcus, Elizabeth Rosenzweig and Marcelo M. Soares

32. LNCS 14715, Design, User Experience, and Usability: Part IV, edited by Aaron Marcus, Elizabeth Rosenzweig and Marcelo M. Soares

33. LNCS 14716, Design, User Experience, and Usability: Part V, edited by Aaron Marcus, Elizabeth Rosenzweig and Marcelo M. Soares

34. LNCS 14717, Culture and Computing, edited by Matthias Rauterberg

35. LNCS 14718, Distributed, Ambient and Pervasive Interactions: Part I, edited by Norbert A. Streitz and Shin'ichi Konomi

36. LNCS 14719, Distributed, Ambient and Pervasive Interactions: Part II, edited by Norbert A. Streitz and Shin'ichi Konomi

37. LNCS 14720, HCI in Business, Government and Organizations: Part I, edited by Fiona Fui-Hoon Nah and Keng Leng Siau

38. LNCS 14721, HCI in Business, Government and Organizations: Part II, edited by Fiona Fui-Hoon Nah and Keng Leng Siau

39. LNCS 14722, Learning and Collaboration Technologies: Part I, edited by Panayiotis Zaphiris and Andri Ioannou

40. LNCS 14723, Learning and Collaboration Technologies: Part II, edited by Panayiotis Zaphiris and Andri Ioannou

41. LNCS 14724, Learning and Collaboration Technologies: Part III, edited by Panayiotis Zaphiris and Andri Ioannou

42. LNCS 14725, Human Aspects of IT for the Aged Population: Part I, edited by Qin Gao and Jia Zhou

43. LNCS 14726, Human Aspects of IT for the Aged Population: Part II, edited by Qin Gao and Jia Zhou

44. LNCS 14727, Adaptive Instructional System, edited by Robert A. Sottilare and Jessica Schwarz

45. LNCS 14728, HCI for Cybersecurity, Privacy and Trust: Part I, edited by Abbas Moallem

46. LNCS 14729, HCI for Cybersecurity, Privacy and Trust: Part II, edited by Abbas Moallem

47. LNCS 14730, HCI in Games: Part I, edited by Xiaowen Fang
48. LNCS 14731, HCI in Games: Part II, edited by Xiaowen Fang
49. LNCS 14732, HCI in Mobility, Transport and Automotive Systems: Part I, edited by Heidi Krömker
50. LNCS 14733, HCI in Mobility, Transport and Automotive Systems: Part II, edited by Heidi Krömker
51. LNAI 14734, Artificial Intelligence in HCI: Part I, edited by Helmut Degen and Stavroula Ntoa
52. LNAI 14735, Artificial Intelligence in HCI: Part II, edited by Helmut Degen and Stavroula Ntoa
53. LNAI 14736, Artificial Intelligence in HCI: Part III, edited by Helmut Degen and Stavroula Ntoa
54. LNCS 14737, Design, Operation and Evaluation of Mobile Communications: Part I, edited by June Wei and George Margetis
55. LNCS 14738, Design, Operation and Evaluation of Mobile Communications: Part II, edited by June Wei and George Margetis
56. CCIS 2114, HCI International 2024 Posters - Part I, edited by Constantine Stephanidis, Margherita Antona, Stavroula Ntoa and Gavriel Salvendy
57. CCIS 2115, HCI International 2024 Posters - Part II, edited by Constantine Stephanidis, Margherita Antona, Stavroula Ntoa and Gavriel Salvendy
58. CCIS 2116, HCI International 2024 Posters - Part III, edited by Constantine Stephanidis, Margherita Antona, Stavroula Ntoa and Gavriel Salvendy
59. CCIS 2117, HCI International 2024 Posters - Part IV, edited by Constantine Stephanidis, Margherita Antona, Stavroula Ntoa and Gavriel Salvendy
60. CCIS 2118, HCI International 2024 Posters - Part V, edited by Constantine Stephanidis, Margherita Antona, Stavroula Ntoa and Gavriel Salvendy
61. CCIS 2119, HCI International 2024 Posters - Part VI, edited by Constantine Stephanidis, Margherita Antona, Stavroula Ntoa and Gavriel Salvendy
62. CCIS 2120, HCI International 2024 Posters - Part VII, edited by Constantine Stephanidis, Margherita Antona, Stavroula Ntoa and Gavriel Salvendy

https://2024.hci.international/proceedings

Preface

Preliminary scientific results, professional news, or work in progress, described in the form of short research papers (4–11 pages long), constitute a popular submission type among the International Conference on Human-Computer Interaction (HCII) participants. Extended abstracts are particularly suited for reporting ongoing work, which can benefit from a visual presentation, and are presented during the conference in the form of posters. The latter allow a focus on novel ideas and are appropriate for presenting project results in a simple, concise, and visually appealing manner. At the same time, they are also suitable for attracting feedback from an international community of HCI academics, researchers, and practitioners. Poster submissions span the wide range of topics of all HCII thematic areas and affiliated conferences.

Seven volumes of the HCII 2024 proceedings are dedicated to this year's poster extended abstracts, in the form of short research papers, focusing on the following topics:

- Volume I: HCI Design Theories, Methods, Tools and Case Studies; User Experience Evaluation Methods and Case Studies; Emotions in HCI; Human Robot Interaction
- Volume II: Inclusive Designs and Applications; Aging and Technology
- Volume III: eXtended Reality and the Metaverse; Interacting with Cultural Heritage, Art and Creativity
- Volume IV: HCI in Learning and Education; HCI in Games
- Volume V: HCI in Business and Marketing; HCI in Mobility and Automated Driving; HCI in Psychotherapy and Mental Health
- Volume VI: Interacting with the Web, Social Media and Digital Services; Interaction in the Museum; HCI in Healthcare
- Volume VII: AI Algorithms and Tools in HCI; Interacting with Large Language Models and Generative AI; Interacting in Intelligent Environments; HCI in Complex Industrial Environments

Poster extended abstracts were accepted for publication in these volumes following a minimum of two single-blind reviews from the members of the HCII 2024 international Program Boards, i.e., the program committees of the constituent events. We would like to thank all of them for their invaluable contribution, support, and efforts.

July 2024

Constantine Stephanidis
Margherita Antona
Stavroula Ntoa
Gavriel Salvendy

26th International Conference on Human-Computer Interaction (HCII 2024)

The full list with the Program Board Chairs and the members of the Program Boards of all thematic areas and affiliated conferences of HCII 2024 is available online at:

http://www.hci.international/board-members-2024.php

HCI International 2025 Conference

The 27th International Conference on Human-Computer Interaction, HCI International 2025, will be held jointly with the affiliated conferences at the Swedish Exhibition & Congress Centre and Gothia Towers Hotel, Gothenburg, Sweden, June 22–27, 2025. It will cover a broad spectrum of themes related to Human-Computer Interaction, including theoretical issues, methods, tools, processes, and case studies in HCI design, as well as novel interaction techniques, interfaces, and applications. The proceedings will be published by Springer. More information will become available on the conference website: https://2025.hci.international/.

General Chair
Prof. Constantine Stephanidis
University of Crete and ICS-FORTH
Heraklion, Crete, Greece
Email: general_chair@2025.hci.international

https://2025.hci.international/

Contents – Part IV

HCI in Learning and Education

Al-Ahadeeth: A Visualization Tool of the Hadiths' Chain of Narrators 3
    Hamada R. H. Al-Absi, Devi G. Kurup, Amina Daoud,
    Jens Schneider, Wajdi Zaghouani, Saeed Mohd H. M. Al Marri,
    and Younss Ait Mou

Designing for Self-Regulated Learning: A Dual-View Intelligent
Visualization Dashboard to Support Instructors and Students Using
Multimodal Trace Data in Classrooms 9
    Michael Brown, Megan Wiedbusch, Milouni Patel, Evan Naderi,
    Sophia Capello, Andrea Llinas, Roger Azevedo, and Ancuta Margondai

Evaluation of Augmented Reality Applications for the Teaching-Learning
Process 20
    Omar Cóndor-Herrera, Carlos Ramos-Galarza,
    Mónica Bolaños-Pasquel, and Clemencia Marcayata-Fajardo

AlgoTutor: An Integrated Learning Platform for Data Structures
and Algorithms with Real-Time Guidance and Interactive Visualizations 29
    Gadepalli Chandan Sashank, Zong Wei Tan,
    and Owen Noel Newton Fernando

Early Prediction of Mathematics Learning Achievement of Elementary
Students Using Hidden Markov Model 39
    Jen-I Chiu and Mengping Tsuei

Generative Artificial Intelligence and Interactive Learning Platforms:
Second Language Vocabulary Acquisition 48
    Sibel Crum, Belle Li, and Xiaojing Kou

Virtual Reality Supporting Physical Education Teaching in Brazilian
Elementary Schools 54
    Carolina de Carvalho Amaral, Ângelo Amaral,
    and Soellyn Elene Bataliotti

Classification Tools to Assess Critical Thinking in Automotive
Engineering Students 66
    Carlos Alberto Espinosa-Pinos, Paulina Magally Amaluisa-Rendón,
    and Noemi Viviana Rodríguez-Ortiz

Bioindicators of Attention Detection in Online Learning Environments 75
    *Jaffer Hassan, Javier Berdejo, Sakyarshi Kurati, Anh Dinh,
    Andrew Garcia, Katherine A. Shoemaker, and Dvijesh Shastri*

Adaptive Learning Environments: Integrating Artificial Intelligence
for Special Education Advances 86
    *Janio Jadán-Guerrero, Karla Tamayo-Narvaez, Elena Méndez,
    and María Valenzuela*

On-Demand Internationalization for Learning Management System
Moodle 95
    Tina John and Anna Lena Möller

Examining the Impact: Pencil-and-Paper Versus Touch-Screen
Assessments in Augmented Reality Learning 103
    NaYeon Kang and Jung Hyup Kim

Developing a Teacher Self-Reflection E-portfolio Platform
for the Improvement of Noticing Skills of Childcare Teachers 109
    Soojung Kim and Yun Gil Lee

Dishonesty Tendencies in Testing Scenarios Among Students with Virtual
Reality and Computer-Mediated Technology 114
    *Tanja Kojić, Alina Dovhalevska, Maurizio Vergari, Sebastian Möller,
    and Jan-Niklas Voigt-Antons*

Towards Blockchain-Based Incentives for STEM Education 123
    Myles Lewis and Chris Crawford

Exploring Media Modalities for Cultural Heritage Learning on Social
Platforms: A Comparative Analysis of Short Videos, Nine-Grid Pictures,
and Sequential Pictures 135
    Qiang Li, Tianqi Wu, and Zhen Chen

Enhancing Searching as Learning (SAL) with Generative Artificial
Intelligence: A Literature Review 143
    Kok Khiang Lim and Chei Sian Lee

Learning Beyond the Classroom in the AI Era: A Generation Z Perspective 156
    Kok Khiang Lim and Chei Sian Lee

Collaboration of Digital Human Gestures and Teaching Materials
for Enhanced Integration in MOOC Teaching Scenarios 169
    Yaxin Liu, Xiaomei Nie, and Zhiyong Wu

Enhancing an App for Sustaining Motivation in Learning 176
Tetsuya Nakatoh, Mamiko Miyagi, Ayana Ukegawa,
and Aoiko Motoyama

Multi-dimensional Three-Dimensional Space Learning
in Human-Computer Interaction 180
Li Ou Yang, Yunyi Zhuang, and Jie Ling

Integrating Collaborative Learning into Youth Art Education: Preservation
and Innovation of Guangzhou's Polo Birth Culture 192
Li Ou Yang, Jinrong Liu, Ying Guo, and Jie Ling

Learning Foreign Language Vocabulary Through Task-Based Virtual
Reality Immersion 203
Ethan Seefried, Mariah Bradford, Swagatalaxmi Aich,
Caspian Siebert, Nikhil Krishnaswamy, and Nathaniel Blanchard

ContextVis: Envision Contextual Learning and Interaction with Generative
Models 214
Bo Shui, Chufan Shi, Yujiu Yang, and Xiaomei Nie

Designing a Tangible Interactive Learning System for Children's Art
Education: A Multi-Sensory Design Approach 225
Yuwen Sun and Lin Lin

Verification of Novel Summarization in Arousing Reading Interests 235
Hiroya Toyama, Junjie Shan, and Yoko Nishihara

STEAM Teaching Research Based on Real and Virtual Technology:
A Case Study of 3D Printing Replication and Holographic Interactive
Display of Ancient Light-Transmitting Bronze Mirrors 243
Wei Xiong, Liang Hao, and Jian Rao

Research on the Practice of New Media Literacy Education in the Context
of Integrated Online Education 251
Lin Yu and Jingyuan Shi

Design and Evaluation of a Gamified Generative AI Chatbot for Canvas
LMS Courses 259
Ramin Zandvakili, De Liu, Andy Tao Li, Radhika Santhanam,
and Scott Schanke

Design Strategies for Children's Science Popularization Books Based
on Interactive Narrative 265
Yue Zhao and Li Ou Yang

HCI in Games

Picky Monster: Examining the Effects of Visual Reinforcements Through
Gamified Avatars and Personalized Goal Setting on Reducing Sugar
Consumption 279
    Yun-Hsuan Chou, Yu-Chen Wang, Amanda J. Castellanos,
    Hadar Natanson, and Pei-Yi Patricia Kuo

Application of Digital Game-Based Learning in Popular Science
Education: A Case Study on Taiwan Butterfly Ecology Conservation 290
    Wen Huei Chou and Bing Shuan Chuang

CheMate: Anthropomorphic-cues-Mediated Experiential Learning Game
Using Generative AI 301
    Fengsen Gao, Ke Fang, and Wai Kin Chan

A Streamlined Game Logic and Locomotion Authoring System for VR
Escape Rooms 312
    Gerick Jeremiah Niño N. Go, Jed Laszlo O. Jocson,
    and Eric Cesar E. Vidal Jr.

Make NPC More Realistic: Design and Practice of a Hybrid Stealth Game
NPC AI Framework Based on OODA Theory 321
    Zhiyue Lin, Zetao Zhang, Xing Sun, and Hai-Tao Zheng

A Study of Ethics Education Game Design Based on a Reflective
Framework 329
    Guozhang Ma, Ping Li, Ke Fang, Yueer Mao, and Chu Zhang

Peadom: An Endogenous Educational Game to Learn Hybridization
and the Framework to Guide It 337
    Yueer Mao, Ping Li, Yuan Zeng, and Zhiyue Huang

Ourhotel: A Two-Player Cooperative Game Designed for Young Couples
in Long-Distance Relationships 348
    Xiaoke Pu, Ruoxin You, and Wei Huang

Research into the Development of Game Assets by Independent Artists
for a Valve's Workshop Game Dota 2 359
    Nicolas C. Romeiro, André Salomão, Flávio Andaló,
    Letícia Maria Fraporti Zanini, Fabíola Borges, Jacob Neto,
    and Milton Luiz Horn Vieira

The Effects of Enriched Narratives on Presence and Motion Sickness
in Game-Guiding 370
    Chian Shing Wang and Cheng-Jhe Lin

An Educational Simulation Game Framework and Practice Based
on Complex Adaptive Systems Theory: For Fostering Systems Thinking 377
    Chu Zhang, Ping Li, Ke Fang, Yueer Mao, and Guozhang Ma

Design and Application of Family Intergenerational Social Game Based
on Proxemics Play Framework 388
    Yueming Zhou and Wei Huang

Author Index 399

HCI in Learning and Education

Al-Ahadeeth: A Visualization Tool of the Hadiths' Chain of Narrators

Hamada R. H. Al-Absi[1]([⊠])(iD), Devi G. Kurup[1](iD), Amina Daoud[1],
Jens Schneider[1](iD), Wajdi Zaghouani[2](iD), Saeed Mohd H. M. Al Marri[3],
and Younss Ait Mou[1]([⊠])(iD)

[1] College of Science and Engineering, Hamad Bin Khalifa University, Doha, Qatar
{haalabsi,dkurup,aminadaoud,jeschneider,ymou}@hbku.edu.qa
[2] College of Humanities and Social Sciences, Hamad Bin Khalifa University,
Doha, Qatar
wzaghouani@hbku.edu.qa
[3] College of Shariah and Islamic Studies, Qatar University, Doha, Qatar
saealmarri@qu.edu.qa

Abstract. Hadiths are the records of words, actions, and silent approval attributed to the Prophet Mohammed (PBUH). Their significance is second only to the Holy Quran within the Islamic faith. They have been collected, curated, and published by the most respected Islamic scholars through time. Each Hadith begins with a chain of narrators (sanad), distinguishing them from the main text (Matan), serving as a means for Islamic scholars to assess their strength and veracity. Most people read the approved six books of Hadiths, often focusing solely on the content (Matan) or browsing through topics, neglecting the profound intricacies hidden within the individual narrators' backgrounds. Furthermore, the data is accessed without a visual user interface, imposing limitations due to the purely text-based nature. To alleviate this, we present Al-Ahadeeth, a visualization tool of the chain of narrators of Hadiths. Mapping narrators and narrated-to relations to nodes and edges in a directed graph, we use node size and edge thickness to show occurrence frequencies. Using the concept of generations, we place nodes on concentric rings based on the topological index to compute a 2D layout. Due to the high degree of interconnection in the community of narrators, traditional graph embedding techniques such as multi-dimensional scaling (MDS), t-distributed stochastic neighbor embedding (t-SNE) or uniform manifold approximation and projection (UMAP) tend to map the entire graph to a single cluster and give unsatisfactory results. In contrast, our approach uses the concept of generations to compute the layout of the graph which places nodes on concentric rings to indicate the generation.

Keywords: Hadith · Chain of Narrators · Directed Graph · Visualization

C. Stephanidis et al. (Eds.): HCII 2024, CCIS 2117, pp. 3–8, 2024.
https://doi.org/10.1007/978-3-031-61953-3_1

1 Introduction

In Islam, Hadiths (singular: Hadith; in Arabic: حَديث) are the words, actions, silent approvals, and habits of Prophet Mohammed-Peace Be Upon Him (PBUH). They are considered the second source of Islamic teachings following the Holy Quran [1, 2]. In Arabic, the word "Hadith" in its singular pronunciation form means a "speech" or "report" and its plural form is "Ahadeeth" or "Hadiths" and refers to collections. Scholars have collected, investigated, curated, and published these Hadiths over time, adhering to a strict methodology to ensure the authenticity of each Hadith [3]. An incredibly rich collection of historical information is found in the Kutub al-Sittah—The Six Books. These collections include commentary on the works of Sahih Bukhari, Sahih Muslim, Sunan Abu Dawood, Jami al-Tirmidhi, Sunan al-Sughra, and Sunan ibn Majah and/or Muwatta Malik. In addition to the Hadiths themselves, geographical data and narrators' biographies have likewise been collected and compiled into books such as "The Great History" by Bukhari or al-Jarh wa al-Ta'dil by Abi Hatim, to give just two examples. The usage of this data varies greatly depending on the objective. A Hadith comprises two parts: the "Matn" and the "Sanad". The "Matn" is the body of the Hadith that reports the action or reaction to specific situations, or teachings of the prophet PBUH, and the "Sanad" is the chain of narrators who have transferred the Hadith generation after another from "Al Sahabah" the companions of the Prophet PBUH, who passed these Hadiths to their successors, who are called "Al Tabiun", and this was continued from one generation to another [2].

In the science of Hadith, validating each Hadith's authenticity is of significant importance. Scholars use the "Sanad" to validate Hadiths, a crucial step in preserving the teachings of Prophet Mohammed PBUH. A key criterion in this validation process is examining the narrators' character and the continuity of their chain [4]. Through this process, scholars have examined the trustworthiness and ethical conduct of narrators, categorizing them based on their reliability, and scrutinizing their connections to predecessors and whether these connections have continued to the Prophet PBUH or any of his companions, "Al Sahabah", to establish the Hadiths' authenticity [4]. A major challenge for scholars studying the chain of narrators is the textual nature of the data. Apart from books, scholars utilize both online resources and offline databases, which offer vast and complex collections of literature. This constraint can impair both the accessibility and usability of Hadith data for authentication purposes, underscoring the necessity for improved tools and interfaces. Such advancements would enable more efficient analysis and validation of the chains of narration within Hadith literature. By overcoming these technological barriers, researchers could significantly enhance validation processes, ensuring the preservation and accurate interpretation of Prophetic traditions in contemporary scholarship.

Some researchers have used technological tools to study Hadith narrators, Saeed et al. [5] investigated the construction of narrative networks from the Sahih Muslim book. Using social network analysis techniques, the researchers aimed to discover primary narrators, interaction patterns, and network structural features. The study offered a technique for evaluating narrators and created a tool for narrative network analysis to help scholars and historians comprehend the transmission of hadith. The research identified major narrators using centrality metrics and compared the findings to a comparable investigation on the Sahih Bukhari book. The comparison revealed both parallels and variations in the rankings of renowned narrators across the two surveys. The study emphasizes the possibility for future research to better explore the narrative network. Shukur et al. [6] introduced the Chain of Hadith Narrators Visualizer (CHN), a proto-type designed to visually display the chains of narrators in Hadith literature using Information Visualization methods. Preliminary testing with 20 Islamic education students revealed favorable results, suggesting the efficiency of visual tools in assisting Hadith study. Another article by Siddiqui et al. [7] presented a system to automatically retrieve the Hadith chain of narrators using Named Entity Recognition (NER) and classification, allowing them to construct a net-work to visualize the narrator's chain. They used machine learning trained on an annotated Hadith corpus to identify the names of narrators. One common issue with the above studies, especially when visualizing the chain of narrators is the amount of clutter in the visualizations making them hard to navigate and under-stand or clearly find connections. Furthermore, traditional graph embedding techniques, such as multi-dimensional scaling (MDS) [8], t-distributed stochas-tic neighbor embedding (t-SNE) [9], or uniform manifold approximation and projection (UMAP) [10], often result in unsatisfactory results due to the high degree of interconnection among narrators.

The traditional text-based approach to studying Hadith chains of narrators poses significant challenges in comprehending the intricate relationships and pat-terns within the narration network. Hence, in this paper, we present our Al-Ahadeeth tool which employs the concept of generations to offer a visualization of the chain of narrators that is both apparent and readily accessible. Our tool aims to address these limitations by providing a visual representation and anal-ysis tool that leverages the power of information visualization techniques. By mapping the complex network of narrators as an interactive graph, Al-Ahadeeth enables users to explore the connectivity patterns, identify central figures, and uncover insights that may be obscured in the textual format, making the complex connections of narrators more understandable and visually engaging.

2   Methodology

2.1   Data

We developed this tool using data from the Muslim Scholar Database [11]. Ini-tially, we focused primarily on adding Sahih Bukhari data to the current proto-type. This decision was made strategically, with the goal of refining our approach on a well-defined subset of data before extending to include all six Hadith books. Each narrator in the database is identifiable uniquely by a Muslim Scholar ID, allowing for a direct link to a wide range of metadata. This includes, but is not limited to, biographical and geographical data, which increase the tool's usability and depth of understanding.

The data obtained from the Muslim Scholar Database underwent a thor-ough preprocessing and cleaning process to ensure its suitability for integration into the Al-Ahadeeth tool. This included handling missing or inconsistent data, resolving any conflicts or duplicates, and standardizing the formatting and representation of various attributes.

2.2   Tool Development

Our tool comes in two versions, a web version (https://www.hbku.edu.qa/cse/al-ahadeeth/) and iPad version (https://apps.apple.com/me/app/alahadeeth/id1590736786). To build both versions, we have leveraged the capabilities of a recent UI framework developed, and maintained by Google called **Flutter**. We have chosen this framework among others for its rapid live updates (hot-reload) and cross-platform capabilities. Therefore, a single source code was required to build and deploy both versions. This allowed us to focus on the research aspect of the project rather than on the maintenance of multiple source codes. We have used a CustomPainter to render the graph elements (nodes, edges, generation circles). We have opted for Flutter's Impeller runtime rendering capabilities to improve the rendering performances. That was particularly the case for situations where a large number of nodes, and edges had to be rendered simultaneously.

3   Al-Ahadeeth Tool

The Al-Ahadeeth tool enables users to visually explore the *"Sanad"*. Mapping narrators and narrated-to relations to nodes and edges in a directed graph, we

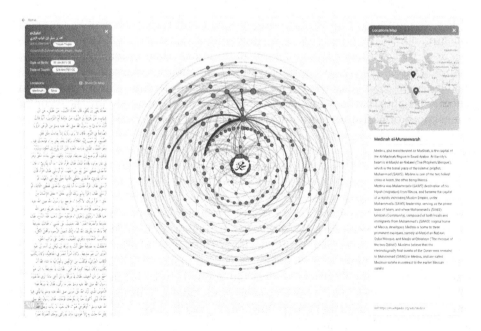

Fig. 1. Al-Ahadeeth tool Interface. Lines in red show the connection between one narrator and others. (Color figure online)

used node size and edge thickness to illustrate occurrence frequencies. Using the concept of generations, we placed nodes on concentric rings based on the topological index and used mass-spring relaxation to avoid edge intersections to compute our 2D layout. The tool provides the full text of the Hadiths (English and Arabic), geolocations of narrators, and short bios. Links to external online sources provide more detailed biographies. Figures 1 and 2 show examples of the tool. The Al-Ahadeeth tool offers a range of user interactions and features to facilitate exploration and analysis of the Hadith chains of narrators. Users can pan and zoom the graph view, enabling them to focus on specific regions or zoom out to observe the overall structure. Additionally, interactive filtering and search capabilities allow users to isolate narrators based on various criteria, such as biographical attributes, geographical regions, or occurrence frequencies. To enhance the user experience and provide contextual information, the tool displays relevant metadata associated with each narrator when hovering over or selecting a node. This includes biographical details, geographical locations, and links to external resources for further exploration. Furthermore, the tool supports the display of the full text of Hadiths, both in Arabic and English translations, allowing users to navigate between the visual representation and the textual content.

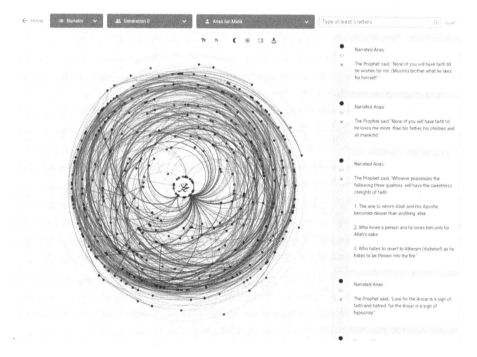

Fig. 2. An example of the Mobile application output when selecting one Narrator (Anas bin Malik). In the middle, the connection between Anas bin Malik and the other narrators is shown. On the right panel, the Hadiths are displayed.

4   Conclusion

In this paper, we presented Al-Ahadeeth, a visualization tool for the chain of narrators, *"Sanad"*, in Hadith literature. Using data from the Muslim Scholar Database, we focused on Sahih Bukhari for the current prototype, intending to eventually expand to include all six Hadith books. Al-Ahadeeth takes an innovative technique, mapping narrators and their relationships onto a directed graph, with node size and edge thickness expressing occurrence frequencies, and nodes positioned on concentric rings to demonstrate generational depth. This methodology not only tackles the problems of standard graph techniques by reducing clutter and improving navigability, but it also expands the user's comprehension by incorporating biographical and geographical material. Furthermore, the tool is available via web and mobile applications. Our tool marks a big advancement in making the complex networks of Hadith narration more accessible and engaging for scholars and enthusiasts alike.

Acknowledgment. This work is part of a research project that is support by Qatar Research, Development and Innovation Council (QRDI) (formerly known as Qatar National Research Fund (QNRF)) under grand number: NPRP13S-0129-200194.

Disclosure of Interests. The authors have no competing interests.

References

1. Dimashqi, A.-H.I.K.: Al Bidaya Wa Al-Nihaya (The Beginning and the End). Dar Al-Kotob Al-Ilmiyah (2002)
2. Swarup, R.: Understanding the Hadith: The Sacred Traditions of Islam. Prometheus Books, Amherst, N.Y. (2002)
3. al Asqalani, I.H.: Nukhbat al-Fikar fi Mustalah Ahl al-Athar. Dar al-Kotob al-Ilmiyah (2002)
4. Khan, I.A.: Muslim scholars' contribution in hadith authentication. J. Islam Asia (E-ISSN 2289-8077) **8**, 345–363 (2011)
5. Saeed, S., Yousuf, S., Khan, F., Rajput, Q.: Social network analysis of hadith narrators. J. King Saud Univ.-Comput. Inf. Sci. **34**(6), 3766–3774 (2022)
6. Shukur, Z., Fabil, N., Salim, J., Noah, S.A.: Visualization of the hadith chain of narrators. In: Zaman, H.B., et al. (eds.) IVIC 2011. LNCS, vol. 7067, pp. 340–347. Springer, Heidelberg (2011). https://doi.org/10.1007/978-3-642-25200-6_32
7. Siddiqui, M.A., Saleh, M., Bagais, A.A.: Extraction and visualization of the chain of narrators from hadiths using named entity recognition and classification. Int. J. Comput. Linguist. Res **5**(1), 14–25 (2014)
8. Borg, I., Groenen, P.J.F.: Modern Multidimensional Scaling. SSS, Springer, New York (2005). https://doi.org/10.1007/0-387-28981-X
9. Van der Maaten, L., Hinton, G.: Visualizing data using t-SNE. J. Mach. Learn. Res. **9**(11) (2008)
10. McInnes, L., Healy, J., Melville, J.: UMAP: uniform manifold approximation and projection for dimension reduction. arXiv preprint arXiv:1802.03426 (2018)
11. Muslim scholar database. https://muslimscholars.info/. Accessed Jan 2023

Designing for Self-Regulated Learning: A Dual-View Intelligent Visualization Dashboard to Support Instructors and Students Using Multimodal Trace Data in Classrooms

Michael Brown[✉], Megan Wiedbusch, Milouni Patel, Evan Naderi, Sophia Capello, Andrea Llinas, Roger Azevedo, and Ancuta Margondai

University of Central Florida, Orlando, USA
michael.brown2@ucf.edu

Abstract. Effective learning analytics dashboards (LADs) should offer both instructors and students valuable insights into student learning. Information about one's learning, as both a product and a process, should be provided to the user as actionable data visualizations and aggregated indicators of learning. However, most dashboards often solely focus on the instructor's perspective, neglecting the impact of providing students with their data in a student view. Furthermore, these dashboards assume instructors are proficient in data analytics and can quickly interpret complicated visualizations in-situ while accounting for context and conditional factors. This challenge is further exacerbated by the lack of theoretically informed learning analytics principles and design choices as many of the dashboards rely primarily on performance-based data, neglecting process and trace data of cognitive, metacognitive, affective, motivational, and social (CAMMS) processes. As such, we are introducing MetaDash, a multimodal self-regulated learning (SRL) dashboard with both an instructor and student view. This dual-view (i.e., instructor and student-facing) dashboard prototype is populated with aggregate and contextualized multimodal trace data grounded within models of SRL, affect dynamics, information processing, cognitive load, and multimodal learning analytics. In this paper, we leverage ideas derived from SRL to identify gaps in current learning analytics dashboards. We then present the design principles and architecture of MetaDash, including how we derived its structure and how it supports our framework. We discuss the affective dynamics and learning analytics on the landing page to understand user engagement and detail how analytics are customized for different phases within the architecture. We highlight the advantages of incorporating real-time data analysis for immediate decision-making. Future research will focus on refining MetaDash through enhancements informed by user and focus group testing, experimental studies, and the integration of user feedback to address challenges and expand the dashboard's functionality and effectiveness.

Keywords: Dashboard · Metacognition · Multimodal · Learning Analytics · Self-Regulated Learning

© The Author(s), under exclusive license to Springer Nature Switzerland AG 2024
C. Stephanidis et al. (Eds.): HCII 2024, CCIS 2117, pp. 9–19, 2024.
https://doi.org/10.1007/978-3-031-61953-3_2

1   Introduction

Learning Analytics Dashboards (LADs) provide insights into student educational data with the explicit goal of optimizing learning processes by methodically collecting, analyzing, examining data, and extracting actionable insights that facilitate a deeper understanding of individual learning patterns and student progress [8,14]. Studies have shown that LADs can significantly increase student engagement with learning technologies and course resources, boosting learning motivation levels due to the novel analytics insights derived from predictive and prescriptive analytics [7]. Thus, it can be inferred that LADs can significantly benefit from integrating frameworks of Self-Regulated Learning (SRL), which empower students to actively engage in the analysis, monitoring, and reflection of their learning processes, enhancing the effectiveness and personalization of educational experiences. SRL is a pivotal component of contemporary education, enabling students to actively engage in learning strategies, and is underpinned by academic self-efficacy beliefs that, along with self-observation, self-judgment, and self-reaction, are essential in the social cognitive framework of self-directed academic learning [15–17].

Within the SRL paradigm, LADs should aim to aid students in effectively managing their learning by providing meaningful feedback and visualizations to assist in monitoring progress, setting goals, and adapting learning strategies. To do so, LADs should integrate data-driven insights into one's cognitive, affective, metacognitive, motivational, and social (CAMMS) processes, offering a holistic view of learner's academic behaviors and attitudes [1]. However, the utility of LADs is often hindered by the complexity of their data visualizations, which can be challenging for users without formal training in data analytics. This underscores the importance of integrating automated and intuitive learning analytics and visualizations that can be "drilled down" to make LADs more user-friendly and effective [9]. Current LADs tend to overlook the holistic learning environment by focusing predominantly on either the student or the instructor and often neglect the inclusion of diverse data sets, such as psychophysiological and online trace data. Moreover, the common emphasis on post hoc rather than real-time analysis impedes the ability to provide timely feedback and support, ultimately restricting the capacity for accurate data interpretation and analyses of learning processes, which is essential for facilitating appropriate interventions and bolstering both student and instructor experiences in the learning environment.

MetaDash has been developed to address the limitations of existing LADs by providing a dual-perspective dashboard prototype catering to both instructors and students [14]. It emphasizes a holistic view of the learning process, incorporating established frameworks of self-regulated learning [16], affect dynamics [2], and multimodal learning analytics [4,10] into its conceptualization and design. MetaDash also focuses on user drill-down capabilities and advanced data processing techniques to enhance data interpretation and decision-making. In the following sections, we first detail MetaDash's architecture and describe the basic page layouts and analytics. Next, we describe the (near) real-time data integration from data collection to visualization pipeline. Finally, we conclude with a discussion on the future enhancements of MetaDash and address challenges arising from practical use cases.

2   Design Principles and Architecture

2.1   Design and Gross-Level Structure

MetaDash is a dashboard designed to evaluate student's CAMMS processes, behaviors, and academic performance in (near) real-time, presenting data insights through a graphical user interface (UI) on a web-based application and is designed to be interactive, with responsive pages that automatically update as new data is received. This application, accessible over any network connection, is developed using Angular, D3.js, and Nest.js. To bridge these functionalities to user experience, MetaDash adapts its interface dynamically.

Both instructor and student are initially provided one of four landing pages based on the phases from Winne's IPT framework [16]. The landing page is determined by the phase the majority of students have been in for the past 10 min and is automatically updated every 2 min to create a dynamic LAD that follows the natural flow of the classroom without requiring manual user input. However, instructors are still able to manually navigate landing pages if they choose. Each landing phase is constructed in a similar layout with a (A) vertical navigation bar on the left to proceed manually to other landing pages, and (D-E) real-time affective data on the right side of the page which we describe in further detail below. The space between these two sections corresponds to the various learning analytics that are specific to each phase, which we will refer to as the Phase Specific (PS) content (B-C). The following section discusses Phase 1 of the instructor landing page (see Fig. 1), emphasizing task definition and introducing Affective Dynamics Learning Analytics to visualize student emotions in real time.

2.2   Affective Dynamics Learning Analytics

Across every landing page in the instructor view, the class's affective dynamics (AD) learning analytics are always present on the right-hand side of the page (see Fig. 1, D-E). The AD section is designed to provide educators with dynamic visualizations of the student's affective states in real time. These states are limited to those as informed by Grasser and D'Mello's [2] Model of Affective Dynamics - engagement, confusion, frustration, and disengagement. According to this model, effective learning occurs when students are challenged, leading to cognitive disequilibrium and confusion, which are essential for deep learning through critical thinking and problem-solving. However, if challenges become too overwhelming without adequate support or resolution, a student may transition from confusion to frustration, indicating that the challenge is perceived as insurmountable and leads to disengagement. These student affective states can be monitored by the instructor both for the class as a whole and for individual students, as described

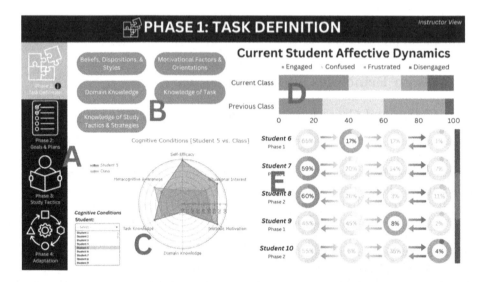

Fig. 1. The above figure showcases the main landing page from the instructors' perspective during phase 1, segmented into three distinct areas for streamlined navigation. Starting from the left, section (A) presents the Phases Navigation Bar (PNB), equipped with phase selection buttons that are visually distinguished by a green, black, and white color scheme. Adjacent to the PNB, the Phase Information (PI) section is bifurcated into subsections (B) and (C). Subsection (B) features user-interactive drill-down buttons leading to detailed domain-specific insights, while subsection (C) displays a radar chart for comparing individual student cognitive metrics against class averages. On the right, the Affective Dynamics (AD) section comprises a dual-bar chart (D) visualizing class-wide affective states across two temporal states—previous and current classes—and a table of donut charts (E), each row representing an individual student's percentage time spent in each affective state. (Color figure online)

next. Affective states are determined by utilizing facial expression data collected via video that are coded using the AFFDEX algorithm [6] which identifies facial landmark movements as Action Units (AUs) through the Facial Action Coding System (FACS) [3].

The AD section is segmented into aggregate class-level data (located at the top of the AD section) and individual student-level data (located below). Aggregate data is updated every five seconds as two horizontal stacked bar graphs representing the proportional frequency of total time across students spent in each affective state: engagement (green), confusion (yellow), frustration (orange), and disengagement (red). Below the bar chart visualizations, the dashboard incorporates a table of donut charts, each row represents an individual student. Each donut chart's proportion represents the percentage of class time the student has spent in that state, refreshing every five seconds concurrently with the bar chart. The chart corresponding to a student's current affective state appears opaque while the other affective states appear more transparent to aid in quick instructor interpretation. This is done so that the most salient information (the current state) is more prominent, but all information is still made readily available. Updates are not provided at a higher frequency to prevent becoming overly cognitively demanding or distracting to the instructor.

2.3   Phase Specific (PS) Learning Analytic Exemplar

Located to the right of the AD segment, each landing phase has a unique set of navigation buttons to drill down pages (Fig. 1, B) and quick and actionable "at-a-glance" learning analytics (Fig. 1, C) of a learner's CAMMS processes corresponding to that specific phase. For example, phase one's PS section is further subdivided into upper and lower segments. The upper segment houses drill-down buttons (Fig. 1, B) that lead to pages filled with specific analytics of the class's cognitive conditions as theorized by Winne [16] (see Fig. 2). Unlike the landing pages which serve to provide quick and actionable "at-a-glance" data, drill-down pages provide more detailed analytics when an instructor or student has specific questions. For instance, the "Beliefs, Dispositions, and Styles" button directs to a page where information from self-reports, such as student's perceptions about studying, is available (see Fig. 2). Additionally, the drill-down buttons would be used if an instructor wishes to understand how they should structure their instruction after a particularly difficult quiz or if they suspect that their students were not effectively using strategies but knew the information. To confirm this, they may choose to examine the "Beliefs, Dispositions, and Styles" drill-down page to examine how one's level of metacognitive awareness (captured via a self-report) related to their quiz score.

In addition to button navigation to drill-down pages, each phase also may contain other at-a-glance visualizations. For example, in our Phase 1 Instructor view landing page, there is a radar chart (Fig. 1, C) that allows instructors to compare a selected student's (via drop-down menu) cognitive condition metrics (represented in blue) against the class average (in orange). This facilitates the identification of personalized instructional strategies by visually comparing individual performance to the class norm.

While we are unable to fully describe the design of each landing page and drill-down page in this paper, each page has been methodically designed using a theory-first approach. Next, we further expand the data side of MetaDash from collection to learning analytics, then proceed to discuss future research directions.

3   Data Management: From Collection to Visualization

The MetaDash data pipeline comprises multiple stages, including data collection, analysis, feature selection and extraction, aggregation, and data processing. Multimodal data is gathered in-situ including eye tracking, log files, self-reports, physiological responses (e.g., EDA, heart rate), and facial expressions. This information is directly collected and synchronized from the student's computer system via iMotions, a human insights software known for its seamless integration of

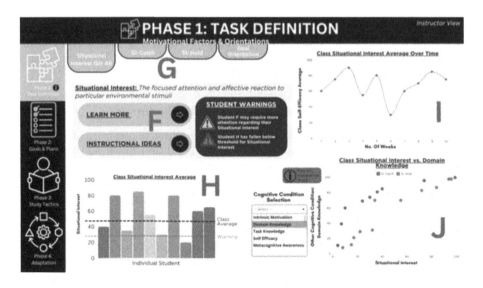

Fig. 2. The above figure presents an exemplar drill-down page. This page is accessible from the "Motivational Factors and Orientations" drill-down cognitive condition button (Fig. 1, B) for the instructor's view of Phase 1. This page provides the user with information about potential motivational factors and orientations, specifically depicting the situational interest page collected via a self-report that is collected once a week. Other conditions can be picked from tabs (G) including sub-constructs of situational interests such as the "holding" situational interest. F shows the instructional aid that is provided to an instructor should they want to learn more about the construct or be given some instructional ideas about how best to support learners. Additionally, this is where they will receive any student-level warnings about this construct. For example, Student H has fallen below the threshold (two standard deviations below the class average) in situational interest and Student F is close to falling below this threshold as well. This is visually depicted in the bar chart (H) where the class average and the warning cutoff are provided to the instructor at-a-glance. Additional information is provided to the instructor to help contextualize these values including a time plot (I) to show any class-level changes in situational interest on a week-to-week basis. Finally, J provides information about situational interest against any of the other cognitive conditions in a scatterplot where each dot is a student (chosen from the drop-down menu to the right of J's graph) so that the instructor may examine the relationships between cognitive conditions to help determine how best to address any potential issues they identified. We have also provided a help button for this visualization that when pressed will provide the instructor with an explanation about the strength and direction of the relationship on the scatterplot and how to interpret this relationship.

diverse data sources and real-time insights provision. Upon collection, the data undergoes preprocessing of time-based alignment of data points by the iMotions engine before being transmitted through a WebSocket for processing (see Fig. 3).

As Fig. 3 depicts, MetaDash harnesses multimodal multichannel data from students, including verbal responses, physiological signals (such as Galvanic Skin

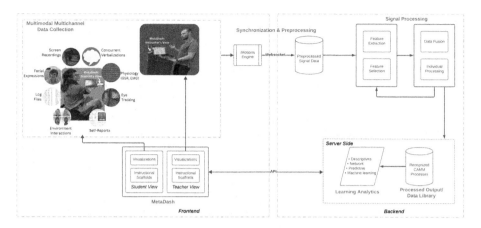

Fig. 3. The above figure is a depiction of the flow of data from the multimedia collection through synchronization and preprocessing to signal processing to learning analytic development and finally visualization.

Response [GSR] and Electromyography [EMG]), eye tracking, self-reports, environmental interactions, log files, facial expressions, and screen recordings. Following this, the signal processing phase extracts and/or selects features from each data channel, transforming them into a new feature space or maintaining their original form for analysis. These features can be examined individually or fused across channels and data types, enhancing the data library with further feature extraction or selection. The entire framework is grounded in established learning theories, ensuring a theoretical basis for the collection and processing of multimodal data such as the integrated Model of Multidimensional SRL Engagement [12] and the Dynamics of the Affective States Model [2]. This theoretical foundation also dictates how the dashboard updates and manages the complexities of real-time analytics. For instance, affective data is updated every second with 60 Hz data, whereas self-report data is refreshed only upon new submissions, reflecting different temporal granularities [12]. Thus, MetaDash functions as both a data-driven and theory-informed LAD, effectively bridging bottom-up data analysis with top-down theoretical insights.

4 Future Research and Direction

4.1 Real-Time Data Utilization and Decision Making

MetaDash's versatility as a LAD is showcased through its applicability across diverse educational settings, including traditional classrooms, online learning environments, and blended learning models. We can imagine a scenario in an AI course where Nina, a diligent student, is studying with MetaDash. As Nina engages with AI course content, MetaDash actively records her screen interaction and her eye movements, captures, and assesses her facial expressions via webcam, and logs keystrokes and mouse actions, extensively monitoring every detail of her learning process. As she progresses into the course content, she becomes stuck on an algorithm problem and starts to randomly click on the course engagement page to find her way out of this learning frustration and get a solution. Her head tilts and her brow furrows in frustration. She starts to think aloud tracking her steps and exclaims that she does not understand why her answer is incorrect. MetaDash detects her confusion through her random keystrokes and mouse actions, it assesses her eye movement patterns coupled with a frown and head tilt, indicating possible confusion and inefficient study strategy deployment. Upon detecting a sudden shift in Nina's affective state, MetaDash sends a context-specific alert to both the instructor and Nina through (near) real-time data-informed visualization that Nina might be struggling with a particular machine-learning algorithm. The instructor may see that Nina isn't the only student struggling and stops the class to offer clarification. Conversely, the instructor may see Nina as one of the few with this confusion and instead choose to monitor before intervening. Guided by MetaDash, Nina is empowered to self-regulate her learning, adjust her approach based on MetaDash's suggestions, and proceed with a clearer understanding of complex AI concepts.

This scenario exemplifies the transformative potential of MetaDash in enhancing personalized learning experiences. In such scenarios, instructors might decide to include additional tasks from the designated problem set that include more complex AI concepts in the next assignment for either the whole class or specific students, without needing to take any additional steps. This supports a personalized learning experience, fostering an environment where Nina and students like her can thrive with the support of real-time data-informed visual analytics and interventions from instructors and educators. Building on these insights, we pivot to exploring future research directions, emphasizing future enhancements informed by user feedback to advance MetaDash's educational utility.

4.2   Challenges and Limitations

While the Dual-View Intelligent Visualization Dashboard concept holds great promise for enhancing instructors' and students' self-regulated learning (SRL) using multimodal trace data, several challenges and limitations must be addressed for successful classroom implementation.

One significant challenge is the complexity of integrating and interpreting multimodal trace data from various sources. This requires sophisticated algorithms and machine learning models capable of analyzing diverse data types and extracting meaningful theoretically-based instructional prescriptions. Ensuring the accuracy and reliability of these algorithms poses a substantial technical challenge, as errors or biases in data analysis could lead to inaccurate interpretations and misinformed decisions by instructors and students. Additionally, safeguarding this sensitive information and ensuring compliance with data protection regulations are paramount to maintaining trust and confidentiality among students, instructors, and educational institutions.

Furthermore, another challenge is designing a Dual-View Dashboard that caters to the diverse needs and preferences of both instructors and students. Instructors may require different visualizations and analytics to monitor class progress, identify at-risk students, and adapt instruction accordingly. In contrast, students may benefit from personalized feedback, goal-setting tools, and interactive learning resources. Balancing these diverse requirements while maintaining usability and accessibility can be daunting for dashboard designers.

In conclusion, while a Dual-View Intelligent Visualization Dashboard offers promising opportunities for supporting SRL in classrooms, addressing the challenges and limitations of data complexity, design considerations, privacy concerns, and user adoption and engagement is crucial for its effective implementation and utilization in educational settings. These challenges can be overcome through collaborative efforts and iterative refinement, paving the way for more effective and personalized learning experiences.

4.3   Future Research

Designing dual-view dashboards for self-regulated learning (SRL) presents a promising avenue for enhancing student success and engagement. One key aspect of future research will involve the refinement and implementation of intelligent multimodal learning analytic dashboards that simultaneously provide dual perspectives for instructors and students.

To do so will require the future development of intelligent algorithms and machine learning models to analyze and interpret multimodal trace data effectively and efficiently. These models will detect patterns, trends, and correlations in students' learning behaviors and processes, enabling predictive analytics and proactive interventions to support SRL. These models may oscillate between the presentation of process data to encourage self-regulation and, under certain instructional conditions, may tutor students on how to enact SRL processes and tutor teachers on how to support students SRL using self-regulated teaching [11]. Moreover, research efforts will focus on ensuring the usability, accessibility, and interpretability of these dashboards for both instructors and students and consider the use of advanced modalities such as augmented reality (AR) and virtual reality (VR) to enhance interaction and engagement. This approach aims to foster adoption and effectiveness in diverse educational contexts, meeting the demands of 21st-century schooling.

Overall, the future of designing for SRL using a Dual-View intelligent visualization dashboard holds great promise for advancing educational technology, promoting student success, and teacher effectiveness in classrooms. Through interdisciplinary collaboration and innovative research endeavors, we can harness the power of multimodal trace data and intelligent analytics to support more effective teaching and learning practices.

5   Conclusion

In this paper, we have detailed the design of a new dual-facing learning analytics dashboard, MetaDash. MetaDash is being designed and developed to provide both instructors and students with a holistic view of learning as not only an outcome but as a dynamic process that incorporates all CAMMS processes. Using this dashboard, instructors will have more contextualized data to make data-driven insights about their students that are grounded within theory and supported by the system to help interpret visualizations. Additionally, students will have (near) real-time access to their learning data to reference during learning challenges and points of reflection or planning. We underscore the importance of enhancing data literacy among educators and students to improve learning outcomes, a challenge our multimodal, theory-driven dashboard design aims to address by offering adaptive, individualized support and actionable insights [5,13]. We highlight many of the current design pitfalls of current systems and outline how our design directly addresses these gaps. Additionally, we detail the flow of data from collection through preprocessing, machine-learning-driven processing, and theory-driven interpretation to data visualization.

Future work on MetaDash will involve user-experience studies, focus groups, and experimental studies on the use of the prototype situated within authentic learning contexts. The design and implementation will be iterative with educator's and student's co-creation. However, we hold that this dual-view dashboard responds to many of the current gaps in the learning analytics dashboards, providing students and instructors with precise and comprehensive actionable data to enhance and support student learning.

Acknowledgements. The research described in this paper was partially supported by funding from the National Science Foundation (DRL#1916417). The authors' opinions, findings, conclusions, or recommendations are those of the authors and do not necessarily reflect the views of the National Science Foundation.

References

1. Azevedo, R.: Using hypermedia as a metacognitive tool for enhancing student learning? the role of self-regulated learning. In: Computers as Metacognitive Tools for Enhancing Learning, pp. 199–209. Routledge (2018)
2. D'Mello, S., Graesser, A.: Dynamics of affective states during complex learning. Learn. Instr. **22**(2), 145–157 (2012)
3. Ekman, P., Friesen, W.V.: Facial action coding system. Environmental Psychology & Nonverbal Behavior (1978)
4. Giannakos, M., Spikol, D., Di Mitri, D., Sharma, K., Ochoa, X., Hammad, R.: Introduction to multimodal learning analytics. In: The Multimodal Learning Analytics Handbook, pp. 3–28. Springer (2022)
5. Lee-Cultura, S., Sharma, K., Cosentino, G., Papavlasopoulou, S., Giannakos, M.: Children's play and problem solving in motion-based educational games: Synergies between human annotations and multi-modal data. In: Proceedings of the 20th Annual ACM Interaction Design and Children Conference, pp. 408–420 (2021)

6. McDuff, D., Mahmoud, A., Mavadati, M., Amr, M., Turcot, J., Kaliouby, R.e.: Affdex sdk: a cross-platform real-time multi-face expression recognition toolkit. In: Proceedings of the 2016 CHI Conference Extended Abstracts on Human Factors in Computing Systems, pp. 3723–3726 (2016)

7. Ramaswami, G., Susnjak, T., Mathrani, A.: Effectiveness of a learning analytics dashboard for increasing student engagement levels. J. Learn. Anal. **10**(3), 115–134 (2023)

8. Schwendimann, B.A., et al.: Perceiving learning at a glance: a systematic literature review of learning dashboard research. IEEE Trans. Learn. Technol. **10**(1), 30–41 (2016)

9. Shabaninejad, S., Khosravi, H., Leemans, S.J.J., Sadiq, S., Indulska, M.: Recommending insightful drill-downs based on learning processes for learning analytics dashboards. In: Bittencourt, I.I., Cukurova, M., Muldner, K., Luckin, R., Millán, E. (eds.) AIED 2020. LNCS (LNAI), vol. 12163, pp. 486–499. Springer, Cham (2020). https://doi.org/10.1007/978-3-030-52237-7_39

10. Sharma, K., Giannakos, M.: Multimodal data capabilities for learning: what can multimodal data tell us about learning? Br. J. Edu. Technol. **51**(5), 1450–1484 (2020)

11. Taub, M., Azevedo, R.: Teachers as self-regulated learners: the role of multimodal data analytics for instructional decision making. New Dir. Teach. Learn. **2023**(174), 25–32 (2023)

12. Wiedbusch, M., Dever, D., Li, S., Amon, M.J., Lajoie, S., Azevedo, R.: Measuring multidimensional facets of SRL engagement with multimodal data. In: Kovanovic, V., Azevedo, R., Gibson, D.C., lfenthaler, D. (eds.) Unobtrusive Observations of Learning in Digital Environments: Examining Behavior, Cognition, Emotion, Metacognition and Social Processes using Learning Analytics, pp. 141–173. Springer, Cham (2023). https://doi.org/10.1007/978-3-031-30992-2_10

13. Wiedbusch, M.D., Azevedo, R.: Modeling metacomprehension monitoring accuracy with eye gaze on informational content in a multimedia learning environment. In: ACM Symposium on Eye Tracking Research and Applications, pp. 1–9 (2020)

14. Wiedbusch, M.D., et al.: A theoretical and evidence-based conceptual design of metadash: an intelligent teacher dashboard to support teachers' decision making and students' self-regulated learning. In: Frontiers in Education, vol. 6, p. 570229. Frontiers Media SA (2021)

15. Winne, P., Azevedo, R.: Metacognition and self-regulated learning. In: The Cambridge Handbook of the Learning Sciences, vol. 3, pp. 93–113 (2022)

16. Winne, P.H.: Cognition and metacognition within self-regulated learning. In: Handbook of Self-regulation of Learning and Performance, pp. 36–48. Routledge (2017)

17. Zimmerman, B.J.: Attaining self-regulation: a social cognitive perspective. In: Handbook of Self-Regulation, pp. 13–39. Elsevier (2000)

Evaluation of Augmented Reality Applications for the Teaching-Learning Process

Omar Cóndor-Herrera[1,3] , Carlos Ramos-Galarza[1,2(✉)] ,
Mónica Bolaños-Pasquel[1] , and Clemencia Marcayata-Fajardo[1]

[1] Centro de Investigación en Mecatrónica y Sistemas Interactivos MIST/Carrera de Psicología/Maestría en Educación mención Innovación y Liderazgo Educativo, Universidad Tecnológica Indoamérica, Av. Machala y Sabanilla, Quito, Ecuador
{omarcondor,carlosramos}@uti.edu.ec,
italo.condor@educacion.gob.ec, caramos@puce.edu.ec
[2] Facultad de Psicología, Pontificia Universidad Católica del Ecuador, Av. 12 de Octubre y Roca, Quito, Ecuador
[3] Ministerio de Educación del Ecuador, Av. Amazonas N34-451 y Av. Atahualpa, Quito, Ecuador

Abstract. Different studies show that A.R. has been implemented in several areas of education with positive and encouraging results, for example, in the teaching of anatomy [1] in the literature [23] for reading comprehension, immersive learning [1], preschool education, creation of educational video games to name a few examples.

Therefore, the present research project aimed to evaluate 3 augmented reality applications used in the learning of human body systems, the applications evaluated were: Virtualiti Tee, Merge Object Viewer and Humanoid 4d.

The evaluation of the platforms focused on determining which one offered the best augmented reality animations, the quality of information on the subject, the design of each application, the best application from the students' perspective, among other aspects evaluated.

The population consisted of 81 people made up of 36 men and 45 women whose age varies between 13 and 16 years of age (Mage = 14,074), the exogenous variables were controlled: gender, socioeconomic level, age and academic level, so these characteristics were homogeneous in all participants.

The intervention project was worked on in 8 sessions with a duration of 40 min each, in the last session the data collection instrument was applied which consisted of a survey, once the instrument was applied, we proceeded with the analysis and processing of the data from which the following results are derived, according to 42% of the students, the best application to study the systems of the body 43% of students consider that the application that has the best animations with augmented reality is Virtualiti Tee and 53% indicated that the application that provides the most complete information on the subject is HUMANOID 4D.

Keywords: Augmented reality · education · innovation · technology

© The Author(s), under exclusive license to Springer Nature Switzerland AG 2024
C. Stephanidis et al. (Eds.): HCII 2024, CCIS 2117, pp. 20–28, 2024.
https://doi.org/10.1007/978-3-031-61953-3_3

1 Introduction

The application of technology can change the way students currently learn, the use of various technological tools has become a powerful motivation to improve the learning process of students, it is evident that the resources and tools to apply in the teaching-learning process have increased significantly and have gradually taken on greater relevance for the educational field. This is mainly due to the ease of use, as well as the availability of technical devices for students [2, 3].

Within those technological resources and tools that are booming augmented reality resources from now on A.R., which based on Martínez-Pérez et al., (2021) defines as a technology which enables the combination of virtual objects and real objects in real time through technological devices, since A.R complements the sensory perception of reality by the student by incorporating computer-generated content into the environment, which allows the student to experience different forms of interactivity between reality and the virtual simultaneously [4–6].

Various studies show that RA has been implemented in several areas of education with positive and encouraging results, for example in the teaching of anatomy [1] en la literatura [7], for reading comprehension, immersive learning, preschool education, educational video game creation [8, 9], emotional intelligence, a [10]. In addition, positive results have been found in favor of learning with the use of technology, to improve motivation, commitment to the design of MOOCs with elements of A.R [11, 12], to name a few examples.

Due to the above, augmented reality (A.R) for the educational field represents an innovative tool in which the teacher can present to their students the contents to be studied by combining them with active teaching methodologies such as gamification or in turn with educational approaches such as STEAM education, it is undeniable that the [13]. Technological tools are powerful instruments at the service of education because the ease and speed that they offer to access information in different formats, contribute to the optimization and improvement of the teaching and learning process [14].

In this context, this research was developed which aimed to evaluate the different characteristics and operation of three augmented reality applications: Virtualiti tee, Merge object viewer and Humanoid 4d, through a comparative analysis of them in order to determine which application of those evaluated is most useful for the student in their learning process.

In the following sections, we expand on the importance of augmented reality technology, the benefits of the use of technology in education, recent studies on the use of R AI in the educational field, and present the main results found in the development of the research.

1.1 Augmented Reality

Augmented Reality A.R. is defined as a technology that enables the combination of virtual objects and real objects in real time through the use of technological devices such as cell phones, A.R. allows reality to be completed without replacing it [15, 16]. Dundeleavy & Dede (2014) they define A.R as the interaction of audio, graphics, text and other virtual elements superimposed on reality where objects can be visualized in real time, for which they use mobile devices such as smartphones and tablets to allow the user to interact with the digital information integrated into the physical space, to access A.R animations they use triggers that are generally immersed in QR codes the user scans code and can display the AR animation [17]. It is worth mentioning that studies related to the subject indicate that teachers have a positive attitude towards the use of AR and trust in its potential to enrich the learning environment [18].

1.2 Benefit of the Use of Technology in Education

Technology applied to education has several benefits for education, the use of resources, devices and different technological elements inserted in the educational field have made it possible to create new forms of production, representation, dissemination and access to knowledge, thus innovating the teaching process [19, 20].

The insertion of these resources and technological devices have made it possible to propose disruptive forms of educational interaction, thus allowing students to get deeply involved and enjoy their learning process, which generates great motivation in students because it is considered that when an individual enjoys performing a task, a positive intrinsic motivation is induced. Significantly improving the learning experience, [20–22]. This aspect could be considered the best option for integration in the field of education because in this way students would learn based on interest and motivation instead of the pressure of study [23].

1.3 Description of the Augmented Reality Applications Evaluated

For the research, 3 augmented reality applications were selected: Virtualiti tee, Merge object viewer and Humanoid 4d, which have similar characteristics, in this case the three applications present animations of A.R on the systems of the human body, a topic that was selected for its importance within the subject, in the same way the applications are compatible with Android and IOS phones, which allowed to evaluate the operation of them by students across the board equitably.

1.4 Virtuality tee

The "Virtualiti tee" app shows different systems of the human body such as the digestive, respiratory, skeletal, renal and circulatory systems, the app allows you to work with augmented reality AR and VR virtual reality experiences, the app uses as a trigger a qr code printed on a t-shirt or the image of the t-shirt that also works as a trigger, In addition, students can look inside organs and systems in 360° and it has a built-in heart rate tracker, in Fig. 1 you can see the augmented reality offered by the application [24].

1.5 Merge Object Viewer

It is an application that works with a cube based on QR codes called merge cube which works as a trigger for the A.R animations as visualized in Fig. 2 in the cube you can visualize the different systems of the human body and other animations, additionally the application works with the merge edu platform and the merge explorer application to complement the learning experience with STEAM lessons [25].

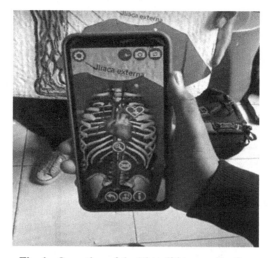

Fig. 1. Operation of the Virtualiti tee application

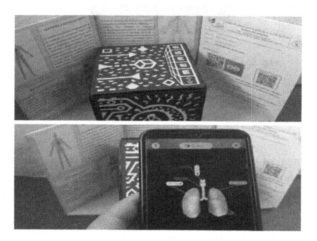

Fig. 2. How the Merge object viewer application works

1.6 Humanoid 4D

It is an application designed by octagon studio which uses cards with images of the human body as triggers, the application allows you to see all the systems of the body in augmented reality, Fig. 3 shows a referential image of the A.R elements of the application [26].

Fig. 3. Operation of the Humanoid 4D application

2 Methodology

2.1 Participants

For the development of this research, we worked with 81 people made up of 36 men and 45 women whose age varies between 13 and 16 years of age (Mage = 14,074), controlling the exogenous variables: gender, socioeconomic level, age and academic level, so these characteristics were homogeneous in all participants.

The participants belonged to the fiscal education system of the city of Quito, Ecuador. All legal representatives of the participants signed the consent for voluntary participation and the ethical standards of research involving human subjects were safeguarded at all times during the research. In addition, this study was approved by the Human Research Ethics Committee of a university in Ecuador.

2.2 Instruments

A constructed survey was designed as an instrument for data collection [27]. Ad-hoc Exclusively for this research, which evaluated different aspects of the applications such as the ease of learning to use the applications, the design, the compatibility with mobile devices, benefits for learning, quality of the augmented reality animations, usefulness of the information provided by the applications, availability of the applications, parameters that served to determine which application of those evaluated is most useful for the student in their learning process.

2.3 Procedure

When the authorities of the institution approved the research and the ethics committee selected the groups of students from the same educational sublevel, the research was then developed and worked on during 8 sessions of 40 min each.

In the first work session, the students were explained the operation and essential concepts about reality, in the subsequent sessions 2 sessions were worked using the Virtualiti tee application, 2 sessions with the Merge object viewer application and 2 final sessions using the Humanoid 4d application, it is worth mentioning that in all the work sessions the same study contents on the systems of the human body worked with were covered different applications.

In the eighth and last working session, the data collection instrument was applied to the students, which consisted of a survey.

This work complied with the ethical standards considered for research involving human subjects, declared in Helsinki and Nuremberg.

3 Results

Figure 4 shows the difference of the students evaluated: 42% consider that Virtualiti Tee is the best application to study the systems of the human body. This preference may suggest that the interface and pedagogical approach that Virtualiti Tee uses are particularly effective or appealing to this particular group of students.

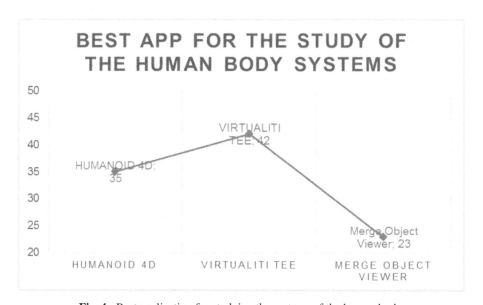

Fig. 4. Best application for studying the systems of the human body.

Figure 5 shows that 43% of students said that Virtualiti Tee has the best augmented reality animations on human body systems. This result highlights the importance of visual quality and immersion provided by animations in teaching the anatomy and systems of the human body.

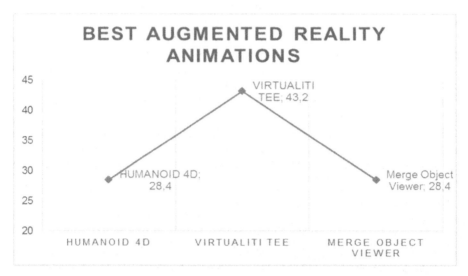

Fig. 5. Best Augmented Reality Animations.

Finally, with regard to the information provided on the subject, Fig. 6 shows that 53% of students consider that Humanoid 4D offers the most complete information about the systems of the human body. This suggests that although the preference for the application

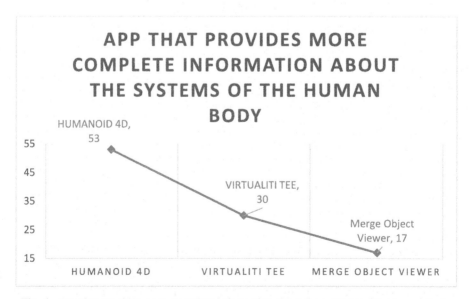

Fig. 6. App that provides more complete information about the systems of the human body.

may vary, the perception of the completeness of the information provided is a crucial factor.

4 Conclusions

In this article we have reported the results of a research that aimed to evaluate three specific applications of Augmented Reality used in the learning of human body systems: Virtualiti Tee, Merge Object Viewer and Humanoid 4d. Areas of evaluation included the animations offered, the quality of the information provided, and the overall design of each application. This approach provides a useful perspective for the selection of effective educational tools in this specific field.

The results of the research indicate that, according to the perception of students, Virtualiti Tee stands out as the best application for studying the systems of the human body (42%), as well as the one that offers the best animations with augmented reality (43%). On the other hand, 53% of students say that Humanoid 4D provides the most complete information on the subject. These student preferences underscore the importance of considering user perceptions and experiences when selecting Augmented Reality tools for anatomy and biology education.

As future research, it is proposed to incorporate other cognitive and emotional variables, such as the level of interest, motivation and perception of difficulty. This can help gain a more complete understanding of how these apps affect not only the knowledge acquired, but also the attitude and engagement of students towards learning.

References

1. Hidalgo-Cajo, B., Hidalgo-Cajo, D., Montenegro-Chanalata, M., Hidalgo-Cajo, I.: Augmented reality as a support resource in the teaching-learning process. Revista Electrónica Interuniversitaria de Formación del Profesorado 24(3), 43–55 (2021)
2. Yusuf, Y.A.M., Ismail, I., Hamzah, W., Amin, M.A.M., Arsad, M.A.M.: A literature review on mobile augmented reality in education. In: Alareeni, B., Hamdan, A. (eds.) ICBT 2021. LNNS, vol. 488, pp. 875–888. Springer, Cham (2021). https://doi.org/10.1007/978-3-031-08090-6_56
3. Cabero-Almenara, J., Fernandez-Batanero, J., Borroso-Osuna, J.: Adoption of augmented reality technology by university students. Heliyon 5(5) (2019)
4. Cabero-Almenara, J., Vásquez-Cano, E., Villota-Oyarvide, W., López-Meneses, E.: Innovation in the university classroom through augmented reality. Analysis from the perspective of the Spanish and Latin American student. Revista Electronica Educare 25(3) (2021)
5. Kaur, N., Pathan, R., Khwaja, U., Sarkar, P., Rathod, B., Murthy, S.: GeoSolvAR: augmented reality based application for mental rotation. In: 2018 IEEE Tenth International Conference on Technology for Education, vol. T4E, pp. 45–52 (2018)
6. Ibañez, M., Delgado, C.: Augmented reality for STEM learning: a systematic review. Comput. Educ. 123, 109–123 (2018)
7. Delneshin, D., Jamali, H., Mansourian, Y., Rastegarpour, H.: Comparing reading comprehension between children reading augmented reality and print storybooks. Comput. Educ. 153, 1–24 (2020)
8. del Rosario-Neira, M., del-Moral, E.: Literary education and reading promotion supported in immersive literary environments with augmented reality. In: OCNOS, vol. 20, no. 3 (2021)

9. Méndez-Porras, A., Alfaro-Velasco, J., Rojas-Guzmán, R.: Educational video games for girls and boys in preschool education using robotics and augmented reality. In: RISTI - Revista Iberica de Sistemas e Tecnologias de Informacao, vol. 2021, no. 42, pp. 472–485 (2021)
10. López, L., Jaen, J.: EmoFindAR: evaluation of a mobile multiplayer augmented reality game for primary school children. Comput. Educ. **149**, 1–42 (2020)
11. Campos, N., Caliz, C., Pérez, J.: Simulation-based education involving online and on-campus models in different European universities. Int. J. Educ. Technol. High. Educ. **17**(8), 1–15 2020
12. Hamada, E.K., Mohamed, E.A., Mohamed, S., Youssef, M.: Virtual reality and augmented reality at the service of increasing interactivity in MOOCs. Educ. Inf. Technol. **25**, 2871–2897 (2020)
13. Cóndor-Herrera, O., Ramos-Galarza, C.: E-learning and M-learning technological intervention in favor of mathematics. In: Zaphiris, P., Ioannou, A. (eds.) Learning and Collaboration Technologies: New Challenges and Learning Experiences. LNCS, vol. 12784, pp. 401–408. Springer, Cham (2021). https://doi.org/10.1007/978-3-030-77889-7_28
14. García-Varcálcel, A., Gómez-Pablos, V.: Project-based learning (PBL): assessment from the perspective of students. J. Educ. Res. **35**(1), 113–131 (2017)
15. Martínez Pérez, S., Bárbara, F., Borroso, J.: Augmented reality as resources for training in higher education. Campus Virtuales **10**(1), 9–19 (2021)
16. Azuma, R.: A survey of augmented reality. Teleoperators Virtual Environ. **6**(4), 355–385 (1997)
17. Cóndor-Herrera, O., Acosta-Rodas, P., Ramos-Galarza, C.: Gamification teaching for an active learning. In: Russo, D., Ahram, T., Karwowski, W., Di Bucchianico, G., Taiar, R. (eds.) IHSI 2021. AISC, vol. 1322, pp. 247–252. Springer, Cham (2021). https://doi.org/10.1007/978-3-030-68017-6_37
18. Hamadah, A., Thamer, A.: Faculty at Saudi Electronic University attitudes toward using augmented reality in education. Educ. Inf. Technol. **24**, 1961–1972 (2016)
19. de Pérez, A.M., Tellera, M.: ICT in education: new learning environments for educational interaction. J. Theory Didactics Soc. Sci. **18**, 83–112 (2012)
20. Cóndor-Herrera, O., Ramos-Galarza, C.: The impact of a technological intervention program on learning mathematical skills. Educ. Inf. Technol., 1–13 (2020)
21. Mirbabaie, M., Stieglitz, S., Brunker, F., Hofeditz, L., Ross, B., Frick, N.: Understanding collaboration with virtual assistants – the role of social identity and the extended self. Bus. Inf. Syst. Eng. **63**(1), 21–37 (2021)
22. Anaya, A., Anaya, C.: Motivating to pass or to learn? Learning motivation strategies for students. Technol. Sci. Educ. **25**(1), 5–14 (2010)
23. Nijhawan, M., Sindhwani, N., Tanwar, S., Kumar, S.: Role of augmented reality and internet of things in education sector. In: Sindhwani, N., Anand, R., Niranjanamurthy, M., Chander Verma, D., Valentina, E.B. (eds.) EAI/Springer Innovations in Communication and Computing, pp. 245–259. Springer, Cham (2023). https://doi.org/10.1007/978-3-031-04524-0_14
24. Curioscope: curioscope.com (2022). https://www.curiscope.com/pages/education
25. Merge: mergeedu.com (2022). https://mergeedu.com/merge-cube?cr=4835
26. Octagon studio: Octagon studio (2019). https://octagon.studio/about-us/
27. Hernandez, R., Fernandez, C., Baptista, P.: Investigation Methodology, 6th edn. McGraw-Hill, Mexico (2014)

AlgoTutor: An Integrated Learning Platform for Data Structures and Algorithms with Real-Time Guidance and Interactive Visualizations

Gadepalli Chandan Sashank$^{(\boxtimes)}$, Zong Wei Tan, and Owen Noel Newton Fernando

Nanyang Technological University, Singapore, Singapore
chandans001@e.ntu.edu.sg

Abstract. AlgoTutor is an innovative educational interactive system designed to transform the learning experience of algorithms and data structures for modern university students in computer science. Despite the growing demand for robust computer science education, mastering these subjects remains challenging due to their inherent complexity. AlgoTutor offers an integrated learning platform featuring interactive modules, diverse materials, a real-time coding compiler, and visual aids to enhance conceptual understanding. By emphasizing critical thinking, retention, and real-time feedback without direct answers, AlgoTutor facilitates a deeper comprehension of fundamental concepts. Additionally, the platform ensures the quality and relevance of instructional materials by leveraging ChatGPT with the GPT4.0 API to provide high-quality responses. With its focus on accessibility and engagement, AlgoTutor aims to make learning data structures and algorithms more enjoyable and effective, ultimately empowering students to master these essential aspects of computer science education.

Keywords: Data Structures and Algorithms · Computer Science Education · Educational Technology · ChatGPT Integration · Learning Platform

1 Introduction

Data structures, serving as a fundamental pillar of computer science, play a crucial role in organizing, processing, and storing data to facilitate efficient access and modification. However, despite their pivotal significance, data structures present formidable challenges within the discipline, stemming from various intrinsic and academic factors. The complexity inherent in data structures arises from their abstract nature and the multitude of operations they support. Students are tasked with comprehending not only the theoretical underpinnings, encompassing the properties and functionalities of diverse data structures such as arrays, linked lists, trees, graphs, and hash tables, but also their practical applications. This multifaceted requirement poses a considerable hurdle for students in mastering the subject matter.

© The Author(s), under exclusive license to Springer Nature Switzerland AG 2024
C. Stephanidis et al. (Eds.): HCII 2024, CCIS 2117, pp. 29–38, 2024.
https://doi.org/10.1007/978-3-031-61953-3_4

Furthermore, the learning trajectory escalates as students delve into algorithms, which constitute another highly intricate concept in computer science aimed at manipulating the data structures. The interdependence between data structures and algorithms exacerbates the learning process, as proficiency in one domain often necessitates mastery of the other. Students are confronted with the task of understanding various algorithmic techniques for sorting, searching, and analyzing algorithms. Each of these techniques presents its own set of challenges, encompassing optimization strategies and the analysis of complexity, including considerations of time and space complexity.

From an academic perspective, conventional teaching approaches may inadequately cater to the multifaceted learning requirements of students grappling with data structures for the initial time. Traditional pedagogical techniques encounter obstacles in capturing students' attention, thereby resulting in subpar learning achievements. In terms of instructional methodologies, the utilization of obscure and intricate abstract data types prevails, often employed to elucidate fundamental principles, which students find challenging to grasp and even more challenging to connect with tangible applications [1, 2]. This disparity constitutes a significant hurdle for many students, as they encounter difficulties in envisaging how abstract concepts of data structures translate into practical programming endeavors.

The necessity for a more interactive and captivating educational methodology is apparent, advocating for an approach that not only imparts the theoretical foundation of data structures but also provides students with opportunities for practical, hands-on engagement. Visual learning resources and interactive platforms, facilitating experimentation with data structures, visualization of their operations, and provision of prompt feedback on coding endeavors, hold the potential to markedly alleviate the hurdles associated with this subject. The evolution of such tools and methodologies is geared towards demystifying the intricate nature of data structures, rendering them more accessible and comprehensible to students across various proficiency levels, thereby enriching the overarching learning milieu in computer science education.

The impetus driving the creation of AlgoTutor stems from the prevalent challenges encountered by learners in mastering data structures and algorithms, coupled with the inherent constraints of existing online educational platforms. Data structures and algorithms, as cornerstone elements of computer science, impose a formidable learning curve owing to their abstract essence and the intricate logic governing their functionalities. Students frequently encounter difficulties in apprehending these concepts, impeded by conventional educational approaches that may inadequately address the practical application of these theories or accommodate varied learning modalities.

KhanMigo Academy [3, 4], despite its encompassing curriculum and adaptive learning technologies, may not furnish the requisite depth necessary for students to confront the intricacies of data structures and algorithms comprehensively. Its broad-based approach, while advantageous for comprehensive learning, might inadvertently overlook specialized areas crucial for individuals aiming to delve deeper into computer science. Similarly, VisualAlgo's unparalleled strength in furnishing visual depictions of abstract concepts [5, 6] may not be supplemented adequately with hands-on coding experiences essential for practical application. Although visualization aids in conceptual comprehension, a singular focus on this aspect may overlook the cultivation of problem-solving abilities and coding proficiency indispensable in real-world scenarios.

AlgoTutor is conceptualized as a remedy to these hurdles, presenting an integrated platform that amalgamates the strengths of existing resources while mitigating their limitations. It endeavors to furnish a more holistic learning encounter by integrating real-time coding practice, interactive visualizations, and personalized feedback. Such an approach not only renders abstract concepts more tangible but also empowers learners to apply theoretical knowledge through practical coding exercises, thereby augmenting their comprehension and retention of material. AlgoTutor endeavors to accommodate diverse learning preferences by incorporating a myriad of academic strategies, ensuring that students can progress at their own pace and in a manner aligning with their individual preferences. In so doing, AlgoTutor endeavors to surmount the prevailing barriers in computer science education, particularly within the realms of data structures and algorithms, thereby fostering a more immersive, efficacious, and inclusive learning milieu.

This paper aims to outline the design and development of an interactive system integrated with ChatGPT that seeks to enhance the educational experience, with a particular focus on data structures in C. The project is guided by a set of foundational principles to ensure its effectiveness and relevance. First, it commits to adhering to contemporary educational standards by ensuring that the content presented aligns with established educational resources widely utilized in the teaching of data structures. Additionally, recognizing the sensitive nature of educational data, the system prioritizes the secure handling of user information to protect privacy and integrity. Moreover, the development approach emphasizes ensuring that the system is compatible across various browsers and devices, thereby broadening accessibility and usability for a diverse user base. Finally, the project underscores the importance of continuous improvement through regular updates and maintenance. This incremental process aims to address any emergent issues quickly and integrate user feedback, thereby maintaining the system's relevance and enhancing the overall learning experience.

2   Literature Review

The integration of ChatGPT within education, particularly in the domains of assessment, student engagement, personalized learning, and coding, introduces a multifaceted outlook on the evolution of learning environments. Examining ChatGPT's potential in these spheres uncovers a spectrum of opportunities and challenges that warrant thorough examination.

Within the domain of assessments, a recent study underscores ChatGPT's capacity to engage in computer science examinations, narrowly passing and showcasing the model's potential in tackling structured problems. The transition from GPT-3.5 to GPT-4 signifies a progression toward approximating the capabilities of an average student, indicative of the continuous refinement of AI models for educational evaluations [7]. While this advancement suggests a promising trajectory for AI-assisted assessments, it also prompts inquiries into the depth of understanding exhibited by these models, questioning whether they truly grasp content or merely replicate learned patterns. Furthermore, ChatGPT exhibits proficiency in elucidating various programming concepts, such as data structures, algorithms, programming languages, and syntax, in a succinct, straightforward manner [8]. Additionally, automated assessment tools driven by Chat-GPT facilitate immediate feedback and grading on assignments, affording educators more time to concentrate on engaging instructional methodologies. This application is particularly advantageous in programming and technical subjects, wherein ChatGPT can evaluate code accuracy and logic [9].

In educational contexts, student engagement and personalized learning emerge as pivotal considerations in the integration of ChatGPT. A study detailing an experiment where students were allocated into groups, one with access to ChatGPT for resolving programming challenges, indicates that ChatGPT augments student engagement by furnishing a responsive and interactive learning milieu. It empowers students to navigate topics at their own pace, pose inquiries, and receive immediate feedback, thereby nurturing a more immersive learning environment [9]. Furthermore, according to another study, students favor the explanations provided by ChatGPT, as evidenced by the statement: "We found that the code explanations generated by GPT-3 were rated better on average in understandability and accuracy compared to code explanations created by students" [10]. However, these findings also underscore the potential for inconsistencies and inaccuracies introduced by ChatGPT [11], which may impact learning outcomes. Moreover, it is imperative to prevent students from relying solely on ChatGPT for obtaining complete answers, as such dependence may impede the development of critical thinking and problem-solving skills [8, 12]. This dichotomy underscores the imperative of a balanced approach in integrating AI tools into education, ensuring that while they serve as valuable resources, they do not overshadow the cultivation of critical thinking and problem-solving competencies fundamental to authentic learning.

Furthermore, the discourse surrounding ChatGPT's integration into education transcends its immediate functional advantages and encompasses broader implications, including academic integrity, the risk of plagiarism, and the influence on students' analytical proficiencies [13]. The advanced capabilities of ChatGPT and similar AI technologies present unparalleled prospects for accessing information, receiving feedback on assignments, and even automating grading processes, potentially liberating educators to allocate more time to engaging instructional techniques and personalized interactions with students.

However, the excitement surrounding these technologies is accompanied by apprehensions regarding their potential impact on the cultivation of critical thinking and problem-solving skills among students. The conundrum lies in leveraging the advantages of ChatGPT to enhance educational experiences while simultaneously implementing measures to mitigate its potential drawbacks. One notable concern is the propensity for ChatGPT to produce inaccuracies [11], as highlighted in a study [14]: "Apart from these different features and capabilities, various limitations have been observed such as; the sometimes generation of incorrect information may rise with biased content etc." As artificial intelligence continues to progress, the educational community faces the challenge of devising innovative strategies to integrate these technologies in a manner that enriches the learning process without compromising the development of essential skills.

The exploration of ChatGPT's application in education reveals a complex landscape where the potential for transformative learning experiences coexists with challenges that need careful navigation. The ongoing development and integration of AI tools in education demand a nuanced approach that maximizes their benefits while addressing the ethical, practical, and pedagogical concerns that accompany their use.

3 AlgoTutor

3.1 System Architecture

The system architecture of the website, as demonstrated in Fig. 1 is meticulously structured to deliver a resilient and dynamic user experience, facilitated through a multi-tiered design. Users engage with the system via a standard web browser on the client side, initiating HTTP requests directed to the server. Meanwhile, the server side is compartmentalized into discrete layers, allowing for streamlined processing and ensuring a distinct separation of concerns.

At the forefront of the server side lies the Front End, also known as the Presentation Layer. This crucial tier is tasked with managing the user interface and presenting content to users, ensuring an intuitive and responsive interaction with the website's features and services. Serving as the gateway, users submit their inputs, such as queries, through the Front End, which then channels them to the Back End via an API layer.

The Back End comprises two core components: the App Logic Layer and the Data Layer. The App Logic Layer serves as the backbone, housing custom APIs and the fundamental application logic responsible for interpreting user requests. Crucially, it incorporates a GCC Compiler, pivotal for compiling user-submitted code—a vital feature for a website emphasizing programming and data structures.

The Data Layer works in concert with the App Logic Layer, offering a structured framework for data management and storage. Leveraging MongoDB, a NoSQL database, it facilitates the storage and retrieval of documents in response to user queries. This implementation is pivotal for efficiently managing educational content and user data, ensuring swift retrieval and robust data handling capabilities.

Integral to the system is the integration of the GPT-3.5 API, which enhances the retrieval process by providing contextually relevant prompts derived from user queries. This component of the architecture leverages the advanced language processing capabilities of ChatGPT to generate dynamic content and facilitate educational interactions.

The architecture delineates a clear pathway from user request to response delivery, ensuring seamless operation of each component to furnish an efficient, secure, and user-friendly experience. The distribution of responsibilities across layers not only facilitates smooth functionality but also guarantees the system's maintainability, scalability, and adaptability to accommodate the website's expanding requirements.

3.2 AlgoTutor Features

The user interface (UI), as demonstrated in Fig. 2 has been meticulously crafted to enrich users' learning encounters while studying data structures and algorithms. Questions are

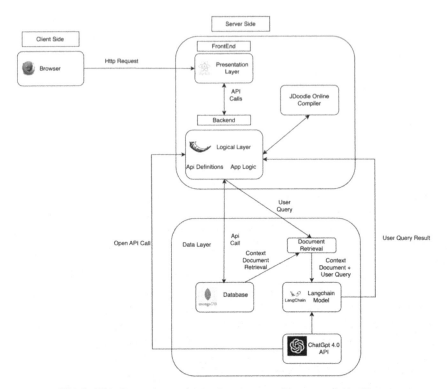

Fig. 1. This figure demonstrates the system architecture of AlgoTutor

systematically categorized into various topics, such as stacks and queues, binary trees, linked lists, and hash tables, enabling focused learning. These problems are meticulously organized by titles and further segmented based on difficulty levels, spanning from 'Easy' to 'Medium' and 'Hard,' thereby empowering users to incrementally challenge themselves in alignment with their skill development.

The system features a search functionality, allowing users to filter and locate specific questions or topics efficiently. This ensures that students can tailor their learning experience to their immediate needs, whether it involves revising known concepts or tackling new, more challenging problems.

In addition to problem-solving, the system integrates a section for multiple-choice questions (MCQs), as demonstrated in Fig. 3 providing an alternative mode of learning and assessment that accommodates varied learning preferences.

The visualization (Viz) component, as demonstrated in Fig. 4 emerges as a prominent feature, offering interactive graphical depictions of data structures in operation. Various visualization functionalities encompass actions such as adding or deleting nodes from a linked list, as well as pushing and popping nodes from a stack or queue. This aids users in comprehending the precise connections between nodes and pointers within the data structure.

Fig. 2. This figure demonstrates the homepage UI of AlgoTutor

Fig. 3. This figure demonstrates the MCQ Page of AlgoTutor

Moreover, a dedicated Concepts section serves as a theoretical companion to the practical exercises, providing users with essential background knowledge and detailed explanations of fundamental principles. This section proves invaluable for users seeking to solidify their theoretical understanding alongside practical application.

The Frequently Asked Questions (FAQ) segment, as demonstrated in Fig. 5 addresses common inquiries and offers additional support, augmenting a comprehensive self-service learning resource. This aspect of the system reflects its user-centered design philosophy, ensuring that learners have prompt access to answers and can surmount obstacles in their learning journey without undue delay.

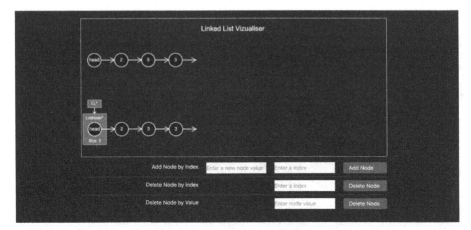

Fig. 4. This figure demonstrates the Linked List Visualization Page of AlgoTutor

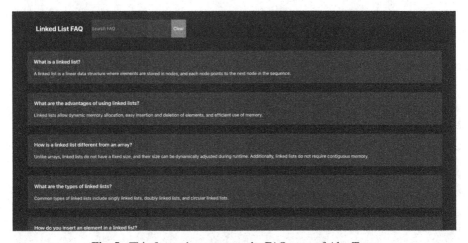

Fig. 5. This figure demonstrates the FAQ page of AlgoTutor

4 Discussion and Future Work

The system, in its current iteration, lays a sturdy foundation for learning data structures and algorithms; nonetheless, it harbors inherent limitations. Foremost among these is the scope of content, which presently addresses fundamental topics like linked lists, binary trees, hash maps, etc., but may lack comprehensive coverage of advanced subjects or the latest advancements in computer science. Additionally, optimizing performance across various devices and browsers necessitates ongoing vigilance to ensure a seamless user experience across all platforms. Furthermore, while the existing knowledge base and FAQs offer substantial support, they may not be exhaustive, potentially leaving users in search of more nuanced or specialized guidance.

Looking towards future enhancements, the platform could significantly improve by expanding its content library to encompass a broader spectrum of topics, incorporating more intricate challenges to serve as a comprehensive educational resource. Improvements to the platform's responsiveness and compatibility with diverse devices and browsers will be pivotal for ensuring accessibility. Transitioning towards a more community-centric model, wherein users contribute to and refine the content, could further enhance the learning experience.

For future endeavors, there exists significant potential to diversify the utilization of AlgoTutor in data structures and algorithms education. Developing mobile applications would render learning more accessible, enabling users to access content anytime, anywhere. Establishing partnerships with educational institutions could extend the platform's reach and integrate it within formal education systems, thereby offering a range of collaborative and feedback opportunities. Implementing gamification could introduce a new dimension of interactivity and enjoyment to learning, enhancing user engagement. Furthermore, a commitment to leveraging user feedback by conducting user studies and actual learning outcomes to inform platform updates will ensure that the system evolves continuously to meet the genuine needs of its users. Such advancements would not only augment the efficacy of the current system but also position the platform as a solid tool in the realm of data structures and algorithms education.

5 Conclusion

AlgoTutor represents a potential step forward in the domain of computer science education, specifically addressing the many challenges associated with learning data structures and algorithms. By integrating the capabilities of ChatGPT within a user-friendly website, AlgoTutor provides a personalized and engaging learning experience for its users. It surpasses the limitations of traditional and current digital learning tools by offering a unique blend of interactive visualization, hands-on practice, and real-time ChatGPT feedback. This innovative approach not only develops a deeper understanding of complex concepts but also cultivates the critical thinking and problem-solving skills essential for success in the field of data structures and algorithms. As a readily available educational resource, AlgoTutor is bound to make a profound impact on learners across various levels, helping them to navigate the intricacies of computer science with greater confidence and competence. Through its commitment to continuous improvement and user-centered design, AlgoTutor stands as a testament to the potential of technology-enhanced learning in the digital age.

References

1. Sun, Y.: Research on teaching reform and innovation of 'data structure and algorithms' in the context of new engineering. In: Yacob, S., Cicek, B., Rak, J., Ali, G. (eds.) Proceedings of the 2023 7th International Seminar on Education, Management and Social Sciences (ISEMSS 2023), vol. 779. Advances in Social Science, Education and Humanities Research, vol. 779, pp. 1654–1662. Atlantis Press SARL, Paris (2023). https://doi.org/10.2991/978-2-38476-126-5_186

2. Patel, S.: A literature review on tools for learning data structures (2014)
3. Kochenderfer, M.: Review of Khan academy's AI tutor. Is Khanmigo any good? Mama Smiles - Joyful Parenting. https://www.mamasmiles.com/khanmigo-review/. Accessed 13 Mar 2024
4. Kshetri, N.: The economics of generative artificial intelligence in the academic industry. Computer **56**(8), 77–83 (2023). https://doi.org/10.1109/MC.2023.3278089
5. Mckinney, J.K.: VisuAlgo: a deep dive into visualizing algorithms and data structures. Medium. https://medium.com/@joe.code.mckinney/visualgo-a-deep-dive-into-visualizing-algorithms-and-data-structures-c26f0604074f. Accessed 13 Mar 2024
6. Loftus, N., Green, C., Narman, H.S.: The cybersecurity packet control simulator: CSPCS. In: 2022 IEEE Global Humanitarian Technology Conference (GHTC), pp. 226–233, September 2022. https://doi.org/10.1109/GHTC55712.2022.9911042
7. Bordt, S., von Luxburg, U.: ChatGPT participates in a computer science exam. arXiv, 22 March 2023. http://arxiv.org/abs/2303.09461. Accessed 12 Mar 2024
8. Rahman, M., Watanobe, Y.: ChatGPT for education and research: opportunities, threats, and strategies. Appl. Sci. **13**(9), 5783 (2023). https://doi.org/10.3390/app13095783
9. Qureshi, B.: Exploring the use of ChatGPT as a tool for learning and assessment in undergraduate computer science curriculum: opportunities and challenges (2023)
10. Leinonen, J., et al.: Comparing code explanations created by students and large language models. In: Proceedings of the 2023 Conference on Innovation and Technology in Computer Science Education, vol. 1, pp. 124–130. ACM, Turku, Finland, June 2023. https://doi.org/10.1145/3587102.3588785
11. Shen, Y., et al.: ChatGPT and other large language models are double-edged swords. Radiology **307**(2), e230163 (2023). https://doi.org/10.1148/radiol.230163
12. Finestrone, F., di Furia, M., Savino, F., Palmisano, L.: HELMeTO 2023 Book-of-abstracts (2024)
13. Tyson, J.: Shortcomings of ChatGPT. J. Chem. Educ. **100**(8), 3098–3101 (2023). https://doi.org/10.1021/acs.jchemed.3c00361
14. Haleem, A., Javaid, M., Singh, R.P.: An era of ChatGPT as a significant futuristic support tool: a study on features, abilities, and challenges. BenchCouncil Trans. Benchmarks Stand. Eval. **2**(4), 100089 (2022). https://doi.org/10.1016/j.tbench.2023.100089

Early Prediction of Mathematics Learning Achievement of Elementary Students Using Hidden Markov Model

Jen-I Chiu(ID) and Mengping Tsuei(⊠)(ID)

Graduate School of Curriculum and Instructional Communication Technology,
National Taipei University of Education, Taipei, Taiwan
mptsuei@mail.ntue.edu.tw.com

Abstract. Elementary students usually felt the fractions and decimals concepts were challenged concepts. This leads to misconceptions due to their symbolic representations and arithmetic rules being distinct from those of integers. This study utilized data mining and learning analytics methods to develop a learning system using a Hidden Markov Model (HMM), focusing on students' misconceptions in fractions and decimals lessons. The study aims to evaluate the efficacy of HMM in predicting students' mathematics achievement by comparing the Mean Squared Errors (MSE) of the HMM and a baseline model. There were seventy-eight fourth-grade students participating in Taiwan. Students answered forty mathematics questions using the system over eighty minutes, 6,246 time-series data points were collected. The baseline model used the ZeroR classifier as a benchmark. The first thirty learning behaviors were sequentially input into both models, calculating MSE relative to the students' mathematics achievement test scores. Subsequently, the Wilcoxon signed-rank test assessed significant MSE differences between models. The results showed that HMM significantly outperformed the baseline model in fractions and decimals, showing lower MSE. Furthermore, in graphical analysis, incorporating sequentially inputted behaviors, revealed a more pronounced reduction in MSE for the HMM model across lessons. These results highlight HMM's effectiveness in early math achievement prediction in elementary education.

Keywords: Hidden Markov Model · Learning Analytics · Mathematics Learning Achievement

1 Introduction

Mathematics plays a vital role in developing students' 21st century skills. However, primary school students encounter challenges when learning fractions and decimals. These lessons differ from the concept of integers in terms of symbolic representation and arithmetic rules, which can often lead to misconceptions that impact their mathematical learning achievements (Aliustaoğlu et al., 2018; Avgerinou & Tolmie, Nahdi & Jatisunda, 2020). When students hold misconceptions or lack relevant knowledge, they may depend on strategies such as trial and error, which can increase cognitive load and have negative effects on learning achievement (Kapur, 2014).

© The Author(s), under exclusive license to Springer Nature Switzerland AG 2024
C. Stephanidis et al. (Eds.): HCII 2024, CCIS 2117, pp. 39–47, 2024.
https://doi.org/10.1007/978-3-031-61953-3_5

Learning analytics make a substantial contribution in predicting students' performance, identifying behavioural patterns, and supporting educational policy-making. The integration of data mining and learning analytics improves the ability of educators to refine instructional designs and enables personalized support on learning platforms (Pardo et al., 2019, and Wang et al., 2020). Within the field of artificial intelligence, the Hidden Markov Model (HMM) is a classic algorithm that is particularly effective for analyzing time-series data. As an interpretable and efficient model, HMM has shown it's potential in providing early warnings. However, to date, there has been less research conducted on the effectiveness of early predicting systems in primary schools (López-Zambrano et al., 2021). Therefore, this study aims to establish a predictive model of student mathematics learning achievement and to verify the effectiveness.

The aim of this study was to develop a mathematics learning system based on unsupervised Hidden Markov Models specifically designed to mine students' learning behaviours in fractions and decimals lessons. The data revealed misconceptions in the learning process and predicted mathematics learning achievement. The results of the study can provide educators with a tool to identify and support students who are struggling with mathematics learning.

2 Literature Review

2.1 Misconceptions in Mathematics

Safriani et al. (2019) suggested that mathematical errors can be categorized according to the causes: procedural errors, principle errors, and conceptual errors. Procedural errors usually arise when students make mistakes inadvertently when solving problems. Principle errors involve the incorrect application of facts and concepts, such as the misuse of formulas. Conceptual errors arise from systematic mistakes in constructing mathematical concepts, thus resulting in misconceptions (Resnick, 1989). Students' knowledge often depends on their previous experiences, which they might use to understand and interpret new information.

Typical errors in learning fractions with the same denominator include ignoring the integer part, directly adding (or subtracting) the integer, numerator, and denominator, or multiplying the integer by both the numerator and denominator (Safriani et al., 2019; Aliustaoğlua et al., 2018). These errors reflected students' misconceptions about the fractions lessons, especially when the questions included the calculation of integers and fractions. In learning equivalent fractions, students may have misconceptions about comparing the value of fractions, such as the misconception that the larger the denominator or numerator, the larger the value of the fraction (Aliustaoğlua et al., 2018; Deringöl, 2019).

In the study of decimals, students may have difficulty in understanding the meaning of the decimal point. For example, they may think that the more decimal places there are, the greater the value is, or that the numbers are aligned to the right in a column form (Mohyuddin & Khalil, 2016). These misconceptions often stem from students' lack of understanding that decimals represent the separation of integer and decimal parts. In addition, students may also have difficulties in reading and converting decimals, for example, reading a number after the decimal point as an integer, or ignoring the decimal point when converting meters to centimeters.

Analyzing the misconceptions originated by the students during the learning process is beneficial for the establishment of the HMM. By categorizing students' errors into misconceptions, it allows HMM to analyze and predict students' learning achievements more precisely during the learning process.

2.2 HMM in Educational Research

The activities of students' learning encompass a sequence of actions over time, rather than specific behaviours at a single moment. To offer personalized learning support, it is vital to analyze students' entire learning progress and understand their needs (Martin & Sherin, 2013; Chen et al., 2019). Early prediction plays a crucial role in e-learning environments. Efficient predictive techniques allow educators to identify at-risk students at an early stage, reducing the likelihood of failure. According to López-Zambrano et al. (2021), research gaps in early prediction systems reveal two crucial areas: firstly, most current studies primarily concentrate on secondary and higher education, while relatively little research has been conducted on primary education. Secondly, the analytical methods used in these studies typically do not include HMM. These findings are noteworthy and warrants further research. The primary stage is a critical period for students to learn foundational skills like reading, writing, and arithmetic. Identifying learning obstacles early in this stage and providing appropriate learning support can facilitate students overcome these challenges.

Both supervised and unsupervised HMMs have their value in data analysis. Supervised HMM are suitable for datasets with tags, like in language processing for part of speech tagging, where texts can be manually tagged for training and prediction (Fwa & Marshall, 2018). Unsupervised HMMs are more practical in analyzing student learning behaviors, as students' internal mental states or learning achievement statuses are difficult to observe directly and thus challenging to label. Tadayon and Pottie (2020) indicated that unsupervised HMMs' predictive capabilities are comparable to supervised HMMs and serve as an effective model training method when labeled data are hard to obtain.

The use of Hidden Markov Models (HMM) in the field of education has begun to gain traction. Pan et al. (2020) used unsupervised HMM to analyze students' flow states during problem-based learning activities. They found that students often exhibited anxious states when opening learning tools and viewing messages, but showed flow states while organizing notes. Additionally, Zeng (2020) analyzed college students' physical education learning achievement using HMM. The study predicted students' mastery of knowledge by collecting formative assessment results, assessing their learning achievement. These studies indicated that HMM has shown potential in the field of learning analytics. However, research on using HMM to predict students' achievement in mathematics, especially in handling complex concepts like fractions and decimals, remains relatively scarce.

Considering the misconceptions that primary school students may develop in learning fractions and decimals lessons, which can lead to increased cognitive load and affect learning achievement. This study aims to use HMM to predict students' learning achievement by coding mathematical misconceptions as data features.

3   Method

3.1   Participants

This study involved 78 primary school students from Taipei, divided across three fourth-grade classes. These classes exhibited similar characteristics in terms of gender ratio and curriculum progress.

3.2   Instruments

The Mathematics Learning System: The mathematics learning system, developed by researchers, features 20 items each on fractions and decimals. Excluding items with difficulty less than .30 or greater than .80 and discrimination below .20 (Agarwal, 1986), the fractions set was left with 19 items, while the decimals set had 18 items. The fractions items averaged a 0.57 difficulty index, ranging from 0.41 to 0.77, and the decimals items averaged 0.51, ranging from 0.31 to 0.80. Discrimination indices were excellent for both sets: fractions averaged 0.84, ranging from 0.46 to 1.0, and decimals averaged 0.85, ranging from 0.48 to 1.0, indicating high quality (Ebel & Frisbie, 1991). The system interface, as shown in Fig. 1, is web-based, utilizing responsive web design for compatibility with various mobile devices and personal computers.

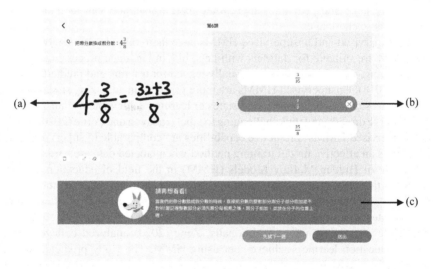

Fig. 1. The Mathematics Learning System Interface: (a) handwriting area, (b) buttons for options, and (c) feedback content

Mathematics Achievement Test. The mathematics achievement test was developed to validate the performance of HMM in predicting students' mathematical achievement. After applying the exclusion criteria (difficulty <.30 or >.80 and discrimination <.20), the fraction test consisted of 14 items, with an average difficulty index of .66 and a range from .50 to .83. The decimal test, comprising 10 items, had an average difficulty index of .59, ranging from .50 to .78. For discrimination, the fraction items had an average index of .69, with a range from .33 to 1.0, and the decimal items had an average of .82, ranged from .44 to 1.0, both demonstrating excellent discriminations (Chase, 1978; Ebel & Frisbie, 1991).

3.3 Data Collection and Model Training

Data Collection and Behavioral Coding: Researchers collected students behavioral sequences through the system to form the dataset for model training. An unsupervised HMM was applied to predict learning achievement states. Parameters of the HMM were initialized randomly and iteratively computed using the Baum-Welch algorithm until convergence. The dataset comprised the students' initial response accuracy, correctness after revision, instances of giving up, and behaviors related to misconceptions in fractions and decimals. These behaviors were further coded into 8 fractional misconceptions and 7 decimal misconceptions, and computation errors, totaling 19 distinct behaviours were coded.

Dataset Description: In this study, a total of 6,246 valid time-series data points were collected, representing the complete dataset. To create the datasets for HMM training and testing, student-based random sampling was employed. Specifically, 80% of students' data, encompassing lessons on both fractions and decimals, were randomly selected to constitute the training set. The remaining 20% of data points were allocated to the test set, ensuring that both subsets maintained continuity in the time-series data.

Data Analysis and Achievement Prediction: The Viterbi algorithm, as indicated by Forney (1975), was employed to predict students' learning achievements in fractions and decimals, with its predictive accuracy validated against the results of the mathematics achievement test. The algorithm's application was based on the formula described by Jurafsky and Martin (2018):

$$V_t(j) = max_{1 \leq i \leq N-1}\left(V_{t-1}(i) \times a_{ij}\right) \times b_j(O_t)$$

where $V_t(j)$ is the probability of the most likely sequence of students' learning achievement levels up to step t that ends in state j; i represents a specific achievement level from the set of all possible levels at time $t-1$, where $1 \leq i \leq N-1$ and N is the total number of achievement levels; a_{ij} is the transition probability from achievement level i at time $t-1$ to state j at time t; $b_j(O_t)$ is the probability of observing the specific learning behavior O_t, given that the student's achievement level is j at time t; The *max* operator selects the maximum probability across all sequences that conclude at achievement level j at time t.

In the context of our study, the hidden states represent different levels of students' learning achievements, while the observed behaviors correspond to the learning behaviours of students during learning tasks. The Viterbi algorithm is applied to determine the most likely sequence of achievement levels based on the observed behaviors.

To evaluate the efficacy of the HMM in predicting mathematical learning achievements, a baseline model was employed as a benchmark. The baseline model, based on

Zohair (2019), employs the ZeroR classifier as a benchmark to evaluate the performance of various machine learning models in small datasets for predicting learning achievements. The ZeroR classifier relies solely on the statistical regularities in historical data, without involving the input and analysis of any additional features. This equation represents a basic performance level that any effective model should be able to surpass. The equation is as follows:

$$Learning\ Achievement = (\frac{Number\ of\ Correct\ Responses}{Total\ Number\ of\ Responses}) \times 100\%$$

Mean Squared Errors (MSE) were employed as a metric of model performance. MSE values, indicative of model fitting accuracy, were computed by processing the initial thirty learning behaviors of students in the test set through both the HMM and baseline models, and correlating these with students' mathematics achievement test scores. A lower MSE value signifies better model fitting. Furthermore, following the recommendations of Son et al. (2015) and Krzystanek et al. (2009), the Wilcoxon signed-rank test was utilized to ascertain the statistical significance of the differences in MSEs between the models. This analysis facilitated an understanding of the HMM's efficiency in early prediction of students' learning achievements.

4 Results

4.1 Graphical Presentation

The graphical representation (Fig. 2.) of the MSE for the HMM and baseline models across the first 100 learning behaviors reveals a notable trend in the predictive accuracy as a function of increasing behavior sequence length. In the fractions lesson, the baseline model commenced with an initial MSE of .81, suggesting a lower accuracy in early predictions. This MSE gradually reduced to .21, indicating an enhancement in predictive performance as the number of behaviors considered increased. The HMM for fractions demonstrated a superior trend, starting with a marginally lower initial MSE of .73 and showing a more pronounced improvement, culminating at a minimum MSE of .11. This suggests that the HMM adapts more efficiently to accumulating data, thereby refining its predictions more rapidly than the baseline model.

Similarly, in the decimals lesson, the baseline model's MSE trended from a maximum of .80 down to .42, whereas the HMM started at a slightly higher initial MSE of .84 but improved to .32. This pattern implies that despite a higher initial error, the HMM is capable of leveraging early behavioral data to achieve greater predictive accuracy over time.

4.2 Comparing the Predictive Performance of HMM and Baseline Models

In evaluating the predictive accuracy of the Hidden Markov Model (HMM) compared to the baseline model in mathematics learning achievement, the first 30 learning behaviors were sequentially input into both models, and the MSE between each set of predictions and the students' mathematics achievement test scores were calculated. These MSE

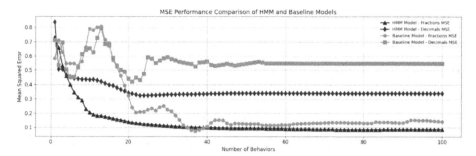

Fig. 2. Comparative performance of HMM and baseline models on behavioral data

values were then subjected to the Wilcoxon signed-rank test to compare the performance of the models. As illustrated in Table 1, the results of the Wilcoxon signed-rank test indicate a significantly lower MSE for the HMM in the fractions lesson ($M = .23$, $SD = .17$) compared to the baseline model ($M = .48$, $SD = .21$; $Z = -4.47$, $p < .001$). Similarly, in the decimals lesson, the HMM ($M = 0.41$, $SD = 0.21$) also exhibited a significant advantage over the baseline model ($M = 0.57$, $SD = 0.10$; $Z = -4.57$, $p < .001$).

Table 1. Results of Wilcoxon signed-rank test for Mean Squared Errors (MSE)

Lessons	Baseline ($n = 30$)	HMM ($n = 30$)	Z
Fractions M (SD)	.48(.21)	.23(.17)	−4.47***
Decimal M (SD)	.57(.10)	.41(.21)	−4.57***

*** $p < .001$.

5   Discussion and Conclusions

The study results demonstrated that the Hidden Markov Model (HMM) was more effective and accurate than the baseline model in predictive primary school students' mathematical achievements in both fractions and decimals lessons. The HMM showed a significantly lower Mean Squared Errors (MSE) with mathematics achievement test scores in these areas, highlighting its potential for early identification of learning difficulties and provision of timely, effective interventions.

Our preliminary results offer educators insights to identify difficulties in students' learning processes and offer opportunities to provide appropriate learning supports for students. Further research could expand the scope of HMM application, including predicting academic achievement in other disciplines or integrating HMM with personalized learning support to establish better learning environments.

Acknowledgments. This work was supported by funding from the National Science and Technology Council of Taiwan (NSTC-112-2424-H-152-001-DR).

References

Agarwal, Y.P.: Statistical Methods, Concepts, Applications and Computations. Sterling Publication, New Delhi (1986)

Aliustaoğlu, F., Tuna, A., Biber, A.Ç.: The misconceptions of sixth grade secondary school students on fractions. Int. Electron. J. Elementary Educ. **10**(5), 591–599 (2018). https://doi.org/10.26822/iejee.2018541308

Avgerinou, V.A., Tolmie, A.: Inhibition and cognitive load in fractions and decimals. Br. J. Educ. Psychol. **90**, 240–256 (2020). https://doi.org/10.1111/bjep.12321

Chen, H., Dai, Y., Gao, H., Han, D., Li, S.: Classification and analysis of MOOCs learner's state: the study of hidden Markov model. Comput. Sci. Inf. Syst. **16**(3), 849–865 (2019). https://doi.org/10.2298/CSIS181002030C

Chase, C.I.: Measurement for Educational Evaluation. 2nd edn. Addison-Wesley (1978)

Deringöl, Y.: Misconceptions of primary school students about the subject of fractions. Int. J. Eval. Res. Educ. **8**(1), 29–38 (2019)

Ebel, R.L., Frisbie, D.A.: Essentials of Educational Measurement (5, th Prentice-Hall, Englewood Cliffs, NJ (1991)

Forney, G.D., Jr.: Minimal bases of rational vector spaces, with applications to multivariable linear systems. SIAM J. Control **13**(3), 493–520 (1975)

Fwa, H.L., Marshall, L.: Modeling engagement of programming students using unsupervised machine learning technique. GSTF J. Comput. **6**(1), 1–6 (2018)

Jurafsky, D., Martin, J.H.: Speech and Language Processing: An Introduction to Natural Language Processing, Computational Linguistics, and Speech Recognition. Prentice Hall (2018)

Kapur, M.: Productive failure in learning math. Cogn. Sci. **38**(5), 1008–1022 (2014)

López Zambrano, J., Lara Torralbo, J.A., Romero Morales, C.: Early prediction of student learning performance through data mining: a systematic review. Psicothema **33**(3), 456–465 (2021)

Martin, T., Sherin, B.: Learning analytics and computational techniques for detecting and evaluating patterns in learning: an introduction to the special issue. J. Learn. Sci. **22**(4), 511–520 (2013). https://doi.org/10.1080/10508406.2013.840466

Mohyuddin, R.G., Khalil, U.: Misconceptions of students in learning mathematics at primary level. Bull. Educ. Res. **38**(1), 133–162 (2016)

Nahdi, D.S., Jatisunda, M.G.: Conceptual understanding and procedural knowledge: a case study on learning mathematics of fractional material in elementary school. J. Phys. Conf. Ser. **1477**(4), 042037 (2020)

Pardo, A., Jovanovic, J., Dawson, S., Gašević, D., Mirriahi, N.: Using learning analytics to scale the provision of personalised feedback. Br. J. Edu. Technol. **50**(1), 128–138 (2019). https://doi.org/10.1111/bjet.12592

Pan, Z., Li, C., Liu, M.: Learning analytics dashboard for problem-based Learning. In: The Seventh ACM Conference on Learning@ Scale, Virtual Event, United States, August 2020. https://doi.org/10.1145/3386527.3406751

Resnick, L.B., Nesher, P., Leonard, F., Magone, M., Omanson, S., Peled, I.: Conceptual bases of arithmetic errors: the case of decimal fractions. J. Res. Math. Educ. **20**(1), 8–27 (1989)

Safriani, W., Munzir, S., Duskri, M., Maulidi, I.: Analysis of students' errors on the fraction calculation operations problem. Al-Jabar: Jurnal Pendidikan Matematika **10**(2), 307–318 (2019)

Tadayon, M., Pottie, G.: Comparative analysis of the hidden Markov model and LSTM: a simulative approach. IEEE Sig. Process. Mag. **29**(1), 22–34 (2020). https://doi.org/10.1109/MSP.2011.942819

Wang, C., Fang, T., Gu, Y.: Learning performance and behavioral patterns of online collaborative learning: impact of cognitive load and affordances of different multimedia. Comput. Educ. **143**, 103683 (2020). https://doi.org/10.1016/j.compedu.2019.103683

Zeng, Y.: Evaluation of physical education teaching quality in colleges based on the hybrid technology of data mining and hidden Markov model. Int. J. Emerg. Technol. Learn. **15**(1), 4–15 (2020). https://doi.org/10.3991/ijet.v15i01.12533

Zohair, A., Mahmoud, L.: Prediction of student's performance by modelling small dataset size. Int. J. Educ. Technol. High. Educ. **16**(1), 1–18 (2019)

Generative Artificial Intelligence and Interactive Learning Platforms: Second Language Vocabulary Acquisition

Sibel Crum[1]([✉]) [iD], Belle Li[2] [iD], and Xiaojing Kou[1] [iD]

[1] Indiana University, Bloomington, IN 47405, USA
sariogul@indiana.edu
[2] Purdue University, West Lafayette, IN 47907, USA

Abstract. This study examines Q-Chat, a new tool developed by Quizlet that integrates ChatGPT API, for its potential for L2 vocabulary learning. As a generative AI tool, ChatGPT has shown significant potential in enhancing language learning through interactive conversations, grammar corrections, and personalized learning experiences. However, challenges such as the learning optimization gap and the knowledge comprehension gap have been identified by previous research, affecting beginners' ability to fully utilize these technologies for language learning. Q-Chat, as an Intelligent Tutoring System enhanced by OpenAI's ChatGPT API, addresses the gaps by offering structured, scaffolded learning experiences that adapt to various learning styles and skill levels. The paper introduces the design principles of Q-chat, detailing how this tool leverages AI-empowered conversational interface to engage and guide learners in a more structured manner of learning. The paper highlights the importance of aligning design of AI-enhanced learning products with pedagogical and learning needs, and the importance of training language educators in understanding AI concepts to ensure meaningful integration of AI in teaching. It calls for future empirical studies to explore the practical implementation of ITSs in L2 classrooms and their impact on students' learning process.

Keywords: Generative Artificial Intelligence · Intelligent Tutoring Systems · Q-Chat · Language Learning · vocabulary Acquisition

1 Background and Purposes

The United Nations Educational, Scientific, and Cultural Organization (UNESCO) [1] defines Artificial Intelligence (AI) as systems capable of processing data and information in ways that resemble intelligent behavior, incorporating "reasoning, learning, perception, prediction, planning, or control." (p. 10). In 2023, AI, particularly generative AI, saw significant adoption, characterized by their ability to create new content across various domains. Generative AI models, such as OpenAI's ChatGPT, leverage large-scale language models for generating human-like text [2, 3]. ChatGPT stands out for its chat functionality, extensive size, and deep machine learning advancements, offering powerful capabilities, user-friendliness, and human-like interactions. This has led to rapid popularity, attracting over a million users globally within five days of its launch [4].

C. Stephanidis et al. (Eds.): HCII 2024, CCIS 2117, pp. 48–53, 2024.
https://doi.org/10.1007/978-3-031-61953-3_6

In language education, AI technologies like ChatGPT offer a broad spectrum of functionalities to enhance learning experiences [5, 6]. These tools span across interactive conversations, grammar and syntax corrections, writing practice, reading comprehension, pronunciation guidance, cultural insights, personalized learning, support for educators, exposure to different dialects in languages, exam preparation, and engaging in quizzes and language games. Advanced polyglot AI models, such as BLOOM, facilitate multilingual contextual translation, aiding in real-time language transition [7]. Specifically emphasizing vocabulary acquisition, Kohnke et al. [8] point out ChatGPT's effectiveness as a tool for enhancing vocabulary learning. It adapts dialogues to various proficiency levels and elucidates vocabulary in learners' native languages. Furthermore, ChatGPT serves as a dynamic dictionary, generating lists of words pertinent to specific topics upon request. Its capacity to provide word explanations within context and furnish additional examples to clarify specific meanings makes it an exceptionally valuable resource for vocabulary acquisition [6].

Despite the wide range of functionalities offered by ChatGPT in language education, particularly in vocabulary acquisition, there are certain limitations that need to be considered. Li, Bonk & Kou. [9] identified two gaps that hinder its effective use: the learning optimization gap and the knowledge comprehension gap. The learning optimization gap arises when learners, particularly beginners, struggle to operate ChatGPT effectively, leading to inadequate or irrelevant answers. This certainly impacts its ability to fully utilize ChatGPT's potential for language learning. The knowledge comprehension gap, on the other hand, happens when there appears to be a mismatch between the materials presented by ChatGPT and learners' ability to understand and absorb the information. This gap could emphasize the challenge of aligning ChatGPT's content with learners' cognitive abilities and prior knowledge, especially for beginners who could struggle to interpret the information correctly.

Quizlet's Q-Chat, built on OpenAI's ChatGPT API, has the potential to bridge the learning optimization and knowledge comprehension gaps identified by Li, Bonk & Kou [9]. Q-Chat stands out from other AI-powered chatbots like ChatGPT by providing a structured, scaffolded learning experience. Instead of being a completely free-form interface, Q-Chat offers a variety of activities that users can choose from, such as "quiz me," "practice with sentences," and "apply my knowledge." This approach guides learners through different levels of Bloom's Taxonomy, encouraging them to go beyond mere memorization and engage in higher-order thinking skills. By providing personalized one-on-one tutoring that adapts to different learning styles and skill levels, Q-Chat assists learners in navigating the platform effectively, asking accurate questions, and receiving relevant answers [10]. Moreover, Q-Chat's adaptive tutoring in material understanding, language learning guidance, and study coaching aligns the presented materials with learners' cognitive abilities and prior knowledge, reducing the knowledge comprehension gap. This facilitates effective independent learning, complementing Quizlet's existing assessment tools.

This paper explores the integration of generative AI in second language (L2) pedagogy, with a specific focus on vocabulary acquisition. By examining the capabilities of ChatGPT, an exemplar of generative AI, and its synergistic collaboration with adaptive learning platforms like Quizlet, the researchers aim to shed light on the transformative potential of these technologies in language education.

2 Intelligent Tutoring Systems

Intelligent tutoring systems (ITSs) are student-facing computerized learning platforms based on instructivist pedagogy, leveraging artificial intelligence (AI) [11] and other technologies to offer personalized and adaptable instruction to students [12] often simulating one-on-one tutoring interactions. Within these systems encompassing various technologies and methodologies, adaptive instruction provides the ability to dynamically adjust instructional content, pacing, and feedback based on individual learner characteristics, such as knowledge level, learning style, and performance by utilizing a data-driven method [12]. Adaptive instruction is a key component of many ITSs, establishing student-centered learning pathways, allowing users to improve learning effectiveness, optimizing instructional design and catering to the diverse needs and abilities of learners.

The traditional method of learning from textbooks confines learners to uniform tasks in a predetermined sequence. The constraints of time and resources often prevent educators from tailoring a curriculum to suit each learner's individual needs [13]. However, contemporary neuroscience research highlights the inherent diversity in how each brain processes information, indicating that personalized learning approaches are essential [13]. AI-powered ITS tailors the instructional and evaluation process to individual learners. By utilizing AI algorithms, ITS assessments can analyze learners' responses, identify their strengths and weaknesses, and dynamically adjust the difficulty level of questions. This adaptive and accessible approach leads to an appropriately challenging learning environment, resulting in a more accurate evaluation of learners' knowledge and skills. As AI continues to improve, it offers the potential to go beyond the boundaries established by teaching through textbooks and lack of personalized teaching. It tracks each learner's development for achieving life goals [14] and adapts educational content to match the unique cognitive profiles of students. This paves the way for fostering equity and accessibility in education.

3 Quizlet Q-Chat: Enhancing Learning Experience Through AI-Powered Tutoring

Quizlet is a well-known learning platform that offers various interactive study resources spanning from the study of Chemistry to L2. It allows users to customize their learning experiences and access a vast database of user-generated content that contributes to efficient and effective learning across various subjects and disciplines. Q-Chat takes the Quizlet platform into a more visible AI space than the former products and offers an entirely adaptable AI tutoring developed upon the foundation of OpenAI's ChatGPT API [15]. As Q-Chat is a relatively new tool in AI in Education (AIED), the authors of this paper are not aware of research publications related to it. Therefore, the paper is based on the authors' experiences as instructional designers and language educators and the information distributed by the Quizlet team through videos and articles.

Q-Chat provides a conversational interface for L2 learners that can facilitate scaffolded learning. Within a sheltered learning environment, learners can select a range of activities. This contrasts with the open-ended interface of ChatGPT. With continuous instruction and assessment, learners can receive real-time feedback and personalized learning experiences that can empower them through bridging learning gaps and improving their understanding. Q-Chat has been designed by incorporating various strategically engineered design principles geared towards enhancing the learning experience such as The Socratic Method that the system asks questions rather than providing answers to learners, engaging them with helpful and friendly feedback, and offering personalized responses [16]. By using Socratic method of teaching and real-time feedback mechanisms, Q-Chat supports active learner engagement and assists deeper comprehension that are critical elements of effective language learning [17]. This innovative model not only increases the effective vocabulary acquisition but also encourages learners to autonomously navigate their language learning journey. Additionally, Q-Chat uses mechanisms to increase learner interest by providing constructive feedback [16]. The platform's interface is easy to use, with simple menus and a clear layout for easy learner navigation. Finally, Q-Chat builds multiple layers of guardrails to protect users (learners) [16].

The integration of AI technologies (ChatGPT API) into Q-Chat, with its well-designed conversational interface, and adaptive activities, marks an important step forward in facilitating L2 vocabulary learning and redefines the process of L2 vocabulary acquisition. This can be considered a significant advancement in leveraging AI-driven methodologies to optimize second language vocabulary acquisition, opening a new era of self-directed L2 learning.

4 Implications for Instructional Designers and Language Practitioners

This conceptual paper proposes that rather than thinking in ITS in binary terms regarding the potential of AI in L2 learning contexts, it is more helpful to consider the conditions and combinations under which AI could assist instructional designers and practitioners and in supporting students more effectively.

To efficiently utilize student-facing AI integration in second language education, instructional designers and L2 educators need to undergo training in AI literacy applicable to educational systems, along with acquiring proficiency in new Internet Connectivity Tools (ICT) skills. The integration of artificial intelligence in classrooms demands that instructors enhance their digital teaching abilities. Ultimately, everyone pedagogically involved with learners needs to understand how to integrate pedagogical strategies and theories into AI systems to ensure meaningful implementation [12]. Ways to leverage AI-powered adaptable assessment needs to be investigated as they provide not only a view of learner progress but also offer valuable insights to educators, assisting them to personalize instructional strategies and interventions.

On the other hand, Holmes [11] contends that "much AIED has been designed (whether intentionally or not) to supplant teachers or to reduce them to a functional role and not to assist them to teach more effectively" (p. 151). It is crucial for educational product developers to closely align with instructional designers and educators, understanding the methodologies they employ to foster a user-friendly approach [18].

Future empirical studies need to prioritize investigating the practical implementation of ITSs in L2 classrooms and evaluating the impact of ITSs on students' self-efficacy, autonomy, and language proficiency. This would include empirical studies of both learner experience with the ITS interface as well as how educators can leverage ITS tools in formal learning context to foster learner-centered environment and to allow them to dedicate more time to provide learners with enriched and enhanced learning experiences.

Disclosure of Interests. The authors have no competing interests to declare that are relevant to the content of this article.

References

1. Liu, B.L., et al.: Harnessing the era of artificial intelligence in higher education: a primer for higher education stakeholders. UNESCO: United Nations Educational, Scientific and Cultural Organization, Venezuela (2023). UNESCO International Institute for Higher Education in Latin America and the Caribbean
2. Jauhiainen, J.S., Guerra, A.G.: Generative AI and ChatGPT in school children's education: evidence from a school lesson. Sustainability **15**(18), 14025 (2023). https://doi.org/10.3390/su151814025
3. Xiao, Y., Zhi, Y.: An exploratory study of EFL learners' use of ChatGPT for language learning tasks: experience and perceptions. Languages **8**(3), 212 (2023). https://doi.org/10.3390/languages8030212
4. Elbanna, S., Armstrong, L.: Exploring the integration of ChatGPT in education: adapting for the future. Manag. Sustain. Arab Rev. **3**(1), 16–29 (2024)
5. Kostka, I., Toncelli, R.: Exploring applications of ChatGPT to English language teaching: opportunities, challenges, and recommendations. TESL-EJ **27**(3) (2023). https://doi.org/10.55593/ej.27107int
6. Li, B., Kou, X., Bonk, C.J.: Embracing the disrupted language teaching and learning field: analyzing YouTube content creation related to ChatGPT. Languages **8**(3), 197 (2023). https://doi.org/10.3390/languages8030197
7. Farrelly, T., Baker, N.: Generative artificial intelligence: implications and considerations for higher education practice. Educ. Sci. **13**(11), 1109 (2023)
8. Kohnke, L., Moorhouse, B., Zou, D.: ChatGPT for language teaching and learning. RELC J. **54**(2), 537–550 (2023). https://doi.org/10.1177/00336882231162868
9. Li, B., Bonk, C.J., Kou, X.: Exploring the multilingual applications of ChatGPT: uncovering language learning affordances in YouTuber videos. Int. J. Comput.-Assist. Lang. Learn. Teach. (IJCALLT) **13**(1), 1–22 (2023)
10. Karatay, Y., Hegelheimer, V.: An overview of new technologies in English language teaching. In: Kurt, G., Başkan, P. (eds.) Educational technology in English Language Teaching. Eğiten Kitap (2023, Preprint). https://www.researchgate.net/publication/375083811_PREPRINT_An_Overview_of_New_Technologies_in_English_Language_Teaching
11. Holmes, W., Bialik, M., Fadel, C.: Artificial Intelligence in Education–Promise and Implications for Teaching and Learning. The Center for Curriculum Redesign, Boston, MA (2019)

12. Lin, C.C., Huang, A.Y.Q., Lu, O.H.T.: Artificial intelligence in intelligent tutoring systems toward sustainable education: a systematic review. Smart Learn. Environ. **10**, 41 (2023). https://doi.org/10.1186/s40561-023-00260-y

13. Annus, N.: Education in the age of artificial intelligence. TEM: technology, education, management. Inf. J. **13**(1), 404–413 (2024). https://doi.org/10.18421/TEM131-42

14. Escotet, M.A.: Looking forward to AI in higher education. LinkedIn (2023). https://www.linkedin.com/pulse/looking-forward-ai-higher-education-miguel-angel-escotet/. Accessed 10 Mar 2024

15. Quizlet: How to get started with an AI tutor. https://quizlet.com/content/how-to-use-an-ai-tutor. Accessed 15 Mar 2024

16. Quizlet: Q-Chat: How We Built That, 11 August 2023. https://www.youtube.com/watch?v=7KwFFqFCwpM. Accessed 15 Mar 2024

17. Quizlet: Q-Chat: Meet your new AI tutor (n.d.). https://quizlet.com/qchat-personal-ai-tutor. Accessed 15 Mar 2024

18. Alam, A: Employing adaptive learning and intelligent tutoring robots for virtual classrooms and smart campuses: reforming education in the age of artificial intelligence. In: Shaw, R.N., Das, S., Piuri, V., Bianchini, M. (eds.) Advanced Computing and Intelligent Technologies. LNEE, vol. 914, pp. 395–406. Springer, Singapore (2022). https://doi.org/10.1007/978-981-19-2980-9_32

Virtual Reality Supporting Physical Education Teaching in Brazilian Elementary Schools

Carolina de Carvalho Amaral[1]([✉]) [iD], Ângelo Amaral[2] [iD],
and Soellyn Elene Bataliotti[3] [iD]

[1] São Paulo State University (UNESP), Rio Claro, SP, Brazil
carolina.c.amaral@unesp.br
[2] University of Campo Limpo Paulista (UNIFACCAMP), Campo Limpo Paulista, SP, Brazil
[3] São Paulo State University (UNESP), São Paulo, SP, Brazil
soellyn.bataliotti@unesp.br

Abstract. Virtual reality allows an immersive learning process which can support elementary school teachers to propose innovative and engaging pedagogical approaches. This work investigates the state of the art related to educational usage of VR through a systematic literature review, evaluating the opportunities to use this technology on physical education classes in Brazilian elementary schools. The main contributions of our work are: (i) a literature review; (ii) the proposal of a VR solution to support physical education teaching and (iii) the discussion on implementation steps.

Keywords: Virtual Reality · Physical Education · Teaching · Elementary School

1 Introduction

Considering the need to propose new ways of supporting educators in the classroom [1], this study evaluates the feasibility of utilizing Virtual Reality (VR) resources as a support for physical education classes in Brazilian elementary schools, exploring their benefits and proposing implementation steps.

Within the scope of this work, virtual reality (VR) is defined as an immersive environment generated by 3D graphic images, representing either a simulation of the real world or an entirely fictional construct, based on immersion, interaction, and engagement principles [2]. Building on this concept, we aim the design proposal of an application wherein Brazilian elementary school students can experience activities through 3D resources modeled in virtual reality [3], contributing to initiatives on enhancing teaching methodologies through the integration of innovative technological solutions.

The main contributions of our work are: (i) a literature review; (ii) the proposal of a VR solution to support physical education teaching and (iii) the discussion on implementation steps.

2 Literature Review and Related Work

We analyzed 54 articles in our systematic literature review on virtual reality supporting physical education teaching. The approach used in the literature review was based on the guidelines proposed by Kitchenham [4] and the research was driven by the questions "How can Virtual Reality support the teaching process?" and "Are the VR research related to elementary teaching currently supporting physical education?", through queries on ACM Digital Library, IEEE Xplore and Redalyc platform. Redalyc was adopted to provide Latin American publications, as our research focus on Brazilian elementary schools, while ACM Digital Library and IEEE Xplore were chosen to address the global state of the art.

The next step was an exploratory analysis classifying the articles on 5 objectives: i) early child education (Ce) support, relating to children under 7 years old, ii) elementary education (Ee) support, iii) other educational levels (Oe) support, iv) Physical Education (PEt) teaching practices and v) other disciplines (Ot) teaching practices.

In addition to these objectives, 4 application domains were considered in our analysis: i) teaching activities, ii) student behavior observation, iii) usage of existing VR applications and iv) proposal or development of new VR applications.

The query used to search the libraries was based on the string "virtual reality AND (education OR teaching)" and its translation to Portuguese, resulting in 90 articles collected, considering the first 30 results from each database, classified by relevance.

As Inclusion Criteria, all 90 returned articles were considered, as they were filtered by publication year between 2019 and 2024. As Exclusion Criteria, during the analysis, 36 articles were identified as non-adherent to VR supporting teaching practices, being removed from this study. This resulted in 17 works returned by ACM, 28 from IEEE and 9 from Redalyc. We classified these 54 resulting articles as 49 analyzed works, listed in Appendix I (Table 1), and 5 related works, listed in Appendix I (Table 2).

The analyzed and related works combine new insights and the status quo of current research, with the concept of an ideal systemic approach, setting key aspects for virtual reality as a supporting tool for elementary schools teaching practices. The synthesis of these works can be found in the next subsections and in Appendix I (Tables 1 and 2) we present their classification.

Considering our literature review, we identified that the usage of virtual reality is a promising strategy to support the teaching process, although its application focused on physical education for elementary education has less publications than the application of VR solutions focused on other disciplines and education levels.

2.1 Analyzed Work

Bicalho et al. [5] present a literature review on virtual reality supporting teaching practices and activities. They work is strictly focused on Brazilian higher education and not related to physical education discipline, whereas we are focused on the analysis of VR to support physical education classes in Brazilian elementary schools, presenting an updated systematic mapping and a classification of the research works.

Zou [6] and Zhang et al. [7] describe the adoption of VR as a tool to support college education, on Physical Education courses to engage the next generation of teachers on this approach. Zhang et al. [7] developed new VR solutions for this purpose, while Cliburn (2023) evaluated how teachers can benefit from VR.

Schuster et al. [8] and Song et al. [9] do not discuss teaching activities, while focusing on a solution design proposal for VR adoption as an education tool. In parallel, Liang [10] and Hahn et al. [11] present similar approaches, also including teaching activities and practices while discussing the risks and implications of integrating VR to existent scholar programs.

Oliveira et al. [12], propose and implement a Virtual Reality environment for early childhood education in Brazilian schools, without focusing on physical education.

Li et al. [13] do not propose a VR solution but evaluate students' expectations through interviews to determine how to benefit from virtual reality in schools, while Barbosa et al. [14] presented a similar study, focused on Brazilian students.

Valero-Franco et al. [15] address gamification aspects of VR adoption, focused on Spanish colleges and Piernas et al. [16] adopts the same model in a study based in Spain and France. Gerini el al. [17] also discuss VR adoption from a gamification perspective, in Italy. Patterson et al. [18] and Zhao et al. [19] implemented VR applications for teaching support, also reinforcing the relevance of gamification, but focused on professional development courses.

Konecki et al. [20], Li et al. [21], Sharma et al. [22], Pirker et al. [23], Zhang [24] and Izard et al. [25] present different pre-existent VR tools, discussing potential usages by teachers, without in-depth analysis.

Fang [26] and Liu et al. [27] study the implementation of pre-existent VR tool in schools in China, evaluating results through student behavior observation, while Li et al. (2020) additionally considers augmented reality in the research scope.

Similar studies were done in Moroccan schools by Talbi et al. [28], while Cerrillo [29] also added augmented reality to the scope and focused on Mexican students and Trindade et al. [30] worked with VR as tool for geography classes in a Brazilian high school.

Melo [31] and Micheline et al. [32] present works discussing the importance of adopting new technologies as teaching aid tools in under-developed countries, while both Beck et al. [33] and Ferreira et al. [34] implemented new VR tools focused on Brazilian high school and college students.

Cibuļska et al. [35], Zhong et al. [36] and Horst et al. [37] detailed technical aspects on VR application development, considering the requirements from teaching support, while Ye [38], Suying et al. [39], Chen et al. [40] and Li [41] also related the experience of developing VR applications for high school and college teaching, with minor focus on technical aspects.

Guo [42], Zhang et al. [43], Zhu et al. [44], Wenjun [45], Wu et al. [46], Xi [47], Pirker et al. [48], Liu et al. [49] and Cabanag [50] present studies focused on teaching practices and the challenges of VR adoption, without propose specific solutions nor develop new software or adopt existing tools, keeping the argument in the theoretical field.

2.2 Related Work

As related work, we considered articles presenting contributions on supporting elementary education teaching trough VR solutions, as summarized in Appendix I (Table 1) and detailed in the next paragraphs.

Fu [51] and Feng et al. [52] presented works on physical education teaching for elementary schools, implementing new VR resources to aid teaching practices. Feng also observed the students' response to evaluate the results.

Garcia et al. [53] developed a VR based videogame to engage students at an Colombian elementary school, prescribing teaching activities and observing the students' behavior, but without focus on physical education.

Shi [54] and Kongsilp et al. [55] do not present any new VR implementation, but both works focus on teaching practices for elementary school, and how teachers can adopt VR solutions, with Kongsilp also prescribing pre-existent solutions.

3 The Proposed Solution Design

Based on the literature review, there is space for the development of VR based applications to support physical education teachers. We propose the implementation of an app with a minimal set of requirements, mitigating the risk and complexity [56], based in an existing 3D and VR development platform such as Unity 3D [3], presenting an avatar who will teach students some movements which they are intended to reproduce.

The proposed application must be deployed to Android smartphones, facilitating its installation process and the execution must be realized using cardboard 3D glasses [57], due to their reduced cost and to the possibility of engaging the students on its assembly.

4 Next Steps and Implementation Challenges

The steps to adopt the VR app in an elementary school include gathering parental authorization for all involved students, followed by a questionnaire to be answered by the children indicating their current level of digital inclusion [14]. Once the students' profile is known, the group must join an activity in which they will assembly their own cardboard VR glasses, aiming for a sense of belonging in relation to the project [57].

With the cardboard glasses assembled, the students will join 3 weekly classes based on VR activities: i) watching a VR-based video, similarly to the proposal of Trindade et al. [30], allowing them to replicate the experience in their home, also engaging the families, ii) a physical education class based on the developed VR app with the students having to reproduce the movements of a 3D VR-based avatar, creating the immersive environment described by Oliveira et al. [12] and iii) a second physical education class, with the same activity after a week interval to verify if the students' answer to VR tools improves or remains the same.

After these activities, a final questionnaire will be answered by the children to register their perception on how the new resources enhanced their experience in the classes, evaluating their overall satisfaction level towards the project and supporting the *plan-build-validate* cycle for educational objects proposed by Bataliotti et al. [58].

Other teachers related to the group will also answer the initial questionnaire to map their level of digital inclusion and closely monitor the students outside of the physical education classes, aiming to identify potential impacts of the VR tools adoption in the children behavior. They will also be interviewed in the end of the project evaluating their perception on students' demand for similar resources in their classes, positive impacts on children relation with technology and potential opportunities to adopt VR-based resources in their own teaching areas.

As implementation challenges, we foresee the relation with other teachers and human risks to the project as the outstanding topics, as the proposed activities depend on time and engagement of teachers from multiple disciplines and may impact their own lesson plans. Another point to be considered is the potential lack of resources of Brazilian elementary schools [2] as the project may require financial support.

5 Conclusion

We presented an innovative approach that considers Virtual Reality as a supporting tool for physical education teaching into elementary schools, based in an extensive literature review which indicates the state of the art on educational VR applications. The main contributions of our work are: (i) a literature review; (ii) the proposal of a VR solution to support physical education teaching and (iii) the discussion on implementation steps.

Appendix I

Table 1. Summary of Analyzed Work.

Authors	Objective					Application Domain			
	Ce	Ee	Oe	Pet	Ot	1	2	3	4
Piernas et al., [16]			x		x	x	x		x
Valero-Franco et al., [15]			x		x	x	x		x
Beck et al., [33]					x	x			x
Barbosa et al., [14]			x		x	x	x		
Ferreira et al., [34]			x		x	x			x
Melo, [31]			x		x	x			
Trindade et al., [30]			x		x	x	x	x	
Cerrillo [29]			x		x	x	x	x	
Zou, [6]			x	X		x			
Zhang et al., [7]			x	X		x	x		x

(continued)

Table 1. (*continued*)

Authors	Objective					Application Domain			
	Ce	Ee	Oe	Pet	Ot	1	2	3	4
Micheline et al., [32]			x		x				
Zhang, [24]			x		x	x			x
Cibuļska et al., [35]			x		x	x			x
Fang, [26]			x		x	x	x	x	
Talbi et al., [28]			x		x	x	x	x	
Li et al., [59]			x		x	x			
Liu et al., [27]			x		x	x	x	x	
Bicalho et al., [5]			x		x	x			
Guo, [42]			x		x	x			
Zhu et al., [44]			x		x	x			
Li et al., [13]			x		x	x	x		
Konecki et al., [20]			x		x	x		x	
Song et al., [9]			x		x				x
Li et al., [21]			x		x	x		x	
Suying et al., [39]			x		x	x			x
Zhang et al., [43]			x		x	x			
Zhu et al., [44]			x		x	x			
Zhong et al., [36]			x		x	x			x
Chen et al., [40]			x		x	x			x
Li, [41]			x		x	x			x
Wejun [45]			x		x	x			
Wu et al., [46]			x		x	x			
Ye, [38]			x		x	x			
Sharma et al., [22]			x		x	x			
Xi, [47]			x		x	x			
M. Schuster et al., [8]			x		x				x
Horst et al., [37]			x		x				x
Pirker et al., [23]			x		x	x		x	
Pirker et al., [48]			x		x	x			
Izard et al., [25]			x		x	x			

(*continued*)

Table 1. (*continued*)

Authors	Objective					Application Domain			
	Ce	Ee	Oe	Pet	Ot	1	2	3	4
Liang, [10]			x		x	x			x
Patterson et al., [18]			x		x	x			x
Zhao et al., [19]			x		x	x			x
Hahn et al.,[11]			x		x	x			
Cliburn, [60]			x		x	x			
Gerini et al., [17]			x		x	x			x
Liu et al., [49]			x		x	x			
Cabanag, [50]			x		x	x			

Objective: Early child education (Ce); Elementary education (Ee); Other educational levels (Oe); Physical Education (PEt) teaching; Other disciplines (Ot) teaching. *Application Domain*: (1) Teaching activities; (2) Student behavior observation; (3) Usage of existing VR applications; (4) Proposal or development of new VR applications.

Table 2. Summary of Related Work

Authors	Objective					Application Domain			
	Ce	Ee	Oe	Pet	Ot	1	2	3	4
García et al., [53]		x				x	x		x
Shi, [54]		x				x			
Feng et al., [52]		x		x		x	x		x
Fu, [51]		x		x		x			x
Kongslip et al., [55]		x				x		x	

Objective: Early child education (Ce); Elementary education (Ee); Other educational levels (Oe); Physical Education (PEt) teaching; Other disciplines (Ot) teaching. *Application Domain*: (1) Teaching activities; (2) Student behavior observation; (3) Usage of existing VR applications; (4) Proposal or development of new VR applications.

References

1. Afonso, G.B., Martins, C.C., Katerberg, L.P., Becker, T.M., Dos Santos, V.C., Afonso, Y.B.: Potencialidades e fragilidades da realidade virtual imersiva na educação. Revista Intersaberes **15**(34) (2020)
2. da Lobato, A.S., Macedo, H.T.: Realidade virtual: recurso de ensino-aprendizagem no ensino fundamental (2020)
3. Rossignoli, G.H., Duarte Filho, N.F.: Jogo Educacional com Foco no Ensino e Aprendizagem da Disciplina de Acionamentos Elétricos Utilizando a Plataforma UNITY. In: 12o CONGRESSO DE INOVAÇÃO, CIÊNCIA E TECNOLOGIA DO IFSP (2021)
4. Kitchenham, B.: Procedures for Performing Systematic Reviews, Keele, July 2004

5. Bicalho, D.R., Piedade, J.M.N., de Lacerda Matos, J.F.: The use of immersive virtual reality in educational practices in higher education: a systematic review. In: 2023 International Symposium on Computers in Education (SIIE), pp. 1–5, November 2023. https://doi.org/10.1109/SIIE59826.2023.10423711

6. Zou, F.: Analysis on the application of computer virtual reality technology in college physical education teaching. In: 2021 International Conference on Internet, Education and Information Technology (IEIT), pp. 491–494, April 2021. https://doi.org/10.1109/IEIT53597.2021.00115

7. Zhang, L., Zhang, L.: Research on innovative teaching method of university physical education courses based on virtual reality technology—taking table tennis course teaching as an example. In: 2021 2nd International Conference on Big Data and Informatization Education (ICBDIE), pp. 653–657, April 2021. https://doi.org/10.1109/ICBDIE52740.2021.00154

8. Schuster, C.M., Moloney, M.J.: The future of virtual reality in education. In: Proceedings of the 13th International Conference on Education Technology and Computers, ICETC 2021, pp. 85–89. Association for Computing Machinery, New York, NY, USA (2022). https://doi.org/10.1145/3498765.3498778

9. Song, N., Feng, Q., Yin, X., Luo, H.: A visual analysis of virtual reality research in education using CiteSpace. In: 2022 4th International Conference on Computer Science and Technologies in Education (CSTE), pp. 255–260, May 2022. https://doi.org/10.1109/CSTE55932.2022.00054

10. Liang, J.: Discussion on practical teaching mode from the perspective of virtual reality. In: 2020 4th International Conference on Artificial Intelligence and Virtual Reality, AIVR 2020, pp. 7–10. Association for Computing Machinery, New York, NY, USA (2021). https://doi.org/10.1145/3439133.3439137

11. Hahn, J., Ward, D., Cabada, E., Wallace, R., Kurt, E., Mischo, B.: Institutionalizing and sustaining virtual reality experiences. In: Proceedings of the 18th Joint Conference on Digital Libraries, JCDL 2019, pp. 325–326. IEEE Press (2020). https://doi.org/10.1109/JCDL.2019.00053

12. de Oliveira, R.E.M., Ferreira, L.R., de Oliveira, J.C.: A pedagogical virtual reality environment for children in early childhood education. In: Proceedings of the 25th Symposium on Virtual and Augmented Reality, SVR 2023, pp. 204–209. Association for Computing Machinery, New York, NY, USA (2024). https://doi.org/10.1145/3625008.3625047

13. Li, Y., Liang, J., Zhou, Y., Zhang, C., Yue, Y., Liang, H.-N.: Understanding the needs of virtual reality for learning and teaching: a user-centered approach. In: 2023 3rd International Conference on Educational Technology (ICET), pp. 7–11, September 2023. https://doi.org/10.1109/ICET59358.2023.10424148

14. Barbosa, F.F., de Ribeiro, É.A.J.: Um Cenário Sobre a Utilização de Realidade Virtual em uma Instituição de Ensino. SAPIENTIAE: Revista de Ciencias Sociais, Humanas e Engenharias 6 (2021). https://www.redalyc.org/articulo.oa?id=572765408006

15. Valero-Franco, C., Berns, A.: Development of virtual and augmented reality apps for language teaching: a case study. RIED-Revista Iberoamericana de Educación a Distancia 27 (2024). https://www.redalyc.org/articulo.oa?id=331475280023

16. Piernas, J.M.P., Meroño, M.C.P., del Asenjo, M.P.F.: Virtual escape rooms: a gamification tool to enhance motivation in distance education. RIED-Revista Iberoamericana de Educación a Distancia 27 (2024). https://www.redalyc.org/articulo.oa?id=331475280019

17. Gerini, L., Delzanno, G., Guerrini, G., Solari, F., Chessa, M.: Gamified virtual reality for computational thinking. In: Proceedings of the 2nd International Workshop on Gamification in Software Development, Verification, and Validation, Gamify 2023. Association for Computing Machinery, New York, NY, USA (2023). https://doi.org/10.1145/3617553.3617886

18. Patterson, K., Lilja, A., Arrebola, M., McGhee, J.: Molecular genomics education through gamified cell exploration in virtual reality. In: Proceedings of the 17th International Conference on Virtual-Reality Continuum and Its Applications in Industry, VRCAI 2019. Association for Computing Machinery, New York, NY, USA (2019). https://doi.org/10.1145/335 9997.3365724

19. Zhao, R., Aqlan, F., Elliott, L.J., Lum, H.C.: Developing a virtual reality game for manufacturing education. In: Proceedings of the 14th International Conference on the Foundations of Digital Games, FDG 2019. Association for Computing Machinery, New York, NY, USA (2019). https://doi.org/10.1145/3337722.3341831

20. Konecki, M., Konecki, M., Vlahov, D.: Using virtual reality in education of programming. In: 2023 11th International Conference on Information and Education Technology (ICIET), pp. 39–43, March 2023. https://doi.org/10.1109/ICIET56899.2023.10111156

21. Li, X., Jiang, Q.: Application of virtual reality technology in English interpretation teaching. In: 2021 2nd International Conference on Information Science and Education (ICISE-IE), pp. 124–127, November 2021. https://doi.org/10.1109/ICISE-IE53922.2021.00035

22. Sharma, M., Kumar, P., Singh, D.K.: The role of virtual reality in education: a comprehensive review of research and application. In: 2023 1st DMIHER International Conference on Artificial Intelligence in Education and Industry 4.0 (IDICAIEI), pp. 1–6, November 2023. https://doi.org/10.1109/IDICAIEI58380.2023.10406461

23. Pirker, J., Loria, E., Kainz, A., Kopf, J., Dengel, A.: Virtual reality and education – the steam panorama. In: Proceedings of the 17th International Conference on the Foundations of Digital Games, FDG 2022. Association for Computing Machinery, New York, NY, USA (2022). https://doi.org/10.1145/3555858.3555899

24. Zhang, X.: The college English teaching reform supported by multimedia teaching technology and immersive virtual reality technology. In: 2019 International Conference on Virtual Reality and Intelligent Systems (ICVRIS), pp. 77–80, September 2019. https://doi.org/10.1109/ICV RIS.2019.00028

25. González Izard, S., Vivo Vicent, C., Juanes Méndez, J.A., Palau, R.: Virtual reality in higher education: an experience with medical students: research into how virtual reality can be used as a powerful training tool for medicine students. In: Eighth International Conference on Technological Ecosystems for Enhancing Multiculturality, TEEM 2020, pp. 414–421. Association for Computing Machinery, New York, NY, USA (2021). https://doi.org/10.1145/ 3434780.3436539

26. Fang, N.: An analysis of oral English teaching in college based on virtual reality technology. In: 2019 International Conference on Virtual Reality and Intelligent Systems (ICVRIS), pp. 1–4, September 2019. https://doi.org/10.1109/ICVRIS.2019.00008

27. Liu, J., Xue, W.: The exploration of teaching reform of virtual reality technology in applied linguistics courses. In: 2022 Global Conference on Robotics, Artificial Intelligence and Information Technology (GCRAIT), pp. 656–660, July 2022. https://doi.org/10.1109/GCRAIT 55928.2022.00143

28. Talbi, K., Zergout, I., Souad, A., ZinebAithaddouchane: Analytical study of virtual reality in Moroccan higher education. In: 2023 7th IEEE Congress on Information Science and Technology (CiSt), pp. 503–507, December 2023. https://doi.org/10.1109/CiSt56084.2023. 10409978

29. Cerrillo, S.R.: Enseñanza de la anatomía y la fisiología a través de las realidades aumentada y virtual. Innovación Educativa 19, 57–76 (2019). https://www.redalyc.org/articulo.oa?id=179 462793004

30. Trindade, M.J.D.S., Dos Santos, C.A.: Realidade Virtual Na Sala De Aula: Prática De Ensino De Geografia. GEOSABERES: Revista de Estudos Geoeducacionais 10, 72–80 (2019). https://www.redalyc.org/articulo.oa?id=552860312007

31. Melo, M.: Uso de tecnologias de realidade virtual imersiva para treino e certificação de competências. PsychTech Health J. **3**, 1–2 (2020). https://www.redalyc.org/articulo.oa?id=688073937001

32. Micheline, S., Yu, X., Sun, C.: Adoption of teaching strategies leveraging on augmented reality & virtual reality in higher education in less developing countries: a case of BURUNDI. In: 2023 International Conference on Intelligent Education and Intelligent Research (IEIR), pp. 1–5, November 2023. https://doi.org/10.1109/IEIR59294.2023.10391255

33. Beck, T.M., da Costa, A.C.: Aplicativo em Realidade Aumentada para o ensino de Desenho Técnico na Educação Profissional e Tecnológica. Vértices (Campos dos Goitacazes) **22**, 224–240 (2020). https://www.redalyc.org/articulo.oa?id=625764627017

34. Ferreira, F.C., Lourenço, A.B., da Cruz, A.J.A., Paza, A.H., Botero, E.R., Rocha, E.M.: Argumentação em ambiente de realidade virtual: uma aproximação com futuros professores de Física. RIED-Revista Iberoamericana de Educación a Distancia **24**, 179–195 (2021). https://www.redalyc.org/articulo.oa?id=331464460009

35. Cibuļska, E., Boločko, K.: Virtual reality in education: structural design of an adaptable virtual reality system. In: 2022 6th International Conference on Computer, Software and Modeling (ICCSM), pp. 76–79, July 2022. https://doi.org/10.1109/ICCSM57214.2022.00020

36. Zhong, Y., Liu, X.: Design and research of virtual reality teaching assistant system for colleges and universities experimental course under the background of wisdom education. In: 2021 International Conference on Intelligent Transportation, Big Data & Smart City (ICITBS), pp. 533–535, March 2021. https://doi.org/10.1109/ICITBS53129.2021.00136

37. Horst, R., Dörner, R.: Virtual reality forge: pattern-oriented authoring of virtual reality nuggets. In: Proceedings of the 25th ACM Symposium on Virtual Reality Software and Technology, VRST 2019. Association for Computing Machinery, New York, NY, USA (2019). https://doi.org/10.1145/3359996.3364261

38. Ye, H.: A review on the application of virtual reality technology in ideological and political teaching. In: 2021 2nd International Conference on Artificial Intelligence and Education (ICAIE), pp. 712–715, June 2021. https://doi.org/10.1109/ICAIE53562.2021.00156

39. Suying, M., Yiping, L., Jinhua, W.: Usefulness of virtual reality-based teaching to course teaching. In: 2021 2nd International Conference on Artificial Intelligence and Education (ICAIE), pp. 605–609, June 2021. https://doi.org/10.1109/ICAIE53562.2021.00134

40. Chen, G., Xie, X., Yang, Z., Deng, R., Huang, K., Wang, C.: Development of a virtual reality game for cultural heritage education: the voyage of 'Gotheborg'. In: 2023 9th International Conference on Virtual Reality (ICVR), pp. 531–535, May 2023. https://doi.org/10.1109/ICVR57957.2023.10169671

41. Li, Y.: Application of virtual reality technology in interior design teaching. In: 2022 International Conference on Education, Network and Information Technology (ICENIT), pp. 217–220, September 2022. https://doi.org/10.1109/ICENIT57306.2022.00054

42. Guo, X.: Research on accounting teaching based on virtual reality technology. In: 2019 International Conference on Virtual Reality and Intelligent Systems (ICVRIS), pp. 36–39, September 2019. https://doi.org/10.1109/ICVRIS.2019.00017

43. Zhang, C., Li, Y., Cai, C.: Application and research of virtual reality technology based on big data in college teaching field. In: 2020 International Conference on Computers, Information Processing and Advanced Education (CIPAE), pp. 35–38, October 2020. https://doi.org/10.1109/CIPAE51077.2020.00017

44. Zhu, X., Li, L.: The function and core analysis of the application of virtual reality technology in ideological and political practice teaching. In: 2021 International Conference on Internet, Education and Information Technology (IEIT), pp. 26–30, April 2021. https://doi.org/10.1109/IEIT53597.2021.00013

45. Wenjun, L.: Research on digital media art teaching based on virtual reality technology. In: 2021 International Conference on Education, Information Management and Service Science (EIMSS), pp. 320–323, July 2021. https://doi.org/10.1109/EIMSS53851.2021.00076
46. Wu, S., Tian, Y., Li, J., Li, F., Feng, Y.: Research on virtual reality exhibition teaching platform in teaching reform of new economics. In: 2022 International Conference on Education, Network and Information Technology (ICENIT), pp. 87–92, September 2022. https://doi.org/10.1109/ICENIT57306.2022.00026
47. Xi, E.: Analyses of current status of domestic research on virtual reality technology in education. In: 2021 5th Annual International Conference on Data Science and Business Analytics (ICDSBA), pp. 588–591, September 2021. https://doi.org/10.1109/ICDSBA53075.2021.00118
48. Pirker, J., Dengel, A., Holly, M., Safikhani, S.: Virtual reality in computer science education: a systematic review. In: Proceedings of the 26th ACM Symposium on Virtual Reality Software and Technology, VRST 2020. Association for Computing Machinery, New York, NY, USA (2020). https://doi.org/10.1145/3385956.3418947
49. Liu, Y., Fan, X., Zhou, X., Liu, M., Wang, J., Liu, T.: Application of virtual reality technology in distance higher education. In: Proceedings of the 2019 4th International Conference on Distance Education and Learning, ICDEL 2019, pp. 35–39. Association for Computing Machinery, New York, NY, USA (2019). https://doi.org/10.1145/3338147.3338174
50. Cabanag, M.: MathVR: teaching vector arithmetic using virtual reality. In: SIGGRAPH Asia 2023 Educator's Forum, SA 2023. Association for Computing Machinery, New York, NY, USA (2023). https://doi.org/10.1145/3610540.3627012
51. Fu, Q.: Virtual reality technology in information teaching. In: 2021 2nd International Conference on Computers, Information Processing and Advanced Education, CIPAE 2021, pp. 1037–1041. Association for Computing Machinery, New York, NY, USA (2021). https://doi.org/10.1145/3456887.3457457
52. Feng, Y., You, C., Li, Y., Zhang, Y., Wang, Q.: Integration of computer virtual reality technology to college physical education. J. Web Eng. 21(7), 2049–2071 (2022). https://doi.org/10.13052/jwe1540-9589.2173
53. García, S.J.P., Garzón, J.: Efectos de un videojuego en el aprendizaje y la motivación de los alumnos en un curso de Ciencias Naturales. Revista Virtual Universidad Católica del Norte, 81–104 (2024). https://www.redalyc.org/articulo.oa?id=194276552005
54. Shi, P.: Research on effective teaching in the vision of virtual reality. In: Proceedings of the 3rd International Conference on Digital Technology in Education, ICDTE 2019, pp. 44–47. Association for Computing Machinery, New York, NY, USA (2020). https://doi.org/10.1145/3369199.3369240
55. Kongsilp, S., Komuro, T.: An evaluation of head-mounted virtual reality for special education from the teachers' perspective. In: Proceedings of the 25th ACM Symposium on Virtual Reality Software and Technology, VRST 2019. Association for Computing Machinery, New York, NY, USA (2019). https://doi.org/10.1145/3359996.3364721
56. Amaral, A., de Rosa, D.F.: Method for assessing the potential impact of changes in software requirements of agile methodologies based projects. In: Mori, H., Asahi, Y. (eds.) HCII 2023. LNCS, vol. 14016, pp. 3–21. Springer, Cham (2023). https://doi.org/10.1007/978-3-031-35129-7_1
57. da Silva, T.V.A., da Freire, A.L.S.: Utilização do Óculos de Realidade Virtual como Proposta Pedagógica para o Ensino Fundamental (2022)
58. Bataliotti, S.E., Rios, G.A., Schlünzen, E.T.M., Schlünzen Junior, K.: A Construção de Objetos Educacionais Acessíveis. J. Res. Spec. Educ. Needs 16(S1), 41–45 (2016). https://doi.org/10.1111/1471-3802.12266

59. Li, L., Wu, X.: Application of virtual reality and augmented reality technology in teaching. In: 2020 15th International Conference on Computer Science & Education (ICCSE), pp. 543–546, August 2020. https://doi.org/10.1109/ICCSE49874.2020.9201763
60. Cliburn, D.C.: Teaching and learning with virtual reality. J. Comput. Sci. Coll. **39**(2), 19–27 (2023)

Classification Tools to Assess Critical Thinking in Automotive Engineering Students

Carlos Alberto Espinosa-Pinos[✉] ⓘ, Paulina Magally Amaluisa-Rendón ⓘ, and Noemi Viviana Rodríguez-Ortiz ⓘ

Universidad Indoamerica, Bolívar 20-35 and Guayaquil, Ambato 180103, Ecuador
{carlosespinosa,paulinaamaluisa,nrodriguez17}@indoamerica.edu.ec

Abstract. Inadequate conflict resolution skills in automotive engineering students can have negative consequences in the workplace. The development of mathematical logical thinking can help students develop critical analysis skills, improve problem-solving ability, develop reasoning skills, and effective communication, enabling them to deal effectively with conflicts and find creative solutions. This research aims to identify predictors of problem-solving ability using classification algorithms. Methodology: In this study, three classification algo-rithms were applied and the KDD process was used to identify predictors of problem-solving ability. The data set includes 60 records of students from the automotive engineering program at Universidad Equinoccial in Quito, Ecuador, to whom three tools were applied: a sociodemographic card, a Shatnawi test related to mathematical logical thinking, and a Watson Glaser test on conflict resolution ability. Results: The best classification model is the K-nearest neighbors' algorithm and its predictive ability is very good, with a true positive rate versus false positive rate AUC of 0.75, along with a good performance in classifying negative cases. The model can be improved with increased sampling, cross-validation, or hyper-parameter adjustment. Conclusion: Age and mathematical logical thinking are strongly associated with conflict resolution ability. In future research it is important to consider additional variables such as experience in problem-solving projects, technical knowledge and communication skills; to explore the use of more advanced machine learning algo-rhythms; to design specific educational interventions based on the development of mathematical logical thinking; or to compare conflict resolution ability between different engineering disciplines.

Keywords: Classification algorithms · machine learning · mathematical logical thinking · psychology · conflict resolution

1 Introduction

In the area of automotive engineering, it is quite frequent that the different works or projects are carried out in multifaceted groups where students have to interact, collaborate and communicate effectively. On the other hand, in the monotony of individuals conflicts inevitably arise, these in some way affect the welfare directly in the social sphere, however, also affect other areas in which individuals interact. Due to the dynamics of

C. Stephanidis et al. (Eds.): HCII 2024, CCIS 2117, pp. 66–74, 2024.
https://doi.org/10.1007/978-3-031-61953-3_8

relationships, different types of conflicts could be generated that will undoubtedly impact on coexistence, causing discomfort and generating negative aspects in relationships, in which there is no respect, nor the presence of other important values, in this sense, the presence of antagonistic situations that generate gaps in human relationships causes discomfort and conflict. Therefore, the purpose of this research is to analyze the conflict resolution capacity of self-motivated student applicants [1].

Conflicts can be understood as anomalies that are related to violence, in this case they are considered as a dysfunctionality of personal relationships and not as something typical of everyday life. From another perspective, conflict can also be understood as a search by people for the satisfaction of unsatisfied needs, so that students' conflict resolution skills are of significant importance [2].

Therefore, conflicts are generated basically due to existing differences in opinions and perspectives, which is fundamentally caused by coexistence, interaction and acceptance of others. At the same time, another of the causes are changes at the level of society, in different areas such as: economic, political, among others. In short, this inevitably affects human relations and generates interpersonal frictions that when they are not solved in an adequate way can lead to violent acts [1]. For this reason, the ability of students to resolve conflicts in an adequate manner and thus not affect group dynamics is transcendental.

Studies on conflict resolution have emphasized the coping styles of the person, as this depends on how the conflict is addressed and also the type of resolution that is given to the problem, which obviously affects the educational environment, in this sense it is beneficial to analyze this issue at the university level [2].

Therefore, the importance of conflict resolution lies in the fact that it is a useful tool that makes it possible for students to resolve their problems effectively and thus the educational environment is not affected. Conflict can also be understood from a positive perspective, which requires that there be no bias on the part of the observer regarding the way in which student conflicts are being developed and, above all, dealt with. In this sense, it is appropriate to analyze the strategies and goals that are proposed in the resolution of conflicts [3].

In automotive engineering students a purely logical mathematical thinking prevails, they must master logical operations; this is decisive for scientific thinking [4]. Measuring logical-mathematical thinking in students helps to identify whether they have a solid foundation in mathematics, since the teaching-learning process in this area is highly complex, therefore the student must be able to generate skills and abilities that allow him/her to identify problems, analyze, organize and interpret data in different formats, as well as find the most appropriate way to communicate information, make critical judgments and apply strategies that allow the construction of his/her knowledge.

Since logical thinking is the basis from which to achieve the development of complex skills essential for the solution of different problems of daily life, it plays a substantial role in strengthening the mathematical ability that is forging such skills in problem solving in the field of automotive engineering, and on the other hand, also for the cognitive processes that students will need to use in solving problem situations, and thus provide solutions and effective responses to the demands of the external environment that often present challenging situations [5]. Automotive engineering is constantly evolving and therefore requires the ability to think creatively and innovatively. Therefore, measuring mathematical logical thinking in students makes it possible to identify their ability to address technical challenges and contribute to innovation in the automotive industry [6]. However, it should be noted that many students have a marked deficit in mathematical logic skills, which is why they have difficulties in relation to the field of mathematics. In this case, when faced with complex situations, they fail to generate an adequate response. The lack of mathematical logic skills of some students is related to difficulties in problem solving. Thus, when students have to face complex reasoning situations, they are unable to provide an effective and adequate response because they are not familiar with putting concepts into practice in the execution of practical problems [6].

On the other hand, in the labor field, there is a high level of problem-solving ability in areas related to intellectual work. For example, a high performance in problem-solving skills is observed in the manufacturing sector or industries related to intellectual work, and low levels of problem-solving skills are found in labor areas, which present a marked routine and daily routine [7]. The level of development of mathematical logical thinking is directly related to the level of problem-solving ability; therefore, most students are at a concrete level of thinking. In addition, the age of the student and the level of motivation in the area of mathematics are considered to be elements closely related to the level of development of logical thinking [8]. "The development of mathematical logical thinking in Costa Rican eleventh grade students in academic day schools and their of achievement in learning mathematics". The objective of this study was to provide empirical evidence regarding the relationship between the development of mathematical logical thinking in Costa Rican eleventh grade students in academic day schools and their level of achievement in mathematics, specifically in the algebraic and geometric areas. The study found a low level of development of mathematical logical thinking, significantly far from internationally accepted parameters. Scales, logical reasoning and mathematical demonstration were the most challenging. The level of achievement in algebra and geometry was also clearly insufficient [9].

The Watson Glaser test is composed of some dimensions, one of them is the inference which is a conclusion, which can be obtained from observed facts, but also from assumptions; assumption is defined as something that is assumed to have no objective basis. On the other hand, each exercise has several premises linked to several proposed conclusions; Interpretation: Each one of the proposed exercises presents a short paragraph followed by several suggested conclusions [10]. It is assumed that everything that appears in the short paragraph is true, but the problem is to judge whether each of the proposed conclusions is logically deduced from the information contained in the paragraph; Evaluation of arguments: A distinction must be made between strong arguments and weak arguments. For an argument to be considered strong, it must be clearly significant and directly related to the issue. An argument is weak if it is not directly related [11]. Thus, the Watson Glaser critical thinking assessment is a test that aims to evaluate a person's critical thinking ability. The test provides a total score that pre-tends to obtain a classification of people according to the critical thinking skills they present. As for the results, it is established that when there is a score of at least 70% on the test it is equivalent to an advanced critical thinking ability; a score of at least 40% is related to a basic level of critical thinking; and a score below 40% indicates problems or a deficient level of critical thinking ability according to the test [2]. Finally, it is important to note that a higher test score may indicate stronger critical thinking skills that are essential for effective conflict resolution.

2 Methodology

This study has used the Knowledge Discovery Database (KDD) process, an automatic process that combines discovery and analysis to extract rule-like patterns as functions of the data. The KDD process consists of multiple layers; its main objective is to extract valuable but non-trivial knowledge from the data it has access to. The stages of the KDD process are described as follows: 1. Identification of the problem and identification of the working domain. 2. 2. Creation of the data set. 3. Data processing. 4. Reduction and projection of the data. 5. Formulation of the KDD objectives. 6. Selection of data mining methods. 7. Evaluation of the discovered patterns. 8. Presentation and visualization. 9. Integration of the discovered knowledge in the system [9] Database and data collection instruments. The data set has 60 records of students of the automotive engineering career of the Equinoccial Technological University, to whom 3 instruments were applied: The first corresponds to a sociodemographic card; the second to a test to determine logical mathematical thinking called Shatnawi test [9]; The third instrument corresponds to the Watson Glaser test related to the measurement of critical thinking and the variable to be predicted is called GOOD_CUALI, which refers to the number of successful responses. As a result of the application of the Watson Glaser test, it is nominal and can be classified as deficient or advanced basic. The predictor variables are gender and marital status, both of nominal type; age, and the 6 dimensions that are part of the test that measure the development of mathematical logical thinking, the latter of quantitative type.

Description of variables Gender refers to how the students studied self-identify, that is, whether they identify themselves as men or women in this specific case. For marital status, there are two options: single or married. Age indicates the years of life of the students, which on average is 22.5 years. The dimensions of the mathematical logical thinking development test are made up of: Generalization, which includes the search for models or modeling as a fundamental component of mathematical logical thinking; deduction, which refers to the process that leads to valid conclusions, as long as the starting premises are also valid. Induction, which is characterized by leading to the finding of models starting from specific cases; the use of symbols and the use of mathematical language, which refers to the process of mathematical generalization, unifying its representation in a concise, precise and clear way. Logical reasoning, which refers to the ability to decide whether or not propositions are logically true; the ability to perform mathematical demonstrations, which is related to the methods used by students to validate their theoretical constructions or to substantiate the results obtained; the global test of logical thinking, represented by DPLM_10, is the global result obtained from applying the Shatnawi test; and the global Watson-Glaser test, called GOOD_CUALI, which is the global value obtained from applying the critical thinking test [10]. Steps to execute the KDD process Fig. 1 shows, first, the data related to the evaluation of critical thinking of the automotive engineering students of the Universidad Tecnológica Equinoccial, of the last seventh and eighth levels, respectively, together with the results obtained from the sociodemographic sheet and the test for the development of mathematical logical thinking applied to the 60 students, are loaded in an Excel sheet. In this study, the development of mathematical logical thinking and its influence on critical thinking was used. The second step is the preparation of the data, that is, storing the values obtained in the mathematical logical thinking and the global assessment in an Excel file in CSV format delimited by commas to make it visible in the JASP statistical application. It is necessary to indicate that in this stage the base is debugged, verifying that the decimal values are defined by dots and the names of the variables are without accents because the native language of the statistical program is English; the type of respective variable is also verified to finally verify that there are no empty cells or any special symbol, both in the data and in the names of the variables as indicated in [12]. In the third step, the data are modeled using JASP to predict the critical thinking of automotive engineering students from the sociodemographic variables, as well as from the dimensions and the overall Shatnawi mathematical logical thinking development test; in this step, there is a sequence of 5 phases: training, test pattern, outcome assessment and knowledge, representation. The cleaned data are divided into two parts: the training phase and the testing phase. According to [13], The K-nearest neighbors' algorithm for building a model in the in-training phase is an algorithm that uses the binary-type decision method to classify the problem.

Visually, the testing stage is reflected in the area under the receiver operating characteristic (ROC) curve, where the selected classifier is shown as a function of the observations related to the categories or dimensions of the target variable to be predicted. See Fig. 1.

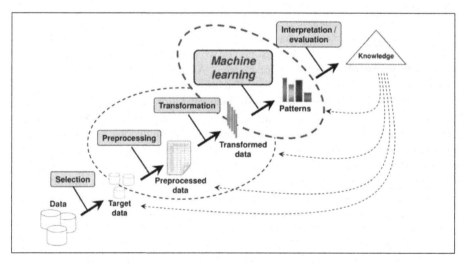

Fig. 1. El process Knowledge Discovery Database (KDD) [13].

To evaluate the performance of the generated learning model, it uses k-fold crossvalidation, to evaluate the performance of the generated learning model. The algorithm divides the data set into K, subsets or folds of the same size, and then the model is entranced k times, each using a different subset as a test and the other K minus 1 subset as training.

3   Results and Discussion

Three classification algorithms were applied such as K-nearest neighbors, random forest, decision tree; of which the best classification model was the first one, i.e., the K-nearest neighbors' model. This can be evidenced in the following Table 1, with the respective evaluation metrics.

Table 1. Classification Algorithm Accuracy.

Algoritmo			Métricas					
K-Vecinos más cercanos	Vecinos más próximos: 3	Ponderaciones: Rank	Distancia: Manhatan	entrenamientos: 48	contrastes: 12	Presición del Contraste: 0.7500		
Árbol de Decisión	Separadores: 6			entrenamientos: 24	contrastes: 36	Presición del contraste: 0.6111		
Bosques Aleatorios	Árboles: 11	Cracterísticas por separador: 3	entrenamientos: 38	validaciones: 10	contrastes: 12	Presición de la validación: 0.50	Presición del contraste: 0.6111	Presición de OBB: 0.5789

Figure 2 shows the ROC curve diagram, where the evaluation of the model's ability to distinguish between the different categories of the variable to be predicted is very good. The rate of true positives versus false positives (1-specificity) under the AUC curve is 0.75, indicating a high discriminant capacity. Still, it could be better in classification, as it is sensitive to the size of the data set.

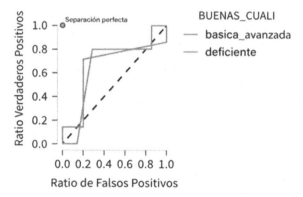

Fig. 2. Diagrama de curvas ROC (JASP 16.0).

The negative predictive value (NPV) is the proportion of negative cases. Correctly classified in relation to all cases classified as negative. In this case, the values are 0.6667,

0.8333 and 07500, respectively for the different classes. A higher NPV indicates that the model is more effective in correctly predicting negative cases. True Negative Ratio (TNR) is the ratio of correctly classified negative cases to all true negative cases. The values provided are 0.8000, 0.7143 and 07571, respectively. A higher RVN indicates that the model is more effective in correctly identifying cases that are truly negative. False Negative Ratio (SNR) is the proportion of negative cases that were incorrectly classified as positive relative to all true negative cases. A lower RFN indicates that the model makes fewer errors in incorrectly classifying negative cases as positive. The false negative ratio RFN and false commission ratio RFO are relatively low, indicating that the model makes fewer errors in misclassifying negative cases as positive and vice versa [14]. The threat score is relatively low, suggesting that the model is effective in minimizing false negative classification errors compared to true negatives. Overall, these indicators show a good performance of the K-nearest-neighbors model as a classifier. See Table 2.

Table 2. All metrics are calculated for each class against all other classes.

Métricas de Evaluación	Basica_avanzada	deficiente	Average / Total
Apoyo	7	5	12
Precisión	0.75	0.75	0.75
Precisión (Valor Predictivo Positivo)	0.83	0.67	0.76
Exhaustividad (Ratio de Verdaderos Positivos)	0.71	0.80	0.75
Ratio de Falsos Positivos	0.20	0.29	0.24
Ratio de Falsos Hallazgos	0.17	0.33	0.25
Puntuación F1	0.77	0.73	0.75
Coeficientes de Correlación de Matthews	0.51	0.51	0.51
Área Bajo la Curva (ABC, AUC)	0.66	0.66	0.66
Valor Predictivo Negativo	0.67	0.83	0.75
Ratio de Verdaderos Negativos	0.80	0.71	0.76
Ratio de Falsos Negativos	0.29	0.20	0.24
Ratio de Falsas Omisiones	0.33	0.17	0.25
Puntuación de Amenaza	1.25	0.80	1.03
Paridad Estadística	0.5	0.50	1.00

4   Conclusions

According to the classification model, K-nearest neighbors, the variables that best allow us to classify Critical Thinking are: Age (AGE) with an individual contribution the classification model of 0.4167; Global Developmental Logical Mathematical Thinking (DPLM_10), Mathematical Demonstration (PP), Logical Reasoning (RR), each with an individual contribution of 0. 25; then, the dimensions of Induction, Deduction, and Use of Symbols and Mathematical Language, with an individual contribution each of 0.1667; next, the dimension Generalization (GG), with an individual contribution to the model of 0.08333. Finally, the variable SEX subtracts precision from the model, and the variable CIVIL has a neutral behavior, so that the two variables are not good predictors. This process was done manually, according to [15], since the variables were removed from the general classifying model to determine their individual impact on the model.

Since age plays a significant role in the classification of critical thinking, specific strategies and programs adapted to different age groups can be developed. This implies addressing in a differentiated manner the needs and characteristics of younger and older students, giving them opportunities for development and practice according to their level of cognitive maturity. The global dimension of the development of mathematical logical thinking has been shown to be an important predictor of critical thinking. Therefore, it can be proposed to implement educational activities and resources that promote the development of skills in this area. This could include mathematical logical reasoning exercises, challenging problems requiring induction and deduction, exploration of symbols and mathematical language in real contexts relevant to automotive engineering. Since both mathematical demonstration and logical reasoning contribute significantly to the classification of critical thinking, specific activities can be designed to promote and develop these skills. This involves providing opportunities for students to practice problem solving using logical demonstration and rigorous mathematical reasoning. It can be proposed to design educational interventions based on the outcomes and variables identified as relevant in the classification model. Then, the impact of these interventions on improving the critical thinking of automotive engineering students should be evaluated. This will allow verifying the effectiveness of the implemented strategies and adjusting them as needed.

In future research on conflict resolution skills in automotive engineering students, it is important to consider additional variables, experience in problem-solving projects, technical knowledge, and communication skills. In addition, the use of more advanced machine learning algo-rhythms that improve classification accuracy could be explored. A longitudinal study analyzing the development of these skills over time would provide valuable information on the factors influencing their improvement.

Disclosure of Interests. The authors have no competing interests to declare that are relevant to the content of this article.

References

1. Aiyub, Suryadi, D., Fatimah, S., Kusnandi: Investigation of Watson-Glaser critical thinking skills of junior high school students in solving mathematical problems. J. Phys. Conf. Ser. **1806**(1) (2021). https://doi.org/10.1088/1742-6596/1806/1/012090
2. Berástegui Arbeloa, G., Galar Idoate, M.: Implementación del algoritmo de los k vecinos más cercanos (K-NN) y estimación del mejor valor local de k para su cálculo [Grado en Ingeniería Informática, Universidad Pública de Navarra (2018). https://academica-e.unavarra.es/xmlui/bitstream/handle/2454/29112/Memoria.pdf?sequence=2&isAllowed=y

3. Ceballos-Vacas, E.M., Rodríguez-Ruiz, B.: How do teachers and students deal with conflict? An analysis of conflict resolution strategies and goals. Revista de Investigación Educativa **41**(2), 551–572 (2023). https://doi.org/10.6018/RIE.547241

4. Ruth, C., Jaime, C., María, V., Julian, S., Nelson, M.: Uso de la Lógica en la Resolución de Problemas de Geometría en un entorno de Lápiz y Papel por Estudiantes de Ingeniería. In: Proceedings of the LACCEI International Multi-Conference for Engineering, Education and Technology, July 2018. https://doi.org/10.18687/LACCEI2018.1.1.108

5. de Romero, J.C.G., Boscán Carroz, M.C., Vinces Centeno, M.R., Barcia Briones, M.F.: Práctica de valores. Una perspectiva de mediación del trabajador social ante los conflictos en las relaciones humanas. Encuentros. Revista de Ciencias Humanas, Teoría Social y Pensamiento Crítico, 19 (septiembre-diciembre), pp. 294–308 (2023). https://doi.org/10.5281/ZENODO.8316312

6. Korshuno I.A., Lubnico S.V., Shirkov N.N.: Adult education and training for the development of problem-solving skills. Obrazovanie i Nauka (2023). https://doi.org/10.17853/1994-5639-2023-6-166-192

7. Martin Guambuguete Rea, C.I., Elizabeth Castro Mayorga III, M., Alberto Espinosa Pinos, C.I., Augusta Sánchez Benítez, C.I., Rodrigo Jordan Bolaños, C.V.: Factores asociados al rendimiento académico: Un análisis mediante regresión logística multivariante en estudiantes del primer nivel del Instituto Superior Tecnológico Tres de Marzo de la Provincia Bolívar, Ecuador. Dominio de Las Ciencias **9**(3), 570–589 (2023). https://doi.org/10.23857/DC.V9I3.3460

8. Ramirez Leal, P., Hernández Suárez, C.A., Prada Núñez, R.: Elements associated with the level of development of mathematical logic thinking in the initial training of teachers. Revista Espacios (2018). https://www-scopus-com.indoamerica.idm.oclc.org/record/display.uri?eid=2-s2.0-85058209032&origin=resultslist&sort=plf-f&src=s&sid=0e084346e4b73c13b93e427effa1918a&sot=b&sdt=b&s=TITLE-ABS-KEY%28desarrollo+del+pensamiento+l%C3%B3gico+matem%C3%A1tico+en+los+estudiantes%29&sl=78&sessionSearchId=0e084346e4b73c13b93e427effa1918a&relpos=0

9. Gonzalo, R.-B.M., Violeta, R.P.N., Hortencia, C.Q.B.: Estrategias educativas en la solución de conflictos escolares en adolescentes. REVISTA COMPLUTENSE DE EDUCACIÓN, 1–16 (2022). https://doi.org/10.5209/rced.80036

10. Rivera, M.-J., Matute, R.: Resolución de conflictos para estudiantes de psicología: Una propuesta de Cultura de Paz Conflict resolution for Psychology students: A culture of peace's proposal. Psicoperspectivas **22**(1), 1–15 (2023). https://doi.org/10.5027/psicoperspectivas-vol22-issue1-fulltext-2769

11. María, S.M.A., Gabriela, B.R.: Design and validation of the software to strengthen logical mathematical thinking (Logical Brain). Revista Internacional de Tecnología, Ciencia y Sociedad, 1–12 (2022). https://doi.org/10.37467/gkarevtechno.v11.2857

12. Thornhill-Miller, B., et al.: Creativity, critical thinking, communication, and collaboration: assessment, certification, and promotion of 21st century skills for the future of work and education. J. Intell. **11**(3) (2023). https://doi.org/10.3390/JINTELLIGENCE11030054

13. Vargas Salazar, G.: El desarrollo del pensamiento lógico-matemático en los estudiantes costarricenses de undécimo año de colegios académicos diurnos y su nivel de logro en el aprendizaje de las matemáticas (2017). https://repositorio.uned.ac.cr/xmlui/handle/120809/1646

Bioindicators of Attention Detection in Online Learning Environments

Jaffer Hassan[1], Javier Berdejo[1], Sakyarshi Kurati[1], Anh Dinh[1], Andrew Garcia[1], Katherine A. Shoemaker[2], and Dvijesh Shastri[1(✉)]

[1] Computer Science and Engineering Technology, University of Houston-Downtown, Houston, TX, USA
{hassanj4,berdejoj1,kuratis1,dinha9,garciaa545}@gator.uhd.edu,
shastrid@uhd.edu
[2] Mathematics and Statistics, University of Houston-Downtown, Houston, TX, USA
shoemakerk@uhd.edu

Abstract. Online classrooms have gained significant prominence in the post-COVID era. While online classes offer advantages, they introduce more distractions that can compromise students' attention to the learning material. Additionally, instructors can find it challenging to gauge student attentiveness when limited to a camera view. The proposed study aims to identify body motion and physiological indicators that can be used to gauge participants' attention in the online meetings. The study explored a set of indicators, including body motion, heart rate, skin temperature, and eye movement. Twenty participants participated in four 30-min long trials consisting of one control and three experimental trials with varying degrees of distractions. Statistical and machine-learning approaches were employed to identify the key indicators of attention. The results reveal that the eye movement, and heart rate showed statistically significant differences between the trials, while the remaining indicators displayed no significant differences.

Keywords: Attention · Virtual Meetings · Video Analysis

1 Introduction

The global pandemic caused by COVID-19 ushered in a large shift towards online learning. The National Center for Education Statistics (NCES) reported that during the pandemic, 77 percent of public schools transitioned to online distance learning, while 84 percent of college students experienced a migration to online-only instruction [1]. It's important to recognize that even before the pandemic-induced paradigm shift, the trend toward virtual learning was already on the rise. Higher education institutions witnessed a surge in online degree programs and enrollments in virtual classrooms [2].

The advantages of online learning are evident. It offers higher accessibility to education, regardless of geographical constraints, and lowers barriers to diverse demographics. A study analyzing enrollment data for an MS degree program at the Georgia Institute of Technology revealed a minimal overlap between online and in-person student populations. This underscores how online options attract individuals who might not otherwise

C. Stephanidis et al. (Eds.): HCII 2024, CCIS 2117, pp. 75–85, 2024.
https://doi.org/10.1007/978-3-031-61953-3_9

pursue the same degree in a traditional setting [2, 3]. Online classes also offer flexibility, enabling students, especially working adults, to engage with learning materials from their places and at their own pace [2].

Despite these merits, online learning presents significant challenges. A U.S. Government Accountability Office report, which examined pre-pandemic data, revealed that students in virtual schools performed academically worse compared to their counterparts in traditional classes. This discrepancy persisted even after accounting for variables like race and economic background [4]. The abundance of distractions, both online and offline, further hindered their learning experiences [5]. In traditional face-to-face learning, instructors gauge student reactions and attentiveness through facial expressions, body language, and class interactions. In the online setting, even with cameras are turned-on during lectures, the limited screen space makes it challenging for instructors to discern facial expressions and obtain a holistic view of students. Consequently, the shift to online learning has generated a substantial body of research dedicated to measuring student attentiveness in this context.

Various methods are employed to assess attention levels in online classrooms. One common approach is the use of grades, which can offer insights into cognitive engagement—defined as a student's willingness to exert mental effort to grasp a subject [6, 14]. However, relying solely on grades has limitations as it does not consider individual intelligence levels or prior subject understanding. Another method involves self-reporting scores, where students assess their own attentiveness during class. While easily administered, this approach may suffer from dishonesty, reluctance to report accurately, or a lack of self-awareness, potentially compromising results [7, 8, 14].

A more objective method involves tapping into students' physiological responses, encompassing heart rate, skin temperature, and EEG signals. For example, in a study conducted in 2022, EEG data was harnessed to construct attention level indices, yielding a 97 percent accuracy rate through the utilization of machine learning techniques [9]. While this approach offers enhanced precision and diminished bias, the collection, analysis, and monitoring of such data are resource-intensive and pose challenges when translating findings into real-world applications.

Eye-gaze is another objective measurement explored for the attention studies. Robal et al. compared a professional grade eye tracking system from Tobii X2-30 with two open-source software-based solutions [6]. They demonstrated that the system outperforms the open-source software-based solutions both in terms of detection performance and processing speed. However, the high-end system was found unsuitable for a large-scale deployment outside a controlled lab setting. Hutt et al. used an external eye-tracking device called EyeTribe to detect participants' attention in a recorded video lecture setting [34, 35]. Bixler et al. extended the study using a high-end tracking device from Tobii called EyeX [36]. Huang1et al. proposed attention detection based on eye vergence information. They also used the Tobii EyeX system [37]. D'Mello et al. developed an intelligent tutoring system (ITS) using Tobii T60™ that aims to promote engagement and learning by dynamically detecting and responding to students' boredom and disengagement [38]. The hardware-based approaches proposed in these studies require the additional hardware device to capture participants' attention.

In recent year, software-based approaches are gaining popularity. The software-based approach is more practical, requiring no additional hardware devices. Hence, it can be used outside the laboratory setup. The approaches employ computer vision and machine learning algorithms to detect affective states, analyzing participants' head and eye movements, as well as facial expressions [10–13]. The study reported in [11] proposed a multimodal computer vision-based system to detect facial expressions through Action Units (AUs) proposed by Paul Ekman [19]. However, they reported the automatic detection of AUs as a major limitation. Computer vision offers a cost-effective, non-intrusive means of monitoring affective states, facilitated by the widespread availability of cameras on various devices and advances in computing power. A comprehensive review of engagement detection in online learning has been documented in [14]. The review classified data related to eye movement, facial expressions, gestures, and posture as foundations of vision-based approaches for automated engagement detection. Within the automatic detection category of the review, most of the referenced work is still in the process of development. The recent developments in vision-based attention detection in online learning utilize pre-existing functionalities found in open-source libraries like DLIB [24] and OpenCV [25] to construct their frameworks. However, they tend to lack comprehensive validation of their frameworks through robust experimental designs. For instance, the convolutional neural networks and eye aspect ratio approach proposed in [15] reported 97 percent accuracy in detecting drowsiness. However, no specifics on the experimental design, length of the videos, or size of the training and test datasets were given. Another example is the reference paper [16], which detailed the system architecture of attentiveness measure using CNN. However, the study lacks an in-depth validation of the proposed architecture. The reference paper [17] presented yet another vision-based student attentiveness monitoring approach. The approach was trained and tested on individual static images, making it less suitable for videos. A computer vision-based attention detection framework discussed in [18] fell short of validating their framework.

In the proposed study, we explored various bioindicators and identified the most effective indicators of attention in online learning environments. The research aimed to answer the following two research questions:

R1. Can bioindicators identify attentive learning sessions from those characterized as distractions?

R2. Can bioindicators differentiate between various distractions, such as those from social media and those from a writing task unrelated to online learning topic?

2 Experimental Design

A total of 20 participants (11 female and 9 male) volunteered for the experiment. Their ages ranged from 18 to 56 years, with a mean age of 27.30 years and a standard deviation of 9.37 years. The experiment featured 4 trials: one control trial and three experimental trials. All four trials required the participants to come to a research lab. The experiment was approved by the institutional review board. The trial orders were counterbalanced using the Latine square design to minimize the order effect [20]. Each visit was approximately 45 to 50 min long and at least a day apart from the last visit.

Five sensors were attached to the participant's body. Specifically, The WitMotion accelerometers (WIT) were attached to the right ankle, right wrist, and chest to collect body motion from the respective body parts. The E4 wristband from Empatica was attached to the left wrist to capture primarily the skin temperature and hand motion. Even though E4 reports electrodermal activity (EDA) and heart rate, our sensor generated erroneous data for these two signals. Hence, we used the Fitbit Versa 4 watch to capture the heart rate and excluded EDA from the analysis. The watch was attached to the participant's right hand. Throughout the experiment, each participant's face was recorded via a Logitech c270 camera. The video recordings were later used to extract the participants' eye-gaze via open-source computer vision software tools. The participants' computer screen was recorded to log their activities in each trial.

Four 30-min long pre-recorded lecture videos from a Data Visualization course were used in the experiment to simulate an online learning environment. The videos were delivered via Zoom – the online meeting platform [21]. The Data Visualization course was chosen for the study as it required no prior background in any specific field of study, making it suitable for the experiment. The study participants had not taken the course before. The content of each video was self-contained requiring no prior knowledge from previously watched videos. The length of the video was chosen as a tradeoff between the following two practical requirements: Data sufficiency to conclude the experiment and accommodation of the participants' busy schedule.

At the beginning of each trial, the sensors were attached to the participants' bodies, followed by a 3-min of relaxation period. The relaxation period aimed to reduce the effects of any stress factors the participants may have carried prior to the day. The length of the relaxation period was determined based on previously conducted experiments of the same type. Next, the participants watched a 30-min lecture video. At the end of the video, they completed a quiz and a post-survey. The quiz data were used to evaluate the participants' learning performance. Each quiz had 5 multiple-choice questions specific to the lecture contents. Hence, the participants would have difficulty answering the question, unless they paid attention to the video. The post-survey questionnaire collected self-reporting of the participants' engagement in each trial.

While the control trial required the participant to focus only on the lecture video, the three experimental trials allowed them to engage in a secondary task simultaneously with the primary task of watching the lecture video. Specifically, in one of the experimental trials, the Writing Trial (Exp_WT), the participants were asked to answer 20 open-ended questions. The question pool was chosen from [22] and was kept sufficiently large so the participants didn't finish answering all of them before the lecture video ended. The questions demanded participants' mental engagement. The writing trial simulated scenarios of drafting an email or working on a homework assignment simultaneously while attending the lecture.

In the second experimental trial, the Social-media Trial (Exp_ST), the participants were instructed to interact with social media channels of their interests (e.g., Facebook or Instagram) while watching the lecture video. This trial simulated scenarios of using social media for matters unrelated to the lecture.

The third experimental trial was a free-activity trial (Exp_FT) in which the participants were given the freedom to partake in various legitimate activities on their phones or computers, such as browsing social media, watching the news, shopping online, writing emails, playing computer games, and more, while watching the lecture video. This trial replicated situations where participants had the option to either engage in secondary activities or simply focus on the lecture.

3 Data Analysis

A total of 80 videos (20 participants × 4 trials) and 400 signals (20 participants × 4 trials × 5 bio measurements) were collected during the experiment. These data were analyzed to extract 10 features as described below. The first and last 2.5 min of data were excluded to ensure that the data reflected participants in a settled state during the trials. In addition, a total of 160 questionnaires (20 participants × 4 trials × 2 questionnaires – quiz and self-report) were collected during the experiment.

3.1 Feature Extraction from Videos

Each video was about 30 min long and recorded at 25 frames/second rate with 640 × 360 pixels resolution. Eye-gaze signals were extracted using an open-source toolkit [23]. The toolkit utilizes various computer vision algorithms from Dlib [24] and OpenCV [25] to extract the eye-gaze locations in pixels and directions from every frame in the face videos. In particular, it uses the Haar feature-based cascade classifiers to detect the face and eyes in each video frame [26, 27]. We utilized the eye-gaze locations (Left_x, Left_y, Right_x, and Right_y) for the analysis. These four signals were generated for every trial of every participant. Next, we computed the variance of each of these four eye-gaze signals, followed by computing the mean of variances in the x-direction and y-direction of the eye-gaze signals.

The analysis resulted in two tabular data-frames of 20 rows representing the participant pool and 4 columns representing the trials – one data-frame for the eye-gaze x-motion (Feature-1) and the other for the eye-gaze y-motion (Feature-2). The variance was chosen as a study variable over the mean because it effectively captures the dispersion of the participants' eye-gaze.

3.2 Feature Extraction from Bioindicators

Signals from three accelerometers, one E4 wristband, and one Fitbit watch were used in the analysis. The signals were timestamped and about 30 min in length. Each accelerometer sensor generates 3-axis output reporting values in the x, y, and z coordinates. The x, y, and z coordinate values were consolidated into an energy signal according to the formulas reported in [29].

Three motion signals (torso, right hand, and right leg) were generated for every trial of every participant. Next, we computed the variance of these signals. Similarly, the participants' skin temperature and left-hand motion were captured via the E4 sensor. The energy signal from the leaft-hand motion data was calculated according to Eq. (3). Finally, the heart rate data was extracted from the Fitbit watch. We computed the variance of each of these six signals, which resulted in six tabular data-frames of 20 rows and 4 columns (Feature-3 to Feature-8).

3.3 Performance Data

The participants' learning performance was assessed via the end-of-lecture quizzes (Feature-9) on a scale of 0 to 5, where 0 represents all wrong answers and 5 represents all correct answers. Their attention to the learning material was evaluated through the self-reported survey. The survey categories were dummy-coded on a scale of 1 to 5, where 1 represents minimal attention to the learning task, and 5 represents complete attention to the learning task (Feature-10).

3.4 Statistical Analysis

A paired Wilcoxon signed-ranked test was used on each of the 10 data-frames to test for feature differences between the trials. This nonparametric test was chosen to account for the small sample size of the data and the lack of normality in the features. A two-sided test was used, where the null hypothesis was that there was no significant differences in the features between trial conditions and the alternative hypothesis suggested the presence of such differences.

3.5 Machine Learning Analysis

Five machine learning (ML) algorithms were used to explore the predictive power of these bioindicators in classifying trials. In particular, Logistic Regression provide parametric approaches for binary classification. KNN offers neighborly insights. Bagging and Random Forest bring the power of ensembles. Support Vector Machines (SVM) is highly effective in handling complex decision boundaries. The aforementioned data-frames were used as predictors. The four trial categories were grouped in two categories (control and experiment) to generate a binary target variable called trial for the classification problem. The data was divided into an 80/20 split via stratified random sampling, having the 80-split for training and the 20-split for testing. The SMOT algorithm [31] was used to tackle the class imbalanced problem that resulted from grouping three experimental trials into one class. The classifiers were modeled on the training set and validated via the 10-fold cross-validation method. To obtain the best performing classifiers, the hyper-parameter tuning was done during the model training. The best performing classifiers were tested on the test set. RStudio and Orange ML [32] were employed for the ML modeling process.

4 Experimental Results

Figure 1 illustrates the participants' quiz scores and self-reported attention scores. It reveals higher quiz scores and self-reported attention in the control trial compared to the three experimental trials. In particular, the mean quiz score for the control trial is 3, while it is 2 or below for the experiment trials. The differences between the control and experiment trials are statistically significant. Specifically, the paired Wilcoxon text reported $p = 0.0074$ when comparing the control (Ctr) and Writing trial (Exp_WT), $p = 0.0124$ for the control and the Social-media trial (Exp_ST), and $p = 0.0093$ for the control and the Free-activity trial (Exp_FT). The score differences between the experimental trials were statistically insignificant.

The mean self-reported attention score for the control trial is above 3, indicating that the participants were engaged about 50% of the time (15 min) on average. The mean scores are around 2 for the experiment trials, suggesting that the participants were less engaged on average during the experiment trials. The self-reported attention score differences between the control and each of the experimental settings are statistically significant. Specifically, the paired Wilcoxon test reported $p = 0.0015$ when coparing tCtr and Exp_WT, $p = 0.0018$ for Ctr and Exp_ST, and $p = 0.0005$ for Ctr and Exp_FT. Overall, the quiz and self-report analysis highlight the fact that each type of secondary activity (writing, social media browsing, or free activity) distracted the participants from their primary task of engaging in online learning, resulting in their poor learning performance. The attention score differences between the experimental trials are statistically insignificant, suggesting that there was not a difference in the distraction levels of the different secondary tasks.

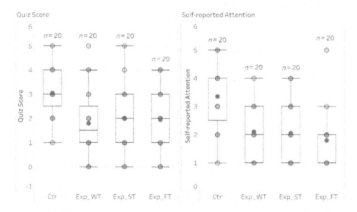

Fig. 1. Boxplots of the quiz scores (left image) and the self-reported attention (right image) for the participant pool (n = 20) group by trials – control (Ctr), Writing (Exp_WT), Social-media (Exp_ST), and Free-activity (Exp_FT). The red dots represent the population mean per trial. Each individual gray dot corresponds to data from a single participant. (Color figure online)

For the accelerometer data, the variance of the left-hand motion of Exp_FT is statistically significantly lower than that of the remaining three trials ($p = 0.0240$ for the Exp_FT and Ctr pair, $p = 0.0121$ for the Exp_FT and Exp_WT pair, and $p = 0.0696$ for the Exp_FT and Exp_ST pair). Furthermore, the variance of the torso motion of Exp_FT is statistically significantly higher than the control trial ($p = 0.0348$). The variances of the right-hand and right-leg motion across the trials are statistically insignificant. In summary, despite certain aspects eliciting favorable results, the accelerometer data essentially reveal insufficient distinctions of the hand, leg, and limb movements among the trials. This suggests that body motion may not serve as a robust indicator for assessing participants' attentiveness in online learning environments. One possible reason is that online learning activities are typically not physically demanding, particularly for non-standing viewers, which may have caused less body movement.

For the physiological data, the mean heart rate variability is lower in the control trial than in the experimental trials. The difference is statistically significant between each pair ($p = 0.0458$ for the Ctr and Exp_WT pair, $p = 0.0490$ for the Ctr and Exp_ST and pair, and $p = 0.0005$ for the Ctr and Exp_FT pair), suggesting that the increased heart rate variability in the experimental trials resulted from the participants' engagement in the secondary activities. The differences between the experimental trials were statistically insignificant. The analysis finds heart rate variability a useful indicator in gauging participants' attention in online learning. The skin temperature variability was higher in the control trial compared to the experiment trials. However, the differences are statistically insignificant, making the sensor unsuitable for assessing the attention task.

The eye-gaze data reveals less eye-gaze variability in the horizontal direction (x-direction) during the control trial compared to the experimental trials. The differences between the control and experiment trials are statistically significant. Specifically, the Wilcoxon test reported p = 0.0256 for the Ctr and Exp_WT pair, p = 0.0946 for the Ctr and Exp_ST pair, and p = 0.0970 for the Ctr and Exp_FT pair. The eye-gaze variability differences in the vertical direction (y-direction) are statistically insignificant across all trials. The findings suggest that when participants engage in activities other than paying attention to an online speaker, they tend to shift their eye gaze horizontally more often than vertically. This discovery is noteworthy because it highlights that secondary activities like writing essays, browsing social media, playing online games, etc., prompt participants to move their eye gaze more horizontally compared to when they are focused on an online speaker. Additionally, it underscores the potential of using a basic webcam in combination with open-source software to assess participants' attention during online meetings. These experimental results validate the study question R1 and R2.

The 10 features were investigated further using machine learning. To gauge the significance of the features, we employed two standard feature ranking methods - chi-square and Information Gain [33]. Both approaches consistently identified the eye-gaze x-motion, and heart rate as the most significant features. This finding aligns with our earlier statistical analysis, where each of those features demonstrated a statistically significant difference between the control and each experimental trial.

Next, we prepared classification models to predict trial type as either control or experiment. Table 1 summarizes the model performance for the classification task. Overall,

Table 1. Model Performance for Trial Classification.

Models	Training Accuracy	Test Accuracy
KNN	85.94%	75.00%
Random Forest	100.00%	93.75%
SVM	87.50%	70.75%
Logistic Regression	71.25%	75.25%
Bagging	98.44%	93.75%

the classification models have superior performance, with the Radom Forest model performing the best with a training accuracy of 100 percent and a test accuracy of 93.75 percent. The results showcase the effectiveness of the machine learning approach in classifying attentive learning sessions from those characterized as distractions, answering the first research question (R1).

5   Conclusion

In this study, we explored various bioindicators in search of robust indicators for assessing participants' attention in online learning environments. Specifically, five contact sensors (three body accelerometers, one E4 wristband, and one Fitbit watch) and a visual camera were used to extract 10 features. Our statistical analysis identified eye-gaze motion, and heart rate as the most significant indicators of attention in the online learning environment. The results from our machine learning analysis aligned with the statistical analysis as it also identified these three features as the key indicators of attention. The analysis revealed that engaging in secondary activities simultaneously with attending online lectures led to a notable increase in participants' eye-gaze movement and heart rate variability when compared to the baseline control trial of attentive learing sessions. We devised five machine-learning classifiers to predict trial type as either control or experiment. Our best-performing model, the Random Forest model, reported 100 percent accuracy for the training dataset and 94 percent for the test dataset. Thus, the study demonstrated the feasibility of predicting attention in online learning. The most significant indicators that our analysis identified require no additional hardware because eye-gaze can be extracted from a webcam, and most smartwatches report heart-rate data. In recent times, both sensors have become ubiquitous. Thus, the study demonstrated the practicality of the proposed approach and the possibility of using it outside the laboratory setup.

As for future work, we plan to perform the analysis with data collection over a more granular level, examining the data over a number of smaller time windows. We anticipate that this approach will offer more nuance to the attention detection challenge. Our ultimate goal is to develop an attention detection system capable of delivering real-time feedback to online presenters regarding participants' engagement.

Acknowledgments. We are grateful to Prof. Ermelinda DeLaViña and the graduate program in Data Analytics at the University of Houston - Downtown for their financial support with the data collection.

The authors have no competing interests to declare that are relevant to the content of this article.

References

1. U.S. Department of Education, National Center for Education Statistics. 2020. Common Core of Data (CCD), "State Nonfiscal Public Elementary/Secondary Education Survey, 2019–20 v.1a and 2020–21

2. Shankar, K., Arora, P., Binz-Scharf, M.C.: Evidence on online higher education: The promise of COVID-19 pandemic data. Manage. Labour Stud. **48**(2), 242–249 (2021)
3. Goodman, J., Melkers, J., Pallais, A.: Can online delivery increase access to education? J. Law Econ. **37**(1), 1–34 (2019)
4. U.S. Government Accountability Office and U.S. Department of Education. 2022. K-12 Education: Department of Education Should Help States Address Student Testing Issues and Financial Risks Associated with Virtual Schools, Particularly Virtual Charter Schools. GAO-22-104444
5. B. Means, J.: Neisler, with Langer Research Associates. 2020. Suddenly Online: A National Survey of Undergraduates During the COVID-19 Pandemic. San Mateo, CA
6. Anderson, A.R., Christenson, S.L., Sinclair, M.F., Lehr, C.A.: Check and connect: the importance of relationships for promoting engagement with school. J. Sch. Psychol. **42**(2), 95–113 (2004)
7. Shernoff, D.J., Csikszentmihalyi, M., Schneider, B., Shernoff, E.S.: Student engagement in high school classrooms from the perspective of flow theory. Sociol. Educ. **73**, 247–269 (2000)
8. D'Mello, S., Lehman, B., Pekrun, R., Graesser, A.: Confusion can be beneficial for learning. Learn. Instr. **29**, 153–170 (2014)
9. Al-Nafjan, A., Aldayel, M.: Predict students' attention in online learning using EEG Data. Sustainability **14**(11), 6553 (2022). https://doi.org/10.3390/su14116553
10. D'Mello, S.K., Craig, S.D., Graesser, A.C.: Multimethod assessment of affective experience and expression during deep learning. Int. J. Learn. Technol. **4**(3), 165–187 (2009)
11. D'Mello, S.K., Graesser, A.: Multimodal semi-automated affect detection from conversational cues, gross body language, and facial features. User Model. User-Adaptive Interact. **20**(2), 147–187 (2010)
12. Kapoor, A., Picard, R.W.: Multimodal affect recognition in learning environments. In: ACM International Conference on Multimedia, New York (2005)
13. McDaniel, B., D'Mello, S., King, B., Chipman, P., Tapp, K., Graesser, A.: Facial features for affective state detection in learning environments. In: Proceedings of the Annual Meeting of the Cognitive Science Society, California (2007)
14. Ali Dewan, M., Murshed, M., Lin, F.: Engagement detection in online learning: A Review. Smart Learn. Environ. **6**, 1 (2019)
15. Deepa, D., Selvaraj, S., Vijaya Lakshmi, D.M., Sarneshwar, S., Vignesh Balaji, N., Vikash, M.: Web application to track student attentiveness during online class using CNN and eye aspect ratio. In: 2022 6th International Conference on Computing Methodologies and Communication (ICCMC) (2022). https://doi.org/10.1109/iccmc53470.2022.9753863
16. Desai, R., Muni, R., Madhani, D., Joshi, A.: Predicting learning behavior using hyper-personalization and attentiveness measure. In: 2022 5th International Conference on Advances in Science and Technology (ICAST), pp. 258–264. IEEE, December 2022
17. Madake, J., et al.: IEEE Pune Section International Conference (PuneCon). Pune, India **2022**, 1–6 (2022). https://doi.org/10.1109/PuneCon55413.2022.10014782
18. Shah, N.A., Meenakshi, K., Agarwal, A., Sivasubramanian, S.: Assessment of student attentiveness to E-learning by monitoring behavioural elements. In: 2021 International Conference on Computer Communication and Informatics (ICCCI), Coimbatore, India, pp. 1–7 (2021). https://doi.org/10.1109/ICCCI50826.2021.9402283
19. Ekman, P.: Emotions revealed. Bmj **328**(Suppl S5) (2004)
20. Richardson, J.T.E.: The use of Latin-square designs in educational and psychological research. Educ. Res. Rev. **24**(2018), 84–97 (2018)
21. Zoom (2023)
22. White, A.: 365 Deep & Thought Provoking Questions to Ask Yourself (& Others) (2023)
23. Agarwal, V.: Automating Online Proctoring Using AI (2023)

24. Dlib github (2023). https://github.com/davisking/dlib
25. OpenCV (2023). https://opencv.org/
26. Viola, P., Jones, M.: Rapid object detection using a boosted cascade of simple features. Proceedings of the 2001 IEEE Computer Society Conference on Computer Vision and Pattern Recognition (CVPR 2001), vol. 1. IEEE (2001)
27. Martynow, M., Zielińska, A., Marzejon, M., Wojtkowski, M., Komar, K.: Pupil detection supported by Haar feature based cascade classifier for two-photon vision examinations. In: 2019 11th International Symposium on Image and Signal Processing and Analysis (ISPA), pp. 54–59. IEEE (2019)
28. Nielsen, N.: Head Pose Estimation (2023). https://github.com/niconielsen32/ComputerVision/blob/master/headPoseEstimation.py
29. Bouten, C.V., Koekkoek, K.T.M., Verduin, M., Kodde, R., Janssen, J.D.: A triaxial accelerometer and portable data processing unit for the assessment of daily physical activity. IEEE Trans. Biomed. Eng. 44 (3), 136–147 (1997)
30. Singh, R.: The Ultimate Guide to Emotion Recognition from Facial Expressions using Python (2023). https://towardsdatascience.com/the-ultimate-guide-to-emotion-recognition-from-facial-expressions-using-python-64e58d4324ff
31. Chawla, N., Bowyer, K., Hall, L., Kegelmeyer, W.: SMOTE: synthetic minority over-sampling technique. J. Artif. Intell. Res. 16(2002), 341–378 (2002)
32. Orange (2023). https://orangedatamining.com/
33. Steinbach, M., Tan, P., Kumar, V.: Introduction to Data Mining. 2nd edition
34. Hutt, S., Krasich, K., R. Brockmole, J., K. D'Mello, S.: Breaking out of the lab: Mitigating mind wandering with gaze-based attention-aware technology in classrooms. In: Proceedings of the 2021 Human Factors in Computing Systems, pp. 1–14, May 2021
35. Hutt, S., Hardey, J., Bixler, R., Stewart, A., Risko, E., D'Mello, S.K.: Gaze-based detection of mind wandering during lecture viewing. In: International Educational Data Mining Society (2017)
36. Bixler, E., Robert, D'Mello, S.K.: Crossed eyes: domain adaptation for gaze-based mind wandering models. In: ACM Symposium on Eye Tracking Research and Applications, pp. 1–12 (2021)
37. Huang, M.X., Li, J., Ngai, G., Leong, H.V., Bulling, A.: Moment-to-moment detection of internal thought during video viewing from eye vergence behavior. In: Proceedings of the 27th ACM International Conference on Multimedia, pp. 2254–2262 (2019)
38. D'Mello, S., Olney, A., Williams, C., Hays, P.: Gaze tutor: a gaze-reactive intelligent tutoring system. Int. J. Hum Comput Stud. 70(5), 377–398 (2012)

Adaptive Learning Environments: Integrating Artificial Intelligence for Special Education Advances

Janio Jadán-Guerrero[1]([✉]), Karla Tamayo-Narvaez[2], Elena Méndez[3], and María Valenzuela[4]

[1] Centro de Investigación en Mecatrónica y Sistemas Interactivos (MIST), Universidad Tecnológica Indoamérica, Av. Machala y Sabanilla, Quito EC170103, Ecuador
janiojadan@uti.edu.ec
[2] Maestría en Educación, mención Pedagogía en Entornos Digitales (MEPED), Ambato, Ecuador
ktamayo3@indoamerica.edu.ec
[3] Maestría en Gestión y dirección de Proyectos, Universidad Galileo, Ciudad de Guatemala, Guatemala
hytfer@galileo.edu
[4] CEMSA, Florida, Sarazota, USA

Abstract. Students with special educational needs are confronted with various barriers that restrict their learning and performance in the educational environment. The lack of accessible and adapted educational resources tailored to their needs based on their disability negatively impacts their ability to interact effectively with both teachers and peers. In this context, Artificial Intelligence emerges as a promising solution to overcome some of these educational barriers by offering personalized tools, speech recognition technologies, and text-to-voice conversion technologies that allow students with disabilities to communicate seamlessly. Artificial Intelligence not only addresses the challenges mentioned previously but also opens up new possibilities for more effective learning and an enriching educational experience. The integration of these technologies could represent a significant advancement towards the creation of more accessible and egalitarian educational environments. This article focuses on identifying challenges from the perspective of teachers and parents, proposing the implementation of adapted educational resources using artificial intelligence. To establish a reference base for the needs and problems of students, a survey was conducted with the participation of 66 teachers and 112 parents in two developing countries, Ecuador and Guatemala. The results obtained offer an opportunity to improve student education by identifying possible solutions in adapting resources and promoting inclusion through the implementation of Artificial Intelligence. A recurring challenge in both countries is the lack of adequate infrastructure, specialized tools, inclusive methodologies, and software to facilitate the learning process in educational institutions.

Keywords: Special educational needs · Artificial Intelligence · Educational barriers · Disabilities · Inclusive methodologies · Adapted Educational Resources

C. Stephanidis et al. (Eds.): HCII 2024, CCIS 2117, pp. 86–94, 2024.
https://doi.org/10.1007/978-3-031-61953-3_10

1 Introduction

Research into adaptive learning environments that integrate artificial intelligence (AI) to advance special education presents a complex and multifaceted problem that requires careful analysis. First, there is the need to effectively personalize the educational experience to meet the individual needs of students with disabilities or special educational needs. This means not only recognizing different learning styles and abilities, but also adapting the environment in real time to the student's responses and progress [1]. Second, there is the challenge of the technical implementation of artificial intelligence in educational platforms. This challenge involves not only the development of the technology itself, but also the design of inclusive content to ensure that the platforms are accessible and usable by individuals with various disabilities [2].

There is also the issue of the technological gap and inequality in access to these advanced resources, which could perpetuate or increase the differences in educational quality between institutions and populations of different socioeconomic levels. Added to this is the training and preparation of teachers to effectively use these technologies in the classroom and adapt to a role where, supported by AI, they can focus more on direct and personalized pedagogical intervention.

Another relevant concern is the evaluation of the effectiveness of adaptive learning environments with artificial intelligence in the context of special education. Defining appropriate success metrics and conducting longitudinal studies to understand the long-term impact of these technologies on the academic and emotional development of students is essential. It is worth reflecting on the ethical implications of the use of AI in special education. Consideration should be given to how the design of these technologies impacts student autonomy and what is necessary to avoid bias and other forms of discrimination that could be instilled or perpetuated by misconfigured AI-based measures [3].

The integration of artificial intelligence into adaptive environments intended for special education, therefore, represents a complex web of challenges ranging from pedagogical personalization to ethical and equity issues, requiring an interdisciplinary and collaborative approach to study and resolution. In this context, this research poses the following research question:

How can artificial intelligence be designed and integrated into adaptive learning environments to effectively and ethically enhance special education, taking into account the diversity of individual needs, teacher preparation, and equity in access to technology?.

2 Related Works

Currently, there has been a growing interest among academics in enhancing education through artificial intelligence (AI), which has generated a variety of research approaches. These approaches include tools such as intelligent tutoring systems designed specifically for special education, the use of natural language processing to improve language teaching, the incorporation of educational robots in learning environments, the application of data mining techniques to predict student performance, speech analysis in collaborative environments, the use of neural networks to evaluate the effectiveness of teaching methods, affective computing to measure students' emotions, and the implementation of recommendation algorithms to personalize the learning process. These areas of research reflect the growing relevance and potential impact of AI in education, particularly in the context of special education [4, 5].

Artificial intelligence (AI) can help students with disabilities learn more effectively. For example, AI resources can be more engaging and motivating than traditional teaching materials, which can help keep students' attention. In addition, AI can provide immediate feedback, which helps students better understand concepts. [6]. The integration of artificial intelligence, Internet of Things (IoT), machine learning, gamification and other technologies in education aims to significantly transform and improve teaching and learning processes. This includes providing more personalized and adaptive learning experiences, enabling continuous monitoring of student progress and offering instant and relevant feedback. The evolution of this concept, known by some authors as Education 5.0, highlights a focus on human learning, fostering the development of social and emotional skills, as well as promoting minimal environmental impact, with special attention to health and safety [7].

The potential of artificial intelligence (AI) in education has not yet been fully exploited. In this context, a study emphasizes the importance of specialized knowledge in technology and pedagogy for its successful implementation, as well as the ability to critically evaluate its ethical aspects. In order to address this need, a scale is introduced to measure such knowledge based on the TPACK framework, and a model is developed to analyze how technological knowledge can enhance teachers' ability to apply the educational benefits of AI. The results suggest that effective integration of AI requires a combined knowledge of technology and pedagogy, as well as proposing an enhanced framework with an ethical focus, called Intelligent-TPACK. [8].

Furthermore, the contribution by Roll (2016) entitled "Evolution and Revolution in Artificial Intelligence in Education" should be considered. In this article, it is mentioned that in a twenty-five year retrospective of artificial intelligence in education (AIED), 47 articles published at key moments (1994, 2004, and 2014) in the Journal of AIED were analyzed to distinguish the usual focuses and scenarios in the field. From these findings, two research avenues are proposed to influence education in the next quarter of a century: an evolutionary one, which improves current classroom practices in collaboration with teachers and expands technological diversity and domains; and a revolutionary one, which seeks to integrate technologies into students' daily lives, supporting their cultures, practices, goals, and communities [9].

Also, the research by Sharma (2021) titled "Artificial Intelligence and Its Implications in Education," where it is indicated that recent advances in computer hardware, software, and online services have contributed to improvements in classrooms and teaching methods, but it is with artificial intelligence (AI) where a true educational revolution is anticipated. AI, which has already caused unprecedented transformations in various sectors, has the capacity to create expert systems with skills such as visual perception, speech recognition, and intellectual behaviors similar to humans. This chapter aims to explore the role of AI in education by analyzing its impact on the market, effects on learning, and presenting case studies of current applications in education such as intelligent content and tutoring systems, in order to improve educational and life outcomes. The chapter concludes by pointing out the problems and challenges faced by the integration of AI in the educational sector [10].

In the same way, the contribution of Jadán (2022) titled "Virtual Assistants for Teaching the English Language" indicates that this study investigates the learning of the English language through Virtual Assistants to overcome the lack of knowledge in innovative methodological strategies. The aim was to create strategies involving virtual assistants to foster technological immersion and motivate students to learn. Using a mixed-methods approach in documentary and field research, and applying inductive-deductive methods, activities were developed that address the four main linguistic skills: "listening, reading, speaking, and writing" with the topic "Jobs". Post-test results with the use of Alexa demonstrated an improvement in student learning and motivation, concluding that virtual assistants are beneficial for the development of English skills [11].

Lastly, the research by Peñaherrera (2022) titled "Implementation of Artificial Intelligence (AI) as an Educational Resource" should be considered. In it, it is mentioned that what once seemed like science fiction is now transformed by Artificial Intelligence (AI) into a reality that we could use in various projects and institutional environments. AI implements methodologies such as Machine Learning, Deep Learning, and Natural Language Processing to teach algorithms to autonomously learn, process information, and execute actions based on large volumes of data. This study explores how AI is revolutionizing teaching and educational management through optimizations in pedagogical processes and adaptive systems that personalize the learning experience to each student's individual profile. The adoption of AI technologies in Educational Institutions promises multiple benefits and is crucial to stay up-to-date in the face of an imminent digital transformation that will redefine interactions in the near future and contribute to progress in teaching and educational marketing.

3   Method

With the objective of inquiring into the perspectives on the difficulties faced by students with disabilities in the educational setting, as well as the challenges they face both in the academic environment and at home, a Design Thinking methodology composed of five phases was implemented [12]:

1. **Empathize**: In this phase, we sought to understand the specific needs and challenges of students with disabilities. Activities were carried out to put ourselves in the students' shoes and understand their perspective.
2. **Define the problem**: In this stage, the data collected in the questionnaire to teachers and parents were analyzed. The main problem posed in the research question was clearly defined, focusing on the use of technology as a possible solution.
3. **Designing solutions**: In this phase, creative ideas were generated and different approaches are explored to address the identified problem. Creativity was encouraged and innovative solutions and the use of Artificial Intelligence that can improve the educational experience of students with disabilities were sought.
4. **Prototyping**: In this stage, prototypes and strategies of the solutions proposed during the ideation phase were developed. These simplified versions were designed with Artificial Intelligence tools.

5. **Evaluate and improve**: In this final phase, the prototypes developed with students with disabilities that teachers use in the educational environment were evaluated.

3.1 Participants

In the research, 66 teachers and 112 parents from two countries, as well as 6 school authorities, participated with the aim of evaluating their opinion on the inclusion of students with disabilities in education, as well as the problems faced by students with disabilities both at school and at home.

3.2 Instruments and Materials

The instruments used in the research were online tools such as Padlet to foster empathy in the groups, as well as MindMeister to categorize problems and online questionnaires using Google Forms. These tools made it possible to obtain data in an agile manner, eliminating the geographical limitations of teachers located in Ecuador and Guatemala. In addition, the artificial intelligence tools described in Table 1, developed as a result of previous research conducted by the teachers, were used.

Table 1. AI tools for education strategies.

Name	Description	Link
StoryBird.ai	Application for creating stories	https://www.storybird.ai
Animated Drawings	Create animations from a drawing	https://sketch.metademolab.com/
Quickdraw	Students can make a drawing and the artificial intelligence can guess what has been depicted	https://quickdraw.withgoogle.com/
Deepl Translator	Automatic translation tool that can facilitate language learning and make educational materials accessible to students with different native languages	https://www.deepl.com/es/translator
Curipod	Platform that enriches the teaching-learning process, potentially useful for adapting learning to the diverse needs of students	https://curipod.com/
Eduaide.ai	Uses advanced AI algorithms to offer a personalized learning experience, adapting educational content to each student's abilities, interests, and learning pace	https://www.eduaide.ai/
Magicschool.ai	Helps teachers to generate detailed lesson plans and educational content adapted to different skill levels and learning styles	https://www.magicschool.ai/

(continued)

Table 1. (*continued*)

Name	Description	Link
Education CoPilot	Assists teachers in designing curricula, lesson plans, and activities, and in tracking their students' progress	https://educationcopilot.com/
Gradescope	AI-based assessment and grading tool that facilitates the grading of assignments, homework, and exams	https://www.gradescope.com/
Formative AI	Provides real-time feedback on student performance, identifying strengths and weaknesses to adjust teaching strategies	https://www.formativeai.com/lander

3.3 Procedure

The research was carried out over a period of one month, during which 66 master's students from two different programs, who also work as teachers in educational institutions, were recruited. The first group consisted of 48 students from the Master's program in Education, while the second group was composed of 18 students from the Master's program in Transformation, belonging to two universities located in Ecuador and Guatemala, respectively.

Following the five-stage Design Thinking methodology, a series of empathy activities were carried out in the first stage for the participants to get to know each other. In the second stage, focused on defining the problem, the research question was addressed, opting to explore the potential of artificial intelligence to solve problems through its application. To this end, a questionnaire was designed that included both closed and open-ended questions.

Since both master's degree programs are taught in virtual mode, we worked with both groups and requested permission to carry out the research. Once the instrument was applied through the educational platforms of each program, the information was processed.

In the prototyping stage, various artificial intelligence tools were used to address different student scenarios and conditions, including physical, language, hearing, visual, and intellectual disabilities. Finally, in the evaluation stage, each group was asked to evaluate their prototypes and strategies to answer the research question.

4 Results and Discussion

The baseline results provide a significant perspective on the perception of teachers in Guatemala and Ecuador regarding the inclusion of students with disabilities in the educational system. Table 2 summarizes the most relevant aspects.

Table 2. Results of the survey application

Category	Result
Importance of Education	74% consider education to be of great importance for people with disabilities
Right of People with Disabilities	79% strongly agree that people with disabilities have the right to access an education system
Difficulties in the Learning	33% consider that it is sometimes true that students with disabilities find it difficult he is learning
Responsibility of the parents	45% do not believe that the responsibility for the education of persons with sensory disabilities should rest solely with the parents
Concern of Educational Institutions for Inclusion	56% think that the different educational institutions should be concerned about the inclusion of students with disabilities in their classrooms
Knowledge of Inclusion Programs	25% are aware of any inclusion program in educational institutions in their country
Attention to Students with Disabilities	34% have attended to students with disabilities in the courses they teach
Deal Different or Special	41% agree in provide a deal different or special to those students with disabilities in assigning and receiving tasks
Taking Exams Specials	42% believe that they are due carry out exams short, partial, and final with characteristics special or different from those traditional for students with disabilities
Extension of Time in Exams	35% consider that it is due enlarge the time assigned to resolve requests to the students with disabilities
Use of special software	44% value the importance of using special software such as support for the students with disabilities in the development of its activity's academics

Within the open-ended questions some teachers report that sometimes they do not realize that they have students with disabilities until they are assessing and seeing their difficulty.

The results of prototypes made with artificial intelligence and evaluations conducted with students with disabilities have shown that Artificial Intelligence offers resources to support the educational strategies of students with disabilities. These resources include mapping their learning plans, detecting their strengths and areas for improvement, identifying the most accessible or challenging subjects, as well as understanding their learning preferences and styles. In addition, AI can personalize learning and improve opportunities for students with the help of their teachers, through intelligent tutoring systems. However, it is important to keep in mind that AI can also widen inequalities and exclude certain people from the educational process, which can lead to a new digital divide. In this sense, it is important to identify affordable and accessible resources for families and teachers working with students with disabilities.

The collaboration between educational professionals, programmers, and AI experts is essential for designing and developing effective and coherent solutions. Teachers and principals should be given enough autonomy to manage their respective classrooms and schools, based on the idea that they know their students' needs best. To fully leverage AI technologies, educators need to acquire new competencies in education. It is fundamental to find a balance between using AI as a support and complementary tool and the value of human relationships in the educational process.

Artificial intelligence has the capacity to improve educational accessibility for students with various disabilities. For example, it can employ voice recognition technology to facilitate the interaction of visually impaired students with academic content. It also enables those with motor disabilities to control devices without the need to use a mouse or keyboard. Furthermore, through eye-tracking technologies, AI can learn patterns and recognize movements to allow more fluid interaction in these cases. Additionally, it offers automatic generation of subtitles for students with hearing impairments and enables the use of translation technology for those who speak different languages.

Overall, each of these AI tools brings distinct advantages to the educational environment, ranging from fostering creativity and personalized learning to aiding in essential teaching tasks like grading and lesson planning. The successful integration of such tools could complement traditional teaching methods, providing both students and educators with enhanced opportunities for growth and development in a digital age.

5   Conclusions

The presence the growth of Artificial Intelligence in education is undeniable and promises an impact significant in the ambit educational. However, it is essential that those develop and introduce are tools are responsible for monitoring the values transmitted to the new generations. Ethics and values they must be a fundamental part of the implementation of Artificial Intelligence in education.

The quick adoption of new technologies in teaching in the systems educational formalities is essential to prepare students for challenges of the world work and changes economic and social. However, innovation should not only be the responsibility of teachers. Individual; must become on a target institutional ingrained in the life of the institution educational.

AI plays a crucial role in adapting the contents educational to the needs and learning pace of each student. Through data analysis, you can identify the strengths and weaknesses of students, which allows provide materials educational personalized to improve understanding and retention of contents heads.

For future research, it is suggested to delve deeper into the impact of artificial intelligence on inclusive education, focusing on the development of specific tools and programs that address the individual needs of students with disabilities. In addition, it could be beneficial to explore how artificial intelligence can reduce inequalities in access to education and improve the quality of instruction for all students, regardless of their abilities. Another area of interest would be to examine the ethical and social challenges associated with the use of artificial intelligence in education, and how these can be effectively addressed to ensure inclusive and equitable education for all. In addition, it would be important to further evaluate and refine strategies for implementing artificial intelligence in educational settings, as well as its long-term impact on the development and academic success of students with disabilities.

Acknowledgments. The authors would like to thank the cooperation of the School Cardenal de la Torre and the Universidad Tecnológica Indoamérica and Universidad Galileo for the support for the development of this work.

References

1. Peñaherrera, W.: Implementación de la Inteligencia Artificial (IA) como Recurso Educativo. Indoamérica (2022). https://repositorio.uti.edu.ec/handle/123456789/4400
2. Ramírez, J.: Artificial intelligence within the interplay between natural and artificial computation: advances in data science, trends and applications. Neurocomputing (2020). https://doi.org/10.1016/j.neucom.2020.05.078
3. Vera, F.: Integración de la Inteligencia Artificial en la Educación superior: Desafíos y oportunidades. Transformar (2023). https://doi.org/10.1016/j.chb.2022.107468
4. Chen, X.: Two Decades of Artificial Intelligence in Education. JSTOR (2022). https://www.jstor.org/stable/48647028
5. Geczy, P.: Challenges and future directions of big data and artificial intelligence in education. Front. Psychol. (2020). https://doi.org/10.3389/fpsyg.2020.580820
6. Saputra, I.: Integration of artificial intelligence in education: opportunities, challenges, threats and obstacles. A literature review. Indonesian J. Comput. Sci. (2023). https://doi.org/10.33022/ijcs.v12i4.3266
7. Rane, N.: Education 4.0 and 5.0: Integrating Artificial Intelligence (AI) for Personalized and Adaptive Learning. SSRN (2023). https://papers.ssrn.com/sol3/papers.cfm?abstract_id=4638365
8. Celik, I.: Towards Intelligent-TPACK: an empirical study on teachers' professional knowledge to ethically integrate artificial intelligence (AI)-based tools into education. Comput. Hum. Behav. **2**(5), 99–110 (2016). https://doi.org/10.1016/j.chb.2022.107468
9. Roll, I.: Evolution and Revolution in Artificial Intelligence in Education. Springer (2016). https://doi.org/10.1007/s40593-016-0110-3
10. Sharma, U.: Artificial Intelligence and Its Implications in Education. IGI Global (2021). https://www.igi-global.com/chapter/artificial-intelligence-and-its-implications-in-education/261505
11. Jadán-Guerrero, J.: Asistentes virtuales para la enseñanza del idioma Inglés. Indoamérica. (2022). https://repositorio.uti.edu.ec/handle/123456789/2744
12. Arias-Flores, H., Jadán-Guerrero, J., Gómez-Luna, L.: Innovación Educativa en el aula mediante design thinking y game thinking. Hamut´ay **6**(1), 82–95 (2019). https://doi.org/10.21503/hamu.v6i1.1576

On-Demand Internationalization for Learning Management System Moodle

Tina John$^{(\boxtimes)}$ and Anna Lena Möller

Technische Hochschule Lübeck, Mönkhofer Weg 239, 23562 Lübeck, Germany
tina.john@th-luebeck.de

Abstract. As part of the BMBF-funded joint project Onlinecampus Pflege, a mobile, freely accessible self-learning offer for professional nurses was developed and tested to promote the competent use of digital technologies in nursing and care with the aim of low-threshold access.

The platform was implemented as an instance of the learning management system Moodle, with learning units that seamlessly combine text, graphics and various gamification elements from the Html5 package. After one year of testing, 485 users with 24 different mother tongues are registered on the platform. The current study aims to provide internationalization through translation. This includes ensuring easy access to the content and the platform by offering it in multiple languages. As a result, AI-assisted simultaneous translation is being developed. The Moodle plugins Auto Multilanguage and H5P Translate add on-demand translation to Moodle's static native language support. Initial results show that the solution developed with sustainability in mind minimizes the effort and cost of creating learning materials that need to be prepared for different languages, while providing maximum accessibility for learners in terms of their native language or, more importantly, the desired language in the learning domain.

The use of AI-powered translations in education and training as well as the effect on the learning performance remains to be discussed.

Keywords: Translation · H5P · Multilingual · Moodle plugin · Professional health care

1 Introduction

As part of the BMBF-funded joint project Onlinecampus Pflege, a mobile, freely accessible self-learning offer for professional nurses was developed and tested to promote the competent use of digital technologies in nursing and care [1–3].

In addition to the aim of imparting learning content that promotes the digital competences of the learners, strong attention is paid to accessibility and low-threshold access to both the topics and the learning environment itself. The target group of professional caregivers can be classified as heterogeneous in terms of age, gender, origin and thus the mother tongue, among other things. Providing learning material in one's own language can greatly reduce comprehension difficulties, especially in the lower performance

C. Stephanidis et al. (Eds.): HCII 2024, CCIS 2117, pp. 95–102, 2024.
https://doi.org/10.1007/978-3-031-61953-3_11

spectrum, or any existing language problems [4]. In order to contribute to low-threshold access to the content and the platform, the learning programme is to be offered in several languages, which will be the subject of this article.

The learning environment was developed as an instance of the learning management system (LMS) Moodle [5] in an iterative process. The media-didactic implementation of the learning content combines various media, which are seamlessly embedded in very small, thematically and didactically self-contained Moodle courses (so-called Learning Nuggets [6]). The media include texts, graphics, interactive videos and diverse gamification elements of the Html5 Package (H5P) [7], which Moodle can natively integrate as a learning activity.

In the era of globalization, mobility, migration, and recruitment of skilled workers, internationalization in human-computer interaction can be expected from any established learning platform. The learning management system Moodle was developed from the very beginning with the aim of being internationally usable. Users can use the platform in their preferred language, reducing the barriers to accessing educational content worldwide. In H5P, internationalization is also implemented through language support via text translation. For both Moodle and H5P content, translations must be created by the learning material creator, the course designer. This procedure is classified as static, requires an enormous amount of work for each micro-learning unit, and the language support is statically limited to the corresponding stored languages. When integrating externally developed Open Educational Resources (OER), all translations for all languages that the Moodle instance is to support must be completed manually.

So far, the learning platform Onlinecampus Pflege has been evaluated in two test phases through quantitative and qualitative data collection. Qualitative data collection in the form of focus groups and teaching and learning events, in which learning on the platform was guided and accompanied, revealed that a native-speaker representation of the learning content but also of the learning environment as a whole is desired.

The aim of this study is the work in progress development of a concept and an implementation of a multi-language option for learning content in Moodle LMS through AI-assisted simultaneous translations.

2 Methodology

2.1 Needs Analysis for the Multi-language Option

Methodology and Results. The Moodle native registration process has been supplemented with additional profile fields for testing the platform, including the indication of the native language.

For the analysis of the native languages, the participants profile data was extracted from the Moodle database and pseudonymized as part of the user analysis. Native languages entered as free text were checked for different spellings of the same language and corrected if necessary. From the corrected data, the absolute frequencies of the specified languages were calculated. Over a period of one year, a total of 485 participants registered on the platform. A total of 24 (cf. Table 1) different native languages are stored in the participant profiles.

Table 1. Mother tongues different from German per frequency with additional information of *DeepL* (see 2.2) *language support* (italic) and languages that are spoken in regions with second language English (underlined).

7	5	4	3	2	1
Russian	Turkish, Polish, *Malayalam*	English, *Albanian, Persian*	Arabic, *Kurdish*	Spanish, Hungarian, *Filipino*	Portuguese, Romanian, French, *Bosnian, Syrian Serbian, Croatian, Ukrainian, Indonesian, Tigrinya, Urdu*

Discussion. From the analysis of the participant profiles, no immediate need for a multi-language option of the target group can be identified due to the very low frequencies per language. Nevertheless, due to the rather high number of different mother tongues, there is a need for it. This assumption is supported by informal impressions gained from the teaching and learning events that have been held. Participants used web browsers' built-in translation capabilities to translate the content into English. It can be assumed that these participants were not native German speakers. The translation into English is an observation but not an indication of the native language of the participants. Under certain circumstances, the choice of English language may be due to technical reasons, as language support of the actual mother tongue may not be offered.

A certain need for a multi-language option for English can be deduced, although Russian was given as a type more often than other languages. Malayalam and Urdu are languages of India, whilst Tigrinya is spoken in Ethiopia and Eritrea, among others. In all the countries mentioned above, and also for the languages of the Philippines and Indonesia, English is a second language, a language of education or a lingua franca. Other clusters were also assessed, with English outperforming all other clusters in absolute numbers.

The request to indicate the mother tongue in the profile data for data collection for the needs analysis of the multi-language option is deemed unsuitable after the analysis. The explicit question regarding the preferred language for the educational offering appears more appropriate [4]. Particularly in regions where diglossia, the use of different languages for different areas of life, is prevalent, the requirement for the desired language is pertinent for the relevant field and not the mother tongue in order to effectively comprehend the necessity.

Conclusion. Based on the needs analysis, English was chosen as a language for the initial conception and implementation of the multi-language option on the platform.

2.2 Appropriate AI-Powered Translation Service

The market currently offers a variety of translation services that offer AI-powered translation between German and English. For the development of the concept and the first implementation, the non-preparation of an API was an exclusion criterion for any service, as manual processing of translations in any form was to be avoided. The cost factor should be kept as low as possible. Established and well-known translation services that offer an API individualize the API usage via a personal API key. Microsoft Translator [8] and Google Translate [9] should be mentioned as examples. For both services, an API key is only provided in conjunction with a service account subscription. DeepL [10] offers an API key with a very transparent and quickly understandable cost model. Without a service subscription as a prerequisite, an API key is provided free of charge for a manageable, yet applicable token quota, which is renewed monthly.

Basically, the concept and the implementation should be designed for the use of a wide range of services. Without considering any other factors for other services, the DeepL API was selected as part of the initial implementation because of the very simple cost model for the API key and the superior accuracy reported in the literature [11, 12]. The API functionality is comprehensive and well documented. Along with essential language support for translation from German to English, DeepL provides various other languages. However, whilst the other two services offer language support for all languages covered in the needs assessment, the choice in DeepL is limited (cf. Table 1, [10, 12]).

2.3 Preliminary Considerations

Moodle Native Language Support. Moodle offers over 800 language packs, which must be installed by the administrator for each Moodle instance. An installation of all language packs should not significantly burden the performance of the instance. The language packs contain all Moodle's native language strings of the graphical user interfaces. Any additional text content that is available as HTML on the client side can be modified by Moodle-native routines so-called filters before display. These filters identify special tag attributes in the code and replace the content according to a custom dictionary built by a set of tags with special attributes. The special tag attributes as well as the custom dictionary are inserted individually by the course designer for each content as in the following example:

```
<span lang="de" class="multilang">Deutscher Text</span>
<span lang="en" class="multilang">English text</span>
```

Although H5P content is also displayed as HTML content on the client side, it is not replaceable via Moodle filter. H5P offers its own static translation mechanism. As with the language pack of the Moodle platform, only static existing elements are translated, but not user-defined texts. In the backend H5P content is available in JSON format, which defines different attributes depending on the respective H5P content type. Moodle also offers a native filter for these parameters as a method within the theme, which is dependent on it and can only be edited in the source code by a developer.

To summarize, Moodle's native language support differs for three different types of content. The language packs can be transferred, but suitable translation methods had to be found for the HTML and H5P content.

Sustainability. When using AI methods that are additionally accessed via web interfaces, performance and energy consumption, which should not be underestimated even in the inference phase where new outputs are generated [13], need to be taken into account compared to local rule-based methods. Performance should remain high, but energy consumption should be low. Therefore, it should be possible to reuse already completed translations.

2.4 Concept and Technical Implementation

The Onlinecampus Pflege is set up monolingually. The Moodle language packs are used to translate the static elements of the platform. All strings to be translated are extracted using the routines or the open-source code from the existing filter functions.

All HTML code is translated using the Deepl API for HTML to the language set by the user. For reasons of efficiency, the translation is only done once on demand and is stored in the Moodle database together with the hash of the original text. And is retrieved from the database on another request. Energy consumption is thus reduced to the minimum necessary. It also provides a way to correct existing translations in the event of inaccurate translations as soon as such an error is detected.

For non-H5P elements, this concept was implemented based on the Moodle filter plugin Multi-Language Content in the Auto Multilanguage plugin [14] for Moodle. Different from HTML content, the H5P parameters are filtered by the theme's method. All attributes used for the H5P content type functionality must not be translated. The DeepL API for XML accepts a list of XML tags to be ignored. Therefore, all functional attributes for all H5P content types used on the platform were identified. Preparation and translation with DeepL API for XML were implemented in the plugin for Moodle H5P Translate [15]. The source code clearly separates, the extraction of the character strings from the translation via the API in a modular manner. Each plugin provides a corresponding menu for configuring the necessary API key and API URL.

3   Results and Discussion

The Moodle course example in Fig. 1 shows two different language versions of the same content. Translation was carried out in the backend without any human interaction by the native Moodle Language Pack for English for the menus, the developed H5P Translate plugin for the H5P content type for interactive video with embedded quiz and by the developed Auto Multilanguage for the remaining content. Figure 1 also shows the special course design of the Onlinecampus Pflege, where all learning material is seamlessly embedded into the page. Although it looks seamless, automatic external translation tools do not have permission to change the embedded content, therefore do not work in the given course design.

The solution presented translates every written word. This does not completely solve the challenge of providing low-threshold access to non-native language learning content. Success depends primarily on the learning media used. To be successful, media need to meet certain requirements in terms of verbal content. They must be prepared without any verbal information that cannot be extracted from the media as text.

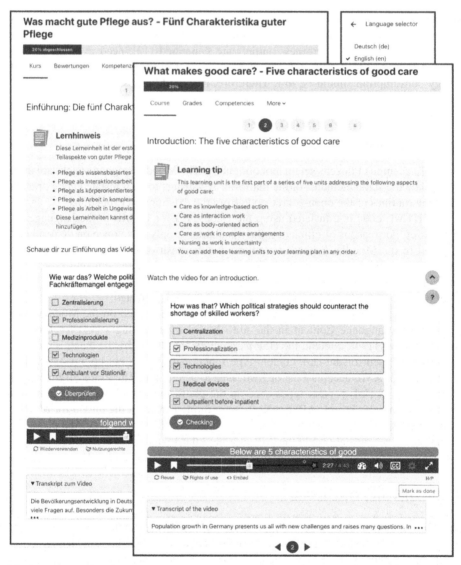

Fig. 1. An example of a Learning Nugget (very small self-contained Moodle course) from the monolingually developed Onlinecampus Pflege (left) and the AI-assisted simultaneous translation (right) with course title, menus, course creator designed texts (HTML) and a subtitled (vtt) interactive video with embedded quiz from the Html5 Package (H5P) with extra video transcript.

Another challenge is the spoken word in audio and video media. The concept and implementation of the multi-language option presented is not able to translate the spoken words within the audio or video, but accessible provided transcripts (in Fig. 1). At this stage, automatic speech recognition (ASR) or audio-visual ASR (AV-ASR) can assist in the preparation of the content and may be integrated in future work for automatic audio and video transcription and translation [16–18]. The video transcription text (vtt) for subtitles in Fig. 1 were prepared for each language using external tools and are embedded in the H5P element as vtt-files, thus not stored in translatable parameter.

Future work will include extensive testing of the multi-language option for English, followed by Slavic languages, where the support for the Cyrillic alphabet might require an effort, and followed by Arabic languages, where the writing direction might require attention. Moodle supports both alphabets in its language packs. Based on the experience gained from this work, special attention should be paid to ensuring the appropriate design of the text field sizes in the H5P activities. In addition, the functionality should be tested for all H5P content types that have not been considered yet, to be able to expand the list of functional H5P attributes accordingly. There are many different H5P content types on the platform, so the list should already capture most of the attributes. At least, there are use cases demanding a filter hindering automatic translations.

As a result of the analysis, DeepL cannot yet be used to cover all native languages from Table 1. Other services support a variety of other languages but use different APIs. Following this circumstance, the various APIs must be examined in further work regarding their usability in the presented concept and appropriate interfaces must be implemented. It is to be expected that any service can be integrated as a replacement for DeepL or in addition. However, for the reasons discussed above, native language support could be less important than support for the language of education.

The multi-language option available on the platform should be evaluated in terms of translation quality and benefits for the learner in a trial. If the quality is insufficient, no positive effect on learning outcomes is to be expected. Comparative studies with speakers of different native languages who learn with and without the multi-language option could shed light on this.

4 Conclusion

The AI-assisted simultaneous translation for a Moodle instance was successfully implemented. Future work will include further features and intensive testing. The process minimizes the effort and cost of creating multilingual learning materials while providing learners with maximum accessibility in their preferred language of instruction. However, the use of AI-supported translation in education and training still needs to be discussed. Quality control is the responsibility of the learning platform provider.

Acknowledgments. This study was funded by Federal Ministry of Education and Research funding guideline INVITE (grant number 21INVI09).

Disclosure of Interests.   The author has no competing interests to declare that are relevant to the content of this article.

References

1. Wullf, S., Borcherding, G., Pengel, J., Meißner, A., Hülsken-Giesler, M.: Onlinecampus Pflege: Für kompetenten Umgang mit digitalen Technologien in der beruflichen Pflege qualifizieren. Zeitschrift für Sozialmanagement **20**(1), 131–138 (2022)

2. Borcherding, G., Hülsken-Giesler, M., Meißner, A.: Digitale Kompetenzen erwerben. Pflegezeitschrift **74**, 38–41 (2021)
3. Möller, A.L., et al.: Gute Pflege mit digitaler Unterstützung ermöglichen – das Weiterbildungsangebot für digitale Kompetenzen in der beruflichen Pflege. In: Boll, S., et al. (eds.) Zukunft der Pflege. Tagungsband der 6. Clusterkonferenz 2023: Mit Pflegeinnovationen die Zukunft gestalten – menschlich, professionell, online, pp. 39–43, Oldenburg, Germany (2023)
4. Benson, C.: Addressing language of instruction issues in education: Recommendations for documenting progress. Background paper for Global Education Monitoring Report 2016 Education for people and planet: Creating sustainable futures for all (2016)
5. Moodle Homepage. https://moodle.org/. Accessed 15 June 2023
6. Bailey, C., Zalfan, M.T., Davis, H.C., Fill, K., Conole, G.: Panning for gold: designing pedagogically-inspired learning nuggets. Educ. Technol. Soc. **9**(1), 113–122 (2006)
7. H5P Homepage. https://www.h5p.org. Accessed 15 June 2023
8. Microsoft Translator. https://learn.microsoft.com/de-de/azure/ai-services/translator/. Accessed 10 Mar 2024
9. Google Translate. https://cloud.google.com/translate/. Accessed 10 Mar 2024
10. DeepL. https://www.deepl.com/translator. Accessed 10 Mar 2024
11. Yulianto, A. & Supriatnaningsih, R.: Google translate vs. DeepL: a quantitative evaluation of close-language pair translation (french to english). AJELP: Asian J. English Lang. Pedagogy **9**(2), 109–127 (2021)
12. Nwakanma, C.I., Njoku, J.N., Kim, D.S.: Evaluation of language translator module for metaverse virtual assistant. 한국통신학회 학술대회논문집, pp. 1779–1780 (2022)
13. de Vries, A.: The growing energy footprint of artificial intelligence. Joule **7**(10), 2191–2194 (2023)
14. Auto Multilanguage Repository. https://github.com/tinjohn/moodle-filter_automultilang. Accessed 19 Jan 2024
15. H5P Translate Repository. https://github.com/tinjohn/moodle-local_h5ptranslate. Accessed 19 Jan 2024
16. Sherstinova, T., Kolobov, R., Mikhaylovskiy, N.: Everyday conversations: a comparative study of expert transcriptions and ASR outputs at a lexical level. In: Karpov, A., Samudravijaya, K., Deepak, K.T., Hegde, R.M., Agrawal, S.S., Prasanna, S.R.M. (eds.) Speech and Computer. SPECOM 2023.LNCS, vol. 14338, pp. 43–56 (2023)
17. Potamianos, G., Neti, C., Gravier, G., Garg, A., Senior, A.W.: Recent advances in the automatic recognition of audiovisual speech. Proc. IEEE **91**(9), 1306–1326 (2003)
18. Ciobanu, D., Secară, A.: Speech recognition and synthesis technologies in the translation workflow. In: The Routledge Handbook of Translation and Technology. Routledge, pp. 91–106 (2019)

Examining the Impact: Pencil-and-Paper Versus Touch-Screen Assessments in Augmented Reality Learning

NaYeon Kang and Jung Hyup Kim[✉]

University of Missouri, Columbia, MO, USA
nkrh7@umsystem.edu, kijung@missouri.edu

Abstract. This research examines the effects of assessments conducted through traditional pencil-and-paper versus touch-screen-based approaches in the context of Augmented Reality (AR) learning. Utilizing AR devices and real-time sensors, we established an educational setting to enhance learner interaction. The assessment methodology was modified to optimize the AR learning environment. In our previous study, participants were equipped with motion sensors to capture their movements, and their learning attitudes were assessed accordingly. We also used the same AR system in the current study. Notably, the key difference from the previous experiment is in assessment methods. In the prior study, questionnaires were administered on paper, and participants received feedback post-experiment. In contrast, the current experiment involved participants receiving questionnaires on a touch screen, with immediate feedback provided after each problem solution. After the AR learning, we asked participants to fill out the Student Satisfaction and Self-Confidence in Learning Scales (SCLS). The results revealed that the student's responses corresponding to two questions: "I enjoyed how my instructor taught the Augmented Reality module" and "It is my responsibility to learn what I need to know from this Augmented Reality module," show significant differences between Pencil-and-Paper and Touch-Screen Assessments in AR Learning.

Keywords: AR Learning · AR Education · Problem-Solving method

1 Introduction

Despite the potential of Augmented Reality (AR) in education, many people are unfamiliar with its usage, posing a potential obstacle. To address this, the study was conducted to enhance the efficacy of the AR learning system. The experiment was performed by integrating the AR device with a motion sensor. Students were equipped with motion sensors to track their movements, and their learning behaviors were examined accordingly. The current study is the follow-up of the previous AR study by Yu, Kim [1]. The primary distinction in this study, as opposed to the prior experiment, lies in the alteration of assessment methods. In the prior year, the questionnaire was paper-based, and participants received feedback after the experiment concluded. In the current year, participants received the questionnaire on a touch screen, obtaining immediate feedback upon solving each problem.

C. Stephanidis et al. (Eds.): HCII 2024, CCIS 2117, pp. 103–108, 2024.
https://doi.org/10.1007/978-3-031-61953-3_12

2   Method

2.1   AR-Based Learning Design

We developed AR modules for biomechanics [2]. The learning content was structured based on the curriculum covered in real engineering lectures, consisting of two parts. Lecture 1 contained 7 scenes, while Lecture 2 included 8 scenes. To enhance learner immersion and understanding, multiple blackboards were used in the lecture setup. The main blackboard was positioned at the front, supplemented by additional blackboards on the sides to provide more detailed information visibility. To closely replicate the actions of an actual instructor, we integrated natural body motions. Furthermore, we introduced lip synchronization in this iteration to heighten the realism of the instructor. Certain scenes featured human models engaged in biomechanical scenarios to facilitate better comprehension.

2.2   Experiment Process

We conducted an experiment with 21 University of Missouri students. Initially, we provided them with a detailed explanation of the experimental procedure. Participants put on HoloLens and 11 motion detection sensors to their upper bodies. Additionally, an eye-tracking device was worn to capture eye movement data, and a real-time location sensor at the waist monitored participant positions. Utilizing these sensors, we recorded real-time responses, which were then applied to the AR system to generate results. As the lecture commenced, participants utilized HoloLens to view the presentation. Following each scene, participants were tasked with solving related problems on a laptop positioned on the table in front of them. To enhance participant comfort, a touch screen was employed for problem-solving. After solving the problem, participants judged their confidence in the solution on a scale from 0 to 100 [3]. They could promptly compare their confidence level with their actual performance. Overconfidence was noted if their confidence score surpassed their performance, while a lower score indicated under-confidence. Upon completing the problem, participants were instructed to move the table to the next predefined point marked with an X. The table was equipped with a sensor, detecting participant movements to trigger the next scene. This sequence was repeated 7 or 8 times during the experiment (Fig. 1).

In the previous study [1], participants needed to answer a paper questionnaire resembling the format depicted in Fig. 2. They addressed the problems presented after each scene, and upon completing all scenes, their questionnaires were graded and received the feedback from the instructor. In the present study, participants were handed with a touch screen questionnaire, illustrated in Fig. 3. Similar to the previous study, participants tackled problems following each scene. However, this time, upon resolving a problem, they promptly received feedback to assess the correctness of their answers and their corresponding confidence levels [4].

In this study, we asked participants to fill out the Student Satisfaction and Self-Confidence in Learning Scale (SCLS) after the experiment [5]. Each statement is rated on a scale of 1 to 5, from strongly disagree to strongly agree. Below are the questions asked to the participants.

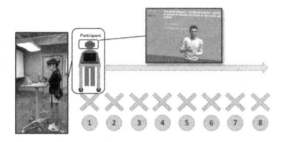

Fig. 1. Experiment setup conditions.

Question 1) Please complete the sentence by filling in the blank

Occupational Biomechanics studies the physical interaction of workers with
their tools, machines, and materials to enhance the worker's performance while
minimizing the risk of (   ).

    a) Failure
    b) Musculoskeletal injury
    c) Momentum
    d) Muscle energy
    e) Physical motion

Fig. 2. Paper form of questionnaire.   **Fig. 3.** Touch screen form of questionnaire

1. The teaching methods used in this Augmented Reality module were helpful and effective.
2. The Augmented Reality module provided me with learning materials and activities to promote my learning.
3. I enjoyed how my instructor taught the Augmented Reality module.
4. The teaching materials used motivating and helped me to learn.
5. The way the virtual instructor taught was suitable to the way I learn.
6. I am mastering the content of the Augmented Reality module.
7. The Augmented Reality module covered critical content necessary for the mastery.
8. I am developing the skills and obtaining the required knowledge to perform in a clinical setting.
9. The Augmented Reality module included helpful resources.
10. It is my responsibility to learn what I need to know from this Augmented Reality module.
11. I know how to get help when I do not understand the concept covered in the Augmented Reality module.
12. I know how to use the Augmented Reality module activities to learn the key concepts of biomechanics.
13. It is the instructor's responsibility to tell me what I need to learn during class time.

3   Results

In general, the SCLS results for 2023 exhibit minor variations compared to those of 2022. Notably, there were significant differences in the responses to question #10 in lecture 1 and question 3 in lecture 2. Question #10, which assesses participants' perception of their responsibility to grasp essential information from the AR learning module, directly correlates with the clarity of the lecture and the learners' comprehension of its content. The analysis of the responses reveals noteworthy differences between 2022 and 2023. Compared to the 2022 SCLS results, a dominant pattern emerged with approximately 40% and 60% of respondents selecting degrees 4 and 5, indicating a high level of clarity in the lecture. However, in 2023, a more even distribution of degrees was observed. There was an increase in the proportion of respondents selecting degrees 2 and 3, accounting for around 20% and 15%, respectively.

While lecture 2 exhibited minimal deviation from the previous year's results, lecture 1 demonstrated a significant difference, particularly in the context of question #10 (Fig. 4).

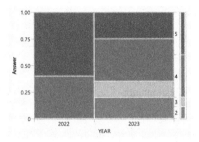

Fig. 4. Mosaic plot of Question #10 of Lecture 1.

The third question, "I enjoyed how my instructor taught the Augmented Reality module," serves as an indicator of the learner's level of interest during the learning process. In 2022, most students expressed enjoyment, with approximately 20% and 40% assigning degrees 4 and 5. Despite a substantial 43% and 5% of respondents giving high enjoyment ratings, there was an increase in the proportion of students who did not find the module enjoyable in 2023. Specifically, students opting for degrees 1 and 2 constituted around 10% and 24%, totaling approximately 33% of the responses (Fig. 5).

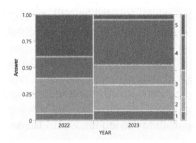

Fig. 5. Mosaic plot of Question #3 of Lecture 2.

4 Discussions

The reduced sense of responsibility in learning during lecture 1 compared to the previous study can be attributed to the influence of the modified immediate feedback system. In the prior study [1], students would engage with a scene and solve problems presented on paper. Upon completing all modules, they received grades and feedback. However, in the current study, participants solved the problems on a computer monitor and received instant feedback. This feedback encompassed information on the correctness of their answers and their corresponding confidence levels. According to Razzaq, Ostrow [6], students who received immediate feedback for each problem solved demonstrated higher performance compared to those who received feedback after completing all problems. Furthermore, Bae [7] reported that the academic achievement of students was found to be higher when utilizing an app providing real-time feedback compared to those without such feedback. Moreover, meaningful outcomes were observed in immediate feedback categories such as 'learning usefulness,' 'interest/motivation,' 'interaction,' 'functionality,' and 'convenience.' These factors play crucial roles in aiding learners in comprehending the material, thereby enhancing the clarity of the lecture. Particularly, 'interaction' exhibited a substantial difference comparing between pencil-and-paper and touchscreen-based assessments.

Collectively, the meaningful interaction results among students receiving immediate feedback suggest a reduced sense of responsibility in their learning interactions with the AR contents, fostering clearer lectures and elevated achievement. However, given the significantly greater difficulty of lecture 2 compared to lecture 1, the impact of feedback was less pronounced. Overall, as lecture 2 demanded a heightened sense of responsibility for learning, participants may have been more influenced by the lecture content itself rather than the feedback, potentially explaining the limited difference from the previous study.

The diminished enjoyment reported by students in lecture 2 compared to the previous study can be attributed to variances in the questionnaire format. In the prior one, the questionnaire was paper-based, allowing participants to preview the questions before they solve. This preview enabled them to identify specific areas to focus on during the lecture, making the problems comparatively easier to solve and heightening interest in the presentation. Conversely, with the touch screen format, participants remain unaware of the problems until each scene concludes. This necessitates a broader focus on the entire lecture rather than specific points, demanding increased concentration and resulting in heightened fatigue, thereby diminishing the overall enjoyment of the lecture. While lecture 1, being relatively straightforward, did not significantly differ from the previous study due to the manageable nature of problem-solving without prior exposure to the questions, lecture 2, being comparatively challenging, accentuated the impact of this feature. Consequently, the shift in assessment methods yielded positive outcomes in the immediate feedback domain but generated negative effects in the learners' interest sector.

5   Conclusion

In our quest to transform education, we integrated Augmented Reality into our teaching modules, significantly changing our approach to problem-solving. This evolution begs a crucial question: how can we heighten student engagement in lectures while preserving the touch screen's clear, interactive benefits? Our journey began with a traditional paper questionnaire in 2022, where students tackled problems after each section and received graded feedback post-lecture. Yet, 2023 marked a shift to an interactive touchscreen format, offering instant feedback and noticeably boosting students' comprehension. Despite this progress, we encountered an unexpected challenge: student interest waned as they lost the ability to preview questions. Now, our mission is clear - we must innovate once more to make lectures captivating, keeping the touchscreen's clarity-enhancing virtues intact.

References

1. Yu, C.-Y., et al.: Developing an Augmented Reality-Based Interactive Learning System with Real-Time Location and Motion Tracking. Springer, Cham (2023)
2. Guo, W., Hyup Kim, J.: Investigating academic performance using an AR-based learning environment with retrospective confidence judgments. In: Proceedings of the Human Factors and Ergonomics Society Annual Meeting. SAGE Publications Sage CA, Los Angeles, CA (2022)
3. Mostowfi, S., et al.: The effect of metacognitive judgments on metacognitive awareness in an augmented reality environment. In: International Conference on Human-Computer Interaction. Springer (2023). https://doi.org/10.1007/978-3-031-35017-7_22
4. Guo, W., Kim, J.H.: How metacognitive monitoring feedback influences workload in a location-based augmented reality environment. In: International Conference on Human-Computer Interaction. Springer (2021). https://doi.org/10.1007/978-3-030-77932-0_14
5. Smith, S.J., Roehrs, C.J.: High-fidelity simulation: factors correlated with nursing student: satisfaction: and self-confidence. Nurs. Educ. Perspect. **30**(2), 74–78 (2009)
6. Razzaq, R., Ostrow, K.S., Heffernan, N.T.: Effect of immediate feedback on math achievement at the high school level. In: International Conference on Artificial Intelligence in Education. Springer (2020)
7. Bae, J.-H.: Effectiveness of learning flow and academic achievement on learning activities with real-time feedback utilizing a smart clicker app in higher education. J. Korea Academia-Ind. Cooperation Soc. **15**(9), 5543–5552 (2014)

Developing a Teacher Self-Reflection E-portfolio Platform for the Improvement of Noticing Skills of Childcare Teachers

Soojung Kim[1] and Yun Gil Lee[2]([✉])

[1] Hannam University, 70 Hannamro, Daedeok-gu, Daejeon 34430, Korea
[2] Hoseo University, 20, Hoseo-ro, 79beon-gil, Baebang-eup, Asan-si,
Chungcheongnam-do 31499, Korea
yglee@hoseo.edu

Abstract. The objective of this study is to develop a system that provides early childhood teachers with video clips of their classroom teaching practices. This system is designed to aid teachers in self-reflection regarding the interactions observed in these videos. Furthermore, it aims to enable teachers to analyze and make informed decisions based on their interpretations. To streamline the process of facilitating teachers' self-reflection through recorded teaching practices, experts in teacher education have collaborated to develop web-based teaching portfolios. Specifically, the SRP developed for this study is based on a web-based portfolio platform that is centered on artificial intelligence. This platform is tailored to effectively support teacher's cognitive process training in self-reflecting on their teaching behaviors. The SRP is expected to serve as an effective tool for enhancing teachers' cognitive processes related to supporting play. It will allow teachers to record, reflect upon, and share their self-reflection processes using the e-portfolio platform.

Keywords: Teacher self-reflection · E-portfolio platform · Noticing skills · Childcare teachers

1 Introduction

For infants and toddlers, the classroom serves as a dynamic environment where they engage in play according to their interests, facilitating learning through this play. It is crucial for teachers to offer appropriate interaction and support for play, enabling young children to enhance their learning experiences. This involves identifying meaningful moments in children's play situations and understanding the dynamics of their play [1]. However, observing meaningful play, interpreting these observations, and making informed decisions about instructional support in a classroom filled with infants and toddlers engaging in diverse interests requires a high level of professional expertise. These cognitive processes are typically mastered by highly trained teachers [2]. Enhancing the professionalism of teachers to effectively support play among infants and toddlers has become increasingly urgent and challenging, particularly in the context of the Fourth Industrial Revolution [3].

© The Author(s), under exclusive license to Springer Nature Switzerland AG 2024
C. Stephanidis et al. (Eds.): HCII 2024, CCIS 2117, pp. 109–113, 2024.
https://doi.org/10.1007/978-3-031-61953-3_13

This study focused on utilizing self-reflection as a method to aid teachers in making decisions in early childhood classrooms [4]. The objective of this research is to develop a system that provides early childhood teachers with video clips of their classroom teaching practices. These clips are intended to assist teachers in reflecting on the play interactions observed in the videos, enabling them to analyze and make decisions based on their interpretations. The self-reflection process for teachers involves consultation. The system developed in this study for teacher self-reflection is named the teacher self-reflection portfolio (SRP), and it is summarized in Fig. 1.

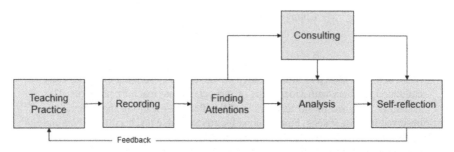

Fig. 1. SRP process

2   Importance of the Teacher Self-Reflection Portfolio (SRP)

The SRP process begins with the occurrence of a teaching practice, which is then recorded by a third party. The recorded video clip is subsequently reviewed by the teacher. During this review, the teacher engages in reflection, observing which aspects of the children's behavior or learning they focused on during the teaching practice. This reflection allows the teacher to analyze their attention and provides an opportunity to assess their teaching practice based on their areas of focus. Additionally, the teacher can reflect on whether their teaching practice was a result of their cognitive attention or whether it was a habitual and unconscious action (perhaps disregarding or being indifferent to the signals exhibited by the children).

In particular, the SRP aims to integrate the consultation process with experts during self-reflection to verify the teacher's focus. This ensures the examination of whether their teaching practice was influenced by such focus and whether it was appropriate. Enriching the self-reflection process with consultation provides valuable feedback to the teacher, applicable in future similar play situations or interactions with the same child. Many previous studies have shown that this series of self-reflection processes, based on video footage of teaching behavior, can effectively improve teachers' professionalism [5].

Considering the current emphasis on play-based curricula in childcare settings, where preplanned and directed curriculums by teachers are discouraged, it becomes essential for teachers to pay attention to the interests, engagements, and thoughts of the children, striving to follow and build upon these ideas. This child-centered approach is critical for the successful implementation of a childcare curriculum. As facilitators of a play-based curriculum, educators in these settings actively work on analyzing and refining their cognitive processes to focus on, interpret, and support children's play. This dedication is based on an understanding of the children's thoughts during daily play interactions. They are committed to further developing their ability to engage with and foster children's learning through play (for additional insights, refer to related research).

To facilitate convenience in the process of providing teachers with opportunities for self-reflection by recording teaching practices, experts in teacher education have collaborated to develop web-based teaching portfolios. Notably, according to White and his colleagues, when videos of teaching practices were stored using an e-portfolio, it was found through research that children's learning could become more vivid [6]. Based on these findings, platforms such as Storypark [7], EduCa [8], and SeeSaw [9] have been commercially developed and widely distributed among educators.

3   Developing a Teacher Self-Reflection E-portfolio Platform

Interestingly, the SRP, which is developed for this study, is based on a web-based portfolio platform that is centered on artificial intelligence (AI). This platform aims to effectively support the cognitive process training of teachers' self-reflection on their teaching behaviors. The system configuration of the SRP is depicted in Fig. 2.

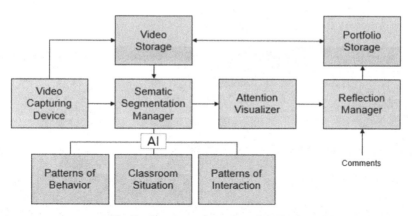

Fig. 2. System configuration of the SRP

First, the classroom play situation involving teachers and children is recorded using a video capturing tool, with automatic storage of the recorded footage. Subsequently, the stored video image is segmented into categories such as children, teachers, and the surrounding environment using the Semantic Segmentation Manager. In this segmented image, AI is used to identify meaningful scenes—those requiring attention—in both the play behavior of infants and toddlers and the supportive behavior patterns of teachers (Fig. 3). The Attention Visualizer is employed to visually represent teachers so that they can intuitively check both their behaviors and those of the infants requiring attention. Furthermore, the Reflection Manager provides a platform for teachers to document their

Fig. 3. Patterns of teachers identified by AI

reflections. Here, they can reflect on observations regarding children's play, including insights into children's interests and hidden intentions.

Figure 4 illustrates the design concept of the Self-Reflection E-portfolio Platform developed through this research. Within a single screen, teachers can share the full version of a recorded play video while simultaneously being able to quickly locate segments of meaningful moments identified by AI. This enables teachers to more effectively self-reflect on the child's play they observed, the decisions they made at that moment, and evaluate whether the follow-up teaching practices were appropriate. This sequence of cognitive processes is designed to be integrated into a single web-based interface, allowing the cognitive decision-making process, which is based on noticing skills, to be recorded incrementally and saved as a portfolio.

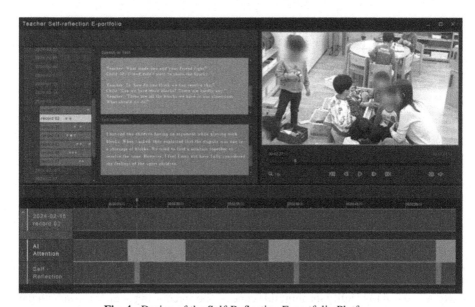

Fig. 4. Design of the Self-Reflection E-portfolio Platform

4 Conclusion and Discussion

By utilizing the SRP, childcare teachers will be able to interpret the play of infants and toddlers during their interactions, to reflect on how they supported the children's play based on these interpretations, and to determine whether the support method needs improvement. The SRP is expected to be an effective system for supporting and improving teachers' cognitive processes related to supporting play. It enables teachers to record, reflect upon, and share their self-reflection processes through the e-portfolio platform, fostering continuous improvement in their play support practices.

Acknowledgments. This work was supported by the Ministry of Education of the Republic of Korea and the National Research Foundation of Korea (NRF-2023S1A5A8076560).

References

1. Woo, H.K.: A study on the infant and toddler teachers practice for play support based on the infant-centered·play-oriented curriculum. Korean J. Child Educ. Care **22**(2), 31–45 (2022)
2. Downer, J.T., López, M.L., Grimm, K.J., Hamagami, A., Pianta, R.C., Howes, C.: Observations of teacher–child interactions in classrooms serving Latinos and dual language learners: applicability of the Classroom Assessment Scoring System in diverse settings. Early Childhood Res. Q. **27**(1), 21–32 (2012)
3. Lee, S.I., Han, J.H.: Collaborative implementation process of the toddler class curriculum created by toddlers and teachers together. J. Child. Literat. Educ. **23**(4), 225–257 (2022)
4. Gamoran Sherin, M., Van Es, E.A.: Effects of video club participation on teachers' professional vision. J. Teach. Educ. **60**(1), 20–37 (2004)
5. White, E.J., Rooney, T., Gunn, A.C., Nuttall, J.: Understanding how early childhood educators 'see' learning through digitally cast eyes: Some preliminary concepts concerning the use of digital documentation platforms. Australas. J. Early Childhood **46**(1), 6–18 (2021)
6. STORY PARK Homepage. https://au.storypark.com. Accessed 11 Mar 2024
7. Edu-Ca Homepage. https://geteduca.com. Accessed 11 Mar 2024
8. SeeSaw Homepage. https://seesaw.com. Accessed 11 Mar 2024

Dishonesty Tendencies in Testing Scenarios Among Students with Virtual Reality and Computer-Mediated Technology

Tanja Kojić[1]([envelope]), Alina Dovhalevska[1], Maurizio Vergari[1], Sebastian Möller[1,3], and Jan-Niklas Voigt-Antons[2]

[1] Quality and Usability Lab, TU Berlin, Berlin, Germany
`tanja.kojic@tu-berlin.de`
[2] Immersive Reality Lab, Hamm-Lippstadt University of Applied Sciences, Lippstadt, Germany
[3] German Research Center for Artificial Intelligence (DFKI), Berlin, Germany

Abstract. Virtual reality (VR) systems have the potential to be an innovation in the field of e-learning. Starting with fully functional e-classes, VR technologies can be used to build entire e-campuses. The power of VR is that it allows for stronger contact with students than computer-mediated technology. Deceptive behaviour, both verbal and nonverbal, refers to intentional activities designed to deceive others. Students often engage in dishonest practices to make progress.

Whether it is cheating on an exam, copying another student's essay, or inflating their GPA, the motivation for cheating is rarely simply a lack of preparation. Even though some may see academic dishonesty as an asset, the reality is that it can have major consequences.

This poster demonstrates the findings from a study of students' deceitful behaviour during a test in VR and in real-life situations. For this user study, 22 volunteers were invited to test, with each experiment involving exactly two participants and the examiner present in the room. Students were invited to take two tests: one in VR and one on a laptop. Their goal was to score as many points as possible by simulating a real-world online exam. Participants were requested to complete questionnaires during and after each experiment, which assisted in collecting additional data for this study. The results indicate that the amount of cheating that happened in VR and on a laptop was exactly the same.

Keywords: Virtual Reality · User Experience · e-Learning

1 Introduction

Numerous VR research studies were focused on the technical aspect, to improve the software and hardware for better human-machine interaction and user

T. Kojić and A. Dovhalevska—Contributed equally to this publication.

© The Author(s), under exclusive license to Springer Nature Switzerland AG 2024
C. Stephanidis et al. (Eds.): HCII 2024, CCIS 2117, pp. 114–122, 2024.
https://doi.org/10.1007/978-3-031-61953-3_14

experience. Fewer such were done to underline the possible impact of VR on already existing fields of human occupation [23].

Academia has long been using VR technologies in the process of learning. For example, VR systems are being widely used for surgical simulators, allowing medical students and doctors to practice the conduction of virtual operations [23]. VR systems can be a potential breaking-through medium in the development of e-learning. Starting from fully operated e-classes, VR technologies can be used for creating entire e-campuses [23]. The power of VR is in providing more powerful interaction with a student than computer-mediated technology. In dealing with human-machine interaction, human behaviour should be thoroughly analysed in the new learning environment. One of the main tasks of universities is to guarantee fair treatment for each student, as well as fair chances and possibilities on the way to gaining a degree.

Deceptive behaviours, both verbal and non-verbal, refer to intentional actions aimed at misleading others [9]. Referring to Wang et al. [25], South Dakota State University scientists Hicks and Ulvestad classify that "nonverbal cues are clues of deceit that are expressed through facial expressions, eye movements, and body language. [And] verbal cues are linguistic clues of deceit that are expressed in an individual's statement, such as stuttering, differentiation in pitch, etc." [16]. For example, a person may lie about their qualifications or experience during an interview in order to gain a job advantage over others, or a person may smile while lying to make the lie appear more believable. The studies of deceptive behaviours [8,11,20] have played a significant role in the field of psychology, providing valuable insights into the motivations behind these actions, as well as the ways in which they can be detected. Researchers [1,7,14] have found that deceptive behaviours are often the result of a complex interplay between individual and situational factors, and that these behaviours can have significant consequences for both the deceiver and the deceived. It is not uncommon for students to engage in deceptive behaviours in order to get ahead. "Cheating has always been a problem in academic settings, and with advances in technology such as cell phones, and more pressure for students to score well so that they get into top-rated universities, cheating has become an epidemic" [4].

1.1 Related Work

Much research on deceptive behaviour included experiments in which people were observed either telling a lie or telling the truth. Such studies helped to gather information about non-verbal and verbal signs of lying. Gozna, Vrij and Bull [13] compared deceptive behaviour in everyday life and in high stake scenarios. Students were put in an imaginary situation, where they were required to lie about their plagiarized essays. Additionally, participants were interviewed with the questionnaires in an attempt to understand the personal perception of deceptive behaviours under both conditions [13].

Greene and Saxe [14] conducted research on the reasons why academic cheating behaviour appears in the first place. The goal of the study was to "explain how students, who believe that cheating is wrong, are nevertheless able to engage in cheating behaviour" [14]. As to be expected, students reported more cheating done by their fellow students than by themselves. They also believed that if their peers cheat more, then they can justify their own deceptive behaviour, making it more ethically appropriate. This phenomenon was explained with 2 theories: the uniqueness bias and the theory of downward comparison. Like many other scientists, in their definition of uniqueness bias Monin and Norton refer to the work of Goethals et al. from 1991 [12], and define it as "the tendency for people to underestimate the proportion of others who can or will perform desirable actions [...]. In practice, those who perform a desirable behaviour underestimate the number of others as good as them, whereas those who perform an undesirable behaviour overestimate the number of others as bad as them" [19]. Referring to a work of Wills from 1991 [26], Greene and Saxe explained the theory of downward comparison as "people will compare themselves to others who are worse off than they are, in order to appear better themselves" [14]. Moreover, it was established during this study that students thought their classmates benefit more from cheating. Meaning that they personally would get the same result without cheating, but others needed cheating to pass. This allowed them to again rationalize their deceptive behaviour [14].

University exams are inevitably connected with stress in students' life. And since "human beings are radically social by nature" [3], one of the best ways to cope with stress is having friends.

Human behaviour in VR and real life has been widely compared in many experimental studies and research papers. For example, Özgür Gürerk and Alina Kasulke [15] studied the difference in charitable behaviour in real and virtual environments, Rajaram Bhagavathula et al. [5] − compared pedestrian behaviour.

Various research studies were done to find out how students cheat and why they cheat. Furthermore, the targeted environment to detect deception was either virtual reality or real-world circumstances. To the best of our knowledge, there is no research that compares students' cheating behaviour using both VR and computer-mediated technology. And while other researchers focused more on having a virtual observer in their studies, the current study was conducted under conditions of a real observer being present in the room under both conditions.

1.2   Research Questions

The goal of the present study was to compare the possible deceptive behaviour of students using VR and computer-mediated technology. Through our experiment, we seek to answer whether virtual reality would have an impact on students' deceptive behaviour during exams.

RQ1: Will students cheat more or feel the urge to cheat more during a test in virtual reality, than while doing it on a laptop?

RQ2: Will a pair of participants, who were familiar with each other, feel more relaxed and at ease to cheat during a test?

RQ3: And on the contrary, will a pair of participants, who were not familiar with each other, cheat neither in VR nor on a laptop?

2   Method

"There are, in principle, three ways to catch liars: (1) by observing how they behave (the movements they make, whether they smile or show gaze aversion, their pitch of voice, their speech rate, whether they stutter, and so on), (2) by listening to what they say (analysing the speech content), and (3) by measuring their physiological responses" [22].

2.1   Data Collection

The participants were invited to the Quality and Usability Lab on a campus of TU Berlin. Each experiment was held with exactly 2 participants and the researcher present in the room. Students were asked to take 2 tests - one in VR and another on a laptop. Their goal was to gain as many points as possible by putting themselves into the situation of a real online exam. In order to gather data, the history of the VR browser and the laptop browser were checked after each participant, and the screens on both laptops were recorded as well.

2.2   Participants

Participants were 22 students from respective Berlin universities, with an average mean of 11 semesters of study time. Among them, 14 males with a mean age of 26 and 7 females with a mean age of 26. One participant preferred not to specify gender. On a scale from 1 to 5, participants' average VR experience score was 2. All students had participated in online exams before and estimated their level of anxiety during an exam as 3 out of 5.

2.3   Study Setup

On average, one experiment took around 40 min. After reading an information sheet about the present study, students were asked to sign a consent form and fill out the Demographics. Both first and second tests were defined as conditions of "Laptop" and "VR". To minimize order-effects [2] on the results of the study, conditions were randomized using the Latin squares system [10]. Before each test, a short instruction was given in which it was explained how participants can navigate through the test, how much time they have, and in the case of VR, how to use a controller. The examples of how participants had seen the tests on a laptop and in VR are illustrated in Figs. 1 and 2.

After each test (in VR and on a laptop) participants filled out the SAM [6] and IPQ [17] forms and evaluated how they were feeling during the experiment and after it. The students were asked to fill out the questionnaires "Self-perception of Lying" and "Perception of Others Lying" at the end of the experiment after the study goal was revealed to them. Hence, they had an opportunity to reflect on their feelings and thoughts during the experiment to describe them.

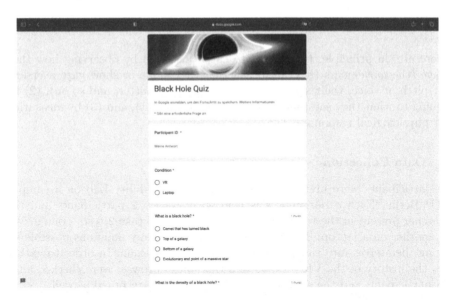

Fig. 1. Example of a quiz "Black Hole", which participants should have done on a laptop

Fig. 2. Example of a quiz "Milky Way and Solar System", which participants should have done in VR

3   Results and Discussion

The data from the SAM and IPQ questionnaires were analyzed in order to find the significant differences between the conditions of "Laptop" and "VR". Therefore, independent samples t-tests were run with open statistical software "jamovi" [21]. As a result, conditions of "VR" and "Laptop" were significantly different in the following questions (Table 1 and 2):

Table 1. Independent Samples T-Test

Question	Statistic	df	p
In the computer generated world I had a sense of "being there"	-3.727^a	42.0	< .001
Somehow I felt that the virtual world surrounded me	-6.653	42.0	< .001
I did not feel present in the virtual space	-4.723	42.0	< .001
I had a sense of acting in the virtual space, rather than operating something from outside	-7.456	42.0	< .001
I felt present in the virtual space	-6.452	42.0	< .001
How aware were you of the real world surrounding while navigating in the virtual world (i.e. sounds, room temperature, other people, etc.)?	-4.313	42.0	< .001
I was not aware of my real environment	-3.389	42.0	0.002
I still paid attention to the real environment	3.900	42.0	< .001
I was completely captivated by the virtual world	-4.688	42.0	< .001
How real did the virtual world seem to you?	-2.451	42.0	0.018

Present research demonstrated that cheating occurred among 5 pairs of participants who were familiar with each other. Among them:

- 2 students who cheated only in VR;
- 2 students who cheated only on a laptop;
- 6 students who cheated under both conditions.

Contrary to the previous data, the other 5 pairs of participants were as well familiar with each other but did not cheat. This result could be supported by the answers received in questionnaires, which indicated a high percentage of participants feeling guilt after deception. Further findings indicated 1 pair of students who were not familiar with each other and likewise did not cheat.

Within 11 subjects, who did not cheat but had an urge to, were 3 students who thought about it in VR, and 5 - who thought about it while doing tests both in VR and on a laptop. They reported several reasons why they did not cheat. Such as the fact that this would indicate their lack of intelligence, or simply because they were observed. Mol stated that "the observer triggers feelings of being watched, which activates a concern for reputation and a desire to abide by the norm of honesty" [18], And the majority of the students were worried about being caught in deception.

Table 2. Group Descriptives

Question	Condition	Mean	SD
In the computer generated world I had a sense of being there	Laptop	2.18	1.532
	VR	3.64	1.002
Somehow I felt that the virtual world surrounded me.	Laptop	1.73	1.032
	VR	3.82	1.053
I did not feel present in the virtual space.	Laptop	1.73	1.032
	VR	3.36	1.255
I had a sense of acting in the virtual space, rather than oper	Laptop	1.55	0.800
	VR	3.59	1.008
I felt present in the virtual space.	Laptop	1.86	1.037
	VR	3.77	0.922
How aware were you of the real world surrounding while navigat	Laptop	2.09	1.065
	VR	3.50	1.102
I was not aware of my real environment.	Laptop	2.09	1.231
	VR	3.27	1.077
I still paid attention to the real environment.	Laptop	3.82	1.259
	VR	2.50	0.964
I was completely captivated by the virtual world.	Laptop	1.64	1.049
	VR	3.00	0.873
How real did the virtual world seem to you?	Laptop	1.95	1.327
	VR	2.86	1.125

4   Conclusion

Considering the rapid development and expansion of VR innovations, it is beneficial for researchers to focus on having VR technologies in the educational paradigm. In 2002 Walsh wrote that "with a strong theoretical foundation established, high quality experiments can be designed which measure the effects of VR systems. It may be appropriate to test some aspects of VR systems with captive audiences such as university students, while other aspects will need study in the richness of real world environments" [24]. Our study is among others to contribute to a better understanding of students' deceptive behaviour in VR compared to real life.

Certain limitations were met during this research study. Due to ethical reasons, we had to inform the participants in the consent form about screen recording. It could potentially influence the behaviour of subjects during tests. A part of the participants of this study was familiar with the researcher since they studied at the same university. This also means that they were not feeling as intimidated by the researcher as they would be by a professor or teaching assistant. Moreover, since it was not a real exam, there was no feeling of being put under pressure.

Future research directions for this paper include investigating the effects of a researcher's presence on participant behavior in virtual reality, examining the impact of VR proficiency on study results, and exploring psychological group dynamics by involving more than two subjects simultaneously.

References

1. Ackerman, P.D.: The effects of honor-grading on students' test scores. Am. Educ. Res. J. **8**(2), 321–333 (1971)
2. Atmanspacher, H., Römer, H.: Order effects in sequential measurements of non-commuting psychological observables. J. Math. Psychol. **56**(4), 274–280 (2012)
3. Bailey, D., Wolfe, D.M., Wolfe, C.R.: With a little help from our friends: Social support as a source of well-being and of coping with stress. J. Sociol. Soc. Welfare **21**(2), Article 8 (1994). https://doi.org/10.15453/0191-5096.2137. https://scholarworks.wmich.edu/jssw/vol21/iss2/8
4. Batool, S., Abbas, A., Naeemi, Z.: Cheating behavior among undergraduate students. Int. J. Bus. Soc. Sci. **2**(3), 246–254 (2011)
5. Bhagavathula, R., Williams, B., Owens, J., Gibbons, R.: The reality of virtual reality: A comparison of pedestrian behavior in real and virtual environments. Proc. Hum. Factors Ergon. Soc. Ann. Meeting **62**, 2056–2060 (2018). https://doi.org/10.1177/1541931218621464
6. Bradley, M.M., Lang, P.J.: Measuring emotion: the self-assessment manikin and the semantic differential. J. Behav. Ther. Exp. Psychiatry **25**(1), 49–59 (1994). https://doi.org/10.1016/0005-7916(94)90063-9
7. Bunn, D.N., Caudill, S.B., Gropper, D.M.: Crime in the classroom: an economic analysis of undergraduate student cheating behavior. J. Econ. Educ. **23**(3), 197–207 (1992)
8. De Paulo, B.M.: Nonverbal aspects of deception. J. Nonverbal Behav. **12**(3), 153–161 (1988)
9. DePaulo, B.M., Lindsay, J.J., Malone, B.E., Muhlenbruck, L., Charlton, K., Cooper, H.: Cues to deception. Psychol. Bull. **129**(1), 74–118 (2003)
10. Dénes, J.H., Keedwell, A.D.: Latin squares: New developments in the theory and applications, Annals of Discrete Mathematics, vol. 46. Academic Press, Amsterdam (1991). paul Erdős (foreword)
11. Ekman, P., Friesen, W.V.: Detecting deception from the body or face. J. Pers. Soc. Psychol. **29**(3), 288–298 (1974). https://doi.org/10.1037/h0036006
12. Goethals, G.R., Messick, D.M., Allison, S.T.: The uniqueness bias: Studies of constructive social comparison. Lawrence Erlbaum Associates, Inc. (1991)
13. Gozna, L., Vrij, A., Bull, R.: The impact of individual differences on perceptions of lying in everyday life and in a high stake situation. Personality and Individual Differences - PERS INDIV DIFFER **31**, 1203–1216 (2001). https://doi.org/10.1016/S0191-8869(00)00219-1
14. Greene, A.S., Saxe, L.: Everybody (else) does it: Academic cheating (1992)

15. Gürerk, Ö., Kasulke, A.: Does virtual reality increase charitable giving? an experimental study. Public Policy (Topic), BHNP (2018)
16. Hicks, C., Ulvestad, N.: Deception detection accuracy using verbal or nonverbal cues. J. Undergraduate Res. **9**, 9 (2011). https://openprairie.sdstate.edu/jur/vol9/iss1/9
17. iGROUP: IPQ - Integrated Performance Questionnaire. http://www.igroup.org/pq/ipq/download.php. Accessed 17 Feb 2023
18. Mol, J., van der Heijden, E., Potters, J.: (not) alone in the world: Cheating in the presence of a virtual observer. Exp. Econ. **23**, 961–978 (2020). https://doi.org/10.1007/s10683-020-09644-0
19. Monin, B., Norton, M.I.: Perceptions of a fluid consensus: uniqueness bias, false consensus, false polarization, and pluralistic ignorance in a water conservation crisis. Pers. Soc. Psychol. Bull. **29**(5), 559–567 (2003). https://doi.org/10.1177/0146167203251523
20. Phillips, M.C., Meek, S.W., Vendemia, J.M.: Understanding the underlying structure of deceptive behaviors. Personality Individ. Differ. **50**(6), 783–789 (2011)
21. The jamovi project: jamovi. [Computer Software] (2022). https://www.jamovi.org
22. Vrij, A., Edward, K., Roberts, K.P., Bull, R.: Detecting deceit via analysis of verbal and nonverbal behavior. J. Nonverbal Behav. **24**(4), 239–263 (2000). https://doi.org/10.1023/A:1006610329284
23. Walsh, K.: Virtual reality for learning: some design propositions (2001). https://aisel.aisnet.org/amcis2001/13
24. Walsh, K.R., Pawlowski, S.D.: Virtual reality: A technology in need of is research. Commun. Assoc. Inf. Syst. **8**(1), 20 (2002). https://doi.org/10.17705/1CAIS.00820
25. Wang, G., Chen, H., Atabakhsh, H.: Criminal identity deception and deception detection in law enforcement. Group Decis. Negot. **13**, 111–127 (2004). https://doi.org/10.1023/B:GRUP.0000021838.66662.0c
26. Wills, T.A.: Similarity and Self-esteem in Downward Comparison. Lawrence Erlbaum Associates, Inc. (1991)

Towards Blockchain-Based Incentives for STEM Education

Myles Lewis[(✉)] and Chris Crawford

Department of Computer Science, University of Alabama, Tuscaloosa, USA
mlewis16@crimson.ua.edu

Abstract. The field of computer science is expanding at an unprecedented rate, with technology becoming increasingly integral to nearly every industry. To meet the growing demand for computer scientists, there is a pressing need to address challenges in computer science education and prepare students effectively. Simultaneously, the emergence of blockchain technology has brought about new opportunities as a disruptive technology that is recently being explored in the education sector. Blockchain technology, known for its decentralized and secure nature, offers unique advantages for motivating and engaging students. This paper explores the integration of blockchain technology into gamified learning environments to enhance STEM education. By employing blockchain's unique properties such as decentralization, immutability, and transparency, the research aims to increase student engagement and motivation. The study discusses various components of a gamification framework, including goal orientation, achievement, reinforcement, competition, and fun orientation, illustrating how blockchain can be leveraged to improve educational outcomes. It highlights practical applications and proposes a novel approach to incentivize learning through digital rewards, fostering a dynamic and interactive educational experience.

Keywords: Blockchain · Gamification · Engagment · Immersive Learning

1 Introduction

The field of computer science is expanding at an unprecedented rate, with technology becoming increasingly integral to nearly every industry. To meet the growing demand for computer scientists, there is a pressing need to address challenges in computer science education and prepare students effectively. While STEM education tools have emerged, the transition to more advanced computer science topics often leads to declining student engagement and motivation.

Blockchain technology and gamification are two opportunities for universities to enhance the educational experience of its students. Gamification involves the integration of game elements and mechanics into non-game contexts to create an interactive and immersive learning experience. Researchers have used these

C. Stephanidis et al. (Eds.): HCII 2024, CCIS 2117, pp. 123–134, 2024.
https://doi.org/10.1007/978-3-031-61953-3_15

gamification principles in many types of systems such as enterprise information systems [1] and web application [2].

Simultaneously, the emergence of blockchain technology has brought about new opportunities and possibilities in various domains outside of finance, especially in education [3]. Researchers have approached incorporating blockchain technology into education in a number of ways: to secure learner's educational information [4,5], leveraging blockchain as the subject of study to improve on cybersecurity education [6–8], integrating blockchain with other emerging technologies (AR/VR, Metaverse, Artificial Intelligence, etc.) [9–11], and a way to target diverse age groups for an educational application [5]. Though fundamentally, blockchain promotes collaboration due to its decentralized nature and trustless data interaction between multiple entities for retrieving, editing and transmitting information. Its core features, such as decentralization, immutability, and transparency, have opened doors for innovative applications in education.

An overlapping characteristic for both blockchain technology and gamification is the capability to foster an engaging, active learning environment. By combining the motivational aspects of gamification with the unique properties of blockchain, it becomes possible to create transparent and trustworthy systems that reward and recognize learners' achievements and progress [12].

This research seeks to bridge this gap by harnessing the potential of blockchain technology to enhance student engagement and motivation as they matriculate through their education. In particular, this work aims to address existing challenges by integrating blockchain-based incentives into gamified learning environments.

2   Background

Gamification refers to implementation of game design elements into non-gaming activities which can expand to the context of education [13]. The goal of gamification is to harness the motivational and engagement incentives and transmute these features into an enjoyable instructional experience. Through research, Lee and Hammer [14] establishes that schools have been utilizing game design elements such as giving points to students based upon the completion and accuracy of assignments, which are then converted into achievable badges and/or milestones known as grades. This system gives students positive feedback for desired grades and punishes for undesired grades. Based on these grades, the system can grant students to level up known as graduating to the next level.

Furthermore, there are many approaches and models that are developed when developing systems to increase motivation and engagement. The Octalysis Framework suggests that almost every game is "enjoyable" because it appeals to specific core sentiments within humans to motivate players to towards certain goals [15]. In the Self-Determination Theory model, game developers can better understand the intrinsic nature of participants to better develop engaging systems to make them more enjoyable, as well [16]. By giving students choices and autonomy in their learning, creating a supportive and connected classroom community, and helping them feel competent and successful, it can make learning more enjoyable and motivating. Within the Game-Based Learning Design Framework [17], the systems emphasizes the importance of aligning game mechanics with the learning objectives and ensuring that learners are actively engaged in meaningful activities within the game-based environment.

Practical applications of gamification in educational contexts aimed to leverage multiple game design elements to enhance the student experience. Nah et al. [13] identified five main components that are essential in establishing a gamification framework in the educational space Table 1. This framework constructs components that in combination with blockchain technology can further enhance the experience of students and/or users of the system to achieve increased levels of motivation and engagement.

Blockchain technology, known for its decentralized and secure nature, offers unique advantages for motivating and engaging students as it is continually explored. Through leveraging blockchain technology, this paper explores its application in enhancing certain gamified components. The core features of blockchain technology are suited for educational systems. When referring to Table 1, blockchain technology has a correlation to each component.

2.1 Blockchain in Higher Education

Just recently, the emergence of blockchain technology has presented new opportunities for innovation in various domains, including higher education. Originally developed as the underlying technology behind cryptocurrencies, blockchain is a decentralized and transparent ledger system that ensures secure and immutable record-keeping. Its unique properties, such as decentralization, immutability, smart contract automation, consensus algorithms and transparency, have sparked interest in exploring its potential applications in education.

As noted in a preliminary systematic literature review on blockchain's application in educational spaces presented by Kamišalić [18], current use cases for blockchain revolve around certification verification [19–21] and data management [22,23] purposes. Systems that rely on blockchain for certification verification systems have a primary objective of confirming and verifying degrees. While Data management systems are categorized to gather, report and assess data in automated processes to facilitate better security and privacy [24].

In educational spaces, different mechanisms within blockchain help foster engagement and motivation for students. Turkanović et al. presented a system called "EduCTX," which leverages the tokenization capabilities of blockchain for students to earn tokens (as credits) as a way for students to have a visual representation of their academic progress as they matriculate through their major [21]. Han et al. proposed a novel blockchain-based solution for handling students information and educational resources on-chain to alleviate third party interaction and eliminate unwanted fees for information exchanges (e.g. official transcripts) [20]. "Blockchain for education: Lifelong learning passport" a solution for maintaining secure, long-lasting academic records that can follow a student throughout their education lifespan and career was proposed in research by

Gräther et al. to potential challenge the current data retrieval and transmission process revolving around resumés and CV [25].

Table 1. Essential components in gamification platforms [13].

Components of a Gamification Framework	
Goal Orientation	This involves structuring educational games with multiple layers of goals (long-term, medium-term, short-term) to gradually increase the challenge and match it as the player grows in skills and knowledge. This progression helps sustain motivation and engagement by providing a clear path from beginner to mastery levels.
Achievement	Recognizing players' achievements through badges, trophies, or other forms of acknowledgment boosts their sense of gratification, motivation, and engagement. This principle suggests that incorporating systems to celebrate achievements can enhance learning outcomes in educational games.
Reinforcement	Based on the behavioral learning model [26], reinforcement through rewards (tangible or intangible) and feedback supports learning. Positive reinforcement encourages players, while negative feedback provides corrective insights, aiding in achieving learning goals more efficiently.
Competition	Competition, driven by intrinsic rewards and engaging challenges, is crucial for maintaining or enhancing focus and engagement in learning tasks. Clear, explicit rules and the opportunity for players to create their own rules within the game can boost motivation and facilitate active learning through discovery [27, 28].
Enjoyment	Enjoyment and fun are essential for deep engagement, often leading players to lose track of time. An educational game must incorporate fun elements to effectively motivate and engage learners, making the learning process enjoyable and effective

The integration of blockchain technology with gamified learning environments presents a promising approach to incentivize users and increase engagement in educational settings. By combining the motivational aspects of gamification with the unique properties of blockchain, it becomes possible to create transparent, secure, and decentralized systems that enhance user participation and recognition.

3   Our Approach

Blockchain technology can significantly enhance a gamified learning platform by providing secure, transparent, and immutable records of achievements, facilitating automated and fair reward mechanisms, and enabling new forms of engagement and interaction among learners. This integration can lead to a more engaging, rewarding, and effective learning experience.

3.1   Goal Orientation

Blockchain technology's objective tracking features enhance the user's goal orientation as they matriculate through the system. Blockchain provides a robust solution for securely monitoring and authenticating goal achievements across different timeframes, including long-term, medium-term, and short-term objectives. The use of a transparent and unchangeable ledger ensures that both learners and educators possess a definitive and trustworthy record of educational progress. This capability not only streamlines the progression from one competency level to another but also safeguards the integrity of recorded goals and achievements against unauthorized alterations (Fig. 1).

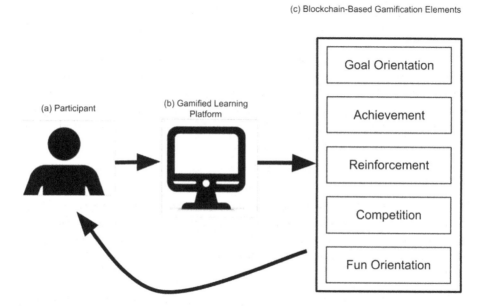

Fig. 1. The relationship between user, gamified learning environment and blockchain-based incentives.

Yusup et al. harness the cryptographic strengths of blockchain to protect sensitive information recorded on the blockchain, including personal, familial, financial, and health-related details, especially within educational settings [4]. Through blockchain's authorization features, students gain direct access to their information, reducing the expenses related to accessing personal records. On another front, MetaEdu [10] utilizes blockchain to create a secure database for storing student information, thereby enabling a tailored, AI-driven approach to adapt to each learner's unique educational needs. This forward-thinking method places students at the helm of their learning experience, empowering them to navigate their educational path effectively.

3.2 Achievement

The implementation of blockchain for the issuance of digital accolades such as badges, certificates, or tokens aligns seamlessly with the demands for recognition in the realm of educational gaming. These digital tokens of achievement, securely logged on the blockchain, offer an immutable and verifiable history of a learner's accomplishments. This not only motivates learners by acknowledging their progress but also enriches their educational narrative by providing tangible evidence of their achievements that they can present or utilize elsewhere.

Yusup et al. developed a system that incentivizes students with Enrichment Cumulative Points for participation in campus activities, employing tokenization to enhance student engagement [4]. Similarly, research by Latifah and Fauziah utilized gamification techniques to teach students in business and business information technology about complex blockchain topics. They adapted their approach from a classroom-based game to a web-based application in response to the challenges posed by the pandemic [29].

Yfantis and Ntalianis [30] explored the effectiveness of incorporating blockchain-based gamification elements such as token-based rewards and automated adaptive feedback into educational settings. This method enhances the appeal of learning about blockchain, significantly increasing motivation for learners of all ages. Their work highlights the importance of both intrinsic and extrinsic motivation in fostering engagement.

3.3 Reinforcement

Blockchain technology offers powerful mechanisms for both positive reinforcement and providing constructive feedback in educational contexts. It facilitates the distribution of digital rewards, such as tokens or points, and records detailed feedback, creating an immutable ledger of accomplishments and learning paths. Smart contracts enable the automatic issuance of rewards based on specific achievements or actions within educational games, ensuring a transparent and equitable system. Additionally, blockchain can document areas for improvement or corrective actions, allowing learners to personalize their development and reference their progress for future improvement.

The concept of automated admission aid exemplifies the fusion of student assessment, administration, and registration processes through blockchain technology. Awaji's study [24] highlights the potential for blockchain to streamline educational administration and assessment processes efficiently. Moreover, Mitchell et al. [31] introduced dAppER, an automated system for quality assurance in education that develops exams and their evaluation criteria through logical processes. Ghaffar [32] proposed a blockchain-based system for the verification of students' educational records, simplifying the university admission process through a unified platform.

In addition to blockchain's administrative and feedback capabilities, recent research has explored the synergistic application of artificial intelligence (AI) and blockchain in education, aiming to deliver personalized feedback. This is highlighted by MetaEdu's [10] AI-powered framework and the Edu-Metaverse [11] platform, both of which focus on creating adaptive learning environments tailored to individual students' needs and learning styles.

3.4 Competition

Blockchain technology offers a unique advantage in enhancing competition within educational contexts by providing a secure, transparent platform for recording, validating, and comparing scores, achievements, and rankings. Its immutable nature ensures that once data is recorded, it cannot be altered, thereby guaranteeing the integrity and fairness of the competition. Furthermore, blockchain enables the adoption of decentralized governance models, wherein participants have the power to propose or vote on competition rules. These rules can be seamlessly implemented and enforced via smart contracts, ensuring that the competition operates fairly and transparently according to community consensus.

Research has underscored how educational systems that incorporate blockchain technology bolster user confidence in the system's fairness and reliability. This increase in trust directly impacts learners' motivation and engagement, leading to enhanced educational outcomes. The secure and transparent characteristics of blockchain play a pivotal role in augmenting user confidence, which in turn fosters a deeper engagement with the learning material. Students are more inclined to invest effort and participate actively when they trust the system's capability to accurately record and reward their achievements.

The potential of blockchain to transform the educational landscape is further illustrated by Tepelidis et al., who proposed the creation of a multi-blockchain system dedicated to the verifiable documentation of academic credentials [5]. Such a system not only simplifies the process of verifying academic achievements across different institutions but also establishes a foundation of trust among educational entities, employers, and other relevant parties. This foundational trust is vital for the recognition and validation of online and gamified learning experiences. It indirectly promotes greater engagement among users and fosters positive educational outcomes by making learning more interactive, engaging, and, most importantly, trustworthy.

3.5 Fun Orientation

Blockchain technology can significantly enhance the enjoyment and engagement aspects of gamified learning by introducing innovative interaction and reward mechanisms. For example, the possibility of earning cryptocurrencies or Non-Fungible Tokens (NFTs) for achieving certain milestones introduces a novel and enticing layer of rewards, making the educational process more stimulating and engaging. Furthermore, blockchain facilitates peer-to-peer exchanges or trading within the educational game environment, fostering a community-driven atmosphere that amplifies the fun and collaborative aspect of learning.

Mittal et al. [33] exemplify this approach by integrating a game-based method to deepen players' understanding of blockchain technology and improve their cybersecurity capabilities. Similarly, the "Discover DaVinci" app [34] innovatively combines augmented reality (AR) with blockchain, offering a unique, interactive learning experience that allows users to explore art history. The integration of blockchain with popular gaming platforms like Minecraft [35] to educate about Bitcoin and other cryptocurrencies provides a compelling mix of entertainment and educational value, facilitating a comprehension of digital finance (Fig. 2).

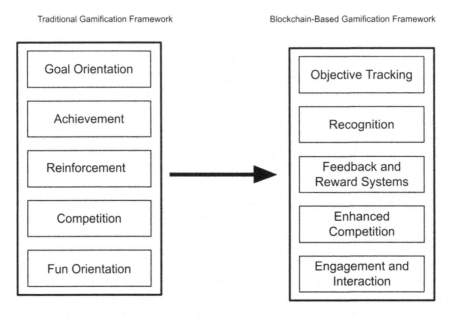

Fig. 2. The transformation of traditional gamification elements to incorporate blockchain technology.

Thompson et al. introduced "NFTrig [36]," an application that utilizes Google Blockly and NFTs [8] for instructing both blockchain principles and mathematics, presenting inventive strategies to captivate students with blockchain technology within their existing educational framework. These methods offer practical, hands-on experiences through interactive and familiar platforms, enhancing students' learning. They illustrate the versatility of blockchain as a tool that can be seamlessly integrated with current educational resources, demonstrating its practical application and relevance to enhancing educational engagement and learning outcomes.

4 Discussion

Blockchain's security protocols ensure the authenticity and integrity of digital certificates, assuring students of the value and recognition of their achievements. These digital certificates can serve as a tangible representation of their skills and accomplishments, boosting their self-esteem and motivation to excel in computer science. Moreover, the decentralized nature of blockchain ensures transparency and immutability, assuring students that their achievements are verifiable and cannot be tampered with. Tokenization plays a pivotal role in incentivizing students. By assigning tokens for completing coding assignments, achieving milestones, or demonstrating mastery of specific concepts, students receive tangible rewards for their efforts. These tokens can be exchanged for various educational benefits, such as access to advanced coding tutorials, exclusive workshops, or even scholarships. The introduction of tokens creates a gamified environment, where students are motivated to accumulate and utilize tokens to enhance their learning experiences. The public ledger, a fundamental component of blockchain technology, adds an element of transparency and competition to the educational ecosystem. Students can view their progress and achievements on the blockchain's public ledger, fostering a sense of accomplishment and healthy competition among peers. This transparency also allows educators and institutions to identify struggling students early and offer personalized support, further enhancing the overall learning experience. Also, new programming languages are being leveraged to automate the data transmission and state of information on chain by programmers [37]. Programmers can build education application leveraging underlying blockchain capabilities to promote more customization of these decentralized applications. Therefore, gamified learning application on networks can access blockchain features via coding languages. Coding languages such as:

- Solidity, a statically-typed programming language for Ethereum
- Pact, a programming language used for smart contract development on the Kadena network
- Liquidity, a high-level typed smart contract language for Tezos blockchain
- Algorand's SDK is compatible with Python and Javascript

To implement this conceptual design, existing STEM education applications can be enhanced with blockchain technology seamlessly. Students would create digital identities on the blockchain, which would store their achievements, progress, and tokens. Digital certificates would be issued for successful completion of courses or projects, all recorded on the blockchain ledger. As students advance in their computer science journey, they can unlock new challenges and opportunities by utilizing their earned tokens.

In conclusion, this research seeks to assist computer science education by harnessing blockchain technology to elevate student engagement and motivation. By integrating digital certificates, tokenization, and a public ledger into STEM education applications, we can create a dynamic educational ecosystem that rewards and empowers students at every level of their computer science journey. This application holds the potential to inspire a new generation of computer scientists who are proficient in coding and simultaneously motivated and passionate about their field. Therefore, blockchain-based incentives can bridge the gap between introductory and advanced computer science education, ensuring that students remain engaged, motivated, and well-prepared for the challenges and opportunities of the digital age.

References

1. Swacha, J.: Gamification in enterprise information systems: what, why and how. In: 2016 Federated Conference on Computer Science and Information Systems (FedCSIS), IEEE (2016) 1229–1233
2. Zichermann, G., Cunningham, C.: Gamification by design: implementing game mechanics in web and mobile apps. O'Reilly Media, Inc. (2011)
3. Liu, S., Ba, L.: Blockchain technology and its application prospect in higher education. In: 2021 13th International Conference on Education Technology and Computers, pp. 237–242 (2021)
4. Yusup, M., Sunarya, P.A., Lutfiani, N., Nabila, E.A., et al.: A blockchain-based framework gamification for securing learners activity in merdeka belajar-kampus merdeka. In: 2022 4th International Conference on Cybernetics and Intelligent System (ICORIS), pp. 1–6. IEEE (2022)
5. Tepelidis, A., Mitsopoulou, E.E., Patenidis, A.T., Votis, K., Tzovaras, D.: A multi-blockchain system for verifiable academic credentials. In: International Conference on Remote Engineering and Virtual Instrumentation, pp. 917–926. Springer, Cham (2023). https://doi.org/10.1007/978-3-031-42467-0_86
6. Irudayam, L., Breitinger, F.: Teaching blockchain in k9-12: Instruction materials and their assessment. arXiv preprint arXiv:2211.05933 (2022)
7. Benson, K.C., Tran, B., Jonassen, L.: Pedagogy of blockchain: training college students on the basics of blockchain. Int. J. Eng. Res. Technol 7(5), 17–25 (2018)
8. Tsai, Y.C., Huang, J.Y., Chiou, D.R.: Empowering young learners to explore blockchain with user-friendly tools: a method using google blockly and nfts. arXiv preprint arXiv:2303.09847 (2023)
9. Mourtzis, D., Angelopoulos, J., Panopoulos, N.: Metaverse and blockchain in education for collaborative product-service system (pss) design towards university 5.0. Procedia CIRP 119, 456–461 (2023)
10. Cui, L., Zhu, C., Hare, R., Tang, Y.: Metaedu: a new framework for future education. Discover Artif. Intell. 3(1), 10 (2023)
11. Wu, T., Hao, F.: Edu-metaverse: concept, architecture, and applications. Interactive Learning Environments, pp. 1–28 (2023)
12. Parizi, R.M., Dehghantanha, A.: On the understanding of gamification in blockchain systems. In: 2018 6th International Conference on Future Internet of Things and Cloud Workshops (FiCloudW), pp. 214–219. IEEE (2018)
13. Nah, F.F.-H., Telaprolu, V.R., Rallapalli, S., Venkata, P.R.: Gamification of education using computer games. In: Yamamoto, S. (ed.) HIMI 2013. LNCS, vol. 8018, pp. 99–107. Springer, Heidelberg (2013). https://doi.org/10.1007/978-3-642-39226-9_12
14. Lee, J.J., Hammer, J.: Gamification in education: what, how, why bother? Acad. Exchange Q. 15(2), 146 (2011)

15. Economou, D., Doumanis, I., Pedersen, F., Kathrani, P., Mentzelopoulos, M., Bouki, V.: Evaluation of a dynamic role-playing platform for simulations based on octalysis gamification framework. In: Workshop Proceedings of the 11th International Conference on Intelligent Environments, pp. 388–395. IOS Press (2015)
16. Deci, E.L., Ryan, R.M.: Self-determination theory: a macrotheory of human motivation, development, and health. Can. Psychol. **49**(3), 182 (2008)
17. Van Staalduinen, J.P., De Freitas, S.: A game-based learning framework: Linking game design and learning outcomes. Learning to play: exploring the future of education with video games **53**, 29–45 (2011)
18. Kamišalić, A., Turkanović, M., Mrdović, S., Heričko, M.: A preliminary review of blockchain-based solutions in higher education. In: Uden, L., Liberona, D., Sanchez, G., Rodríguez-González, S. (eds.) LTEC 2019. CCIS, vol. 1011, pp. 114–124. Springer, Cham (2019). https://doi.org/10.1007/978-3-030-20798-4_11
19. Liu, Q., Guan, Q., Yang, X., Zhu, H., Green, G., Yin, S.: Education-industry cooperative system based on blockchain. In: 1st IEEE International Conference on Hot Information-Centric Networking (HotICN). IEEE 2018, pp. 207–211 (2018)
20. Han, M., Li, Z., He, J., Wu, D., Xie, Y., Baba, A.: A novel blockchain-based education records verification solution. In: Proceedings of the 19th Annual SIG Conference on Information Technology Education, pp. 178–183 (2018)
21. Turkanović, M., Hölbl, M., Košič, K., Heričko, M., Kamišalić, A.: Eductx: a blockchain-based higher education credit platform. IEEE Access **6**, 5112–5127 (2018)
22. Matzutt, R., Pennekamp, J., Wehrle, K.: A secure and practical decentralized ecosystem for shareable education material. In: 2020 International Conference on Information Networking (ICOIN), pp. 529–534. IEEE (2020)
23. Priya, N., Ponnavaikko, M., Aantonny, R.: An efficient system framework for managing identity in educational system based on blockchain technology. In: 2020 International Conference on Emerging Trends in Information Technology and Engineering (ic-ETITE), pp. 1–5. IEEE (2020)
24. Awaji, B., Solaiman, E., Marshall, L.: Blockchain-based trusted achievement record system design. In: Proceedings of the 5th International Conference on Information and Education Innovations, pp. 46–51 (2020)
25. Gräther, W., Kolvenbach, S., Ruland, R., Schütte, J., Torres, C., Wendland, F.: Blockchain for education: lifelong learning passport. In: Proceedings of 1st ERCIM Blockchain Workshop 2018, European Society for Socially Embedded Technologies (EUSSET) (2018)
26. Betts, B.W., Bal, J., Betts, A.W.: Gamification as a tool for increasing the depth of student understanding using a collaborative e-learning environment. Int. J. Continuing Eng. Educ. Life Long Learn. **23**(3–4), 213–228 (2013)
27. Eleftheria, C.A., Charikleia, P., Iason, C.G., Athanasios, T., Dimitrios, T.: An innovative augmented reality educational platform using gamification to enhance lifelong learning and cultural education. In: IISA 2013, pp. 1–5. IEEE (2013)
28. Gibson, D., Ostashewski, N., Flintoff, K., Grant, S., Knight, E.: Digital badges in education. Educ. Inf. Technol. **20**, 403–410 (2015)
29. Latifah, H., Fauziah, Z.: Blockchain teaching simulation using gamification. Aptisi Trans. Technopreneurship (ATT) **4**(2), 184–191 (2022)
30. Yfantis, V., Ntalianis, K.: Using gamification to address the adoption of blockchain technology in the public sector of education. IEEE Eng. Manage. Rev. **50**(4), 139–146 (2022)

31. Mitchell, I., Hara, S., Sheriff, M.: dapper: decentralised application for examination review. In: 2019 IEEE 12th International Conference on Global Security, Safety and Sustainability (ICGS3), pp. 1–14. IEEE (2019)

32. Ghaffar, A., Hussain, M.: Bceap-a blockchain embedded academic paradigm to augment legacy education through application. In: Proceedings of the 3rd International Conference on Future Networks and Distributed Systems, pp. 1–11 (2019)

33. Mittal, A., Gupta, M., Chaturvedi, M., Chansarkar, S.R., Gupta, S.: Cybersecurity enhancement through blockchain training (cebt)-a serious game approach. Int. J. Inf. Manage. Data Insights 1(1), 100001 (2021)

34. Suvajdzic, M., Oliverio, J., Barmpoutis, A., Wood, L., Burgermeister, P.: Discover davinci–a gamified blockchain learning app. In: 2020 IEEE International Conference on Blockchain and Cryptocurrency (ICBC), pp. 1–2. IEEE (2020)

35. Baláž, A., Madoš, B., Pietriková, E.: Extending minecraft for teaching bitcoin cryptocurrency. In: IEEE 21st World Symposium on Applied Machine Intelligence and Informatics (SAMI). IEEE 2023, 000161–000168 (2023)

36. Thompson, J., Benac, R., Olana, K., Hassan, T., Sward, A., Khan Mohd, T.: Nftrig: Using blockchain technologies for math education. In: International Conference on Intelligent Sustainable Systems, pp. 609–624. Springer (2023)

37. Lewis, M., Crawford, C.: Architectural design for secure smart contract development (2024). arXiv preprint arXiv:2401.01891

Exploring Media Modalities for Cultural Heritage Learning on Social Platforms: A Comparative Analysis of Short Videos, Nine-Grid Pictures, and Sequential Pictures

Qiang Li[⊠], Tianqi Wu, and Zhen Chen

Shenyang Aerospace University, Shenyang, China
qiangli@sau.edu.cn

Abstract. In the digital era, short videos have emerged as a dominant medium on modern social media platforms. Their rapid development and extensive reach mark them as key tools for information dissemination and entertainment. However, the rise of short videos hasn't eclipsed other media forms. Text, sequential images, nine-grid pictures, and animations continue to thrive alongside video content. This paper explores the emotional response, learning effectiveness, and cognitive load associated with various media used during learning cultural heritage on social platforms. Our study focused on three media: video, nine-grid pictures, and sequential pictures. These were used to present identical learning materials to three separate groups of participants (Groups A, B, and C). Post-exposure, interviews were conducted to gather participant feed-back and encourage questions about their experience. The findings revealed diverse opinions across the groups. Group A felt that short videos might not provide in-depth explanations for complex topics. They noted that the scrolling nature of videos and animations could hinder consistent information absorption and fail to offer a clear view of content context. Group B found the nine-grid format offered better control over reading pace, promoting a more subjective and coherent learning experience. Conversely, Group C indicated a lower inclination to explore and learn within this interactive format. This study reveals key implications for cultural heritage learning. By comparing various media formats such as videos and nine-grid pictures, it identifies effective methods for presenting heritage content, enhancing public engagement and understanding. The findings suggest formats like the nine-grid picture are more efficient for coherent content delivery, aiding in preserving and disseminating cultural heritage knowledge. This research also underscores the integration of modern technology with traditional learning, providing a foundation for future explorations in optimizing educational strategies for heritage preservation and dissemination.

Keywords: Media Modalities · Cultural Heritage · Learning Outcomes

C. Stephanidis et al. (Eds.): HCII 2024, CCIS 2117, pp. 135–142, 2024.
https://doi.org/10.1007/978-3-031-61953-3_16

1 Introduction

In modern society, with the popularization of smart phones and the improvement of Internet bandwidth, people's attention is increasingly short and fast-paced lifestyle. Short video platforms such as TikTok and Kuaishou have risen rapidly. They have become the mainstream social media in modern society, attracting users through short and vivid video content, and accurately matching user interests through algorithm recommendation function, greatly improving the efficiency of content transmission and user engagement. The short video platform covers a wide range of user groups of almost all ages and interests, and has become one of the important platforms for information dissemination, entertainment and social interaction.

In contrast, XiaoHongshu, as a platform with the theme of community sharing and knowledge popularization, is different from short video platforms in terms of content form and user positioning. With text, pictures and long videos as the main forms, Xiao-Hongshu focuses on users' sharing and recommendation of products and lifestyles, so it is more suitable for users seeking in-depth information and product purchase advice. Its advantage is that the content quality is relatively high, and users' real evaluation and recommendation of products and services have high credibility; Why in the era of short video, there are still other types of graphic software to flourish is the origin of our research. This paper takes Tiktok and XiaoHongshu as examples to analyze the advantages and disadvantages of different interactive media in the presentation and dissemination of knowledge culture.

In order to better spread traditional cultural heritage, people are increasingly using online platforms to learn various cultural knowledge. Some have added traditional Chinese cultural background to the game to spread cultural knowledge, and more museums have added information display interfaces about cultural heritage [1, 2]. In this context, we conducted an in-depth study of the different effects of different forms of media when learning about cultural heritage on social platforms. The purpose of this study is to explore the differences in emotional response, learning efficiency and cognitive load of three media forms, video, picture and sequence picture, in order to better guide and optimize the design and dissemination of educational content.

Different from the traditional one-way communication, interactive media requires the active participation of users, who can communicate and interact with the media through clicking, sliding, input and other ways. This form of media often includes interactive websites, apps, social media platforms, etc., that not only provide information, but also adapt content based on user feedback and behavior, resulting in a more personalized and user engaged experience. In informal learning time, different media forms of different social platforms can meet the user's relaxed and fragmented learning style to adapt to the fast pace of modern life. Users can access knowledge anytime and anywhere, breaking the time and space limitations of traditional learning. Learning includes brain memory learning of knowledge and culture and body movement learning of dance and sports. The learning methods include active exploration independent learning, passive listening imparted learning, long-term concentrated learning and fragmented informal learning. In this paper, what kind of interactive media is most suitable for users to use social media to actively explore knowledge related to cultural heritage during informal learning time? What are the learning effects, cognitive load, and emotions associated with using different media?

Firstly, we'll focus on emotional responses. Learning the same content about cultural heritage in the interactive interface of short videos, nine-grid pictures and serial pictures can trigger a variety of emotions, including excitement, curiosity, anxiety or frustration. We will analyze the triggering and modulating effects of different media forms on participants' emotions and explore their impact on the learning experience. Study the learning effect of users under different emotions.Secondly, we will examine the impact of various forms of media on learning efficiency. Different forms of media may have different effects on learning, including comprehension, information retention and knowledge transfer. We will compare the advantages and disadvantages of the three forms of media in terms of learning efficiency to find the most suitable form of media for learning cultural heritage on social platforms. Finally, we will examine the effects of various forms of media on cognitive load. Cognitive load during learning refers to the cognitive stress that an individual is subjected to when processing information and completing tasks. We will analyze the effects of different forms of media on cognitive load and explore their potential impact on learning outcomes and learning experiences.

Through comprehensive research on the emotional response, learning efficiency and cognitive load in the process of learning cultural heritage on social platforms in three media forms, video, nine-grid picture and serial picture, we aim to provide valuable references for educators and content creators to optimize the design and communication strategies of educational content, and improve the learning experience and effect.

2 Literature Review

Firstly, in terms of emotion, studies have shown that people's emotions during learning can affect their concentration and memory effect, and good emotions can better improve learning efficiency. There is a relationship between interface design aesthetics and emotional design. Interface design layout affects user emotions [3, 4] and arouses emotions during use to drive user emotions [5]. Secondly, in terms of cognitive load, (the relationship between cognitive load and interactive interface) an intuitive interface can reduce the cognitive load of viewers. Studies have found that different lecture viewing strategies will affect people's cognitive load [6]. Finally, in terms of learning effect, interface layout will affect users' learning effect [7]. Studies have pointed out the impact of interactive multimedia learning on students' sports and volleyball skills learning skills [8]. The potential of multimedia to support complex fine motor skills learning [9]. Interactive video lectures have been found to improve learning comprehension and memory [10]. The impact of informal learning on formal learning [11].

According to the study of different interaction modes, dynamic media such as video and animation can provide vivid and intuitive learning experience [12], while static pictures can enhance learners' understanding and memory of abstract concepts through clear visual presentation. In addition, the study of video forms also found that different forms of video have different learning effects [13], cognitive load and mood. Affective studies have shown that perceived aesthetics and usability have a positive impact on learners' emotional states and an important impact on learners' intrinsic motivation.

The existing research on classroom teaching between video images and text shows that the video medium has better results in classroom teaching [14]. Based on the research of different video forms, the paper analyzes the cognitive load of learning effects of different forms of video such as picture-in-picture, voice-over and lecture capture, and finds that the learning effects of lecture capture and picture-in-picture are better than those of voice-over [15]. Studies have shown that hand-drawn lecture videos are rated as the most attractive and supportive recall performance for individuals with low prior knowledge of the content material [16]. Informal learning takes place in a self-directed, self-determined learning environment, is primarily problem-solving oriented and self-directed, and is related to empirical knowledge. To sum up, different forms of interactive media have different roles and influences in informal learning, which is of great significance for designing and optimizing educational content. Different interactive media convey different interactive emotions. Studies on emotions show that perceived aesthetics and usability have a positive impact on learners' emotional states. The influence of learners' emotional state on learning results is small, but it has a greater impact on learners' intrinsic motivation, including motivation to continue using materials [17]. The main factors affecting memory include learners' emotions, cognitive load, etc. Users of different interactive media will have different emotional performance [18]. Deliberate emotional design when designing multimedia interfaces will enable learners to have better learning emotions [19]. Studies have shown that viewers with different lecture viewing strategies will have different cognitive loads [20]. Studies have found that learning effect is mainly related to learners' emotional cognitive load, and media forms with low cognitive load and higher emotional value are more conducive to user learning.

The three forms of interactive media play different roles in the field of education and learning, each with a set of advantages and limitations. Choosing the right form of interactive media requires weighing various factors, including the complexity of the learning content, the learning habits and needs of users, and so on. Educators and content creators should have the flexibility to use different forms of media according to the specific situation to provide the best learning experience and results.

3   Methods and Materials

3.1   Experimental Method and Materials

The study recruited college students from different backgrounds and ages and divided them into three groups: Group A (video format), Group B (nine-grid image format), and Group C (sequential image format). Each group of participants received the same learning material with the same content and different forms related to cultural heritage. In this experiment, the images of five ridges and six beasts of Taiji Temple were selected, and corresponding interactive interfaces were designed to introduce the symbolic pictures of the names of various gods and beasts. The corresponding interactive interfaces were shared with each group member for learning. The learning time of each group member was recorded and participants were interviewed after receiving learning materials. Qualitative data were collected on their emotional responses to various media formats, perceived learning effectiveness and cognitive load, and the findings revealed a diversity of views across the groups (Fig. 1).

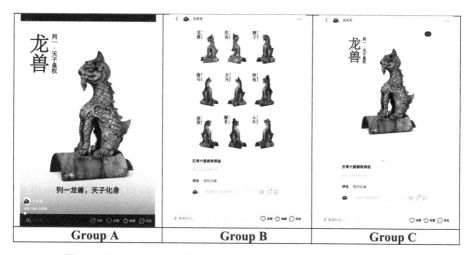

Fig. 1. Screen shots of different interactive forms used in the experiment

3.2   User Interview

Group A. Member 1 expressed concern about the deep interpretation of short videos, pointing out the possibility of information overload and lack of context. "I think that the speed of the video is not fully compatible with my memory speed, and there may be the phenomenon of pausing or playing the video backwards, and I may have certain emotional agitation. I think that I cannot control the learning rate subjectively, but I think that the cognitive load is small, but I think that the memory effect is not very good due to the high fluency of the video." Group A member 2 "I think that the viewing rate of short videos and the low cognitive load will reduce their memory effect, and they are easy to enter the flow state. When they watch videos, they have little mood fluctuation, but they will feel frustrated after the video is played." Group A member 3 "I think that watching relevant science knowledge in the way of video feels good and has a high mood. However, after asking questions about their memory points, it was found that the memory effect of watching short videos was not good, but the experimenters believed that the cognitive load of short videos was low in the process of watching, and the emotions were high and the concentration was high. If it was used as fragmented entertainment reading, it could play a good time." Group A members generally had a memory rate of about 40%.

Group B. Member 1, "I think the nine-grid picture format can control the reading rhythm, and I like the intuitiveness of the nine-grid. For the nine divine beasts we selected, the coherence and order of the nine-grid can just meet their intuitive understanding of the correlation. It is helpful for memory, but because it is the first contact with the knowledge, they think it is interesting and exploratory, so they think it is very interesting because their emotions are high. The memory effect test shows that the memory effect is good, but because the first contact with the relevant knowledge, they think the cognitive load in the process of watching is large. If you brush to this interface at random and non-subjective learning, you will think that this interface is less attractive to them and will not look at it for a long time" Member 2 of Group B "I think that the form of nine-grid pictures is very intuitive and continuous, and thinks that such a continuous interface is more conducive to the memory of the content, but because it displays all the content intuitively, its exploration will decline. At the same time, the intuitive presentation will also reduce the user's cognitive load. This contributes to a subjective and coherent learning experience." Group B member 3 "I believed that the form of nine-grid pictures was very attractive to them, and rich content would make them have a strong desire to explore. During the viewing process, they were happier, and the operation without turning the page left and right was more conducive to improving their concentration, and the result of memory test was better." Group B generally had a memory rate of about 65%.

Group C. Member 1 of Group C "showed a low tendency to explore and learn in the interactive format of sequential pictures. In the process of page turning for unknown knowledge." Member 2 of Group C "I believed that repeated page turning from left to right in the process of memory would affect its memory effect and reduce the continuity of content. The learning effect was tested and found that the effect was general." Group C Member 3 "I believed that the page-turning interface was more controllable and intuitive. The supervisor controlled the memory rate and learning time, and believed that the cognitive load in the process of watching was lower. However, turning the page several times will make them think that watching is less interesting and more compulsory learning is lower mood but better learning effect." The memory rate of group C was generally about 5%.

4   Results and Discussion

For three different forms of interactive media (video, nine-grid picture, and sequential picture), we conducted a comparative study of emotion, cognitive load, and learning outcomes.

4.1   Emotional Impact

Participants in the video form group generally experienced more positive emotions during the learning process because video was able to provide a vivid visual and auditory experience, increasing the enjoyment and attraction of learning. Participants in the nine grid group may feel more neutral because the nine grid form provides a structured presentation of information but lacks the vividness of the video form. Participants in the picture-by-picture group may feel slightly anxious or upset because the learning process requires moving through the images gradually, and the information is presented relatively slowly, which can lead to impatience or anxiety.

4.2   Effects of Cognitive Load

The video format group had a relatively low cognitive load because video was able to present multiple information at the same time, reducing the cognitive load on memory and comprehension. The nine-grid picture group also had a lower cognitive load because the information was presented in a structured way and participants could more easily untangle logical relationships. The cognitive load may be slightly higher in the picture-by-picture format group because the learning process requires a step-by-step look through the pictures and may require more cognitive effort to understand the information.

4.3   Influence of Learning Effect

The video-based group usually shows more moderate learning results because video provides multiple sensory inputs and is more likely to capture the attention and interest of the participants, but because there is less subjective control, mind wandering or teaching and absorbing different frequencies may occur. The learning effect of the nine-grid group was better, because the structured, intuitive and orderly presentation of information helped participants better understand the learning content. Learning in the picture-by-picture group may be slightly less effective than in the other two groups because the learning process is relatively slow, which may lead to reduced information retention and comprehension.

5   Conclusion

The choice of different media formats will produce different emotional response, learning effect and cognitive load when users learn educational content. Educators and content creators should carefully consider the strengths and limitations of each format to optimize the learning experience for different audiences. Future research could explore strategies for integrating multiple media formats to improve learning outcomes and engagement in cultural heritage education.

Funding This study was funded by Shenyang Philosophy and Social Funding This study was funded by Shenyang Philosophy and Social Science Planning Project (SY202236Y).

References

1. Li, Q., Wang, P., Liu, Z., et al.: Using scaffolding theory in serious games to enhance traditional Chinese murals culture learning. Comput. Animation Virtual Worlds **35**(1), e2213 (2024)
2. Li, Q., Wang, P., Liu, Z., et al.: How generous interface affect user experience and behavior: evaluating the information display interface for museum cultural heritage. Comput Animation Virtual Worlds **35**(1), e2212 (2024)
3. Wang, J., Hsu, Y.: The relationship of symmetry, complexity, and shape in mobile interface aesthetics, from an emotional perspective—a case study of the smartwatch. Symmetry **12**(9), 1403 (2020)
4. Lim, Y.M., Ayesh, A., Stacey, M.: The effects of menu design on users' emotions, search performance and mouse behavior. In: 2014 IEEE 13th International Conference on Cognitive Informatics and Cognitive Computing, pp. 541–549. IEEE (2014)
5. Li, J., Luo, C., Zhang, Q., et al.: Can emotional design really evoke emotion in multimedia learning? Int. J. Educ. Technol. High. Educ. **17**(1), 1–18 (2020)
6. Costley, J., Fanguy, M., Lange, C., et al.: The effects of video lecture viewing strategies on cognitive load. J. Comput. High. Educ. **33**, 19–38 (2021)

7. Zhang, M., Hou, G., Chen, Y.C.: Effects of interface layout design on mobile learning efficiency: a comparison of interface layouts for mobile learning platform. Library hi tech **41**(5), 1420–1435 (2023)

8. Gunawan, G., Firmansyah, D., Widiastuti, W.: Effect of interactive multimedia learning to learn skills of students sports volleyball. J. Educ. Health Sport **9**(9), 263–270 (2019)

9. Papastergiou, M., Pollatou, E., Theofylaktou, I., et al.: Examining the potential of web-based multimedia to support complex fine motor skill learning: an empirical study. Educ. Inf. Technol. **19**, 817–839 (2014)

10. Hung, I.C., Chen, N.S.: Embodied interactive video lectures for improving learning comprehension and retention. Comput. Educ. **117**, 116–131 (2018)

11. Rogers, A.: The base of the iceberg: Informal learning and its impact on formal and non-formal learning[M]. Verlag Barbara Budrich, 2014

12. Berney, S., Bétrancourt, M.: Does animation enhance learning? a meta-analysis. Comput. Educ. **101**, 150–167 (2016)

13. Zhuang, W., Zeng, Q., Zhang, Y., et al.: What makes user-generated content more helpful on social media platforms? insights from creator interactivity perspective. Inf. Process. Manage. **60**(2), 103201 (2023)

14. Désiron, J.C., de Vries, E., Bartel, A.N., et al.: The influence of text cohesion and picture detail on young readers' knowledge of science topics. Br. J. Educ. Psychol. **88**(3), 465–479 (2018)

15. Chen, H.T.M., Thomas, M.: Effects of lecture video styles on engagement and learning. Educ. Tech. Res. Dev. **68**, 2147–2164 (2020)

16. H'mida, C., Degrenne, O., Souissi, N., et al.: Learning a motor skill from video and Static Pictures in physical education students—effects on technical performances, motivation and cognitive load. Int. J. Environ. Res. Public Health **17**(23), 9067 (2020)

17. Chen, C.M., Sun, Y.C.: Assessing the effects of different multimedia materials on emotions and learning performance for visual and verbal style learners. Comput. Educ. **59**(4), 1273–1285 (2012)

18. Heidig, S., Müller, J., Reichelt, M.: Emotional design in multimedia learning: differentiation on relevant design features and their effects on emotions and learning. Comput. Hum. Behav. **44**, 81–95 (2015)

19. Chen, C.M., Wu, C.H.: Effects of different video lecture types on sustained attention, emotion, cognitive load, and learning performance. Comput. Educ. **80**, 108–121 (2015)

20. Chen, C.M., Wang, H.P.: Using emotion recognition technology to assess the effects of different multimedia materials on learning emotion and performance. Libr. Inf. Sci. Res.. Inf. Sci. Res. **33**(3), 244–255 (2011)

Enhancing Searching as Learning (SAL) with Generative Artificial Intelligence: A Literature Review

Kok Khiang Lim[✉] [iD] and Chei Sian Lee[iD]

Wee Kim Wee School of Communication and Information, Nanyang Technological University, Singapore, Singapore
w200004@e.ntu.edu.sg, leecs@ntu.edu.sg

Abstract. Searching as Learning (SAL), a learning process with potential knowledge gain during searches in a digital environment, is an emerging field in human-computer interaction research, especially with recent technological advancements in generative artificial intelligence (GenAI). According to SAL, the act of searching for the information itself can be a valuable learning experience. Many studies have investigated SAL's learning perspective and facets supported by traditional search systems (e.g., web browsers), to access, search, and retrieve information to fulfill users' learning intentions. However, the applications of GenAI, as well as their roles and disruption to the existing SAL process, are unclear. To address this gap, this study aims to shed light on the applicability of GenAI in enhancing the SAL process by conducting a systematic literature review.

First, we seek to define the concepts of 'learning' and 'searching' by examining the components of SAL in the literature and then detailing how SAL would have occurred. Next, the systematic literature review, guided by PRISMA, uses the PICO (Population, Intervention, Comparison, and Outcome) framework to develop searchable keywords and guide the literature review. Five major databases were searched, and literature that fulfilled the PICO's criteria was included for review. Preliminary analysis shows that GenAI could improve and ease SAL human-computer interfaces that inevitably change the process and influence users' learning behavior, such as how information is retrieved and consumed. Consequently, these opportunities posed concerns about information reliability, accuracy, and long-term effects on user behavior.

Keywords: Searching as Learning · digital environment · generative artificial intelligence

1 Introduction

Information seeking is a prevalent online activity that people engage in daily to access, retrieve, or use information in ways that satisfy their information needs, from undirected searching of information to formal search of actionable information [1]. Such activities are often iterative and open-ended [2], and typically require people to sense-make and understand the information retrieved to navigate the information environment for the required results [3]. Indirectly, the learning aspect of search leads to understanding and acquiring knowledge. This is termed searching as learning (SAL). Search systems, such as web browsers, are used as an interface to support people's interaction with information retrieval and enable the SAL process. However, the relevancy and accuracy of the search results would largely depend on users crafting the right keywords, formulating their search queries, and interpreting search results [4].

Accordingly, recent advancements in technologies like generative AI (GenAI) that can accept conversational-like queries and reply with contextually aware and direct answers have presented the opportunity to use GenAI applications in enhancing SAL [1, 5]. An example of the GenAI application is ChatGPT, which eliminates query hurdles most users face using traditional search systems and responds with human-like replies that are more intuitive to relate to the queries. Studies have been conducted to understand GenAI applications to enhance learning, such as learning languages [6], students' perception of GenAI [7], and attitudes and usage of GenAI in learning [8]. Notwithstanding the advantages and benefits of GenAI, researchers have also expressed concerns about the ethical usage and potential risks posed by GenAI, especially integrating it into the learning process and education [9, 10].

Nonetheless, despite the interest in using GenAI to enhance SAL, there is a lack of reviews to examine the state of influence of GenAI on SAL. Guided by the concept of SAL, this study aims to conduct a systematic review focusing on how GenAI have changed the SAL paradigm and influenced human-computer interaction behavior. The findings would contribute to SAL's field of knowledge from the HCI perspective by highlighting the associated concerns.

The PICO (Population, Intervention, Comparison, and Outcome) framework is used to develop the research question based on the scope of this review [11]. The population includes individuals who use GenAI for searching; Intervention refers to the use of GenAI for searching; Comparison involves the usage of alternative search systems; and Outcome encompasses the resultant, such as processes, behavior, and human-computer interaction, from the use of advanced search system, as well as the challenges and concerns. Hence, this review aims to answer the following research question. To what extent does GenAI enhance the SAL process and the consequences, challenges, and concerns faced?

2   Related Work

2.1   Concept of Searching as Learning

Searching as learning (SAL) is a concept deeply rooted within information science, highlighting the intrinsic connection between information seeking behaviors and knowledge acquisition [12]. Extant literature on this topic has revealed many aspects of understanding, from how individuals engage in causal search activities to enhancing their cognitive processes and knowledge of the subjects they are searching for [1]. One prominent aspect of describing the SAL concept is the *Guided Inquiry*, based on the research finding grounded in a constructivist approach to learning – the information search process [13]. The model posits that individuals develop learning and understanding during the search process through six stages of inquiry: initiation, selection, exploration, formulation, collection, and presentation.

Furthermore, past studies on SAL emphasize the importance of metacognition in the search process [14, 15]. Metacognition refers to the process of thinking and understanding about one's thinking and learning [14]. Individuals who engage in metacognitive activities during search tasks have demonstrated higher levels of learning and information retrieval skills [14, 16]. This underscores the assumption that effective searching goes beyond simply finding relevant information but involves self-regulation, monitoring, and evaluating one's search behavior to optimize learning outcomes [15]. Additionally, technology has played an essential role in facilitating searching as learning, influencing information seeking behaviors, and providing new opportunities for interactive and collaborative learning experiences [17].

2.2 Technology Advancement in Searching as Learning

The advent of advanced technologies, like GenAI, has ushered in a new era of learning pedagogy. GenAI utilizes large language models to translate text, answer questions, summarize texts, and generate text output, making itself a valuable searching and learning tool [5]. A notable example of a GenAI application is ChatGPT, which is capable of generating tailored responses to users' prompts and questions in a human-like conversational manner [18]. In the context of searching as learning, ChatGPT serves as a multifaceted resource. It enables users to seek information in real-time and respond with answers instantly [19]. These generated responses in a conversational manner further enhanced the learning experience by simulating dialogue and promoting user engagement [19].

Moreover, the utilization of ChatGPT in searching as learning facilitates personalized learning. By tailoring the generated responses to individual prompts and queries, ChatGPT can adapt to each learner's specific needs and preferences, thus offering a customized approach to knowledge acquisition [5, 20]. Furthermore, ChatGPT's ability to generate content in various styles and formats, such as providing summaries, explanations, programming codes, or generating creative responses, enhances its versatility as a learning tool [19, 20]. Through its integration with learning platforms, ChatGPT is set to revolutionize traditional information retrieval and dissemination methods, paving the way for more interactive and immersive learning experiences [5, 19].

3 Methodology

3.1 Literature Search

The systematic literature review method, based on the PRISMA 2020 guidelines [21], is used to guide the selection, evaluation and synthetization of existing literature in a reproducible process to address the research question [22]. This method has been used to, for example, review user trust in AI-enabled systems from an HCI perspective [23] and evaluate the theories and approaches supporting the SAL [12].

The keywords for the search query were devised based on the scope of the research question and their related terms. Further, the keywords were expanded to include synonyms and alternate spellings, which were then concatenated using Boolean operators (OR/AND) to obtain a focused yet comprehensive search. The keywords for the searches include: "searching as learning" OR "searching to learn" OR "learning in search" OR "search as learning process" OR "SAL" AND "generative artificial intelligence" OR "generative AI" OR "generative pre-trained transformer" OR "ChatGPT" OR "AI Chatbot" OR "AI-assisted chatbot" OR "GAI" OR "GenAI" OR "GPT".

The search in the title, abstract, and keywords was conducted across five major databases (ACM Digital Library, ScienceDirect, Scopus, Web of Science, and Google Scholar) for the period between January 2020 and January 2024, to coincide with the launch of GenAI in mid-2020 [24]. In addition, backward and forward citation searches were also conducted from the identified literature references at the end of January 2024 [25]. Endnote, a reference database program, was used as the bibliographic management tool to capture referencing details and manage citations [25].

3.2   Selection Criterion and Process

The inclusion and exclusion criteria were developed to ensure that relevant studies were included within the scope of this review. The inclusion criteria were as follows: 1) studies that were conducted between the years 2020 and 2024; 2) written in English; 3) published in peer-reviewed journals; 4) available in full-text; 5) relevant to SAL; and 6) not belongs to grey literature. The exclusion criteria were: 1) studies that were duplicates; 2) grey literature; 3) not written in English; 4) studies not related to SAL; and 5) studies related to conceptual, working discussion, or literature review. These criteria were then used to screen the records (titles, abstracts, and keywords) retrieved from the databases and for full-text screening during the initial searches and eligibility assessment. In addition, PICO was used as the selection criteria to screen the records further to ensure the quality of the selected studies.

The selection process is shown in Fig. 1. The searches from the five databases returned 1,687 records, while the citation searches yielded another 57 records (see Fig. 1). After removing the duplicated records ($n = 175$) and screening the title and abstracts based on PICO and inclusion/exclusion criteria, a total of 34 records were sought for full-text retrieval and assessed for inclusion eligibility. Following the final assessment of the full text, only 11 studies remained and were accepted for inclusion in this study.

3.3   Data Extraction and Analysis

Data was extracted from the included literature using eight pre-defined categories to address the research questions [25]. These include the year of publication, geographical location of data collection, study context, sample characteristics, terminology related to SAL, research methods, outcomes, and concerns. Common themes from the extracted data were then clustered together for narrative synthesis as meta-analysis could not be performed due to the heterogeneity of the literature. Data was extracted by the first author and cross-verified by the second author. Consensus was used to resolve any disagreement during the analysis.

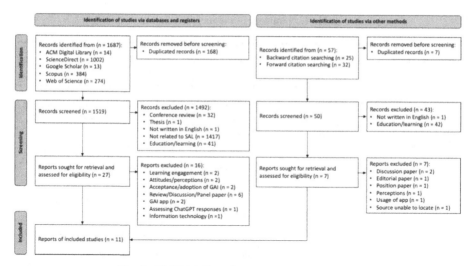

Fig. 1. PRISMA flow diagram for report selection

4   Results

Table 1 shows the summary of the included studies. The 11 studies were conducted in 2023 across the world, from Europe to Asia. Samples involved in the studies were mainly university students, except for studies by Jo [26], Jo and Park [27], and Murgia, Abbasiantaeb, Aliannejadi, Huibers, Landoni, and Pera [28], where workers and 4th-grade children were involved. Four of the 11 studies had relatively small sample sizes, between 41 and 64 [28–31], while the rest had samples above 100. About the SAL process, most of these studies used various terms, such as knowledge sharing, knowledge acquisition, and knowledge discovery, to describe the use of GenAI during the SAL process (see Table 2 for the definitions).

Among the 11 studies, four studies examined or investigated users' intention and behavior to use GenAI for information searches [26, 27, 32, 33], and six were related to evaluating the use of GenAI [19, 28, 30, 31, 34, 35], and the last investigated the impact of GenAI on students' narrative intelligence [29]. All studies have reported positive outcomes on the beneficial use of GenAI to facilitate and support users' search and discover information easily and faster, thus enabling learning or decision-making during the process, except for Niedbał, Sokołowski and Wrzalik [19]'s findings where some felt GenAI lack the benefits during the learning process.

Conversely, these studies highlighted a broad range of concerns arising from using GenAI. Four studies raised the implications of ethical considerations like data and personal privacy, security, and transparency [26, 27, 32, 34], three questioned the accuracy and reliability of information from GenAI [28, 32, 35], and six concerned on the long-term effect, resulting in over-reliance on GenAI, poor quality of knowledge acquisition or hindered the development of query formulation and thinking skills [28–31, 34, 35].

Table 1. Summary of the included studies.

Author / Year / Country	Sample	Study Purpose / Key Outcome
Duong, Vu and Ngo [32] 2023 Vietnam	1389 university students	Examine students' intentions and behaviors to use ChatGPT for learning, with moderation effect of *knowledge sharing*. ✓ The ease of use increased students' intention and use of ChatGPT for learning, and utilizing ChatGPT to facilitate knowledge sharing further reinforces the intention to use it in actual behaviour. ⊘ Concerns on the reliability and accuracy of information from ChatGPT, risks, such as data privacy breaches, and inappropriate use of ChatGPT.
Jo [26] 2023 Republic of Korea	645 university students and office workers	Examine user engagement with ChatGPT based on 13 variables which include *knowledge acquisition*. ✓ Knowledge acquisition and application have a tangible impact on utilitarian benefits and individual impact, which affects user behavior and satisfaction. ⊘ Suggest enhancing data security to foster trust which directly influences user retention.
Jo and Park [27] 2023 Republic of Korea	351 workers	Examine workers' use of ChatGPT in daily tasks and factors, such as *information support* and *knowledge acquisition*, that influence the usage. ✓ Both the information support and knowledge acquisition influence users' perception of ChatGPT utilitarian benefits, which shapes their intention to use. ⊘ Ethical considerations like data privacy, transparency, and fairness. ⊘ Technical constraints which may discourage usage.

(continued)

Table 1. (*continued*)

Murgia, Abbasiantaeb, Aliannejadi, Huibers, Landoni and Pera [28] 2023 Italy	55 students from 4th grade	Explore the feasibility of whether ChatGPT can adapt to support children's *information discovery*. ✓ ChatGPT could support children's information discovery by adapting the language literacy level to the children. ⊘ The ease of query formulation may be detrimental to children development of query formulation, and information pollution may be difficult for children to spot.
Niedbał, Sokołowski and Wrzalik [19] 2023 Poland	231 university students	Evaluate the extent to which ChatGPT can be applied in the *learning process*. ✓ Most students reported that ChatGPT enables them to quickly find information in the learning process and its efficiency in obtaining correct answers. ⊘ About half of the respondents indicated that they did not use ChatGPT for learning purposes, and some stated that it lacked benefits in the learning process.
Pellas [29] 2023 Greece	64 undergraduates	Investigate the effect of generative AI on students' *narrative intelligence* and self-efficacy. ✓ The use of generative AI platforms can substantially enhance both narrative intelligence score and self-efficacy, but it may not entirely replace or replicate the creative aspect of humans. ⊘ Concerns on long-term effects of using generative AI platforms.
Rahman, Sabbir, Zhang, Moral and Hossain [33] 2023 Bangladesh	344 university students	Examine the variables of the acceptance model, such as *perceived informativeness*, to understand its influence on attitudes toward using ChatGPT. ✓ Perceived informativeness is significant in understanding students' attitudes towards using ChatGPT for learning and predicts their intention to use it. It suggests that ChatGPT provides useful information for decision-making. ⊘ Moderating effect of trust on acceptance of ChatGPT which may impact the usage.

(*continued*)

Table 1. (*continued*)

Songsiengchai, Sereerat and Watananimitgul [34] 2023 Thailand	120 students from 1st year pre-service teachers	Explore the potential of ChatGPT to facilitate personalized learning and compare *learning effectiveness* among the students after implementing AI. ✓ Students who interacted with AI significantly improved their language skills. ⊘ Implications on the ethical considerations related to data security, privacy, responsible use of AI, and the long-term effect on learning.
Wandelt, Sun and Zhang [35] 2023 China	102 postgraduate students	Examine the potential of ChatGPT, such as *knowledge discovery*, for education and research. ✓ ChatGPT enabled time saving and improved efficiency in acquiring knowledge and discovering information. ⊘ Concerns on the safe and reliable usage, leading to over-reliance on the ChatGPT for information.
Yilmaz and Karaoglan Yilmaz [31] 2023 Turkey	41 undergraduates	Examine student's use of ChatGPT to *acquire knowledge* during learning. ✓ ChatGPT provided fast and mostly correct answers, improved thinking skills, facilitated tasks, and increased self-confidence. ⊘ No significant effect on increase motivation when students were given challenging tasks. ⊘ Concerns about the poor quality of knowledge acquisition, such as laziness, unable to answer questions or give incomplete answers which lead to anxiety.
Yilmaz and Karaoglan Yilmaz [30] 2023	45 undergraduates	Examine the effect of ChatGPT on students' *thinking skill*, self-efficacy and motivation toward lesson.

Table 2. Terms related to the description of the SAL process.

Term	Definition
Knowledge acquisition	Gathering new insights and knowledge through interactions with an AI system [36]
Knowledge sharing	In the context of ChatGPT, it served as a tool to facilitate the exchanges of insights and data with users [37, 38]
Knowledge discovery	Derive the exact knowledge from the relevant information the user is after [39]
Information discovery	Activities on the network through iterative search and repeated expansion to identify relevant information [39]
Information support	The delivery of relevant and helpful information to provide guidance and advice for problem-solving within the AI context [40]
Perceived informativeness	The perception that an entity can deliver pertinent, in-depth, and accurate information on any problem, attribute, or policy [41]
Narrative intelligence	Cognitive capacity to comprehend, craft and navigate narratives [42]

5   Discussion

The review highlighted the multifaceted role of GenAI in enhancing SAL processes. Firstly, GenAI provides users with a capable tool to ask conversational-like questions without the need to formulate keywords, search for information, and receive personalized feedback in real-time. By leveraging GenAI, users have quick access to information, seek explanations on complex concepts, and receive guidance on problem-solving, thereby facilitating a deeper understanding of the search topics. Further, by providing tailored responses to users' queries, GenAI enables students to engage with complex topics more effectively, enhancing their learning and retention of information presented to them. In addition, GenAI's ability to generate personalized feedback and explanations contributes to a more interactive and engaging learning experience, thereby boosting students' critical thinking skills, improving self-efficacy, and encouraging their active participation in knowledge acquisition and discovery.

On the contrary, user resistance and potential misuse of GenAI emerge as a critical consideration in the context of learning and education. While GenAI offers numerous advantages and benefits for information retrieval and learning, concerns were raised regarding the responsible use of GenAI tools, the need for critical evaluation of generated content, and the risk of overreliance on automated solutions. Addressing these challenges requires a balanced approach emphasizing the importance of human-AI collaboration, co-existing with GenAI, ethical considerations in GenAI usage, and developing digital toolkits as well as digital literacy skills to guide students in fact-checking, navigating, and utilizing GenAI effectively in their learning process. Hence, by acknowledging the benefits of GenAI and addressing the challenges, educators and researchers can harness the potential of advanced technologies to enhance the SAL process from the HCI perspective, in particular information retrieval, knowledge acquisition, and personalized learning experiences, while mitigating the risks and challenges associated with GenAI usage.

This literature review has two limitations. Firstly, the concept of SAL may need to be reconceptualized in light of advanced technologies such as GenAI. SAL process is well suited for a traditional search system built for efficient information search and retrieval through repeated queries, retrieving and evaluating search results to find satisfying answers, and possibly learning during the process [43]. In contrast, an advanced search system can generate contextualized and direct answers to users' non-structured queries [44]. In other words, the learning aspect within the search is different. It changes the metacognition process because there may be less need for the user to understand the results to conduct further searches as the retrieved results were informative enough for immediate consumption. Hence, to ensure that the identified studies were relevant to SAL and minimize the biases, the retrieved studies were screened for concepts or definitions relevant to the operationalization of the SAL process.

Secondly, although GenAI is a rapidly growing area of interest with extant studies related to the education domain, there are limited studies available that are specific to the field of SAL. The small number of studies included for review is a well-acknowledged limitation [45, 46]. This is attributed to the nascent topic and relatively new technology launched in November 2022 [5]. An example of past studies that faced similar limitations includes the review by [47] on the use of AI in pharmacy education, which included only seven articles for review. Nonetheless, the diverse countries and outcomes from the studies provide converging findings on GenAI's role in enhancing the SAL process.

6   Conclusion

This review identifies a gap in existing literature with limited studies examining the impact of GenAI towards the SAL process and how it would change the SAL paradigm and influence human-computer interaction behavior. Overall, the findings show that GenAI offered opportunities to enhance the SAL process through efficient human-computer interaction to retrieve usable and relevant results that enable learning. Consequently, the same capability could also erode users' skills development and pose ethical concerns as the usage becomes more prevalent. Hence, future studies are needed to understand the long-term effect on users' SAL behaviors and formulate policies to guide the ethical usage of GenAI for searching and learning.

Acknowledgments. This research is supported by the National Research Foundation, Singapore under its AI Singapore Programme (AISG Award No: AISG-GV-2023-013).

Disclosure of Interests. The authors have no competing interests to declare that are relevant to the content of this article.

References

1. Choo, C.W., Detlor, B., Turnbull, D.: Information seeking on the web: an integrated model of browsing and searching. First Monday **5** (2000). https://doi.org/10.5210/fm.v5i2.729
2. Wildemuth, B.M., Freund, L.: Assigning search tasks designed to elicit exploratory search behaviors. In: Proceedings of the Symposium on Human-Computer Interaction and Information Retrieval, pp. 1–10 (2012). https://doi.org/10.1145/2391224.2391228
3. Vakkari, P.: Searching as learning: a systematization based on literature. J. Inf. Sci. **42**, 7–18 (2016). https://doi.org/10.1177/0165551515615833
4. Dhillon, M.K.: Online information seeking and higher education students. In: Chelton, M., Cool, C. (eds.) Youth Information- Seeking Behavior II: Context, Theories, Models, and Issues, pp. 165–205. Scarecrow Press, Lanham (2007)
5. Chiu, T.K.F.: Future research recommendations for transforming higher education with generative AI. Comput. Educ. Artif. Intell. **6**, 100197 (2024). https://doi.org/10.1016/j.caeai.2023.100197
6. Song, C.P., Song, Y.P.: Enhancing academic writing skills and motivation: assessing the efficacy of ChatGPT in AI-assisted language learning for EFL students. Front. Psychol. **14**, 1260843 (2023). https://doi.org/10.3389/fpsyg.2023.1260843
7. Malmström, H., Stöhr, C., Ou, A.W.: Chatbots and other AI for learning: a survey of use and views among university students in Sweden. Chalmers Stud. Commun. Learn. High. Educ. **1** (2023). https://doi.org/10.17196/cls.csclhe/2023/01
8. Abdaljaleel, M., et al.: A multinational study on the factors influencing university students' attitudes and usage of ChatGPT. Sci. Rep. **14**, 1983 (2024). https://doi.org/10.1038/s41598-024-52549-8
9. Stahl, B.C., Eke, D.: The ethics of ChatGPT – exploring the ethical issues of an emerging technology. Int. J. Inf. Manag. **74**, 102700 (2024). https://doi.org/10.1016/j.ijinfomgt.2023.102700
10. Wu, X., Duan, R., Ni, J.: Unveiling security, privacy, and ethical concerns of ChatGPT. J. Inf. Intell. (2023). https://doi.org/10.1016/j.jiixd.2023.10.007
11. Pollock, A., Berge, E.: How to do a systematic review. Int. J. Stroke **13**, 138–156 (2018). https://doi.org/10.1177/1747493017743796
12. Gimenez, P., Machado, M., Pinelli, C., Siqueira, S.: Investigating the learning perspective of searching as learning, a review of the state of the art. In: 31st Brazilian Symposium on Computers in Education, pp. 302–311 (2020). doi:https://doi.org/10.5753/cbie.sbie.2020.302
13. Kuhlthau, C.: Guided inquiry: school libraries in the 21st century. Sch. Libr. Worldw. **16**, 1–12 (2001). https://doi.org/10.29173/slw6797
14. Flavell, J.: Metacognition and cognitive monitoring: a new area of cognitive-developmental inquiry. Am. Psychol. **34**, 906–911 (1979). https://doi.org/10.1037/0003-066X.34.10.906
15. Pressley, M.: Metacognition and self-regulated comprehension. In: Farstrup, A.E., Samuel, S.J. (eds.) What Research Has to Say About Reading Instruction, pp. 291–309. International Reading Association, Newark (2002)
16. Hoyer, J.v., Pardi, G., Kammerer, Y., Holtz, P.: Metacognitive judgments in searching as learning (SAL) tasks: Insights on (mis-) calibration, multimedia usage, and confidence. Proceedings of the 1st International Workshop on Search as Learning with Multimedia Information, pp. 3–10. Association for Computing Machinery, Nice (2019)
17. Marchionini, G.: Exploratory search: from finding to understanding. Commun. ACM **49**, 41–46 (2006). https://doi.org/10.1145/1121949.1121979
18. https://openai.com/blog/chatgpt/
19. Niedbał, R., Sokołowski, A., Wrzalik, A.: Students' use of the artificial intelligence language model in their learning process. Procedia Comput. Sci. **225**, 3059–3066 (2023). https://doi.org/10.1016/j.procs.2023.10.299

20. American Psychological Association. https://www.apa.org/monitor/2023/06/chatgpt-lea rning-tool

21. Page, M.J., et al.: The PRISMA 2020 statement: an updated guideline for reporting systematic reviews. Syst. Rev. **10**, 89 (2021). https://doi.org/10.1186/s13643-021-01626-4

22. Fink, A.: Conducting Research Literature Reviews: From the Internet to Paper, 2nd edn. Sage Publications, Thousand Oaks (2005)

23. Bach, T.A., Khan, A., Hallock, H., Beltrão, G., Sousa, S.: A systematic literature review of user trust in AI-enabled systems: an HCI perspective. Int. J. Hum.–Comput. Interact. 40, 1–16 (2022). https://doi.org/10.1080/10447318.2022.2138826

24. Floridi, L., Chiriatti, M.: GPT-3: Its nature, scope, limits, and consequences. Mind. Mach. **30**, 681–694 (2020). https://doi.org/10.1007/s11023-020-09548-1

25. Bandara, W., Miskon, S., Fielt, E.: A systematic, tool-supported method for conducting litera-ture reviews in information systems. In: ECIS 2011 Proceedings 19th European Conference on Information Systems, pp. 1–13. AIS Electronic Library (AISeL)/Association for Information Systems (2011). https://eprints.qut.edu.au/42184/

26. Jo, H.: Understanding AI tool engagement: a study of ChatGPT usage and word-of-mouth among university students and office workers. Telematics Inform. **85**, 102067 (2023). https:// doi.org/10.1016/j.tele.2023.102067

27. Jo, H., Park, D.H.: AI in the workplace: examining the effects of ChatGPT on information support and knowledge acquisition. Int. J. Hum.-Comput. Interact. (2023). https://doi.org/10. 1080/10447318.2023.2278283

28. Murgia, E., Abbasiantaeb, Z., Aliannejadi, M., Huibers, T., Landoni, M., Pera, M.S.: ChatGPT in the classroom: a preliminary exploration on the feasibility of adapting ChatGPT to support children's information discovery. In: Adjunct Proceedings of the 31st ACM Conference on User Modeling, Adaptation and Personalization, pp. 22–27 (2023). doi:https://doi.org/10. 1145/3563359.3597399

29. Pellas, N.: The effects of generative AI platforms on undergraduates' narrative intelligence and writing self-efficacy. Educ. Sci. **13**, 1155 (2023). https://doi.org/10.3390/educsci13111155

30. Yilmaz, R., Karaoglan Yilmaz, F.G.: The effect of generative artificial intelligence (AI)-based tool use on students' computational thinking skills, programming self-efficacy and motivation. Comput. Educ. Artif. Intell. **4**, 100147 (2023). https://doi.org/10.1016/j.caeai.2023.100147

31. Yilmaz, R., Karaoglan Yilmaz, F.G.: Augmented intelligence in programming learning: exam-ining student views on the use of ChatGPT for programming learning. Comput. Hum. Behav. Artif. Hum. **1**, 100005 (2023). https://doi.org/10.1016/j.chbah.2023.100005

32. Duong, C.D., Vu, T.N., Ngo, T.V.N.: Applying a modified technology acceptance model to explain higher education students' usage of ChatGPT: a serial multiple mediation model with knowledge sharing as a moderator. Int. J. Manag. Educ. **21**, 100883 (2023). https://doi.org/ 10.1016/j.ijme.2023.100883

33. Rahman, M.S., Sabbir, M.M., Zhang, D.J., Moral, I.H., Hossain, G.M.S.: Examining students' intention to use ChatGPT: does trust matter? Aust. J. Educ. Technol. **39**, 51–71 (2023). https:// doi.org/10.14742/ajet.8956

34. Songsiengchai, S., Sereerat, B.O., Watananimitgul, W.: Leveraging artificial intelligence (AI): Chat GPT for effective English language learning among Thai students. Kurdish Stud. **11**, 359–373 (2023). https://doi.org/10.58262/ks.v11i3.027

35. Wandelt, S., Sun, X., Zhang, A.: AI-driven assistants for education and research? a case study on ChatGPT for air transport management. J. Air Transp. Manag. **113**, 102483 (2023). https:// doi.org/10.1016/j.jairtraman.2023.102483

36. Al-Sharafi, M.A., Al-Emran, M., Iranmanesh, M., Al-Qaysi, N., Iahad, N.A., Arpaci, I.: Understanding the impact of knowledge management factors on the sustainable use of AI-based chatbots for educational purposes using a hybrid SEM-ANN approach. Interact. Learn. Environ. **31**, 7491–7510 (2023). https://doi.org/10.1080/10494820.2022.2075014

37. Arif, M., Qaisar, N., Kanwal, S.: Factors affecting students' knowledge sharing over social media and individual creativity: an empirical investigation in Pakistan. Int. J. Manag. Educ. **20**, 100598 (2022). https://doi.org/10.1016/j.ijme.2021.100598

38. Bouton, E., Tal, S.B., Asterhan, C.S.C.: Students, social network technology and learning in higher education: visions of collaborative knowledge construction vs. the reality of knowledge sharing. Internet High. Educ. **49**, 100787 (2021). https://doi.org/10.1016/j.iheduc.2020.100787

39. Proper, H.A., Bruza, P.D.: What is information discovery about? J. Am. Soc. Inf. Sci. **50**, 737–750 (1999). https://doi.org/10.1002/(SICI)1097-4571(1999)50:9%3c737::AID-ASI2%3e3.0.CO;2-C

40. Lee, C.T., Pan, L.-Y., Hsieh, S.H.: Artificial intelligent chatbots as brand promoters: a two-stage structural equation modeling - artificial neural network approach. Internet Res. **32**, 1329–1356 (2022). https://doi.org/10.1108/INTR-01-2021-0030

41. Holzwarth, M., Janiszewski, C., Neumann, M.M.: The influence of avatars on online consumer shopping behavior. J. Mark. **70**, 19–36 (2006). https://doi.org/10.1509/JMKG.70.4.019

42. Randall, W.L.: Narrative intelligence and the novelty of our lives. J. Aging Stud. **13**, 11–28 (1999). https://doi.org/10.1016/S0890-4065(99)80003-6

43. Rieh, S.Y., Collins-Thompson, K., Hansen, P., Lee, H.-J.: Towards searching as a learning process: a review of current perspectives and future directions. J. Inf. Sci. **42**, 19–34 (2016). https://doi.org/10.1177/0165551515615841

44. Tayan, O., Hassan, A., Khankan, K., Askool, S.: Considerations for adapting higher education technology courses for AI large language models: a critical review of the impact of ChatGPT. Mach. Learn. Appl. **15**, 100513 (2024). https://doi.org/10.1016/j.mlwa.2023.100513

45. Slyer, J.T.: Unanswered questions: implications of an empty review. JBI Evid. Synth. **14**, 1–2 (2016). https://doi.org/10.11124/JBISRIR-2016-002934

46. Yaffe, J., Montgomery, P., Hopewell, S., Shepard, L.D.: Empty reviews: a description and consideration of Cochrane systematic reviews with no included studies. PLoS ONE (2012). https://doi.org/10.1371/journal.pone.0036626

47. Abdel Aziz, M.H., Rowe, C., Southwood, R., Nogid, A., Berman, S., Gustafson, K.: A scoping review of artificial intelligence within pharmacy education. Am. J. Pharm. Educ. **88**, 100615 (2024). https://doi.org/10.1016/j.ajpe.2023.100615

Learning Beyond the Classroom in the AI Era: A Generation Z Perspective

Kok Khiang Lim[(✉)] and Chei Sian Lee

Wee Kim Wee School of Communication and Information, Nanyang Technological University, Singapore, Singapore
w200004@e.ntu.edu.sg, leecs@ntu.edu.sg

Abstract. Digital technology is essential in enabling Generation Z (Gen Z) students to continue learning beyond the classroom through informal learning. The duality of digital technology effectively engages and supports Gen Z students in their learning, and it also fosters procrastination behavior due to the self-regulated digital environment. Research on the relationship between both ends of digital technology and its effect on learning from the perspective of Gen Z in the AI era is limited. This study integrates perspectives from two widely accepted frameworks, the technology acceptance model and personal motivation factors, to investigate Gen Z students' dichotomy relationship between engagement in digital technology and procrastination behavior.

A sample of 391 students from a local university responded to the survey. Descriptive statistics, factor analysis, and structural equation models were applied to analyze the data. The results show that most Gen Z students are receptive to new and innovative technology, while their perceptions and attitudes towards technology usage are not significant. These findings could be attributed to Gen Z students' accustomization to the technology environment and were consistent with their characteristics. Further, the study observed that Gen Z students heightened personal motivation is associated with an increased likelihood of procrastination, which positively and indirectly influences technology usage. This is a significant finding as it diverged from previously established knowledge between motivation and procrastination and unveiled a novel insight into Gen Z students' counterintuitive learning behavior. Hence, this insight underscores the need for future studies to reevaluate existing theories and investigate the interplay between motivation factors and procrastination tendencies to explain Gen Z's learning behavior.

Keywords: Digital technology · informal learning · procrastination

1 Introduction

Young adults, in particular Generation Z (or Gen Z), born between 1997 and 2012 [1], are regarded as the first true digital natives [2]. They are comfortable and adept with technology to perform tasks, proficient in social media to communicate and interact, and accustomed to instant information access to find answers. These characteristics are attributed to Gen Z's developmental years. They grew up in an environment where

C. Stephanidis et al. (Eds.): HCII 2024, CCIS 2117, pp. 156–168, 2024.
https://doi.org/10.1007/978-3-031-61953-3_18

digital technology is prevalent and integrated into almost every aspect of their daily lives [2], such as education in which Gen Z often use it for research, online learning and collaborations with their peers on projects [3]. In other words, Gen Z's approach to learning and acquiring knowledge differs from previous generations [4].

The recent technological innovation in generative artificial intelligence (GenAI) has propelled digital technology into the AI era. GenAI is capable of generating content based on users' prompts (e.g., writing text, creating digital art, or composing music) that is intelligible to understand and indistinguishable from human creations [5]. Many software applications have since developed around GenAI to boost functional productivity or enhance the usability of software applications. These tools were integrated into our day-to-day lives, ranging from customer service chatbots that provide natural conversational experiences (e.g., Starbucks' chatbot) to AI writing assistance that guides users' writing styles (e.g., Grammarly).

Notwithstanding, the new digital technology has also reshaped the education landscape. Schools and academic institutions have institutionalized digital technology as part of the curriculum to better engage and support Gen Z students in their learning [6], while Gen Z students have lauded the conveniences and accessibility of learning materials afforded by technology [7]. In particular, digital technology has also played an essential role in learning beyond the classroom [8, 9], termed digital informal learning in this study. Gen Z students learn and acquire knowledge through digital informal learning to complement or fill the gaps in their formal learning [10–12]. In addition, as the nature of work is changing rapidly in the AI era, continuous learning has become necessary to remain relevant. Thus, informal learning is crucial in preparing students for these changes [13].

Conversely, the digital technology environment also fostered undesirable learning behaviors. Gen Z students may be tempted or distracted by digital technology, such as social media or video gaming, over academic tasks, as it satisfies immediate gratification [14, 15]. Others lack the self-regulation or self-control ability to manage their learning process [16]. In addition, Gen Z students may also be reluctant to use digital technology if it interrupts their current learning habits, threatens their perceived self-efficacy, or is annoyed by the digital technology's product usability or functionality [17]. Inevitably, these actions evoke Gen Z students' unnecessary postponement or delay in completing their learning tasks, known as procrastination behavior [18].

The dual nature of digital technology characteristics thus posed a challenge for human-communication interaction research to understand the association of procrastination and other factors influencing Gen Z students' usage of digital technology. This is a critical concern where the applications of digital technology for learning are widely proliferated and institutionalized, especially AI, which has significantly changed learning modalities [6, 19]. Extant studies have examined and identified factors that motivate the use of digital technology and the acceptability of technology for learning [20, 21]. Few have evaluated the effect of procrastination behavior concerning the usage and acceptability of digital technology [16], particularly within the digital informal learning environment. This study explored how Gen Z students engaged in digital informal learning by examining the factors, specifically technology acceptance, personal motivation, and procrastination behavior, influencing technology usage. Hence, the research questions are as follows: RQ1: What are the types of digital platforms, and to what extent do Gen Z students use them as part of their digital informal learning? RQ2: How do Gen Z students' technology acceptance, personal motivation, and procrastination behavior influence their use of technology for digital informal learning? To address the research questions, the theoretical framework from the technology acceptance model (TAM), procrastination behavior theory, and personal motivational framework will be used to operationalize the constructs and guide the study.

2 Literature Review

2.1 Digital Informal Learning and Technology Acceptance Model

Informal learning is generally conducted outside formal education and beyond the classroom that results from daily activities related to work, family, or leisure [10], as well as to supplement formal learning materials and curriculum [11, 22]. It is unstructured or unorganized regarding objectives, time, or learning support [23]. Informal learning allows students to actively discover, explore, expand their knowledge, and solve immediate problems [10, 11]. Students have control over the content they want to learn, the objectives they wish to achieve, and the choice of learning resources over the many learning platforms [11]. Digital platforms, such as social media and media content-sharing sites, have enabled informal learning to be performed online. Past studies have found digital technology to be an effective learning platform that provides engaging, flexible, and accessible learning materials [24–26]. YouTube, for example, besides providing entertainment, has a role in teaching and learning due to its ability to deliver multi-modalities (e.g., audio, visual, and graphics media) learning content [27–29].

Extant studies have applied different models to explain the factors influencing students' usage of digital technology for learning [20, 30]. The Technology Acceptance Model [TAM; 31], grounded in the Theory of Reason Action [TRA; 32], is a useful framework to conceptualize and determine the factors that might affect the usage of technology in the educational domain [20, 33]. It has been widely used to address users' attitudes and beliefs over their acceptance of digital technology. TAM hypothesized the relationship based on two beliefs and one attitudinal factor: perceived ease of use, usefulness, and attitude toward technology [34]. Perceived ease of use refers to the degree to which a user expects technology to be free from efforts, while perceived usefulness is the extent to which a user believes it would enhance job performance [34]. Attitude toward technology is the extent to which an individual feels about using the technology during a task [34].

Among the two beliefs, perceived usefulness has shown to be the most robust predictor of technology adoption [35, 36] as it concerns the overall impact (process and outcome) of technology. Perceived ease of use, meanwhile, only relates to the process and, thus, a logical subset of the perceived usefulness [34]. Past studies have shown that usage of digital technology depends on the acceptance of technology, and if applied effectively, it would reinforce their perception of usage [20, 30]. Thus, this study will adopt TAM as a reference to examine its influence on technology usage.

2.2   Motivation and Procrastination Behavior Towards Digital Informal Learning

Motivation, in a learning context, alludes to the student's intrinsic drive to engage in learning to achieve positive academic outcomes [37]. It encompasses a multifaceted construct, such as self-efficacy, task value, and intrinsic goals [38, 39]. Self-efficacy refers to students' belief in their capability to perform tasks effectively [38]. Task value denotes the perceived importance and relevance of the task, while intrinsic goals present satisfaction from the learning process and attainment [39]. In particular, motivated students are self-regulated, which helps them achieve the learning outcomes [40, 41]. Students would also be proactive in setting goals, managing their learning activities, and exercising effective learning strategies, such as using digital technology during their learning process [20, 21]. In contrast, the lack of motivation may result in delaying the completion of tasks, producing poor-quality work, or even low confidence in using digital technology, which affects the overall learning outcomes [20, 21].

Procrastination behavior is defined as the tendency always or nearly always to put off tasks [42]. In other words, it is an irrational behavior that delays planned tasks despite possible adverse outcomes [43, 44]. Procrastination is a perennial problem among students, even among university students, as learning becomes more self-regulated [43, 45]. Rozental and Carlbring [46] found that half of the surveyed student population reportedly engaged in habitual procrastination. Steel's (2007) profiling of procrastinators shows they have poor time management skills or disorganization in their academic tasks, while Howell, Watson, Powell and Buro [47]'s finding shows that procrastinators mostly fail to follow through with their plans or intentions.

Besides affecting students in traditional classroom-based learning, it is a significant problem affecting students who use digital technology [18, 48]. A past study found that a digital learning environment has a higher degree of learning freedom, limited supervision and guidance by instructors, and offers lower social interactions than classroom-based learning [18]. Thus, the demands on self-regulation, motivation, and efforts required by the students are also significantly higher [49–51]. Further, procrastinating students could harbor irrational beliefs about their inability to complete tasks or have lower self-efficacy in executing tasks [43, 48, 52]. In addition, the characteristics and functionality of digital technology also evoke procrastination behavior if students harbor negative perceptions, such as disrupting their routine learning habits, does not serve practical learning purposes, or the learning materials or activities are less stimulating and comprehensible [17, 48]. In contrast, when the digital technology implemented to host the learning is not disruptive, students are less likely to procrastinate and tend to accomplish tasks on time [48].

Therefore, against this backdrop, understanding the competing effect of motivation and procrastination behavior within the digital technology context would provide greater insight and explain Gen Z students' overall use of digital technology.

2.3   Conceptual Model for This Study

Most past studies discussed the association of technology acceptance with factors such as motivation or procrastination [16, 51]. Few have integrated these factors to investigate their correlation to understand and explain the dynamics influencing Gen Z students' technology usage. Hence, based on the identified gaps, the conceptual model is suggested in Fig. 1 with the following hypotheses:

H_1: Technology acceptance is negatively associated with procrastination behavior.
H_2: Technology acceptance is positively associated with digital informal learning.
H_3: Personal motivation is negatively associated with procrastination behavior.
H_4: Personal motivation is positively associated with digital informal learning.
H_5: Procrastination behavior is positively associated with digital informal learning.

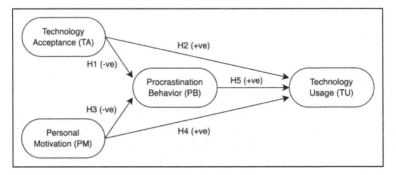

Fig. 1. Conceptual model and hypotheses

3 Method

3.1 Data Collection

This study was approved by the institutional review board (IRB-2023–232) and the online survey was conducted between April and June 2023. Convenience sampling was used to recruit Gen Z students from a local university aged between 21 and 26, studying part-time or full-time, regardless of nationality. A total of 391 participants were recruited, of which 305 were valid after filtering off responses that failed attention checks in the survey, aged 27 and beyond, or had missing values of measurement items exceeding 10% [53].

The participants were first asked to recall their most recent course taken in the past semester(s) and that they had engaged in digital informal learning to fulfill or supplement their formal learning. This information would then guide the participants to answer the remaining questions in four sections pertaining to digital informal learning: (1) technology use for learning, (2) technology acceptance, (3) personal motivational factor, and (4) procrastination behavior. The survey ended with the demographic questions, and participants were compensated for their time and effort through a local online payment system.

3.2 Measures

The research instrument, comprised of 65 items, was based on the adaptation of developed scales and measurements used in prior research to collect participants' self-reporting data. The constructs were from the technology acceptance model [34], motivational beliefs framework [38, 54], pure procrastination scale [55], and the measures for technology usage for learning platforms and activities were adapted from Thompson [56] and Lai et al. (2012) studies, respectively. In addition, a 1-item attention filter question was included to check the data reliability [57]. The collected data was randomly split into two datasets for exploratory factor analysis (EFA) and confirmatory factor analysis (CFA) to examine the validity of the measured scales and validate the conceptual model, respectively. The structural equation model (SEM) was then applied to evaluate the model's significance and the relationships' hypotheses. The evaluation threshold for the model fit is based on the criteria of CFI $> .95$, RMSEA $< .05$, including a 90% confidence interval, and SRMR $< .08$ [58].

Using the first randomly split data, EFA validated a six-factor model that omitted the sub-scale, intrinsic goal orientation, under the personal motivation factor. CFA evaluated the second half of the randomly split data and showed that the model is within the recommended threshold [58], where $\chi 2(256) = 298.906$, $p < .05$; TLI $= .980$; CFI $= .983$; RMSEA $= .033$, 90% CI [.010, .048]; SRMR $= .062$. Finally, the structural model was constructed for the hypothesized paths, and similarly, the model fit is within the recommended threshold [58], $\chi 2(259) = 445.272$, $p < .001$; TLI $= .989$; CFI $= .990$; RMSEA $= .040$, 90% CI [.031, .048]; SRMR $= .061$.

4 Data Analysis and Results

4.1 Descriptive Statistics

From the 305 valid responses, 33.4% were male ($n = 102$) and 66.6% were female ($n = 203$), with ages ranging from 21 to 26 ($M = 22.9$, $SD = 1.38$). Of these, 97.1% (n = 296) were full-time Gen Z students, and 2.9% (n = 9) attended part-time. 87.5% ($n = 267$) were undergraduates; the remaining 12.5% were postgraduates ($n = 38$). Meanwhile, 42.0% ($n = 128$) were from STEMM discipline, and 58.0% ($n = 177$) were from non-STEMM. Regarding the learning environment that the participants would relate to during the online survey, most reported that their instructional formats were conducted online (62.0%, $n = 189$), and 38.0% ($n = 116$) attended in-class courses. Also, more than half of the course duration lasted over three months (51.5%, $n = 157$), with the remaining (48.5%, $n = 148$) ranging between three months to a week. Lastly, out of the 305 responses, 69.8% ($n = 213$) reported having procrastination tendencies, 27.9% ($n = 85$) had a lower tendency to procrastinate, and 2.3% ($n = 7$) were neutral about their procrastination tendency.

Among the seventeen types of digital informal learning platforms surveyed, the top three frequently used were academic social networks (79.7%, e.g., ResearchGate) with an average of approximately three hours per week ($M = 2.86$, $SD = 1.38$, skewness $= .34$, kurtosis $= -.54$), video content sharing platforms (78.7%, e.g., YouTube) at a similar average of approximately three hours per week ($M = 2.84$, $SD = 1.39$, skewness

= .43, kurtosis = −.45), and social messaging (70.2%, e.g., WhatsApp, Telegram) at close to three hours per week ($M = 2.68$, $SD = 1.44$, skewness = .55, kurtosis = −.48). Notably, over half of the surveyed Gen Z students (52.0%, $n = 159$) widely used artificial intelligence at close to three hours per week ($M = 2.11$, $SD = 1.39$, skewness = 1.04, kurtosis = 0.19), with ChatGPT as the commonly reported platform.

4.2 Structural Equation Model

The results of SEM for the conceptual model are presented in Fig. 2. Technology acceptance (TA) had a significant negative direct association ($\beta = -.28$, $p < .005$) with procrastination behavior (PB), but the association with technology usage (TU) was not significant. Hence, H1 was supported while H2 was not. Meanwhile, personal motivation (PM) had a positive association with PB ($\beta = .21$, $p < .05$) and TU ($\beta = .24$, $p < .05$), resulting in H3 not being supported, while H4 was supported. Lastly, PB had a significant positive association ($\beta = .09$, $p < .001$) with TU. Thus, H5 was supported.

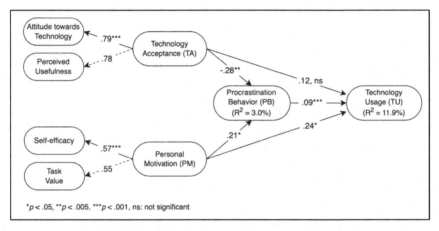

Fig. 2. Standarized estimate of the structural model.

5 Discussion

To address RQ1, we identified that of the seventeen common digital informal learning platforms, over 78% of Gen Z students were frequent users of academic social networks and video content-sharing platforms. These findings were unsurprising as they reflected the characteristics of Gen Z students who leverage digital technology to perform their formal learning, such as reviewing articles and seeking additional learning content to supplement their formal curriculum [59]. In addition, AI, which gained recent popularity with the launch of ChatGPT in November 2022, was also widely adopted by Gen Z students (52%). This shows that Gen Z students were quick to accept and assimilate new technology and innovation into their learning process if the digital platforms were deemed useful and relevant. The findings further amplify the digital native characteristics of the Gen Z cohort [60]. Nonetheless, future studies should examine the factors further to gain deeper insights into Gen Z's drive and motivation to adopt digital technology.

Regarding RQ2, the overall results from the SEM analysis indicated that the research model adequately explained Gen Z students' behavior and supported the hypotheses that technology acceptance and personal motivation, mediated by procrastination behavior, were positively associated with using digital technology for informal learning. TA is negatively associated (H1) with PB, consistent with previous findings that Gen Z students with positive TA would likely exhibit a lower PB as Gen Z students perceived that technology could effectively assist them in learning tasks [17, 48]. However, TA association (H2) with TU was not significant, contrasting with past studies' findings [20, 61]. One plausible reason is that digital technology has been tightly coupled with our environment over the past few decades, and consequently, Gen Z grew up in this digital environment. Technology was a fundamental and central part of their daily lives, and they had fewer concerns about their perception of technology [60].

Meanwhile, PM is positively associated with and directly influences (H4) TU. This aligns with similar studies where motivation is essential to technology usage due to the highly self-regulated environment [21]. However, PM (H3) had a marginally significant positive effect on PB. The finding was unexpected as previous studies have shown that low personal motivation causes procrastination behavior [51, 62]. A possible explanation, according to Chu and Choi [63], is that the behavior observed is a form of active procrastination, such that Gen Z students made the deliberate decisions to procrastinate given their higher ability to manage time, stronger self-efficacy beliefs, and positive learning styles [63], or that the task might be deemed unappealing (i.e., low task value) that does not require immediate attention [64].

Lastly, the indirect effects of TA and PM mediated by PB (H5) were significant and positively associated with TU with lower effects when compared to the direct influences. The findings show that PB plays a vital role in influencing Gen Z students' effort and perseverance in using digital technology in their learning.

5.1 Implications

There are important theoretical implications. This study empirically shows that Gen Z students are likely to learn differently from past generations based on two findings. First, this study observed the traits of active procrastination among Gen Z students, which contradicted most past studies. This is an important finding as it changes the fundamental understanding of behavioral research and warrants a rethink from Gen Z's perspective. Second, this study observed Gen Z students' diminishing effects of perceived usefulness and attitude toward technology usage. This contradicts past studies and could be attributed to Gen Z's exposure to technology throughout their developmental years. Hence, future studies could review TAM and Gen Z's traits and characteristics to better model the users' behavior.

Regarding practical implications, Gen Z students were observed to be quick in adopting and accepting the use of technology for learning. Hence, the finding underscores the importance for researchers and academics to keep abreast of new and innovative digital technology within the educational domain to provide a timely evaluation of the impact and develop policies or guidance to regulate the use of new technology in education.

5.2 Limitations

This study is not without limitations. First, the Gen Z students were recruited from a local university. Their cultural and societal background may influence their learning preferences and characteristics. Hence, the findings should not be generalized across Gen Z students in different countries. Second, although this study took a broad approach to evaluate Gen Z students' technology usage behavior instead of focusing on specific, the results provided a better understanding of the overall digital technology landscape. Nonetheless, despite these limitations, the findings contributed to the body of knowledge on the influences of factors on Gen Z students' utilization of technology to support their informal learning.

6   Conclusion

This study offers a fresh perspective on how Gen Z students engaged in digital informal learning by examining technology acceptance and personal motivation factors mediated by Gen Z's procrastination behavior. In particular, this study provides two preliminary insights that contradict earlier studies. First, Gen Z students' early exposure to technology diminished the effects of predictors towards technology usage, perceived use of technology, and attitude. Second, Gen Z students exhibit active procrastination behavior that influences technology usage despite displaying positive motivation. These two findings indicate that Gen Z students will likely learn differently from past generations. This stems from the fact that Gen Z students are raised in a digital environment, possess a more intuitive understanding of digital technology to quickly embark on it. Thus, they could often use it widely in most aspects of their learning. In contrast, students of past generations had to learn and adapt to digital technology before applying it to their learning, which could slow down their adoption or rejection of digital technology for learning. Therefore, future behavioral research would need to factor in the context of Gen Z characteristics.

Acknowledgments. This research is supported by the Ministry of Education, Singapore under its Tertiary Education Research Fund (Award MOE2023-TRF-028). Any opinions, findings, conclusions, or recommendations expressed in this material are those of the author(s) and do not reflect the views of the Ministry of Education, Singapore.

References

1. Dimock, M.: Defining generations: Where millennials end and generation Z begins. Pew Research Center (2019). https://www.pewresearch.org/short-reads/2019/01/17/where-millennials-end-and-generation-z-begins/

2. Parker, K., Igielnik, R.: On the cusp of adulthood and facing an uncertain future: what we know about gen Z so far. Pew Research Center (2020). https://www.pewresearch.org/social-trends/2020/05/14/on-the-cusp-of-adulthood-and-facing-an-uncertain-future-what-we-know-about-gen-z-so-far-2/

3. Alruthaya, A., Nguyen, T.-T., Lokuge, S.: The application of digital technology and the learning characteristics of generation Z in higher education. In: Australasian Conference on Information Systems 2021 Proceedings. (2021). https://aisel.aisnet.org/acis2021/65

4. Prensky, M.: Digital natives, digital immigrants Part 1. On the Horizon **9**, 1–6 (2001). https://doi.org/10.1108/10748120110424816

5. Chui, M., et al.: The Economic Potential of Generative AI: The Next Productivity Frontier. McKinsey & Company, Chicago (2023)

6. Haleem, A., Javaid, M., Qadri, M.A., Suman, R.: Understanding the role of digital technologies in education: a review. Sustain. Oper. Comput. **3**, 275–285 (2022). https://doi.org/10.1016/j.susoc.2022.05.004

7. Bernacki, M.L., Greene, J.A., Crompton, H.: Mobile technology, learning, and achievement: advances in understanding and measuring the role of mobile technology in education. Contemp. Educ. Psychol. **60**, 101827 (2020). https://doi.org/10.1016/j.cedpsych.2019.101827

8. Green, J.S.: Literature Review in Informal Learning with Technology Outside School. Futurelab Series. Futurelab, London (2004)

9. Tannenbaum, S.I., Beard, R.L., McNall, L.A., Salas, E.: Informal learning and development in organizations. In: Kozlowski, S.W.J., Salas, E. (eds.) Learning, Training, and Development in Organizations, pp. 303–331. Routledge/Taylor & Francis Group (2010)

10. Boekaerts, M., Minnaert, A.: Self-regulation with respect to informal learning. Int. J. Educ. Res. **31**, 533–544 (1999). https://doi.org/10.1016/S0883-0355(99)00020-8

11. Lange, P.G.: Informal learning on YouTube. In: The International Encyclopedia of Media Literacy, pp. 1–11 (2018)

12. Perna, L.W., et al.: Moving through MOOCs: understanding the progression of users in massive open online courses. Educ. Res. **43**, 421–432 (2014). https://doi.org/10.3102/0013189X14562423

13. Hager, P.: Lifelong learning and the contribution of informal learning. In: Aspin, D., Chapman, J., Hatton, M., Sawano, Y. (eds.) International Handbook of Lifelong Learning, pp. 79–92. Springer, Dordrecht (2001)

14. Rozgonjuk, D., Kattago, M., Täht, K.: Social media use in lectures mediates the relationship between procrastination and problematic smartphone use. Comput. Hum. Behav. **89**, 191–198 (2018). https://doi.org/10.1016/j.chb.2018.08.003

15. Dela Vega, M.G.A., Flores, R.B., Magusib, A.J.M.: 'Connected ka pa ba?': a study on how social media usage affects face-to-face interactions within the home. Asian J. Media Commun. **1**, 83–92 (2017). https://doi.org/10.20885/asjmc.vol1.iss1.art7

16. Türel, Y.K., Dokumacı, O.: Use of media and technology, academic procrastination, and academic achievement in adolescence. Participat. Educ. Res. **9**, 481–497 (2022). https://doi.org/10.17275/per.22.50.9.2

17. Xiao, Y., Spanjol, J.: Yes, but not now! why some users procrastinate in adopting digital product updates. J. Bus. Res. **135**, 685–696 (2021). https://doi.org/10.1016/j.jbusres.2021.06.066

18. Svartdal, F., Dahl, T.I., Gamst-Klaussen, T., Koppenborg, M., Klingsieck, K.B.: How study environments foster academic procrastination: overview and recommendations. Front. Psychol. **11**, 54090 (2020). https://doi.org/10.3389/fpsyg.2020.540910

19. Crompton, H., Burke, D.: Artificial intelligence in higher education: the state of the field. Int. J. Educ. Technol. High. Educ. **20**, 22 (2023). https://doi.org/10.1186/s41239-023-00392-8

20. Lai, C., Wang, Q., Lei, J.: What factors predict undergraduate students' use of technology for learning? a case from Hong Kong. Comput. Educ. **59**, 569–579 (2012). https://doi.org/10.1016/j.compedu.2012.03.006

21. Aguilera-Hermida, A.P.: College students' use and acceptance of emergency online learning due to COVID-19. Int. J. Educ. Res. Open **1**, 100011 (2020). https://doi.org/10.1016/j.ijedro.2020.100011

22. He, T., Zhu, C.: Digital informal learning among Chinese university students: the effects of digital competence and personal factors. Int. J. Educ. Technol. High. Educ. **14**, 44 (2017). https://doi.org/10.1186/s41239-017-0082-x

23. Yu, H., Liu, P., Huang, X., Cao, Y.: Teacher online informal learning as a means to innovative teaching during home quarantine in the COVID-19 pandemic. Front. Psychol. **12**, 596582 (2021). https://doi.org/10.3389/fpsyg.2021.596582

24. Patmanthara, S., Febiharsa, D., Dwiyanto, F.A.: Social media as a learning media: a comparative analysis of YouTube, WhatsApp, Facebook and Instagram utilization. In: International Conference on Electrical, Electronics and Information Engineering, pp. 183–186 (2019). https://doi.org/10.1109/ICEEIE47180.2019.8981441

25. Zhou, Q., Lee, C.S., Sin, J.S.C., Lin, S., Hu, H., Ismail, M.F.F.B.: Understanding the use of YouTube as a learning resource: a social cognitive perspective. Aslib J. Inf. Manag. **72**, 339–359 (2020). https://doi.org/10.1108/AJIM-10-2019-0290

26. MacLeod, L., Storey, M.A., Bergen, A.: Code, camera, action: how software developers document and share program knowledge using YouTube. In: 23rd IEEE International Conference on Program Comprehension, pp. 104–114 (2015). doi:https://doi.org/10.1109/ICPC.2015.19

27. Bonk, C.J.: YouTube anchors and enders: the use of shared online video content as a macro-context for learning. Asia-Pacfic Collab. Educ. J. **7**, 13–24 (2011). http://publicationshare.com/pdfs/201103.pdf

28. Lee, C.S., Osop, H., Goh, D.H.L., Kelni, G.: Making sense of comments on YouTube educational videos: a self-directed learning perspective. Online Inf. Rev. **41**, 611–625 (2017). https://doi.org/10.1108/OIR-09-2016-0274

29. Lim, K.K., Lee, C.S.: Informal learning trends on YouTube during the COVID-19 pandemic: a topic modeling analysis. Proc. Assoc. Inf. Sci. Technol. **60**, 1049–1051 (2023). https://doi.org/10.1002/pra2.941

30. He, T., Zhu, C., Questier, F.: Predicting digital informal learning: an empirical study among Chinese University students. Asia Pac. Educ. Rev. **19**, 79–90 (2018). https://doi.org/10.1007/s12564-018-9517-x

31. Davis, F.D.: Perceived usefulness, perceived ease of use, and user acceptance of information technology. MIS Q. **13**, 319–340 (1989). https://doi.org/10.2307/249008

32. Fishbein, M., Ajzen, I.: Belief, Attitude, Intention, and Behavior: An Introduction to Theory and Research. Addison-Wesley, Reading (1975)

33. McGill, T.J., Klobas, J.E.: A task–technology fit view of learning management system impact. Comput. Educ. **52**, 496–508 (2009). https://doi.org/10.1016/j.compedu.2008.10.002

34. Davis, F.D.: User acceptance of information technology: system characteristics, user perceptions and behavioral impacts. Int. J. Man Mach. Stud. **38**, 475–487 (1993). https://doi.org/10.1006/imms.1993.1022

35. Yousafzai, S.Y., Foxall, G.R., Pallister, J.G.: Technology acceptance: a meta-analysis of the TAM: part 1. J. Model. Manag. **2**, 251–280 (2007). https://doi.org/10.1108/17465660710834453

36. Lee, Y.H., Kozar, K.A., Larsen, K.R.T.: The technology acceptance model: past, present and future. Commun. Assoc. Inf. Syst. 12, 50 (2003). https://doi.org/10.17705/1CAIS.01250

37. Cook, D.A., Artino, A.R., Jr.: Motivation to learn: an overview of contemporary theories. Med. Educ. **50**, 997–1014 (2016). https://doi.org/10.1111/medu.13074

38. Bandura, A.: Social cognitive theory. In: Vasta, R. (ed.) Annals of Child Development: Six Theories of Child Development, vol. 6, pp. 1–60. JAI Press, Greenwich (1989)
39. Pintrich, P.R.: The role of goal orientation in self-regulated learning. In: Boekaerts, M., Pintrich, P., Zeidner, M. (eds.) Handbook of Self-regulation, pp. 452–502. Academic Press, San Diego (2000)
40. Kemp, A., Palmer, E., Strelan, P.: A taxonomy of factors affecting attitudes towards educational technologies for use with technology acceptance models. Brit. J. Educ. Technol. **50**, 2394–2413 (2019). https://doi.org/10.1111/bjet.12833
41. Albelbisi, N., Yusop, F.: Factors influencing learners' self-regulated learning skills in a massive open online course (MOOC) environment. Turk. Online J. Dist. Educ. **20**, 1–16 (2019). https://doi.org/10.17718/tojde.598191
42. Rothblum, E.D., Solomon, L.J., Murakami, J.: Affective, cognitive, and behavioral differences between high and low procrastinators. J. Couns. Psychol. **33**, 387 (1986). https://doi.org/10.1037/0022-0167.33.4.387
43. Steel, P.: The nature of procrastination: a meta-analytic and theoretical review of quintessential self-regulatory failure. Psychol. Bull. **133**, 65–94 (2007). https://doi.org/10.1037/0033-2909.133.1.65
44. Senécal, C., Julien, E., Guay, F.: Role conflict and academic procrastination: a self-determination perspective. Eur. J. Soc. Psychol. **33**, 135–145 (2003). https://doi.org/10.1002/ejsp.144
45. Ferrari, J.R.: Procrastination as self-regulation failure of performance: effects of cognitive load, self-awareness, and time limits on 'working best under pressure.' Eur. J. Pers. **15**, 391–406 (2001). https://doi.org/10.1002/per.413
46. Rozental, A., Carlbring, P.: Understanding and treating procrastination: a review of a common self-regulatory failure. Psychology **5**, 1488–1502 (2014). https://doi.org/10.4236/psych.2014.513160
47. Howell, A.J., Watson, D.C., Powell, R.A., Buro, K.: Academic procrastination: the pattern and correlates of behavioural postponement. Pers. Individ. Differ. **40**, 1519–1530 (2006). https://doi.org/10.1016/j.paid.2005.11.023
48. Cheng, S.-L., Xie, K.: Why college students procrastinate in online courses: a self-regulated learning perspective. Internet High. Educ. **50**, 100807 (2021). https://doi.org/10.1016/j.iheduc.2021.100807
49. Elvers, G.C., Polzella, D.J., Graetz, K.: Procrastination in online courses: performance and attitudinal differences. Teach. Psychol. **30**, 159–162 (2003). https://doi.org/10.1207/S15328023TOP3002_13
50. Klingsieck, K.B., Fries, S., Horz, C., Hofer, M.: Procrastination in a distance university setting. Dist. Educ. **33**, 295–310 (2012). https://doi.org/10.1080/01587919.2012.723165
51. Rakes, G.C., Dunn, K.E.: The impact of online graduate students' motivation and self-regulation on academic procrastination. J. Interact. Online Learn. **9**, 78–93 (2010). https://www.learntechlib.org/p/109409/
52. Bridges, K.R., Roig, M.: Academic procrastination and irrational thinking: a re-examination with context controlled. Pers. Individ. Differ. **22**, 941–944 (1997). https://doi.org/10.1016/S0191-8869(96)00273-5
53. Bennett, D.A.: How can I deal with missing data in my study? Aust. New Zealand J. Public Health **25**, 464–469 (2001). https://pubmed.ncbi.nlm.nih.gov/11688629/
54. Pintrich, P.R., de Groot, E.V.: Motivational and self-regulated learning components of classroom academic performance. J. Educ. Psychol. **82**, 33–40 (1990). https://doi.org/10.1037/0022-0663.82.1.33
55. Steel, P.: Pure Procrastination Scale (PPS) APA PsycTests (2010). https://doi.org/10.1037/t10499-000

56. Thompson, P.: The digital natives as learners: technology use patterns and approaches to learning. Comput. Educ. **65**, 12–33 (2013). https://doi.org/10.1016/j.compedu.2012.12.022
57. Kung, F.Y.H., Kwok, N., Brown, D.J.: Are attention check questions a threat to scale validity? Appl. Psychol. **67**, 264–283 (2018). https://doi.org/10.1111/apps.12108
58. Hu, L.T., Bentler, P.M.: Cutoff criteria for fit indexes in covariance structure analysis: conventional criteria versus new alternatives. Struct. Eq. Model. Multidisc. J. **6**, 1–55 (1999). https://doi.org/10.1080/10705519909540118
59. Carraro, K., Trinder, R.: Technology in formal and informal learning environments: student perspectives. Glob. J. Foreign Lang. Teach. **11**, 39–50 (2021). https://doi.org/10.18844/gjflt.v11i1.5219
60. Blocksidge, K., Primeau, H.: Adapting and evolving: generation Z's information beliefs. J. Acad. Librariansh. **49**, 102686 (2023). https://doi.org/10.1016/j.acalib.2023.102686
61. Sprenger, D.A., Schwaninger, A.: Technology acceptance of four digital learning technologies (classroom response system, classroom chat, e-lectures, and mobile virtual reality) after three months' usage. Int. J. Educ. Technol. High. Educ. **18**, 8 (2021). https://doi.org/10.1186/s41239-021-00243-4
62. Yang, C.-Y., Lai, A.-F., Chen, M.-C., Hwang, M.-H., Li, C.-Y.: An investigation on procrastination in the e-learning environment. In: 2012 8th International Conference on Information Science and Digital Content Technology (ICIDT2012), pp. 616–620 (2012)
63. Chu, A.H.C., Choi, J.N.: Rethinking procrastination: positive effects of "active" procrastination behavior on attitudes and performance. J. Soc. Psychol. **145**, 245–264 (2005). https://doi.org/10.3200/SOCP.145.3.245-264
64. Hensley, L.C.: Reconsidering active procrastination: relations to motivation and achievement in college anatomy. Learn. Individ. Differ. **36**, 157–164 (2014). https://doi.org/10.1016/j.lindif.2014.10.012

Collaboration of Digital Human Gestures and Teaching Materials for Enhanced Integration in MOOC Teaching Scenarios

Yaxin Liu, Xiaomei Nie(✉), and Zhiyong Wu

Shenzhen International Graduate School, Tsinghua University, Shenzhen, Guangdong, People's Republic of China
yx-liu22@mails.tsinghua.edu.cn, nie.xiaomei@sz.tsinghua.edu.cn

Abstract. Intelligent-driven digital humans, typically taking text or voice as input, achieve realistic human-like images or models with driven facial expressions, lip synchronization, and body movements, and have already been widely used in short video production and other fields. This technology also offers a novel solution to the issues of teachers' reluctance to appear on camera and the lengthy recording process in MOOCs. However, using digital humans for teaching requires educational adaptation in MOOC scenarios. This paper, starting from the teacher's indicative functions in teaching, enhances the interaction between digital humans and the virtual teaching environment based on existing intelligent-driven digital human technology. We record digital human poses based on the BVH skeletal structure, using text scripts and corresponding Power-Points (PPTs) as the initial input, and then complete the synthesis of collaborative gestures through three steps of Data Preparation, Data-driven Pose Generation and Collaborative Gesture Synthesis. The first step obtains the timing and position information of keywords, which will be used for the generation of inverse kinematics(IK)-controlled gesture animation in the third step. After stitching and rendering, the digital human will behaviorally emphasize key teaching information. Future work will focus on integrating varied collaborative gestures, incorporating spatial and temporal input data, and calculating relative distances and orientations in complex scenes. This will establish a robust mapping between objects and gestures, enhancing the collaboration between digital humans and educational materials in 3D space.

Keywords: Digital Human · Collaborative Gesture Generation · MOOC

1 Introduction

A virtual digital human is a digital avatar with a real person's appearance and behavioral characteristics. Early virtual digital humans mainly focused on the similarity of appearance to real people, relying on modeling and rendering software such as Maya and UE to achieve animation effects in film, television, games,

C. Stephanidis et al. (Eds.): HCII 2024, CCIS 2117, pp. 169–175, 2024.
https://doi.org/10.1007/978-3-031-61953-3_19

and other fields. Recently, a series of artificial intelligence algorithms, such as speech synthesis [6], image generation [3,12], and GPTs, have promoted the development focus of virtual digital humans from digital appearance to intelligent behavior and thinking. Intelligence-driven digital humans typically take voice or text scripts as input to achieve natural animation effects by driving the synchronous synthesis of facial expressions [14], lips [11], and body movements of 2D photos or 3D digital human models, which have already been widely used in live broadcasts, short video production to facilitate efficient digital content production. MOOC is a digital carrier of teachers' teaching content. Digital humans that integrate multiple intelligent-driven algorithms can not only effectively reduce the time teachers spend re-recording but also provide novel solutions to the issues of teachers' reluctance to appear on camera.

Algorithmic solutions for intelligently generating synchronized gestures often extract the prosodic and semantic information contained in speech and text to achieve natural gestures accompanying speech [5,15]. Recently, researchers have been exploring some application-oriented gesture-generation solutions. Tenglong Ao's GestureDiffuClip [1] uses text, video, and motion prompts to create stylized co-speech gestures, expanding the digital human gesture application domain. Cheng Yang's Freetalker [13] system incorporates speaker gestures during silence and non-spontaneous behaviors into co-speech gesture generation, allowing for natural digital human performances in Ted talks.

Using digital humans for teaching requires educational adaptation in MOOC scenarios. It is indicated that the presentation of the teacher's image is more in line with learners' preferences and promotes attention investment [4,9]. Moreover, the teacher's gestures function as visual cues that facilitate learners' focus on salient aspects of the instructional content [4]. Effective collaboration of digitally generated gestures with teaching materials is vital for enhancing the use of digital humans in MOOC production. Traditional gesture categories include symbolic, metaphorical, rhythmic, and indicative gestures [10]. In the context of teaching, indicative gestures, which are often triggered by speech keywords, provide directional information and reflect collaboration with the external environment. Other gesture types synchronize with the teacher's speech content. Based on the above, this paper starts from the perspective of enhancing the ability to convey teaching content, merging data-driven production of gestures that synchronize speaking voices and indicative gestures generated from keywords and orientation information, to realize digital humans' collaborative expression with external teaching materials.

2   Method

The application of digital human technology-empowered teaching scenarios mainly includes two major elements: digital human and teaching environment, which respectively represent the roles of teachers and classrooms in real teaching. The former requires first having appropriate digital assets, such as teachers' digital clones, and combining them with effective driving methods. The teaching environment includes teaching materials that directly convey teaching materials and backgrounds that do not directly convey information. Collaborative gestures are mainly used between driving methods and teaching materials.

Based on the above structure, to reduce the complexity of realizing digital human collaboration with teaching materials, the following conditions are set in advance:

1. While the 3D digital human is well-suited for exploring a more enriching and varied 3D instructional environment, the current teaching materials do not account for complex and diverse 3D elements. Instead, the initial approach uses standard 2D PowerPoint (PPTs) presentations as the input medium.
2. The collaboration of digital humans and teaching materials will take place in 3D space. To comply with the laws of physical observation, it is necessary to first plan and construct the overall scene so that the position of the whiteboard where the digital human and teaching materials are connected is relatively fixed (Fig. 1).

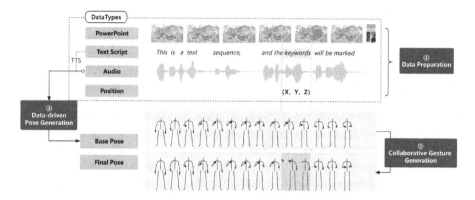

Fig. 1. Based on the consistency of text, audio, and corresponding action sequences in time length, realizing collaborative gestures mainly includes three key steps: data preparation, data-driven pose generation, and collaborative gesture synthesis.

2.1   Data Preparation

We developed a data collection platform using Python Django for the backend and Vue.js for the frontend, which facilitates the integration of text scripts, PPTs, audio, keywords, and target positions. The platform allows teachers to upload text scripts and corresponding PPTs, with each page of the scripts demarcated using a "[page]" token. Next, Teachers are required to highlight keywords in the text and mark the corresponding emphasis coordinates on the PPT slides. Combined with the previously preset scene layout, the relative coordinates of the target point in the 3D space based on the digital human root node can be calculated. Additionally, the backend employs Text-to-Speech (TTS) technology to generate audio files, which are then processed using Google's Speech-to-Text

SDK to obtain precise timestamps for each character. This allows for the determination of the start and end times of keyword occurrences within the audio. The final data will be stored in the database in the form of [page number, keywords, time range, target 3D coordinates].

2.2   Data-Driven Pose Generation

Dataset. We select Chinese drama clips as the data source, referring to the BEAT [7] dataset, and achieve data collection by recording the model's voice and facial expressions and motion capture to obtain the model's movements. After data collection, we engaged in a refinement process that involved realigning certain joints' normal directions and rectifying any discrepancies, thereby upholding data integrity. To date, we have processed 2.25 h of data for a female speaker, using the Facial Action Coding System(FACS) for facial discretization with 51 channels and BVH files for skeletal structure and motion capture, with 63 joints and corresponding feature channels for position and rotation. This dataset serves as the basis for model training.

Model. The overall model architecture is based on the baseline model CAMN [7]. We aimed to predict facial expressions and poses concurrently, a task made possible by the data's dimensionality. However, unlike the BEAT dataset, we omitted emotional labeling and TextGrid creation, citing challenges in precise emotional annotation and issues with the Montreal Forced Aligner, such as missing words, during Chinese TextGrid generation. In the training phase, we treat audio and speaker ID as input and output spliced time series of facial and body action feature channels. Inspired by audio-driven pose generation techniques [8], we compensate for the absence of text input by dividing audio features into low-dimensional and high-dimensional components. The low-dimensional features are encoded using the original WavEncoder in the CAMN framework, while the high-dimensional features are extracted using a pre-trained Chinese Wav2Vec [2] Model. Gesture actions are then generated via Bi-LSTM. We employed an A100 GPU to train the model for 100 epochs, saving the corresponding parameter file for subsequent predictions. Following simple dimension segmentation and data preparation, we produced a base gesture sequence for further processing.

2.3   Collaborative Gesture Synthesis

The paper leverages Blender's Python API for automated collaborative gesture synthesis, defining gestures through time intervals including [start frame, end frame] and target positions [x, y, z]. The collaborative gesture is designed as three steps: pointing, holding, and retracting phases, with a target frame marking the end of pointing and a 5-frame delay for the holding phase's end. IK-based collaborative gesture synthesis is conducted from the Base Pose, using an extruded bone as an IK controller to control the RightForeArm and RightArm joints. Generating collaborative gesture animations involves setting IK controller position keyframes, with the controller's initial and final positions synchronized at the Base Pose's RightForeArm joint tail for seamless data integration. Short keyword intervals allow shared start and end frames for gestures, with retracting before the end for a natural transition. IK-driven skeleton data is then merged into the Base Pose to synthesize the complete collaborative action (Fig. 2).

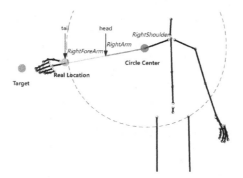

Fig. 2. The figure shows part of the structure of the skeleton. Each joint includes a head and a tail. When the target location cannot be reached, the IK controller locates the intersection between the line connecting the RightShoulder Joint's tail to the target position and the circle with the RightShoulder Joint's tail as the center and the arm length as the radius.

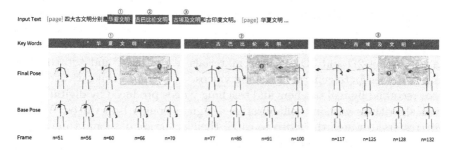

Fig. 3. This is a figure showing hand movements within the time frame corresponding to the keyword through pointing to emphasize the target location.

3   Results

In order to verify the feasibility of the above method, we used 2 pages of PPT and corresponding text scripts for testing. According to the system process, we get the final pose as shown in Fig. 3. Within the time frame that requires collaboration, the arms point to the target position, achieving the expected goal of collaborative gestures. Compared with actions without collaborative gestures (base pose), it seems to be more effective in guiding readers to see the key information in the teaching materials.

4 Future Work

The paper presents a system for coordinating digital human gestures with educational materials in teaching scenarios. After uploading text scripts and teaching materials, the system utilizes data preparation, data-driven pose generation, and IK-based collaborative gesture synthesis to create indicative gestures guided by spatial orientation, achieving natural gesture expression for digital humans in MOOCs. In both the short and long term, the system requires further refinement:

Currently, gesture direction changes in spliced areas can lead to unnatural expressions, and the range of IK-controlled gestures is limited. In practical teaching, emphasizing key points often involves more nuanced actions, such as circling, multiple clicks, and drawing lines, in addition to simple pointing. Future work will involve collecting and clustering various pointing methods used in existing MOOCs to enhance the diversity and naturalness of digital human gestures.

Next, we hope to achieve collaboration between teacher roles and 3D teaching materials in MOOC production in a 3D environment. We will sort out and encode the ways in which objects and teachers collaborate in 3D scenes, and automatically generate and match gesture sequences for collaborative expression by giving attributes such as size and category of 3D teaching materials as well as time and position information existing in the scene, which would broaden the application scenarios of digital humans.

Finally, we will do some validity verification work to make some solid demonstrations. Eye tracking technology is often considered a common means of detecting attention information, and there are also some methods to evaluate MOOC teaching including prior and post-test knowledge questionnaires, cognitive load questionnaires, and learning satisfaction questionnaires. We will choose a course as a test, using 2D and 3D teaching materials respectively, and add collaborative gesture design to generate teaching videos. At the same time, we use MOOC videos recorded by real teachers and teaching videos produced by digital human-driven algorithms without collaborative design as comparison videos. And then invite testers to watch the video to catch their attention data and time spent in key areas, and to fill out questionnaires and scales after watching. The effectiveness of the collaborative design of digital human gestures and teaching materials in supporting MOOC content will be verified by analyzing the quantitative and qualitative data obtained.

Acknowledgments. This work was supported by a research grant from Shenzhen Key Laboratory of next generation interactive media innovative technology (Funding No: ZDSYS20210623092001004), and the Center for Social Governance and Innovation at Tsinghua University, a major research center for Shenzhen Humanities & Social Sciences Key Research Bases, and was done when interned at Zhipu AI.

References

1. Ao, T., Zhang, Z., Liu, L.: GestureDiffuCLIP: gesture diffusion model with CLIP latents (2023). arXiv:2303.14613
2. Baevski, A., Zhou, H., Mohamed, A., Auli, M.: wav2vec 2.0: a framework for self-supervised learning of speech representations (2020)
3. Betker, J., et al.: Improving image generation with better captions (2023)
4. Kar, P., Chattopadhyay, S., Chakraborty, S.: Gestatten: estimation of user's attention in mobile MOOCs from eye gaze and gaze gesture tracking. Proc. ACM Hum.-Comput. Interact. **4**(EICS), 72:1–72:32 (2020). https://doi.org/10.1145/3394974
5. Kucherenko, T., et al.: Gesticulator: A framework for semantically-aware speech-driven gesture generation. In: Proceedings of the 2020 International Conference on Multimodal Interaction, pp. 242–250 (2020). https://doi.org/10.1145/3382507.3418815. arXiv:2001.09326
6. Li, Y.A., Han, C., Raghavan, V.S., Mischler, G., Mesgarani, N.: StyleTTS 2: towards human-level text-to-speech through style diffusion and adversarial training with large speech language models (2023). https://doi.org/10.48550/arXiv.2306.07691. arXiv:2306.07691
7. Liu, H., et al.: BEAT: a large-scale semantic and emotional multi-modal dataset for conversational gestures synthesis (2022). https://doi.org/10.48550/arXiv.2203.05297. arXiv:2203.05297
8. Liu, X., et al.: Learning hierarchical cross-modal association for co-speech gesture generation (2022). https://doi.org/10.48550/arXiv.2203.13161. arXiv:2203.13161
9. Mayer, R.E., Fiorella, L., Stull, A.: Five ways to increase the effectiveness of instructional video. Educ. Tech. Res. Dev. **68**(3), 837–852 (2020)
10. McNeill, D.: Gesture and thought. University of Chicago Press (2008). https://doi.org/10.7208/9780226514642
11. Prajwal, K.R., Mukhopadhyay, R., Namboodiri, V., Jawahar, C.V.: A lip sync expert is all you need for speech to lip generation in the wild. In: Proceedings of the 28th ACM International Conference on Multimedia, pp. 484–492 (2020). https://doi.org/10.1145/3394171.3413532. arXiv:2008.10010
12. Rombach, R., Blattmann, A., Lorenz, D., Esser, P., Ommer, B.: High-resolution image synthesis with latent diffusion models (2022). arXiv:2112.10752
13. Yang, S., Xu, Z., Xue, H., Cheng, Y., Huang, S., Gong, M., Wu, Z.: Freetalker: controllable speech and text-driven gesture generation based on diffusion models for enhanced speaker naturalness (2024). http://arxiv.org/abs/2401.03476. arXiv:2401.03476
14. Zhang, W., et al.: SadTalker: learning realistic 3D motion coefficients for stylized audio-driven single image talking face animation (2023). arXiv:2211.12194
15. Zhi, Y., et al.: LivelySpeaker: towards semantic-aware co-speech gesture generation. In: 2023 IEEE/CVF International Conference on Computer Vision (ICCV), pp. 20750–20760. IEEE, Paris (2023)

Enhancing an App for Sustaining Motivation in Learning

Tetsuya Nakatoh[(⊠)] [iD], Mamiko Miyagi, Ayana Ukegawa, and Aoiko Motoyama

Nakamura Gakuen University, 5-7-1 Befu, Jounan-ku, Fukuoka 814-0198, Japan
nakatoh@nakamura-u.ac.jp

Abstract. In this paper, we present the development of a mobile learning application de-signed for studying for the national examination for registered dietitians. The authors, affiliated with a registered dietitian training institution, have previously ad-dressed shortcomings in existing learning methods by providing an online learning application that resolves these issues and facilitates effective learning. However, a notable challenge has been identified in maintaining student motivation for individual study. To address this issue, we propose a mechanism for sustaining motivation and have implemented it in the existing online learning application. This paper not only describes the newly introduced features but also presents an analysis of the evaluation through surveys.

Keywords: Online Learning · Sustaining Motivation · Smartphone App · Registered Dietitian

1 Introduction

Dietitians play a crucial role as specialists in providing nutritional guidance, meal management, and support to individuals facing challenges with their diet, such as those undergoing illness, elderly individuals struggling with meals, and those aiming for health maintenance. In Japan, dietitians are nationally certified by the Ministry of Health, Labour and Welfare, requiring education at accredited institutions and successful completion of the national dietitian examination. This examination encompasses highly specialized questions across ten domains, demanding comprehensive knowledge.

While regular study proves highly effective, challenges arise from the necessity to carry textbooks and allocate time for dedicated study, hindering overall learning. As members of a dietitian training institution, we were concerned about the limitations of daily learning methods and existing online learning platforms. To overcome these challenges, we developed an online learning prototype application [1] aimed at promoting comprehensive learning. While the application proved effective, a new challenge emerged: sustaining motivation for the learning process itself.

This study introduces three new features focused on maintaining motivation for learning into the practical learning application developed in previous research. To assess the effectiveness of these features, we enlisted participants preparing for the national dietitian examination (final-year students at dietitian training facilities) to utilize the

C. Stephanidis et al. (Eds.): HCII 2024, CCIS 2117, pp. 176–179, 2024.
https://doi.org/10.1007/978-3-031-61953-3_20

application. The evaluation of the effectiveness of this initiative is based on their survey responses.

2 Method

Firstly, we will provide an explanation of the learning application [1] developed by the authors for the national examination for registered dietitians. Prior to developing this application, the authors investigated the features of existing learning applications designed for the national dietitian examination. These applications were designed to confirm knowledge in each field by providing past examination questions and their answers. Past examination questions effectively captured the required knowledge for registered dietitians, and learning based on these questions proved meaningful. However, the challenge arose from the fact that these questions were presented in a multiple-choice format, leading to memorization of question-answer patterns through repetitive learning, hindering the acquisition of appropriate knowledge.

In response to these challenges, the following mechanisms were devised:

1. Presenting questions in a true/false format and changing the question patterns with each session.
2. Displaying correct answers and explanations concurrently with the user's response.

These mechanisms largely addressed the identified issues. A learning application equipped with these features, along with a system for creating question data used within the application, was developed and implemented in educational settings.

In this study, three additional features aimed at maintaining motivation for studying were incorporated into this exam preparation application.

The first feature is a display of accuracy rankings, fostering a sense of competition among learners and elevating motivation. The second feature is an individual accuracy display, updating and presenting accuracy rates with each response to enhance motivation for achieving higher accuracy. The third feature is an encouragement message display. If the accuracy rate is high, a randomly selected encouragement message with humor is displayed. This feature aims not only to maintain motivation through positive reinforcement but also to introduce a relaxation effect through humor.

For evaluation purposes, these three features were implemented as separate functionalities within the application. Each time the application is used, one of these features is randomly available for use, allowing participants to try out all features. A survey was conducted among national examination candidates (final-year students at registered dietitian training institutions) to assess how each feature contributes to motivation maintenance.

3 Data Generation Process

We downloaded PDF files of past questions for the national examination for registered dietitians from the Ministry of Health, Labour and Welfare's website and semi-automatically converted them into text. After conversion, we visually inspected and corrected format distortions caused by symbol corruption or line breaks before transforming the content into CSV format. To rephrase the questions into a suitable format for a one-question-one-answer structure, we explored various methods and implemented pattern-based transformations. For instance, for multiple-choice questions like "Which of the following is correct? Please choose one," we displayed only one option and changed the question to "Is the following statement correct?" This resulted in the generation of five questions. Some questions were deemed unsuitable for the one-question-one-answer format, such as those affected by changes in "Dietary intake standards for Japanese people" [2] rendering them inappropriate, questions without a determined correct answer, questions involving charts or tables, and those presenting complex conditions in applied problems.

Over a span of six years from the 30th to the 35th national examination, we performed these operations and generated questions for a total of 1,200 items [1]. Additionally, for this study, we added questions from the 36th and 37th national examinations. As for the explanatory text, we extracted and utilized content created collaboratively by faculty members from the author's affiliated university, ensuring each explanation corresponds to a single question.

4 Results

A survey was conducted after participants were invited to utilize the implemented application for optional learning. Out of 39 users, responses were obtained from 18 individuals. The results of the aggregated survey responses are illustrated in graphs. Figure 1 depicts the summary of satisfaction levels. The proportion of responses indicating satisfaction (including satisfied and very satisfied) with each feature was significantly higher ($p < .001$). Figure 2 presents the aggregated responses to the question "Was it effective in maintaining motivation?" Here too, the proportion of responses indicating effectiveness in maintaining motivation was significantly higher ($p < .001$).

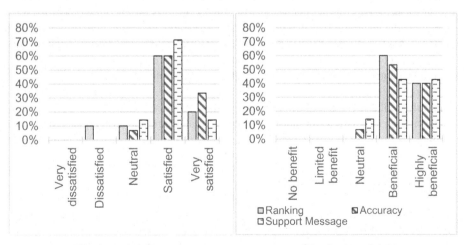

Fig. 1. Satisfaction   **Fig. 2.** Beneficial

Furthermore, insights gleaned from open-ended survey responses revealed the following. Comments regarding the ranking feature included statements such as "My motivation increased when I ranked higher" and "I felt motivated to strive for better rankings." These responses align with our expectations. Regarding the accuracy display feature, while it was intended to show "the user's accuracy at that moment," many users interpreted it as "the accuracy of that specific question," thus the conclusion regarding the intended functionality was inconclusive. Regarding the encouragement message display feature, voices expressing enjoyment in solving problems while anticipating messages were observed.

5 Conclusion

Based on the analysis results, it can be inferred that each feature contributed to maintaining motivation. Insights from the open-ended survey responses suggest the following: The ranking display feature appeared to enhance users' competitiveness, thereby contributing to motivation maintenance. Regarding the accuracy display feature, examples of misinterpretation were observed from the free-text responses in the survey. While the utility was not compromised, improvements in presentation methods are warranted to avoid misunderstandings. Additionally, since the feature "accuracy of that specific question" seemed beneficial as perceived by some users despite the misunderstanding, it will be considered for future implementation. The encouragement message display feature received high praise. Considering feedback indicating a desire for a wider range of messages, plans to expand the variety of messages are underway. Furthermore, suggestions such as "displaying history of incorrect questions" and "expanding explanations" were also noted. It is imperative to enhance the utility of the application by implementing these suggestions as additional features in the future.

Disclosure of Interests.   The authors have no competing interests to declare that are relevant to the content of this article.

References

1. Harada, H., et al.: A mobile learning app using past exam questions. In: 2023 14th IIAI International Congress on Advanced Applied Informatics (IIAI-AAI), Koriyama, Japan, pp. 754–755 (2023). https://doi.org/10.1109/IIAI-AAI59060.2023.00161
2. Dietary intake standards for Japanese people. https://www.mhlw.go.jp/stf/seisakunitsuite/bunya/kenkou_iryou/kenkou/eiyou/syokuji_kijyun.html. (Japanese)

Multi-dimensional Three-Dimensional Space Learning in Human-Computer Interaction

Li Ou Yang[1] , Yunyi Zhuang[1] , and Jie Ling[2(✉)]

[1] Guangzhou Academy of Fine Arts, Guangzhou, Guangdong, China
[2] Zhongkai University of Agriculture and Engineering, Guangzhou, Guangdong, China
47219382@qq.com

Abstract. This study deeply explores the application and efficacy of multi-dimensional three-dimensional space learning in the field of human-computer interaction (human-computer interaction) technology. Three-dimensional space learning plays an important role in cultivating students' spatial cognitive abilities and creativity. At the same time, human-computer interaction technology provides extensive support through multimedia and multi-sensory input, thereby enriching and improving the teaching process. This study takes 20 college students majoring in art education as the research subjects, and uses comprehensive research methods such as questionnaires, observations, evaluations, and feedback to collect data. Subsequent analysis procedures included descriptive statistics, analysis of variance, and correlation analyzes to interpret the data. Research results show that with the support of HCI, multi-sensory three-dimensional space learning can significantly improve students' spatial imagination, creativity, understanding and mastery of three-dimensional space, while also improving students' learning interest, motivation, participation and satisfaction. The results of this study have important implications for design paradigms in both elementary education and HCI fields. This study highlights the advantages, limitations, influencing factors and operating mechanisms of multi-sensory three-dimensional spatial learning under human-computer interaction. Advocate for future exploration of the design principles, implementation strategies, applicability, and scalability of this educational model.

Keywords: three-dimensional space learning · human-computer interaction · multi-dimensional · learning results · learning experience

1 Introduction

In today's era of digitalization and virtualization, the application of human-computer interaction technology in the field of education has attracted increasing attention. Especially in three-dimensional space learning, the development of human-computer interaction technology provides new possibilities and opportunities for education. Three-dimensional space learning refers to a learning method that involves multiple senses, allowing students to better understand and apply three-dimensional space concepts. It not only involves visual perception, but also involves the participation of multiple senses such as hearing and touch. Through the interaction of these senses, three-dimensional space learning can help students understand and experience the characteristics and concepts of three-dimensional space more deeply.

This study aims to deeply explore the application and effect of multi-dimensional three-dimensional space learning in human-computer interaction, and explore its importance and research significance in the field of education. By cultivating cognitive abilities and creativity in three-dimensional space learning, we can provide students with richer and more diverse learning experiences, thereby improving their learning motivation and engagement.

In order to achieve the above goals, this study adopted a comprehensive research method, including questionnaire survey, observation, evaluation, etc. By collecting and analyzing students' feedback and learning data, we can more comprehensively understand the role and effect of human-computer interaction in multi-dimensional three-dimensional space learning, and provide theoretical support and guidance for future educational practice.

In this article, we will first introduce the background and motivation of the research, and then outline the importance and research significance of multi-dimensional three-dimensional space learning in human-computer interaction. Finally, we will briefly introduce the purpose and methods of this study to pave the way for subsequent content.

2 Literature Review

Past research has achieved a series of important results in the application of human-computer interaction technology in the field of education, providing useful inspiration for multi-dimensional three-dimensional space learning. For example, the "Theoretical Foundation and Practical Framework of Social Experiments in Artificial Intelligence Education" The implementation of social experiments in artificial intelligence education is of great significance to promote the development of education in the intelligent era, and also provides a theoretical basis and practical guidance for in-depth discussions in the field of artificial intelligence education. It provides a useful reference for future related research and practice [1]. "Human-Computer Collaborative Teaching: Path Design Based on Virtual Avatars, Digital Twins and Educational Robot Scenarios" analyzes the application forms of human-computer collaborative teaching in physical space, virtual space and hybrid space, and proposes a framework and path for human-computer collaborative teaching. The design provides theoretical support for the practice of multi-dimensional three-dimensional space learning [2]. In addition, the Human-Machine Bidirectional Feedback Mechanism Model and Implementation Principles for Intelligent Education Applications constructs a human-machine bidirectional feedback mechanism model for intelligent education applications, explores ways to solve the human-machine relationship dilemma faced by artificial intelligence educational applications, and provides a multi-dimensional and three-dimensional Guidance is provided for the implementation of spatial learning [3, 4]. At the same time, "Artificial Intelligence + Education: Key Technologies and Typical Application Scenarios" introduces the key technologies and typical application scenarios of artificial intelligence in the field of education, providing technical support and reference for the application of human-computer interaction technology in three-dimensional space learning [5, 6]. Finally, «Research on the Core Theory of Robot Education in Primary and Secondary Schools" puts forward the core theory of robot education in primary and secondary schools, stimulates students' interest in learning through fun and interactive teaching models, improves students' innovation ability and teamwork ability, and provides a multi-dimensional three-dimensional space Learning by practice provides experimental validation [7].

In summary, past research has provided rich experience and inspiration for the application of human-computer interaction technology in multi-dimensional three-dimensional space learning. However, there are still some shortcomings in existing research. First, most of the existing research focuses on specific fields or technologies, and the comprehensive exploration of multi-dimensional three-dimensional space learning is not enough. Secondly, some studies lack comprehensive consideration of factors such as learning motivation, interest, and satisfaction, resulting in a lack of comprehensive understanding of students' learning experience. Therefore, future research can be carried out from the following aspects: first, in-depth exploration of the application effects of different human-computer interaction technologies in multi-dimensional three-dimensional space learning; second, based on students' learning motivation, interest, satisfaction and other factors, carry out more Comprehensive and in-depth research; the third is interdisciplinary cooperation and research to promote the development of the field of multi-dimensional three-dimensional space learning and provide more useful inspiration and suggestions for educational practice.

3   Research Methods

3.1   Research Objects and Samples

The research subjects of this study are college students aged 18–25, and the sample size is 20 people. Participants will be recruited from college students majoring in art education to ensure that they have a certain foundation in understanding and creating three-dimensional space (Fig. 1).

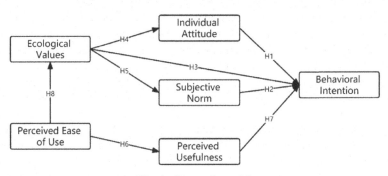

Fig. 1. Research model

3.2   Research Methods Adopted

This study adopted a method that combined questionnaire survey and experimental observation.

Questionnaire survey: In order to understand participants' cognition, experience and satisfaction with three-dimensional space learning, a questionnaire covering multiple aspects was designed. The questionnaire covers evaluation of spatial imagination, creativity, mastery of three-dimensional space, learning interest, motivation, participation and satisfaction.

Experimental Observations: A series of experiments were designed to evaluate participants' performance in three-dimensional space learning. Experiments include flat-to-three-dimensional transformation experiments, creative modeling experiments, etc. Data are obtained by observing the behavior and performance of participants in the experiments.

3.3   Experimental Design

Experiment 1: Exploring the transformation from plane to three-dimensional.

Goal: Improve students' spatial imagination and understanding of three-dimensional space.

step:

1. Theoretical introduction:
   A. The teacher introduces the concept of transformation from plane to three-dimensional, including basic principles such as projection and perspective. Through a brief theoretical explanation, students can understand the three-dimensional effects under different viewing angles.
   B. Display pictures from multiple angles, such as three-dimensional figures under parallel projection and perspective projection, so that students can understand the shapes and characteristics of three-dimensional objects under different viewing angles through observation.
2. Practical operations:
   A. Provide some simple three-dimensional object models, such as cubes, cylinders, etc., and let students observe and judge their three views. B. Students can freely rotate and observe these three-dimensional objects and understand their shapes and characteristics from different angles.
   B. Students try to draw front, side and top views of the three-dimensional objects they observe to deepen their understanding and grasp of three-dimensional space.
3. Discussion and summary:
   A. Students share their observations and judgments, conduct peer discussions, and explore the key points and methods of transforming planes into three dimensions.
   B. The teacher guides students to summarize the basic principles and methods of transforming from plane to three-dimensional, and strengthens students' understanding of three-dimensional space.

Through this experiment, students will gradually master the basic principles and methods of plane to three-dimensional transformation through theoretical introduction, practical operations, and discussion and summary, and improve their spatial imagination and understanding of three-dimensional space (Fig. 2).

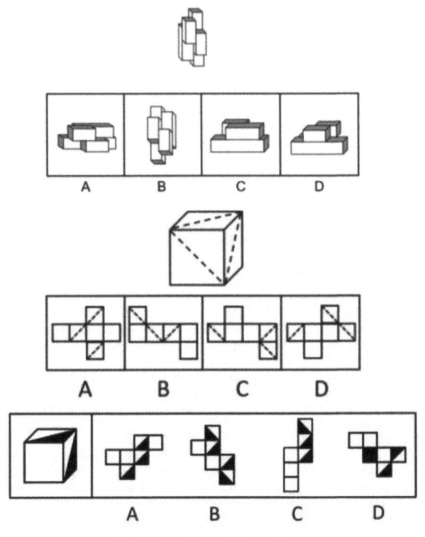

Fig. 2. Stereoscopic spatial perception test

Experiment 2: Diverse construction of three-dimensional objects.
Goal: To enhance students' creativity and mastery of three-dimensional space.
step:

1. Software operation introduction:

A. The teacher guides students to use modeling software (such as Cinema 4D, SketchUp, Rhino, etc.) to introduce how to copy, deform, and place a single three-dimensional object in various ways.

B. The teacher demonstrates the software operation process to let students understand how to use modeling software to construct and edit three-dimensional objects.

2. Practical operations:

A. Students use modeling software to perform practical operations according to the teacher's guidance.

B. Students choose a simple three-dimensional object as a prototype, copy, deform, and place it in various ways to construct a new three-dimensional space scene.

C. Students can try different deformations and placements, use their creativity, and form various three-dimensional space constructions.

3. Three-view drawing:

A. Students draw three views of the constructed three-dimensional object.

B. By drawing three-dimensional views, students B deepen their understanding of the transformation from plane to three-dimensional and consolidate their mastery of three-dimensional space.

C. Teachers give students guidance and feedback during the drawing process to help them improve the three-dimensional view of three-dimensional objects.

Through this experiment, students will master the diverse construction methods of three-dimensional objects through software operation, practical operation and three-dimensional drawing, cultivate creativity, and deepen their understanding and mastery of three-dimensional space (Fig. 3).

Experiment 3: Creative 3D Modeling and Rendering.

Goal: Improve students' creativity and mastery of three-dimensional space, and increase learning interest and satisfaction.

step:

1. Creative design:

A. Students choose a simple three-dimensional object, such as a cube, cylinder, etc., and transform it into another object through imagination for creative design. They can use their imagination to give three-dimensional objects different forms and functions, and determine modeling solutions.

2. Modeling and Rendering:

A. Students use modeling software (such as Cinema 4D, SketchUp, Rhino, etc.) to model creatively designed objects. They need to translate the design concept into a concrete 3D model, adding appropriate materials, textures and details to make it come to life.

B. After the modeling is completed, students perform rendering operations and use the rendering function provided by the software to present the modeling work with realistic effects. They can adjust light, shadow and perspective to enhance the expressiveness and realism of their work.

3. Display and share:

A. Students display their creative modeling works and share design concepts and modeling processes. They can explain where their ideas came from, their design

Fig. 3. Multi-dimensional observation of three-dimensional space

ideas, and the challenges and solutions they encountered during the modeling process.

B. Other students and teachers conduct peer evaluation and discussion of the works, and provide feedback and suggestions. By sharing and communicating with each other, students can inspire each other and stimulate more creativity and ideas.

Through this experiment, students will have the opportunity to transform their imagination into specific three-dimensional modeling works through the whole process of creative design, modeling and rendering, and share and communicate with others, thereby enhancing their creativity and understanding of three-dimensional space. Mastery, as well as learning interest and satisfaction (Fig. 4).

3.4   Data Collection and Analysis Process

Data collection: First, a questionnaire survey was conducted through an online questionnaire platform to collect participants' subjective evaluations of three-dimensional space

Fig. 4. Diverse construction of three-dimensional objects

learning. Secondly, arrange the experimental scene, conduct experimental observations on the participants, and record their behavior and performance in the experiment.

Data analysis: The collected questionnaire data will be subjected to statistical analysis, including descriptive statistics and correlation analysis, to explore the relationship between participants' perceptions and evaluations of different aspects of three-dimensional space learning. The experimental observation data will be qualitatively analyzed, and the participants' performance in the experiment will be summarized and summarized to evaluate the experimental effect and the participants' learning performance.

By combining data from questionnaires and experimental observations, this study aims to comprehensively understand participants' performance and experience in multi-sensory three-dimensional space learning, and provide practical suggestions and guidance for improving students' spatial imagination, creativity and learning motivation.

4 Research Results

4.1 Sample Characteristics

In the past semester, 70% of the participants had not taken a course related to three-dimensional space. The age range of the participants ranged from 18 to 25 years old, and all were college students.

4.2 Main Findings

Before learning multi-dimensional three-dimensional space in human-computer interaction, participants' ability to master three-dimensional views of objects was only 26%. After learning multi-dimensional three-dimensional space in human-computer interaction, participants' ability to master three-dimensional views of objects increased to 95%.Data show that in three-dimensional space learning, spatial imagination, creativity, the ability to understand three-dimensional space, the ability to master the transformation of plane to three-dimensional space, and learning interest are more important. 90% of the participants believed that the three-dimensional space classroom combined with human-computer interaction can improve the understanding of three-dimensional space in terms of spatial imagination, creativity, understanding of three-dimensional space, mastery of the transformation from plane to three-dimensional, and interest in learning. master.

4.3 Reactions and Observations

Participants showed high learning enthusiasm and participation in multi-dimensional three-dimensional space learning in human-computer interaction. Experimental results showed that students showed more creative thinking and spatial imagination when using modeling software and participating in class discussions. In the process of learning three-dimensional space, students' understanding of three-dimensional objects has been significantly improved, and they have a deeper understanding of the transformation from plane to three-dimensional.

In summary, the research results show that through multi-dimensional three-dimensional space learning in human-computer interaction, students' spatial imagination, creativity, understanding of three-dimensional space and mastery of the transformation from plane to three-dimensional space have been significantly improved, and Students are more interested in and satisfied with this teaching model.

5 Discussion

5.1 Interpretation of Research Results

Research results show that through multi-dimensional three-dimensional space learning in human-computer interaction, students' spatial imagination, creativity, understanding of three-dimensional space and mastery of the transformation from plane to three-dimensional space have been significantly improved, and their learning interest and satisfaction have been significantly improved. The degree has also increased. This shows that human-computer interaction technology plays an important role in three-dimensional space learning, providing students with a richer, more intuitive, and more interactive learning experience.

5.2 Analyze the Impact of HCI on Students' Learning Outcomes and Learning Experience

Human-computer interaction technology provides students with a more diverse and flexible learning method, allowing them to understand the concept of three-dimensional space more intuitively. Through interaction with the software, students can perform practical operations in the virtual environment, thereby deepening their understanding of three-dimensional space. In addition, human-computer interaction technology also provides real-time feedback and guidance to help students correct mistakes in time and improve learning efficiency.

5.3 Relationship Between Research Results and Existing Theories

The results of this study are consistent with previous research and support the effectiveness of human-computer interaction technology in the field of education. At the same time, the research results have further enriched and expanded relevant theories and provided empirical support for the application of human-computer interaction technology in three-dimensional space learning.

5.4 Limitations and Future Directions

The limitation of this study is that the sample size is small and limited to college students, so the generalizability of the research results is limited. Future research can expand the sample size to include students of different ages and educational stages to verify the robustness of the findings. In addition, the impact of different human-computer interaction methods on learning effects can be further explored, and more specific teaching guidance and suggestions can be put forward based on teaching practice to further optimize the teaching model of three-dimensional space learning.

6 Conclusion

This study conducted an in-depth discussion on the application of human-computer interaction technology in multi-sensory three-dimensional space learning, made a series of important discoveries, and put forward some valuable insights and suggestions in the fields of education and human-computer interaction.

First, through the collection and analysis of experimental data, we found that multidimensional three-dimensional space learning in human-computer interaction significantly improves students' spatial imagination, creativity and understanding of three-dimensional space. In particular, students' ability to master the three views of objects before human-computer interaction learning was low, only 26%, but after the learning, it increased to 95%. This shows that human-computer interaction has an important impact on students. Significant promotion effect on spatial cognitive ability.

Secondly, experimental results show that participating in three-dimensional space classes with human-computer interaction can greatly increase students' learning interest and satisfaction. Data show that 90% of students believe that a three-dimensional space classroom that combines human-computer interaction can improve spatial imagination, creativity, understanding of three-dimensional space, mastery of the transformation from plane to three-dimensional, and learning interest. Mastery of three-dimensional space. This shows that human-computer interaction technology has great potential in improving educational experience and learning motivation.

Taken together, the findings of this study not only have important implications for the field of basic education, but also provide strong support for the application of human-computer interaction technology in education. By providing a richer and more vivid learning experience, the three-dimensional space learning model combined with human-computer interaction is expected to become an important development direction of education in the future. In addition, this study also provides some valuable ideas and directions for future related research. However, we are also aware that this study has certain limitations. First, the sample size was small and failed to cover student groups of all ages and educational backgrounds, so the findings may be affected by sample bias. Secondly, although the experimental design takes into account a variety of factors, there may still be other influencing factors that are not considered. Therefore, future research can further expand the sample size and adopt more diversified research methods to verify and improve the conclusions of this study.

To sum up, through continuous exploration and innovation, we believe that human-computer interaction technology will bring more possibilities and opportunities to the field of education, and provide better solutions for improving students' learning effects and experience.

Acknowledgments. The project originates from Guangdong Province's First-Class Course "Fundamentals of Design (Three-Dimensional Space)".

References

1. Bao, T., Ke, Q., Ma, X.: Theoretical foundation and practical framework of social experiments in artificial intelligence education. Audio-visual Educ. Res. **44**(01), 54–60 (2023). https://doi.org/10.13811/j.cnki.eer.2023.01.008
2. Huang, R., Liu, D., Ahmed, T., et al.: Human-machine collaborative teaching: path design based on virtual avatars, digital twins and educational robot scenarios. Open Educ. Res. **29**(06), 4–14 (2023). https://doi.org/10.13966/j.cnki.kfjyyj.2023.06.001.Victor
3. Dong, Y., Li, X., Zheng, Y., et al.: Human-machine two-way feedback in intelligent education applications: mechanism, model and implementation principles]. Open Educ. Res. **27**(02), 26–33 (2021). https://doi.org/10.13966/j.cnki.kfjyyj.2021.02.003
4. Pan, C., Guo, Z.: Influencing mechanism of public willingness on green packaging. Packaging Eng. **40**(3), 136–142 (2019)
5. Lu, Y., Ma, A., Chen, P.: Artificial intelligence + education: key technologies and typical application scenarios. Dig. Teach. Prim. Secon. Schools (10), 5–9 (2021)
6. Wang, G.: Holiday gift packaging design. Art Observation **2**, 12 (2003)
7. Zhong, B.: Research on the core theory of robot education in primary and secondary schools - new classification of robot teaching models. Audio-Visual Educ. Res. **37**(12), 87–92 (2016). https://doi.org/10.13811/j.cnki.eer.2016.12.012

Integrating Collaborative Learning into Youth Art Education: Preservation and Innovation of Guangzhou's Polo Birth Culture

Li Ou Yang[1] , Jinrong Liu[1] , Ying Guo[1] , and Jie Ling[2(✉)]

[1] The Guangzhou Academy of Fine Arts, Guangzhou 510261, Guangdong, China
[2] Zhongkai University of Agriculture and Engineering, Guangzhou 510220, Guangdong, China
47219382@qq.com

Abstract. The Cantonese Porcelain technique, as the essence of Chinese ceramic art, not only showcases the exquisite skills of traditional Chinese craftsmanship, but also symbolizes the openness and cultural integration of Guangzhou. However, due to changes in usage habits, the heritage of Cantonese Porcelain skills is facing the risk of decline. Similarly, the Polo Birth Culture festival, a symbol of local cultural heritage and community unity, is under threat of being forgotten, especially as the use of Cantonese by the younger generation declines. In the context of globalization and social change, the transmission and popularization of traditional intangible cultural heritage such as Guangzhou's is particularly critical. The purpose of this study is to explore the application of collaborative learning in youth art education, and apply collaborative learning in it to promote the inheritance of Polo Birth Culture culture with the medium of Cantonese Porcelain, a folk skill. Through collaborative learning, we create an educational environment that promotes interaction, participation and in-depth understanding of culture. This study conducted in-depth interviews and observations with two groups (n = 20 per group) aged 13 to 17 years to compare the effects of traditional teaching methods with collaborative workshops using Cantonese Porcelain techniques as a medium in improving cultural understanding and engagement. The study found that, compared with traditional teaching methods, collaborative learning significantly enhanced students' engagement and cultural identity, deepening their insights into Polo Birth Culture culture and Cantonese Porcelain techniques. These key findings not only provide a new perspective for the modern dissemination and popularization of Guangzhou's intangible cultural heritage, but also confirm the practical application value of collaborative learning in youth cultural education, opening up a new way for the protection and inheritance of local culture.

Keywords: Collaborative learning technology · Folk culture inheritance · Cantonese Porcelain technique · Youth art education · Polo Birth Culture culture

C. Stephanidis et al. (Eds.): HCII 2024, CCIS 2117, pp. 192–202, 2024.
https://doi.org/10.1007/978-3-031-61953-3_22

1 Introduction

"Guangzhou Zhijin colored porcelain" is referred to as Cantonese Porcelain. As one of the glazed colored porcelain, it is painted with colorful patterns on the white porcelain surface and then baked. The development of Cantonese Porcelain is gradually becoming less optimistic, its market share is decreasing, and the heritage of Cantonese Porcelain skills is facing a crisis. Also as a folk belief, the Polo Birth Culture festival is also facing the same crisis due to the development and change of The Times. In June 2010, the Polo Birth Culture festival was listed in the third batch of national intangible cultural heritage list and declared as a world-class intangible cultural heritage. Guangzhou is a city with a long history and diverse cultures, with rich intangible cultural heritage. Protecting these heritages helps maintain the cultural identity of local residents, promote local culture, and promote community cohesion and identity.

Collaborative learning emphasizes that students work together to accomplish tasks and achieve learning goals through cooperation and interaction. This style of learning emphasizes mutual support, communication and working together among students to achieve better academic outcomes and personal development. Collaborative learning advocates that students become contributors and autonomous decision makers in their learning, and it is a process of communicating, cooperating and sharing with each other [1]. American instructional design expert Barnassey succinctly summed it up. Starting from the assumption of the future of design, he distinguished four generations of design methods, of which the fourth generation is the design placed in it [2]. Therefore, the application of collaborative learning technology to collaborative learning was studied. Two control groups (20 people in each group) aged 13 to 17 were set up for in-depth interview and observation, and the effects of traditional teaching methods mainly based on consultative and consultative education and collaborative workshops using Cantonese Porcelain skills as media on improving cultural understanding and participation were compared. The results of the study were comprehensively analyzed from the aspects of participation, knowledge mastery, interaction of learning environment, creative expression, depth of cultural understanding, teamwork process, role assignment and commitment, and collaborative effect evaluation.

It is found that compared with traditional teaching methods, students will feel the richness and diversity of culture more deeply by applying learning experience design, and the cultural identity of Guangzhou Zhijin porcelain and Polo Birth Culture festival will be significantly improved. This process of in-depth understanding and participation helps to form a positive cultural identity, prompting students to better cherish and pass on their own cultural heritage.

2 Research Background

2.1 Cantonese Porcelain Skills

Cantonese Porcelain, also known as "Guangdong Zhijin colored porcelain", as a kind of glazed porcelain, it is painted with rich patterns on the white porcelain surface and fired, with a tight composition, rich color, resplencent and brilliant features [3]. According to historical records, Cantonese Porcelain came into being in the prosperous trade of the

Qing Dynasty. Although its history is only more than three hundred years, it has become the protagonist of Chinese porcelain foreign trade goods in just a few years, and it has gone to the world and given the name of "world official kiln".

With the advent of the digital age, people are increasingly dependent on fast-consuming cultural products, and they may not understand or pay enough attention to traditional handicrafts such as Cantonese Porcelain porcelain, which requires time and energy to appreciate. In addition, the education of traditional handicrafts in the education system may be insufficient, coupled with the impact of low- cost industrial products on traditional handicrafts in the market, which also challenges the inheritance and development of traditional art forms such as Cantonese Porcelain porcelain. To enhance the public's understanding and appreciation of Cantonese Porcelain porcelain, it is necessary to promote the spread and development of Cantonese Porcelain intangible cultural heritage through education, media publicity and cultural activities.

2.2 Guangzhou Polo Birth Culture Culture

Guangzhou Polo Birth Culture culture not only exists as a temple sacrifice activity, it gradually combines with folk entertainment, connects the Marine culture with the local culture, and combines worship to the gods and folk blessing in a "more earth" form, which is illustrated by the oral transmission of the folk song "The first to visit Polo, the second to marry a wife". However, in recent years, due to the changes of people's modern lifestyle and other reasons, people's sense of identity and participation in Borneo traditional culture has declined, especially the younger generation's understanding of Borneo culture has gradually weakened. Chen Xinhe and Guan Xiying pointed out in their Research on the Protection and Activation of National Polo Birth Culture from the Perspective of Cultural Space Theory that this phenomenon was caused by insufficient protection, inadequate infrastructure, insufficient publicity and unattractive temple fair symbols, and put forward some suggestions on the activation of Polo Birth Culture to be solved through education, community participation and policy support. Combining the folk stories and folk culture elements of Polo Birth Culture with them, the influence and spreading power of Polo Birth Culture folk festival culture are improved [4].

2.3 Learn Collaborative Techniques

Learning collaboration technology covers many aspects such as technology development, educational practice, and the impact on learning outcomes. Current research focuses on how collaborative technologies can be designed and used more effectively to support learning and teaching activities, and how these technologies affect student learning outcomes, teacher teaching methods, and the overall structure of the education system. His current research focuses on learner engagement and experience, learning outcomes, and the integration of technology within them, where maintaining a high level of student engagement and motivation in online and distance learning environments is an ongoing challenge. As well as developing effective online assessment and feedback mechanisms to quantify learning outcomes and provide timely feedback, further research and innovation are still needed.

3 Strategies for the Application of Collaborative Learning Techniques in Youth Art Education

3.1 Collaborative Learning Technology Framework

The application of collaborative learning technology to promote the inheritance of Polo Birth Culture culture through Cantonese Porcelain skill education is explored in the form of collaborative workshops mediated by Cantonese Porcelain skill. Research and prepare Cantonese Porcelain porcelain painting tools as a material package. Teenagers use Cantonese Porcelain as a material medium to create, and draw the story of Guangzhou Polo Birth Culture culture and related pattern elements. A research framework related to the study was developed based on the related concepts of collaborative learning (Fig. 1).

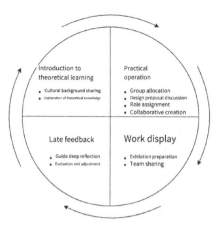

Fig. 1. Table 1. Collaborative learning technology framework

As shown in the chart, the curriculum of the whole collaborative workshop forms a complete circular pattern from theoretical practice to theory, from theoretical output to feedback, which can promote teenagers' cognitive ability, skill development, critical thinking, sociability and creativity. Through theoretical learning, teenagers can acquire the necessary knowledge system and theoretical foundation to help them understand part of the knowledge background and elements. Practical operation further deepens the understanding of these knowledge, so that young people's understanding from conceptual understanding to practice. Collaborative learning encourages interaction and communication among teenagers, helping them to establish effective cooperative relationships and improve teamwork skills. The practical part of it revolves around collaboration, with Karl Smith mentioning the importance of assigning clear roles in a collaborative learning environment to facilitate interaction between students and effective collaboration within teams. Role assignment helps to clarify the responsibilities of each member and ensure that the team works efficiently, while also improving student engagement and motivation [5]. Skills of Cantonese Porcelain also have their steps, so the roles of students in collaborative workshops should be assigned correspondingly (Fig. 2).

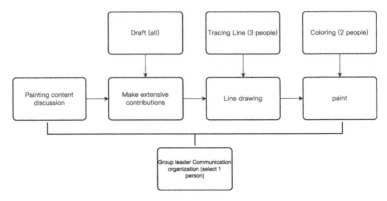

Fig. 2. Table 2. Role assignment framework

3.2 Research Methods

In order to improve reliability and validity, the study was conducted by a controlled experiment. Compared the effects of traditional teaching methods and collaborative workshops using Cantonese Porcelain skills as media in improving cultural understanding and participation, interviews and observation methods were used for in-depth exploration, qualitative data were collected while quantitative data was collected, and comprehensive analysis was carried out from multiple perspectives.

A controlled experiment will be used to evaluate and compare the effects of traditional teaching and collaborative workshops on adolescents' cultural understanding and engagement, and then propose a hypothesis that collaborative workshops mediated by Cantonese Porcelain skills can more effectively improve adolescents' cultural understanding and engagement. Adolescents aged 13–17 years old were selected as the target group of the experiment, and 40 participants from the target group were selected by random sampling method in the experiment to ensure the representativeness of the research objects. Then they were divided into groups and randomly assigned to two control groups with 20 participants in each group. During the teaching process, the study was carried out using the learning experience design framework. After the study, the results of the study were compared, the effects of the two education methods were discussed, and the initial hypothesis was supported or refuted according to the data analysis results. Key factors, such as reliability, validity, durability and ethical considerations, were also considered during the research process to ensure the depth and breadth of the research while maintaining scientific rigor.

This paper will focus on youth interview data and youth behavior during the participation process, and explore the role of collaborative workshops in promoting youth's understanding and cognition of Polo Birth Culture culture, compared with traditional teaching. The questions of the interview are divided into four parts around the learning experience framework, and the four parts explore the degree of participation, interaction and understanding of collaborative workshops for teenagers (Table 1).

The framework for collaborative learning technology is divided into sections focusing on different aspects of learning with Cantonese Porcelain skills. The first two items

Table 1. The role of collaborative workshops in promoting young people's understanding and awareness of Polo Birth Culture culture

• Item 1: Have you ever attended a similar course before joining this course?
• Item 2: Through this learning experience, what new understanding or discovery do you have about Guangzhou's characteristic intangible cultural heritage?
• Item 3: How did you communicate with each other during the collaboration? How did you feel?
• Item 4: Did you have any unforgettable experience in the process of collaboration, or did you encounter any difficulties? How did you solve it?
• Item 5: Were there any particularly useful or effective strategies during the discussion?
• Item 6: What was your biggest takeaway from the discussion?
• Item 7: How do you feel about integrating Cantonese Porcelain skills into teaching in the course? How does it affect your learning experience?
• Item 8: Where do you think collaborative workshops could be improved?

assess the youths' initial cultural understanding by comparing current and past learning experiences. Items 3–6 evaluate the effects of collaborative workshops on students' learning outcomes. The next part, items 7 and 8, deals with students' experiences, including challenges and memorable moments, and their perceptions of integrating Cantonese Porcelain skills into the curriculum. The final sections gather feedback on teaching and curriculum improvements. Observations during the workshops aim to assess adolescents' engagement, interaction, learning effectiveness, and appreciation of culture. Data are collected, coded, and analyzed to understand the impact of learning design on student outcomes, with a special focus on aspects like participation, skill mastery, and cultural identity. This approach combines quantitative ratings with qualitative observations to explore how educational design influences learning effectiveness and cultural connection.

4 Research Process

Research will be conducted in the form of collaborative workshops and in the form of traditional lectures. The observations and question sets of the research will be analyzed in relation to their own level of engagement and understanding of the learning content.

During the practice of the collaborative workshop, the venue was selected in Shipai Primary School, Panyu District, Guangzhou. In order to ensure the smooth progress of the activity, the venue was arranged in advance and a special Cantonese Porcelain skills learning package was prepared. At the same time, the participating students were divided into groups of 5. After the venue was arranged, the activity officially began. First of all, we spent 5 min to explain before class with PPT, including the cultural elements of Guangzhou Polo Birth Culture and the production steps of Cantonese Porcelain. After the presentation, the students began to assign roles and draw preliminary sketches. Each group determined their roles and drew their understanding of the Polo Birth Culture on scratch paper. The time was limited to 10 min. After the sketch is finished, the students enter the formal creation stage. In this stage, group members collaborate with each other according to the assigned roles, or swap roles according to the actual situation to complete the work together. In this process, the role of teachers is mainly to manage classroom discipline, guide students' teamwork and explain Cantonese Porcelain techniques, aiming to enhance students' learning efficiency and understanding depth while helping each other (Figs. 3 and 4).

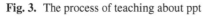

Fig. 3. The process of teaching about ppt   **Fig. 4.** The process of student listening

Throughout the practice, we also recorded the students' learning state with careful observation. First of all, the overall state of each group was recorded and expressed in numerical form. Secondly, additional records are made for the special situation of students, so as to facilitate the comprehensive analysis in the later stage. After the work was completed, we interviewed students in small groups and collected their feedback information for analysis to further improve our teaching methods and feedback mechanisms.

In the traditional teaching process, the classical lecture method will be adopted, and the basic knowledge such as the historical background, development process and iconic elements of Guangzhou Polo Birth Culture culture will be introduced in detail with the help of PPT presentation. An appreciation assignment will be arranged after the lecture, and students will be encouraged to express their understanding and knowledge of the culture through writing descriptions or sharing personal feelings.

In order to better grasp students' learning status and class participation, record their learning activity and enthusiasm during the lecture. At the end of the course, students are interviewed to gain insight into the impact of traditional teaching methods on their learning engagement and understanding. Then the practical conclusions of the two are compared and analyzed, and the results of practice are obtained.

5   Research Results

5.1   Comprehensive Data Analysis

By comparing the participation of students in the collaborative learning environment and the traditional teaching mode and analyzing the understanding degree of Guangzhou Polo Birth Culture culture, this study will deeply study the effects of these two teaching methods. In the experimental group, the average scores of the four groups will be used as the basis for data analysis; In the control group, the analysis will be based on the class performance of 20 teenagers as a whole.

Figure 5 presents the mean observational ratings of the collaborative workshop and compares them with those of the traditional teaching mode. In this way, the aim is to quantitatively assess the influence of different teaching modes on the level of youth's participation in the curriculum and the depth of understanding of Guangzhou Polo Birth Culture culture.

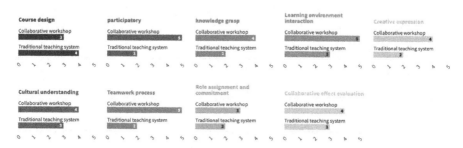

Fig. 5. The average score index of the table was observed

According to the tabled data, compared with traditional teaching methods, collaborative workshops scored 2 to 3 points higher in the three aspects of student engagement, knowledge acquisition and interaction in the learning environment. In the collaborative workshop, students participate in the class by creating art works. This novel teaching method stimulates their curiosity and keeps their enthusiasm high throughout the teaching process. Through the learning centered on Cantonese Porcelain skills, students' hands-on ability, perception and understanding have been significantly improved. The interview data showed that the students who participated in the collaborative workshop had a profound impact on Guangzhou Polo Birth Culture culture and its elements, in particular, they had a deeper understanding of the elements drawn. In contrast, students with traditional teaching methods understand the culture through rational appreciation, and their understanding of the culture is relatively shallow, and sometimes they can't really understand the element knowledge itself.

In terms of the interactivity of the learning environment, students in collaborative workshops show higher interactivity, which correspondingly improves the communication efficiency, cooperation motivation, role adaptation and execution efficiency. In addition, collaborative workshops were rated 1 point higher than traditional teaching methods in terms of cultural recognition. In the process of learning, students not only enhance the application ability of Guangzhou Polo Birth Culture cultural elements, but also have a deeper understanding of culture through discussion and other forms. This understanding is not limited to the knowledge itself, but through the regional culture and traditional skills of Guangzhou, combined with traditional festivals, from cognition to practice to deepen the understanding of Guangzhou regional culture.

In the evaluation of course design, the collaborative workshop is slightly lower than the traditional teaching mode in the score, which is mainly reflected in the feedback of course difficulty. In the course feedback, some students said that it was difficult to combine Cantonese Porcelain techniques to create works, and they thought this method was more challenging, which affected their learning efficiency and enthusiasm to some extent. However, in terms of task completion and satisfaction, as reflected in the student ratings in the class, the collaborative workshop was rated higher than the traditional teaching method. In terms of course completion, collaborative workshops ensured that each group was able to produce work according to the requirements, and that the work exhibited more variety (Figs. 6 and 7).

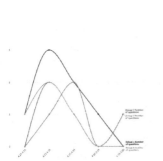

Fig. 6. The number of questions asked by the collaborative workshop group   **Fig. 7.** The completion schedule of the collaborative workshop group

Secondly, I observed the number of questions and progress of the collaborative workshop group, and recorded the progress and questions of the group every 20 min. The research found that the number of questions of the group was mostly concentrated in the early stage, and most of the questions were related to basic skills, and most of the groups cooperated and communicated to solve problems with each other in the later stage. In terms of the completion progress, most of the groups were able to complete the creation according to the time, but the data showed that only the 1st and 4th groups were 100% complete, and the rest were slightly less complete. However, in combination, the groups gradually evolved into mutual communication to solve problems by asking the teachers, which not only promoted the cooperation among the group members, but also promoted the cooperation among the group members. This change not only promoted the cooperation among the group members, but also improved their independent ability to solve problems. The process showed that collaborative workshops provided a platform for students to practice and apply their new knowledge, deepening their understanding and mastery of what was being learned through hands-on and group interaction.

5.2 Specific Case Studies

In recent interviews, a number of groups shared their experiences with the Cantonese Porcelain collaborative workshop, an activity focused on the inheritance of intangible cultural heritage knowledge. Compared with the traditional course form, two groups agreed that this kind of collaborative workshop aroused their curiosity, but a student in the second group did not cooperate. According to the interview, he thought that compared with the previous art course, the operation of Cantonese Porcelain skills was somewhat challenging, and he thought that the control of brush strokes and color moisture was more difficult. However, in general, this novel way of experience enables them to have a deeper understanding of the intangible cultural heritage, and a new understanding of the elements of Polo Birth Culture culture and the historical stories behind it, especially at the image level. This expression is not only reflected in interviews, but also in interviews. In their works, they also show that they have captured the characteristics of Polo Birth Culture cultural elements.

During the learning process, the group members worked with each other step by step to complete the painting work, which not only enhanced teamwork, but also gave them the opportunity to observe and learn from each other's painting skills. However, in the interview process, some groups pointed out that the activity time was a little short and the time arrangement was very tight, especially in the early stage of knowledge explanation, which made it difficult for some participants to quickly devote themselves to the experience. Due to the technical challenges, they were not completely satisfied with the result of the final work. But reviews of the overall learning and experience process were positive. The novelty of the materials and the unique experience of learning made them eager to continue participating in such collaborative workshops, and all four groups hoped for more such learning opportunities in the future (Figs. 8 and 9).

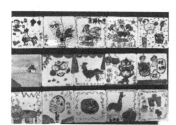

Fig. 8. Final presentation

Fig. 9. First group presentation

6 Conclusion

Collaborative workshops focusing on Cantonese Porcelain skills offer notable benefits over traditional teaching methods by enhancing student engagement, knowledge acquisition, interactivity, creativity, cultural insight, teamwork, and evaluation of collaborative efforts. This approach not only enriches students' understanding of intangible cultural heritage but also ignites their curiosity and passion for artistic creation. By blending Cantonese Porcelain craftsmanship with collaborative learning, students gain a profound appreciation of Guangzhou's cultural heritage through active participation and mutual support, despite the slight challenge in course design due to the craft's complexity. In essence, collaborative learning environments excel in fostering a deep understanding and appreciation of cultural heritage, advocating for the integration of traditional skills with collaborative techniques in educational settings, particularly within cultural and creative arts education, to enhance holistic and deep learning experiences.

Acknowledgments. The project originates from Guangdong Province's First-ClassCourse"Fundamentals of Design (Three-Dimensional Space) (Project Number: 6040324137)". The project is the interim results of the ideo- logical and political demonstration course "Fundamentals of Design (Three-Dimensional Space)" at Guangzhou Academy of Fine Arts in 2021 (Project Number: 6040321061); and Guangzhou Academy of Fine Arts Graduate Program "Cultural Elements and Creative Design Education" (Project Number: 6040122027SFJD).

References

1. Large, A., Beheshti, J., Nesset, V., Bowler, L.: Designing Web portals in intergenerational teams: two prototype portals for elementary school students. J. Am. Soc. Inf. Sci. Technol. **55**(13), 1140–1154 (2004)
2. Wen, G.: On the orientation of instructional design research -- yesterday, today and tomorrow of instructional design research (II). China Audio-visual Educ. (2) (2005)
3. Zeng, Y., Li, H.: Zhijin Color Porcelain Cantonese Porcelain Technology. Guangdong Education Press, Guangzhou (2013)
4. Chen, X.-H., Guan, X.: Study on the protection and activation of national Polo Birth Culture from the perspective of cultural space theory. Comparat. Res. Cult. Innov. **7**(08), 114–119 (2023). (in Chinese)
5. Smith, K.: Learning together and alone: cooperation, competition, and individualization. NACTA J. **23**(3), 23–26 (1979). http://www.jstor.org/stable/43763555. Accessed 2 Mar 2024

Learning Foreign Language Vocabulary Through Task-Based Virtual Reality Immersion

Ethan Seefried$^{(\boxtimes)}$ ⓘ, Mariah Bradford ⓘ, Swagatalaxmi Aich ⓘ,
Caspian Siebert ⓘ, Nikhil Krishnaswamy ⓘ, and Nathaniel Blanchard ⓘ

Colorado State University, Fort Collins, CO 80521, USA
{eseefrie,nkrishna,Nathaniel.Blanchard}@colostate.edu

Abstract. In the rapidly evolving landscape of language learning pedagogy, Virtual Reality (VR) has emerged as a potent tool for enhancing
the educational experience beyond traditional platforms like Duolingo.
This study explores the efficacy of task-based language learning (TBL) in
immersive VR. We conducted an experiment with 27 participants, teaching them 20 Spanish vocabulary words through a VR-enabled cooking
task in Spanish, across three distinct learning conditions: fully immersive VR, traditional non-VR, and mixed modality. The inclusion of VR
did not affect the overall gains; however, analysis of post-experiment
feedback taken three weeks later showed that VR markedly enhanced
engagement and appeal value for participants in the mixed modality,
highlighting VR's potential to enrich the language learning experience.
These results suggest the promise of immersive TBL pedagogy in VR in
making language learning more engaging and effective. Further, the success of the mixed condition indicates future explorations should factor in
when to capitalize on VR and when traditional methods are sufficient.

Keywords: Virtual Reality · Immersion · Task Based Language
Learning

1 Introduction

Learning a new language requires dedication and patience, usually over multiple
years, and a means of learning like a tutor, a class, or a digital learning tool. The
latter is one of the most accessible—for example, in 2022 alone over 500 million
people around the world accessed Duolingo [2]. Duolingo and similar apps have
grown in popularity due to the ease of access and low cost (Duolingo is free with
ads). These apps also focus on short lessons while encouraging users to engage
daily, emphasizing that learners may proceed through the courses at a pace that
fits their lives.

However, despite the success of these apps, how language learning applications best balance engagement and learning gains is an open problem. For example, a side effect of Duolingo's ease of use and accessibility is that many users

C. Stephanidis et al. (Eds.): HCII 2024, CCIS 2117, pp. 203–213, 2024.
https://doi.org/10.1007/978-3-031-61953-3_23

do not end up making much progress learning the language: an informal study highlighted a striking statistic: only 0.01% of users studying Spanish actually complete the course [10].

One potential solution is to refocus language learning around task or game completion, with language learning being a byproduct of task completion—this idea, "task-based language learning" focuses on the intersection of immersive environments and language learning. One popular task-based learning paradigm [3] focuses on kitchen settings [18]. In this work, we combine task-based language learning in a kitchen environment with the immersive nature of Virtual Reality (VR) [4,6].

While other works have examined education or language learning in VR [1, 12,18], there is a surprising dearth of research that examines task-based learning with VR. Our study aims to bridge this gap by introducing participants to a fully immersive virtual environment where they are tasked with cooking fajitas, a Mexican-American dish. 27 participants participated in the learning task in either a VR, mixed modality, or traditional (non-VR) condition. We found that while there were no statistically significant differences in learning outcomes, an analysis of participant survey data showed VR learners were more engaged with the learning task and were generally more interested in returning to the task.

The contributions of our paper are summarized as follows:

- A novel methodology that integrates VR-assisted language learning (VRALL) with Task-based Learning (TBL).
- Qualitative feedback from a post-task survey followed by a post-experiment survey administered three weeks later.
- Design and development of a flexible application framework capable of incorporating multiple languages beyond Spanish, thereby broadening the scope for user language selection, laying the groundwork for future research and application enhancements.

2   Related Works

Language Learning in VR. Immersion has been proven to be the most effective way to learn a second language [7,8]. People can experience much higher language learning results when brought into an environment surrounded by the target language, with a need to engage in it. Similarly, when removed from the environment, many of the learners will see a decrease in their language skills [16,17]. Interactivity has also been found to have a positive impact on learning [16,21].

Language learning has been explored in Augmented Reality (AR) and VR as well. Studies have shown that VR can provide a more immersive and enjoyable method of learning than traditional language learning applications [5] regardless of preferred learning style [15]. AR language learning has also been shown to increase vocabulary, reading, speaking, and writing skills [1,14]. VR can also improve motivation in learners [9]. These applications have often involved interactions where participants can grab objects and be told the word for the object in the target language [5]. Another VR language learning task is a search-and-find task, where participants are given instructions in the target language and tasked with finding the object in the environment [5]. In the realm of VR, one of the most significant benefits is the provision of immediate feedback to users regarding linguistic information. This is particularly relevant in the context of language acquisition and vocabulary development. The research conducted by Miller and Gildea [11] sheds light on the process through which children assimilate new words, primarily through interactive methods such as conversations and writing. They assert that an ideal learning scenario, especially when encountering unfamiliar words in text, involves the availability of an automated system capable of elucidating the meaning of these words within their specific sentential context. This system functions similarly to how one might inquire about the meaning of a new word used in a live conversation [19]. This approach underscores the transformative potential of VR in enhancing language comprehension and acquisition.

Task-Based Language Learning. Task-based learning (TBL) has been a widely recognized instructive approach in language education. It emphasizes practical tasks as the primary means of learning language skills, promoting communication and problem-solving in real-life situations. TBL has shown success in fostering speaking, listening, and comprehension skills by engaging learners in meaningful activities within the target language [3,20].

3   Methods

3.1   Participants

Participants were recruited by word of mouth primarily on campus at Coloardo State University (CSU). A participant was considered eligible for this study if they were 18 years of age or older, were comfortable with wearing a head mounted display (HMD), had correctable-to-normal vision, and had very little prior Spanish knowledge, which could be determined with a pre-test (if a participant scored higher than 50% on the pre-test they were disqualified from participating). In total, 27 eligible participants were recruited, leaving 9 participants to be compared for each given condition. This study was approved by the IRB board at Colorado State University (Fig. 1).

VR Setup. The three-dimensional (3D) VR kitchen environment was constructed with Unity and OpenXR. For hardware, due to its standalone and non-tethering nature, we used a Meta Quest 2, and ported the software physically onto the Quest.

Users were placed into an isolated room with just researchers, where they had the freedom to walk around, rather than rely purely on the teleportation or in game movements of the application.

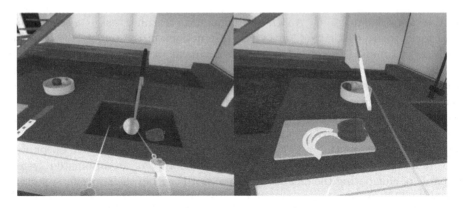

Fig. 1. Two moments captured from participant videos during the VR kitchen task. On the left, a participant is shown washing an onion under virtual water, illustrating the immersive detail of the task environment. On the right, another participant prepares to cut a freshly cleaned pepper, highlighting the application of learned vocabulary and procedures. These images showcase the practical application of language skills in an immersive VR setting.

The Quest 2 had screen recording built in, including audio. While out of scope for this work, these recordings allowed for re-watching of participants videos and conducting analyses of the user experience.

3.2   Language Lesson Conditions

Participants were randomly assigned to one of three conditions: fully real-world, mixed modality, and fully virtual.

Real-World. In the fully real-world segment, we concentrated on traditional learning methods, using Quizlet for the introduction and repetitive reinforcement of vocabulary to make the learning process straightforward. Participants then watched a recorded silent video demonstrating the steps of cooking fish fajitas, with the same steps from the VR environment. For each step in the video, the Spanish sentence was shown on the screen and then the corresponding action was shown, then the sentence and action were shown again, repeating three times before moving on the next step in the recipe, to reinforce the vocabulary. For example, "corte el pescado" would display followed by a video of someone cutting a fish. This approach was crafted as an easy-to-follow baseline to compare with the results from VR learning. Designed to be as simple as possible, we ensured the vocabulary was drilled into participants by showing them the words multiple times before performing the related action in the demonstration. Our objective was to determine if a more immersive VR environment could achieve or approach the learning effectiveness of this baseline, which, while easy to learn from, lacked engagement and might not support long-term retention.

Mixed Modality. In the mixed modality segment, participants began their Spanish vocabulary learning with flash cards utilizing Quizlet in a real-world setting, aiming for a swift and familiar lesson format. This approach leveraged Quizlet's interactive platform to quickly introduce vocabulary, setting the stage for its application in a virtual context. Following the flash card lesson, participants transitioned to the VR environment, specifically to a kitchen setting, to prepare fish fajitas using the vocabulary learned from the flash cards. This phase tested the effectiveness of combining traditional learning with immersive VR tasks in reinforcing language skills. As in the fully virtual segment (described below), participants were oriented to VR controls before starting, ensuring readiness for the immersive task. During the VR cooking task, participants were encouraged to verbalize their thought process, blending learned vocabulary with in-the-moment reasoning. This mixed modality approach aimed to assess how initial real-world learning impacts subsequent application in a virtual setting, focusing on participant engagement and the practical use of newly acquired language skills.

Fully Virtual. In the fully immersive virtual environment, participants engaged exclusively within the VR space, starting with a Spanish vocabulary lesson through the Librarium app. Following this, they were tasked with applying their newly acquired language skills in a VR kitchen setting designed to simulate a real-world cooking scenario. This segment aimed to evaluate the effectiveness of VR in facilitating language comprehension and application, with a focus on participant engagement during the task. Before loading into VR, participants were shown the controls in the real world, and allowed to ask any questions. Once the participants were comfortable with the setting, they were then given the headset. Participants were loaded into the kitchen application in front of a virtual knife and five lemon objects, with which they could see how the controls functioned. After they were comfortable, they were brought into the kitchen and given 10 min to complete a recipe of fish fajitas, where they were given no hints, and the recipe was completely in Spanish. We designed the task to be challenging in order to test participants' ability to assimilate new vocabulary through the use of physical representations and their active application within the task context. As the participants conducted the study they were instructed to think aloud, and they would often say the word in Spanish, followed by what they thought it meant in English, and try and infer their way through the recipe.

3.3 Procedures

The study comprised of six main steps: a pre-test, an initial vocabulary lesson, an applied language learning task, a distraction activity, a post-test, and finally an engagement survey.

Pre-test: Participants completed a pre-test to assess their baseline Spanish vocabulary knowledge. This test consisted of the 20 vocabulary words that would be taught in our Spanish lesson, and was in the form of fill in the blank. The participants were given a word in Spanish, and asked to translate the word into English. A score greater than 10 was deemed too high to continue in the experiment, and we omitted any participants who achieved this.

Vocabulary Lesson. After the pre-test, participants were given a flashcard vocabulary lesson for the 20 terms focused on in this experiment. This lesson took place either on the Quizlet (real, mixed) or Librarium (VR) platforms, depending on the participant's condition as described in Sect. 3.2.

Language Task: After the lesson, participants completed a language task to assess their ability to apply the learned vocabulary. Two-thirds of participants (mixed, VR) were placed in a VR kitchen environment where they were presented with a recipe in Spanish and tasked with completing it. The remaining participants (real) watched a video of the same cooking task being performed in real life (detailed in Sect. 3.2). This setup allowed for a comparison between VR and real-world learning experiences.

Distraction Activity: To allow time between the participants learning the material and taking a test, we constructed distraction activities lasting seven minutes. Participants selected one of two VR games to play: competing in a leader-board of Beat Saber Demo, giving all participants the same song and difficulty, or entering into NFL Pro Era 2, where they could experience VR football. Participants were given a brief introduction to the games, before their seven minutes were started.

Post-Test: A post-test was administered after the distraction activity to assess the learning gains achieved by participants in each condition. The post-test was the same format and vocabulary as the pre-test; however, the word sequence was randomized for each participant.

Engagement Survey: The final step in our procedure was providing participants a post-experiment survey three weeks after participating in the experiment. The survey consisted of a subset of questions from the short-form user engagement scale [13] on the participants' perceived engagement in their lesson and learning task (detailed in Sect. 3.4).

3.4 Data Analysis

In this study, we assess the effectiveness of VR in language learning by analyzing both the participants' engagement and their learning gains. Our method combines subjective evaluations of the learning experience with objective measures of vocabulary acquisition. This approach enables us to explore the dual impact of VR on language learning, assessing not only educational outcomes but also learner engagement and satisfaction.

Survey Analysis. In assessing the participants' preference for learning environments, our survey analysis focused on their experiences in virtual reality versus traditional settings. Three weeks after completing the lesson and tests, participants took a post-study survey which elicited feedback on four factors: focused attention, perceived usability (negative affect), aesthetic appeal, and endurability [13]. This survey includes multiple questions for each factor to get accurate responses. Responses were on a 5-point Likert scale, and responses for the same topic were averaged together. Through this process, we aimed to gauge levels of enjoyment and immersion, providing insights into the overall appeal of VR as a learning medium.

Learning Analysis. To accurately assess the learning gains across the three distinct groups, we employed an ANOVA (Analysis of Variance) to examine the differences in performance outcomes. We define the learning gain of the participant as their pre-test score, subtracted from their post-test score. This statistical analysis enabled us to identify any significant variances in learning achievements among the groups. Moreover, we closely analyzed the mean and median scores of each group to obtain a comprehensive understanding of their overall performance and central tendencies.

4 Results

Table 1. Comparative Analysis of Learning Outcomes Across Conditions. This table presents a summary of the mean, standard deviation, and median learning gains (post-test score - pre-test score), alongside the mean and standard deviation for pre-test and post-test scores. The data is segmented by condition—Full VR, Mixed Modality, and Real World—highlighting the diverse impact of each learning environment on participant performance and gains.

	Full VR	Mixed	Real
Average Pre-Test Score	2.67 ± 2.69	3.78 ± 3.60	3.44 ± 3.13
Average Post-Test Score	12.67 ± 3.90	16.22 ± 5.36	17.78 ± 3.53
Average Learning Gain	10.00 ± 3.67	12.44 ± 4.25	14.33 ± 3.54
Median Learning Gain	13	14	16

To accurately measure the participants' learning gains, defined as the difference between their post-test and pre-test scores, we conducted a thorough analysis of their performance before and after exposure to various learning conditions. The real-world scenario, serving as a baseline, exhibited the highest learning gains with an average increase of 14.33 ± 3.54 on a 20-point scale. The mixed modality closely followed with a gain of 12.44 ± 4.25, as detailed in Table 1, indicating its substantial effectiveness. Conversely, the fully immersive VR group experienced a noticeable decrease in performance with a gain of 10.00 ± 3.67, highlighting potential limitations of excessive immersion without adequate structured learning opportunities. In comparing the learning environments, the immersive Librarium app led participants to encounter vocabulary less frequently than the Quizlet platform, where words could be reviewed multiple times within the same duration. Nevertheless, the tangible interaction with vocabulary in VR suggested a unique potential for enhancing learning, albeit at a more gradual pace.

The diverse range of scores in the real-world group, with no two participants achieving the same result, stood in contrast to the more uniform achievements in the mixed modality. An ANOVA test found no significant difference between groups ($p = .07$, $\alpha = .05$). Thus, in this study we saw no differences in learning gains between conditions. Such statistical evidence bolsters the argument for the balanced integration of VR in educational contexts, especially when aiming for outcomes comparable to real-world learning experiences.

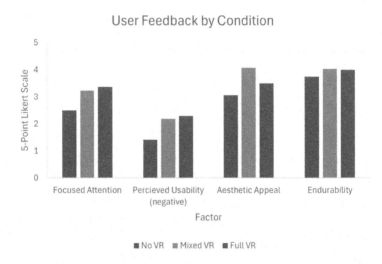

Fig. 2. Average participant ratings by condition: The full VR condition was rated highest for focused attention and perceived usability, whereas the mixed modality scored highest for aesthetic appeal and endurability. A detailed statistical analysis is provided in the subsequent section.

Figure 2 shows the post-task survey results. The full VR condition had the highest reports for focused attention and perceived usability (negative) while the mixed modality condition had the highest scores for aesthetic appeal and endurability. The fully real condition were consistently rated lowest across topic. These findings underscore the advantages that a VR setting can bring to the language learning experience, providing an overall more enjoyable user experience to language learners.

5   Discussion and Future Work

Full immersion, traveling to a place and only speaking/hearing the language being learned, is widely regarded as the best way to learn; however, it is simply not practical for most people. Our experiment supports the idea that VR may provide an alternative path to immersion, and highlights how common immersive tasks like cooking can be used in VR to support language learning.

The results from the fully immersive VR experience highlighted issues with a wholly VR approach: this condition was the most difficult to develop, and was also the one that had the most negative perceived usability by participants. Our takeaway is that the pursuit of full virtual immersion may overshadow the structured learning opportunities, in some cases—the mixed condition was successful because it capitalized on both VR and traditional approaches to language learning. This investigation underscores the feasibility and value of incorporating VR into language learning, revealing that a gradual integration of virtual elements with conventional teaching methods enhanced the educational experience, in this case.

Future studies should aim to refine VR learning environments, explore diverse subject areas, and further investigate the optimal balance between virtual and real-world components. Ultimately, our work lays the groundwork for more immersive, engaging, and effective learning experiences, harnessing the power of virtual reality to enrich educational outcomes.

6   Conclusion

In this study, we have developed and examined a novel method for conducting task-based language learning experiments within virtual reality environments. Our research involved 27 participants in an exploration of how different modalities impact language acquisition across three distinct conditions: fully immersive VR, a hybrid model combining real-world lessons with VR tasks, and a traditional (e.g., not in VR) video that served as a benchmark. Our findings highlight the unique benefits and challenges associated with each learning condition. While the real-world scenario, designed to facilitate easy learning, confirmed its effectiveness as a baseline, the mixed modality approach emerged as a particularly promising model. This blend of traditional and VR learning not only demonstrated substantial learning gains comparable to the real-world condition but also offered insights into optimizing VR's educational potential.

Acknowledgments. Partially supported by the National Science Foundation (NSF) on awards DRL 2019805 and IIS 2303019 to Colorado State University. The views expressed herein do not indicate the position of the U.S. Government.

Disclosure of Interests. The authors have no competing interests to declare that are relevant to the content of this article.

References

1. Barreira, J., Bessa, M., Pereira, L.C., Adão, T., Peres, E., Magalhães, L.: MOW: augmented reality game to learn words in different languages: case study: learning english names of animals in elementary school. In: 7th Iberian Conference on Information Systems and Technologies (CISTI 2012), pp. 1–6 (2012). iSSN: 2166-0735
2. Blanco, C.: 2022 Duolingo Language Report (2022)
3. Buyukkarci, K.: A critical analysis of task-based learning. Kastamonu J. Educ. **17**, 313–320 (2009)
4. Cowie, N., Alizadeh, M.: The affordances and challenges of virtual reality for language teaching. Int. J. TESOL Stud. **4**, 50–65 (2022)
5. Garcia, S., Kauer, R., Laesker, D., Nguyen, J., Andujar, M.: A Virtual Reality Experience for Learning Languages. In: Extended Abstracts of the 2019 CHI Conference on Human Factors in Computing Systems, CHI EA 2019, pp. 1–4. Association for Computing Machinery, New York (2019)
6. Hua, C., Wang, J.: Virtual reality-assisted language learning: a follow-up review (2018–2022). Front. Psychol. **14**, 1153642 (2023)
7. IELTS, I., OET, O.: The benefit of immersive language-learning experiences and how to create them (2021)
8. Kinginger, C.: Enhancing language learning in study abroad. Annu. Rev. Appl. Linguist. **31**, 58–73 (2011)
9. Lan, Y.J.: Chapter one - immersion into virtual reality for language learning. In: Federmeier, K.D., Huang, H.W. (eds.) Psychology of Learning and Motivation, Adult and Second Language Learning, vol. 72, pp. 1–26. Academic Press (2020)
10. London, T.I.L.: Why do so few people complete a Duolingo course? (2022)
11. Miller, G.A., Gildea, P.M.: How children learn words. Sci. Am. **257**(3), 94–99 (1987)
12. Onyesolu, M.O., Nwasor, V.C., Ositanwosu, O.E., Iwegbuna, O.N.: Pedagogy: instructivism to socio-constructivism through virtual reality. Int. J. Adv. Comput. Sci. Appl. (IJACSA) **4**(9), 1–8 (2013)
13. O'Brien, H.L., Cairns, P., Hall, M.: A practical approach to measuring user engagement with the refined user engagement scale (UES) and new UES short form. Int. J. Hum Comput Stud. **112**, 28–39 (2018)
14. Parmaxi, A., Demetriou, A.A.: Augmented reality in language learning: a state-of-the-art review of 2014–2019. J. Comput. Assist. Learn. **36**(6), 861–875 (2020)
15. Pedram, S., Howard, S., Kencevski, K., Perez, P.: Investigating the relationship between students' preferred learning style on their learning experience in virtual reality (VR) learning environment. In: Ahram, T., Taiar, R., Colson, S., Choplin, A. (eds.) IHIET 2019. Advances in Intelligent Systems and Computing, vol. 1018, pp. 275–281. Springer, Cham (2020). https://doi.org/10.1007/978-3-030-25629-6_43
16. Petersen, G.B., Petkakis, G., Makransky, G.: A study of how immersion and interactivity drive VR learning. Comput. Educ. **179**, 104429 (2022)
17. Savage, B.L., Hughes, H.Z.: How does short-term foreign language immersion stimulate language learning? Front. Interdisc. J. Study Abroad **24**(1), 103–120 (2014)
18. Seedhouse, P., Heslop, P., Kharrufa, A., Ren, S., Nguyen, T.: The linguacuisine project: a cooking-based language learning application. EUROCALL Rev. **27**(2), 75–97 (2019)

19. Villena-Taranilla, R., Tirado-Olivares, S., Cózar-Gutiérrez, R., González-Calero, J.A.: Effects of virtual reality on learning outcomes in K-6 education: A meta-analysis. Educ. Res. Rev. **35**, 100434 (2022)
20. Willis, J.: A Framework for Task-based Learning. Intrinsic Books Ltd. (2021)
21. Zhang, D., Zhou, L., Briggs, R., Nunamaker, J.: Instructional video in e-learning: assessing the impact of interactive video on learning effectiveness. Inf. Manag. **43**, 15–27 (2006)

ContextVis: Envision Contextual Learning and Interaction with Generative Models

Bo Shui⑩, Chufan Shi⑩, Yujiu Yang⑩, and Xiaomei Nie⁽✉⁾⑩

Shenzhen International Graduate School, Tsinghua University, Shenzhen, China
{shuib22,scf22}@mails.tsinghua.edu.cn,
{yang.yujiu,nie.xiaomei}@sz.tsinghua.edu.cn

Abstract. ContextVis introduces a workflow by integrating generative models to create contextual learning materials. It aims to boost knowledge acquisition through the creation of resources with contextual cues. A case study on vocabulary learning demonstrates the effectiveness of generative models in developing educational resources that enrich language understanding and aid memory retention. The system combines an easy-to-use Dashboard for educators with an interactive Playground for learners, establishing a unified platform for content creation and interaction. Future work may expand to include a wider range of generative models, media formats, and customization features for educators.

Keywords: Contextual Learning · Interactive Learning Tools · User Interaction · Generative Models

1 Introduction

Recently, generative models have made significant strides in the field of artificial intelligence, demonstrating remarkable capabilities in creating realistic and coherent content across various media formats. These models, such as language models and image generation models, have been widely adopted in the creation of creative resources, offering unique opportunities to enrich materials with contextual information. The deployment of generative models in educational resource development holds considerable promise for augmenting the learning process. It provides learners with an immersive framework that aids in knowledge comprehension and retention.

In this regard, we present the ContextVis system, a workflow that harnesses the capabilities of generative models to craft tailored learning materials and experiences. Through a case study on vocabulary learning, we demonstrate the utility of generative models in generating educational content that supports language development and enhances learning outcomes. The system represents a promising approach to elevate contextual and exploratory learning using generative models and interactive visualizations.

C. Stephanidis et al. (Eds.): HCII 2024, CCIS 2117, pp. 214–224, 2024.
https://doi.org/10.1007/978-3-031-61953-3_24

2 Related Work

2.1 Leveled and Themed Language Learning

Leveled reading, a pedagogical approach characterized by evaluating children's reading skills using specialized instruments and subsequently supplying reading materials commensurate with their ability, has garnered international acceptance and has continued to evolve in recent years [22]. Optimal selection of reading content that presents an appropriate challenge is crucial to fostering advancement in reading proficiency [31].

Empirical evidence suggests that the use of leveled reading materials in English for primary school students learning English as a second language can substantially improve their linguistic capabilities, comprehension skills, and cultural awareness [33]. Renowned publications such as *Reading A-Z* [14], *Geronimo Stilton* [28], and *Oxford Reading Tree* [24] adeptly integrate repetitive sentence structures and captivating illustrations that resonate with the developmental stages of a child's cognition [15,20].

Theme and context play a vital role in language learning. The idea of contextualized learning emphasizes that knowledge is best acquired within the context in which it is used and applied [4]. Learners apply their knowledge in various themes and contexts, deconstructing complex concepts, identifying relationships between elements, and adeptly engaging in problem analysis and resolution [12,27]. For effective learning, the language input should be comprehensible, engaging, relevant, and abundant, focusing more on meaning rather than on grammatical rules [13].

The recent *English Curriculum Standards for Compulsory Education* issued by the Ministry of Education of China in 2022 advocate for English language teaching through leveled and contextual exploration, offering level guidelines and theme examples [18]. Our work utilizes the standards as a foundation for leveled vocabulary and theme references to develop a system that supports both teachers and students in the language instruction.

2.2 Generative Models for Education

Recent advancements in generative artificial intelligence models have been propelled by the growth of available data and model scaling. These models now exhibit capability to generate high-quality content across multi-modalities and demonstrate improved understanding of user instructions, enabling content creation that aligns with human intentions [5]. Notably, empirical evidence has suggested that large generative models are now able to synthesize emergent content that is not only contextually pertinent but also coherent, contingent upon specific prompts [32].

The integration of generative models in the creation of educational resources offers a unique opportunity to enrich learning materials with contextual cues, thereby enhancing the learning experience. They have so far been used in various educational applications, such as storytelling co-creation with specific knowledge

[34], generating reading comprehension quizzes [8], authoring data-driven articles [30], generating coherent comics [11], and creating stories [1,25]. Moreover, the collaboration with human teachers in the creation of educational resources has been shown to be effective in enhancing the quality and alleviating teachers' workload [10].

These studies demonstrate the potential of generative models in creating educational resources that are tailored to specific learning objectives and contexts, as well as integrating generation with human teachers to enhance the quality of the contents. Our work focuses on maintaining the consistency of the learning context in generated story scripts and images for the learning vocabulary.

2.3   Interaction Design for Human-AI Collaboration

Human-AI collaboration is the study of how humans and AI agents work together to accomplish a shared goal [29]. In order to understand and improve this emergent modality of interaction, HCI researchers have proposed a variety of principles, frameworks, and guidelines in recent years [2,6,7,16]. Notably, Amershi et al. have proposed 18 guidelines for Human-AI Interaction, categorized within the sequential phases of initial stage, active interaction, error response, and post-interaction reflection [2]. Cimolino et al. proposed a framework as an analysis tool with four dimensions of the role, supervision, influence and mediation of AI [7].

The domain of AI-assisted design, particularly in graphical and interaction design, has witnessed a significant increase in interest and application since 2016 [26].

Shi et al. proposed that AI can assist designers in Discovering, Visualizing, Creating and Testing, and designers can reciprocally augmenting AI by Training and Regulating [26]. In the teaching process, educators harness AI assistance in lesson planning, thereby liberating themselves from repetitive pedagogical tasks, which in turn fosters innovation in educational content and methodologies [35]. The guidelines for Human-AI interaction laid out in the literature are highly pertinent to our work, as we focus on leveraging AI in the creation, visualization, and validation phases of educational content generation.

3   The ContextVis System

We present the ContextVis system, which leverages generative AI to develop contextual learning materials and experiences. As illustrated in Fig. 1, the workflow comprises three essential components: the back-end platform for processing user input and generating contextual data using Large Language Models (LLMs), as well as generating multi-modal assets through generative models; the database, where the metadata and generated resources are stored; and the front-end platform, featuring a Dashboard for educators and a Playground for learners. It is worth noting that our vision for this system encompasses the ability to receive inputs and generate outputs in multiple media formats, as the models employed can be substituted to accommodate diverse tasks.

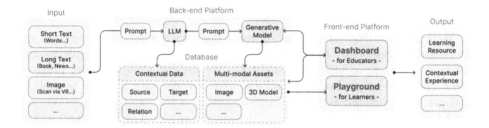

Fig. 1. The general workflow of ContextVis system.

4   Case Study: Contextual Vocabulary Learning

Acquiring English vocabulary can be challenging due to its inherent complexity characterized by contextual nuances, semantic diversity, and an extensive lexicon. Understanding and memorizing grammar rules alongside vocabulary demands a coherent and persistent learning strategy, often requiring prolonged exposure to a variety of linguistic stimuli. This extended engagement with both language inputs and outputs is crucial for reinforcing linguistic knowledge.

The process of vocabulary acquisition can be effectively integrated into the proposed workflow, where the integration of contextual factors plays a crucial role in fostering language development. To this end, we conducted a case study for vocabulary learning which exemplifies the significance of the ContextVis system, shown in Fig. 2. In the workflow, with selected vocabulary in a unit and an optional theme input in the Dashboard, the generative models in the back-end automatically generates a contextually coherent a story script and stickers for each word as output. The generated data and assets are stored in the database on the server for learners to access and explore in the Playground.

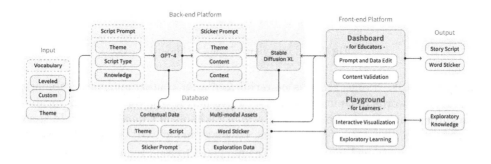

Fig. 2. A case workflow of ContextVis system.

4.1 Dashboard for Educators

To facilitate seamless integration of vocabulary with generative contents, we developed a Dashboard for educators, shown in Fig. 3, with multiple panels allowing educators to input and select the vocabulary, then generate, preview and refine the generated educational resources. By assigning a theme as contextual cue, the generated assets of scripts and stickers are stored in the server and can be exported as teaching materials for classroom use. The Dashboard serves as a pivotal interface within the ContextVis system, offering user-friendly tools and features that empower educators to effectively create tailored educational content.

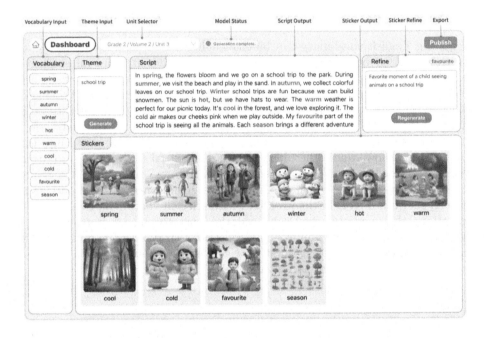

Fig. 3. An overview of the Dashboard.

Story Script. Stories serve as powerful media for contextualizing vocabulary, integrating words organically within cohesive narratives. We extracted vocabulary from English textbooks used in primary schools in China to generate story scripts using the state-of-the-art large language model, GPT-4 [21]. Educators select vocabulary and input in the Theme panel to send request for generation on the server. A model status indicator is shown in the header next to the unit selector to inform the process of generation on the server. When the script is generated, it is displayed in the Script panel with the words highlighted to show their contextual usage. The prompt template and an example script is shown below, in which the words are from a Grade 2 textbook for primary schools:

PROMPT: Generate sentences consisting of the following words with the theme of *<school trip>*, make sure the sentences are easy and short for primary school students learning English as a second language, one sentence for one word and all sentences are contextually related to form an article. And generate a prompt for each word based on the sentence for image generation in stable diffusion. Here are the words: *<spring, ..., cool>*.

OUTPUT:
Word: *"spring"*
Sentence: *"In spring, the flowers bloom and we go on a school trip to the park."*
Sticker Prompt: *"Children on a school trip in a park full of blooming flowers representing spring."*
...
Word: *"cool"*
Sentence: *"It's cool in the forest, and we love exploring it."*
Sticker Prompt: *"A group of students exploring a cool, shaded forest."*

Word Sticker. To further enhance the expressiveness of the generated story script, we incorporated word stickers into the narrative. The Stable Diffusion XL (SDXL) model [23] with two Low-Rank Adaptation (LoRA) modules [9] is employed to accomplish the task, where the LoRA modules fine-tune the SDXL base model to create emoji-like images based on the sticker prompts [19] and accelerate the generation [17]. Using the sticker prompts generated with the script, example of which shown in the OUTPUT section above, the system generates stickers of coherent theme for each word. These stickers are subsequently transmitted to the Dashboard, populating the Stickers panel.

Data Refine and Theme Variants. To encourage divergent thinking and foster customization, educators can further generate variant scripts and utilize alternative prompts, expanding the possibilities for tailoring the output content to specific learning objectives. Upon selecting an item in the Stickers panel, the current prompt associated with the chosen sticker is displayed in the Refine panel. Educators can edit the prompt and regenerate stickers to better fit the intended context, while simultaneously mitigating the risk of generating potentially inappropriate content.

Moreover, by leveraging varied themes and contexts, educators can create more engaging learning contents that not only reinforce vocabulary acquisition but also promote linguistic adaptability, as shown in Fig. 4. By offering a diverse array of learning materials, educators can stimulate more dynamic forms of vocabulary engagement and deepen learners' connections with the language.

Fig. 4. Stickers generated for the same vocabulary in different contexts.

4.2 Playground for Learners

In addition to the generated learning contents, the Playground serves as a platform for learners to engage in interactive exploration. This interactive space offers learners the opportunity to actively review with the concepts and vocabulary introduced in the generated content and to explore more by themselves. It consists of four panels: Vocabulary, Script, Selected and the interactive visualization in the center, as shown in Fig. 5. The Playground is seamlessly synchronized with the Dashboard as the two platforms are interconnected by the data and assets they share in the database on the server. This integration ensures that the learning materials sophisticatedly prepared by educators are available for learners to review and explore extra contents aligning with the theme of the original materials.

Interactive Visualization. Learners select the unit in the header, and the Playground send queries to the database to retrieve the corresponding script and stickers. The Script and Visualization panels are updated with incoming data, so the learner can interact with the stickers to explore the connections between them. The visualization utilizes the D3.js [3] library to create an interactive network, where the stickers attract each other to mimic the context, aiding learners in comprehending the contextual relationship between words and their corresponding usage within the script.

Exploratory Learning. The visualization additionally facilitates a deeper investigation of the interconnections between vocabularies. When the stickers are selected, they are highlighted and appear in the Selected panel, where a maximum of two stickers can be selected at the same time, prompting the user to explore further into the relationship between them. Upon clicking the Explore button, additional vocabulary and stickers will be generated under the

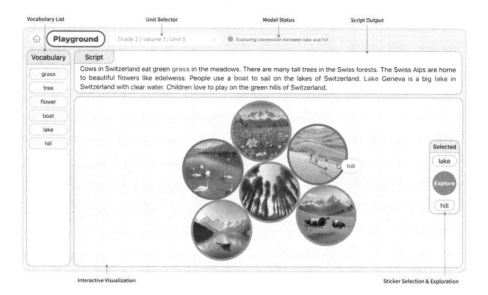

Fig. 5. Explorer view of the Playground.

same context, to establish a connection between the selected items in a pop-up Exploration panel, as shown in Fig. 6. These newly generated elements either act as supplementary materials for the original resources or diverge from the original learning materials, thereby fostering divergent thinking and exploratory learning.

The prompt template and an example output is shown below:

PROMPT: Find the relationship between the following words based on the semantic relevance with the theme of ⟨*Switzerland*⟩. Add related words to make the semantic relevance more consistent. Add a prompt for each word based on the theme for image generation in stable diffusion. Ensure the first and last two words are the input words, for example: "Monitor, Mouse" - "Monitor-Computer-Computer Accessories-Mouse". Here are the two input words: ⟨*lake, hill*⟩.

OUTPUT:
Word: *"geneva"*
Sticker Prompt: *"Cityscape of Geneva, Switzerland, with the iconic Jet d'eau fountain and lake Geneva in the foreground."*
Word: *"chocolate"*
Sticker Prompt: *"Swiss chocolate bars with the Swiss alps mountain in the background."*
Word: *"alps"*

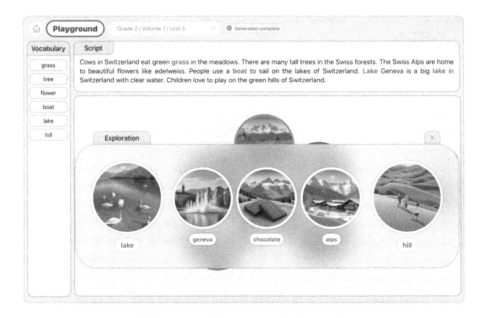

Fig. 6. Example of a relation explored in the Playground.

Sticker Prompt: *"The majestic Swiss alps on a sunny day, with pict uresque ski resorts and chalets"*

5   Discussion

In this article, we presented the ContextVis system, a workflow that leverages generative models for creating contextual learning materials and experiences. Through a case study on contextual vocabulary learning, we have demonstrated the utility of generative models in resource creation and the effectiveness of the system in fostering language development.

The user-friendly Dashboard for educators and an interactive Playground for learners together provide a comprehensive platform for both content creation and engagement. The integration of generative models, contextual cues, and interactive visualizations offers unique opportunities for learners to understand, explore, and retain knowledge. During the development stage, we found that providing competent information such as theme and context to generative models is essential to generate high-quality learning materials.

Future directions for the ContextVis system include expanding the range of generative models and media formats, as well as more in-depth customization options for educators. Overall, the ContextVis system represents a promising approach to enhance contextual and exploratory learning using generative models and interactive visualizations.

Acknowledgements. This work was supported by a research grant from Shenzhen Key Laboratory of Next Generation Interactive Media Innovative Technology (Funding No: ZDSYS20210623092001004) and the Center for Social Governance and Innovation at Tsinghua University, a major research center for Shenzhen Humanities & Social Sciences Key Research Bases.

References

1. Alabdulkarim, A., Li, S., Peng, X.: Automatic story generation: challenges and attempts. arXiv preprint arXiv:2102.12634 (2021)
2. Amershi, S., et al.: Guidelines for human-AI interaction. In: Proceedings of the 2019 CHI Conference on Human Factors in Computing Systems, pp. 1–13 (2019)
3. Bostock, M., Observable: D3 by Observable | The JavaScript library for bespoke data visualization. https://d3js.org/
4. Brown, J.S., Collins, A., Duguid, P.: Situated cognition and the culture of learning. 1989 **18**(1), 32–42 (1989)
5. Cao, Y., Li, S., Liu, Y., Yan, Z., Dai, Y., Yu, P.S., Sun, L.: A comprehensive survey of AI-generated content (AIGC): A history of generative AI from GAN to ChatGpt. arXiv preprint arXiv:2303.04226 (2023)
6. Cila, N.: Designing human-agent collaborations: commitment, responsiveness, and support. In: Proceedings of the 2022 CHI Conference on Human Factors in Computing Systems, pp. 1–18 (2022)
7. Cimolino, G., Graham, T.N.: Two heads are better than one: a dimension space for unifying human and artificial intelligence in shared control. In: Proceedings of the 2022 CHI Conference on Human Factors in Computing Systems, pp. 1–21 (2022)
8. Dijkstra, R., Genç, Z., Kayal, S., Kamps, J., et al.: Reading comprehension quiz generation using generative pre-trained transformers. In: iTextbooks@ AIED, pp. 4–17 (2022)
9. Hu, E.J., et al.: LoRA: Low-rank adaptation of large language models (2021)
10. Ji, H., Han, I., Ko, Y.: A systematic review of conversational AI in language education: focusing on the collaboration with human teachers. J. Res. Technol. Educ. **55**(1), 48–63 (2023)
11. Jin, Z., Song, Z.: Generating coherent comic with rich story using ChatGpt and stable diffusion. arXiv preprint arXiv:2305.11067 (2023)
12. Kloos, C.D., Alario-Hoyos, C.: Educational pyramids aligned: Bloom's taxonomy, the DigCompEdu framework and instructional designs. In: 2021 World Engineering Education Forum/Global Engineering Deans Council (WEEF/GEDC), pp. 110–117. IEEE (2021)
13. Krashen, S.: We acquire vocabulary and spelling by reading: additional evidence for the input hypothesis. Mod. Lang. J. **73**(4), 440–464 (1989)
14. LAZEL: reading A-Z: the online reading program with downloadable books to print and assemble | Reading A-Z. https://www.readinga-z.com/
15. Li, C.: A research into the value and implementation strategy of English picture books for young beginners' English learning based on second language acquisition theory. J. West Anhui Univ. **33**, 134–137 (2017)
16. Lubart, T.: How can computers be partners in the creative process: classification and commentary on the special issue. Int. J. Hum Comput Stud. **63**(4–5), 365–369 (2005)
17. Luo, S., et al.: LCM-LoRA: a universal stable-diffusion acceleration module. arXiv preprint arXiv:2311.05556 (2023)

18. Ministry of Education of the People's Republic of China: English Curriculum Standards for Compulsory Education(2022). Standards for Compulsory Education(2022), Beijing Normal University Press (2022)

19. Norod78: SDXL Emoji LoRA - v1.0 | Stable Diffusion LoRA | Civitai (Sep 2023). https://civitai.com/models/144245/sdxl-emoji-lora

20. Nurhayati, S., et al.: The efficiency of extensive reading using reading AZ on vocabulary enrichment. In: Conference on English Language Teaching, pp. 699–708 (2023)

21. OpenAI, R.: Gpt-4 technical report. arXiv, pp. 2303–08774 (2023)

22. Parents, S.: Learn about leveled reading. https://www.scholastic.com/parents/books-and-reading/reading-resources/book-selection-tips/learn-about-leveled-reading.html

23. Podell, D., et al..: SDXL: improving latent diffusion models for high-resolution image synthesis (2023)

24. Press, O.U.: Oxford Reading Tree: Primary School Literacy Resources. https://global.oup.com/education/content/primary/series/oxford-reading-tree

25. Shi, C., Cai, D., Yang, Y.: LiFi: lightweight controlled text generation with fine-grained control codes. arXiv preprint arXiv:2402.06930 (2024)

26. Shi, Y., Gao, T., Jiao, X., Cao, N.: Understanding design collaboration between designers and artificial intelligence: a systematic literature review. Proc. ACM Hum.-Comput. Interact. **7**(CSCW2), 1–35 (2023)

27. Shui, B., Guo, H., Li, H., Shi, C., Nie, X.: Community tour: an expandable knowledge exploration system for urban migrant children. In: Proceedings of the 22nd Annual ACM Interaction Design and Children Conference, pp. 512–516 (2023)

28. Srl, I.C.S..A.: The philosophy of geronimo stilton. https://geronimostilton.com/WW-en/filosofia/

29. Sturm, T., et al.: Coordinating human and machine learning for effective organizational learning. MIS Q. **45**(3) (2021)

30. Sultanum, N., Srinivasan, A.: Datatales: investigating the use of large language models for authoring data-driven articles. In: 2023 IEEE Visualization and Visual Analytics (VIS), pp. 231–235. IEEE (2023)

31. Wang, l., Zhou, J.: A preliminary Study on the Hierarchical Reading Education Publishing System. View on Publishing, pp. 39–43 (2023)

32. Wei, J., et al.: Emergent abilities of large language models. arXiv preprint arXiv:2206.07682 (2022)

33. Yanman, W.: An empirical study of primary pupils' english reading competence based on English graded readers. Basic Foreign Lang. Educ. **19**, 36–42+110 (2017)

34. Zhang, C., Liu, X., Ziska, K., Jeon, S., Yu, C.L., Xu, Y.: Mathemyths: leveraging large language models to teach mathematical language through Child-AI co-creative storytelling. arXiv preprint arXiv:2402.01927 (2024)

35. Zhang, Y., Tang, L., Ma, C.: Research on the path and countermeasures of artificial intelligence to facilitate teacher development. e-Education Res. **44**, 104–111 (2023)

Designing a Tangible Interactive Learning System for Children's Art Education: A Multi-Sensory Design Approach

Yuwen Sun and Lin Lin[✉]

Nanfang College, Guangzhou, China
2438275230@qq.com

Abstract. This study employed a multi-sensory design approach to design a tangible interactive learning system for children's art education. Through an analysis of current instances of digital art education, a multi-sensory tangible interaction system designed for youngsters between the ages of four and six is proposed.

The design requirements are gathered through an online poll and the design direction are then decided. Subsequently, by adapting the Multi-sensory design method, seven design steps are introduced to facilitate the design process. These steps include selecting target expression, concept exploration, sensory exploration, sensory analysis, user interaction scenarios, model making, and multisensory presentation. This tangible interactive learning system integrates physical desks and interactive screens to offer a comprehensive learning experience. It aims to spark children's curiosity and imagination in art education by incorporating a variety of sensory stimuli. By exploring the application of multi-sensory and tangible interaction systems in children's art education, we hope to incorporate more interactive modalities into art teaching, providing children with diverse learning experiences to better meet their educational needs.

Keywords: Multisensory design · Tangible Interaction · Art Education

1 Introduction

The development of digital technology has permeated various aspects of people's lives, many countries have formulated strategies related to the digital transformation of education. Leveraging digital technology facilitates the establishment of new infrastructure, the opening of shared digital platforms, and the deep integration of digital technology with educational development. The implementation of these strategies has opened up new opportunities for the high-quality development of education and has profoundly impacted children's art education. Early art education serves as a primary resource for children's overall learning and development [1, 2] and fosters future children's learning behavior and attitudes [3]. Therefore, providing children with diverse artistic experiences and opportunities is crucial. Modern education aims to promote multi-sensory interactive experiences in art education through various technologies. Among them, tangible interaction has garnered significant attention in the field of early childhood education

C. Stephanidis et al. (Eds.): HCII 2024, CCIS 2117, pp. 225–234, 2024.
https://doi.org/10.1007/978-3-031-61953-3_25

practice due to its rich sensory experiences involving gestures, movements, or whole-body interactions [4]. Tangible interaction can support children's cognitive processes by expanding their cognitive bandwidth, enabling them to focus on and explore innovative elements [5, 6]. Concrete prototypes in tangible interaction can assist children in completing cognitive processes of imagination [7]. Multi-modal interaction interfaces involving various sensory pathways can effectively engage children's sensory systems, stimulate curiosity, and provide richer cognitive and learning experiences for children in art education [8]. Therefore, tangible interaction technology offers the ability to engage multiple senses, providing a unique opportunity to guide children's cognitive learning through various sensory pathways.

This paper aims to explore the application of multi-modal tangible interaction in art education. In the upcoming chapters, we will provide a comprehensive introduction to art education products associated with tangible interaction, conduct research to define our target users, propose and execute design solutions, and ultimately explore the significance of this design for art education.

2   Previous Works

Below, we analyze four cases that provide us with various insights into experiences of enlightenment through digital art on different levels and in diverse forms.

Taking "TEAMLAB Co-creation! Future Garden" [9] as an example, this immersive art exhibition that exemplifies the core concept of "shared creativity" and "co-creation." It offers children diverse experiences, including interacting with light and shadow and engaging through gestures. This wholehearted interaction allows children to deeply experience the joy of art while playing, prompting them to gain a profound understanding of artistic elements such as light, shadow, and color. *Papier Machine* [10] presents six electronic paper toys in the form of a book, encouraging children to create circuits and produce sounds through folding, assembling, and drawing. This combination of physical and virtual circuits not only ignites children's interest in technology but also expands their understanding of the relationship between circuits and graphics, providing a way to integrate technology with art education. *Peekabook* [11] provides children with a more intuitive and interactive learning experience. *Peekabook* allows children to activate stories through tangible exploration, thereby acquiring knowledge in a more engaging manner. The I/O Brush designed by Kimiko Ryokai [12] connects real-life scenes with a virtual interface, offering children an enjoyable painting learning experience. With this brush, children can capture elements such as colors and textures from the real world and then create in the virtual interface. This innovative painting method not only brings more joy to children's art creation but also helps them intuitively grasp and apply artistic elements. These four cases provide children with different levels of digital art enlightenment experiences. They range from immersive interactive experiences that engage the whole body, practical electronic paper toys, tangible exploration of storybooks, to a combination of the virtual and the real using painting brushes.

These cases showcase innovative applications of multimodal tangible interaction in art education, enhancing children's learning experiences. These cases collectively inspire us to focus on several aspects when designing multimodal interactive devices for children's shape enlightenment. Firstly, immersive interactive experiences are an effective way to stimulate children's interest in learning. They require the creation of various artistic effects through touch and gestures. Secondly, the organic integration of practical activities and electronic elements can enhance children's practical skills. Designing tangible exploration activation stories can convey knowledge more vividly, guiding children to learn in engaging contexts. Finally, the integration of virtual and real elements in design can enhance the learning experience by bridging the gap between the physical world and the virtual interface, thereby fostering children's imagination and creativity.

These four cases offer children various levels of digital art enlightenment experiences. They range from immersive interactive experiences that engage the whole body, practical electronic paper toys, tangible exploration of storybooks, to the combination of virtual and real elements in painting brushes. These cases showcase innovative applications of multi-modal tangible interaction in art enlightenment, enhancing children's learning experiences. These cases collectively inspire us to focus on several aspects when designing multi-modal interactive devices for children's shape enlightenment. Firstly, immersive interactive experiences are an effective way to stimulate children's interest in learning. They require the creation of various artistic effects through touch and gestures. Secondly, the organic integration of practical activities and electronic components can enhance their practical skills. Designing tangible exploration stories can convey knowledge in a more vivid manner, guiding children to learn in engaging contexts. Finally, the integration of virtual and real elements in design can enhance the learning experience by bridging the physical world with the virtual interface, thus fostering children's imagination and creativity.

However, in these studies, there was a lack of effective utilization of multiple sensory channels to enhance learning in the context of art education for children aged 4–6 [13]. Multi-sensory involvement can enrich the learning process and provide powerful support for more comprehensive and in-depth learning. Therefore, we intend to design a tangible multi-sensory interactive art enlightenment system for children aged 4–6. Choosing children aged 4–6 as the target audience for the design is based on the fact that, at this stage, children have already developed a certain level of curiosity and have started to explore. Art, as a highly creative subject, can effectively stimulate children's imagination and creativity.

3   Requirement Gathering

During kindergarten dismissal time, we invited parents of 4–6-year-old children to participate in a survey by scanning a QR code and answering an online questionnaire. We offered small gifts or discount coupons as incentives for participating in the survey. The survey mainly focused on the expectations of parents of 4–6-year-old children regarding this design. A total of 104 valid questionnaires were collected.

The survey revealed that parents' environmental requirements for their children's art education mainly focus on: adequate lighting and colors, a quiet dedicated learning environment, and easily accessible art materials. Regarding the role of parents in children's art enlightenment interactive system, most parents are willing to provide support and

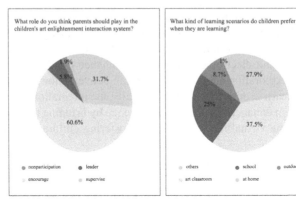

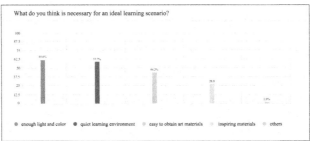

Fig. 1. Survey results

encouragement. These research findings provide guidance for our design of children's art enlightenment education.

4 Summary of Design Goals

Through in-depth research and case analysis, we have identified the following design direction: (1) Create a convenient art enlightenment scenario that offers immersive, multi-sensory interactive experiences and encourages parental assistance and guidance. (2) Utilize a variety of soft fabrics in daily interesting patterns as the primary materials, showcased in the form of fabric patches. (3) Incorporate electronic feedback elements to stimulate children's interest in learning. (4) Emphasize the interactivity and inspiration of the design, stimulating children's creativity and curiosity through touch, observation, and exploration of form.

In selecting the system theme, we opted for points, lines, and surfaces as the focal points of the art learning system. This decision was based on the fact that these basic elements of visual aesthetics, such as points, lines, and surfaces [14], serve as the foundation for children to delve into the world of art. The elements of point, line, and surface can generate various rhythms and patterns through skillful combinations of size, shape, and arrangement, which can stimulate children's artistic awareness.

5   Design Implementation

5.1   Design Method

To fully leverage tangible interaction for providing multisensory stimulation in the Interactive Art Learning System, this paper adopts a multisensory design approach [15] to guide the design process. The Multisensory design approach aims to gather perceptual information through the exploration of multiple senses and explicitly incorporate this process into the design process. This results in a coherent and holistic product that offers users an engaging and rich experience. This approach emphasizes the importance of designing with all sensory modes and proposes eight steps in the design process: Selecting the target expression, Conceptual exploration, Sensory exploration, Sensory analysis, Multisensory mind map, User-interaction scenario, Model making, and Multisensory presentation. We have added a user interface step and, based on our research, adjusted it to seven steps: Selecting the target expression, Conceptual exploration, Sensory exploration, Sensory analysis, User-interaction scenario, Model making, and Multisensory presentation (Fig. 2).

Fig. 2. Design flow

5.2   Design Process

Target Expression. According to the multisensory design process, the first step is to select the target expression. We chose familiarity, curiosity, enjoyment, and "FLOW" [16] as the starting points for the design. This is because familiarity helps children learn and use the system more easily, reducing the time it takes for children to learn a new system and increasing their efficiency in using it. Curiosity helps stimulate children's active participation and increase their interest in the subject. Enjoyment is a positive emotion that motivates children to engage more actively with the system. "FLOW" is included to help children reduce external distractions and increase their focus while using the system.

Conceptual Exploration. The next step, Conceptual Exploration, involves exploring concepts related to the target expression. We conducted searches for relevant concepts in users' life scenarios based on the four concepts mentioned above, resulting in multiple concepts (Fig. 1). Among these concepts, we selected clothing, objects with specific shapes, unfinished objects, bright colors, achievements, and natural environments as the main design scenario objects. These elements are easier to enrich sensory experiences and enhance engagement, thus serving as the primary objects in the design scene (Table 1).

Table 1. Concept exploration and divergent thinking.

Expression	Concept Exploration
Familiarity	school, parks, **clothes**, toys, home, water cups, doors, glasses
Curiosity	**objects of distinctive shapes**, challenging things, **rare things**, un-finished things, blurred photos, magnifying glasses, maps, adventures, encyclopedias
Pleasure	**reward**, emotional resonance, **bright colors**, food, smiling faces, playground, performance
"flow"	**natural environment**, movies, books, musical instruments, painting, sports, beds, exhibitions

Sensory Exploration. The third step is to explore the senses to express familiarity, curiosity, enjoyment, and "FLOW". We explore the possibilities of expressing these concepts through the senses. Based on the conclusions drawn from the second step, we associate the following sensory experiences: the tactile sensation of clothing, distinct tactile sensations, rewarding sounds, unfinished visuals, vibrant colored visuals, and realistic natural environment visuals (Table 2).

Table 2. Sensory exploration.

Expression	Sensory Exploration
Familiarity	the touch of the clothes, familiar faces, often heard mu-sic, familiar taste
Curiosity	prominent graphics, unfinished images, unfamiliar sounds or conversations, different materials
Pleasure	reward sound, bright color picture
"flow"	real natural environment picture

Sensory Analysis. The fourth step combines the senses with the target expression to define how to evoke the target expression. We aim to describe and comprehend the relationship between the sensory characteristics mentioned above and the target expression of the learning system. Clothing is the most common and familiar material in children's lives. Its tactile sensation can evoke feelings of warmth and safety, providing a sense of familiarity. Distinctive graphics, unique textures, and specific sounds can pique children's curiosity and stimulate their desire to explore. Vibrant colors and cheerful sound feedback can bring children a sense of joy. When it comes to the sense of immersion, a system that guides and provides multisensory feedback can help maintain children's focus. The following table summarizes the above content in a graphical form (Fig. 3).

User- Interaction Scenario. Based on the sensory analysis from the previous step, we have decided to create a natural environment-themed setting in the interactive learning

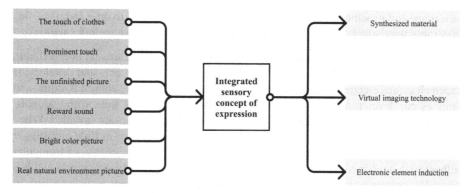

Fig. 3. Sensory analysis

system. We will use a variety of colorful fabrics and electronic components with multiple feedback mechanisms to facilitate children's learning. To ensure that this learning system aligns with children's cognitive characteristics, we have designed the interaction steps of the learning system based on the four stages of cognition: Perception, Processing, Concept Formation, and Inference. This interactive learning system will gradually introduce children to shapes through four stages.

During the perception stage, children's initial processing of information from the external environment is crucial. Therefore, we have designed an activity table made of fabric for children to explore shapes. Inside the activity table, there are four scenes: "Ocean," "Island," "Forest," and "City". Hidden within these scenes are five different shapes: coconut balls (circle), sailboats (triangle), crabs (ellipse), trees (heart), and buildings with square windows (square). This setup combines familiar scenes with various shapes to help children gain initial recognition of shapes. The interaction in this stage involves touching the corresponding shapes with hands.

In the processing and concept formation stages, we primarily focus on enhancing children's learning through manual manipulation and offering abundant sensory feedback.

We have filled the shapes that require exploration with cotton and textured fabrics internally to stimulate children's desire for exploration through tactile experiences. Each time a shape is explored, the electronic components detect it and emit a praising voice to reward the child. Simultaneously, a similar but incomplete puzzle is displayed on the screen to guide children's exploration.

The tangible activity table effectively guides interactions with the shapes, while each appearing fragment on the screen blinks to trigger children's curiosity to touch it. Metaphorically, a voice prompt motivates children to "assist the shape friend in returning to his home," where "home" symbolizes the corresponding shape outline on the screen. This outline also mirrors the color of the respective object, thereby minimizing the learning obstacle. Each time a shape is placed, there are sound effects and friendly praises, accompanied by descriptions of the shape's features. Each shape, whether on the physical activity table or the screen, has its own gameplay and provides positive feedback. During the inference stage, we assess whether children can effectively recognize and utilize shapes. Therefore, we have designed an object on the screen corresponding to each shape and its silhouette with a dashed outline. Children need to drag and place this object into the dashed outline to help them organize and process shape information.

Model Making. Based on the definitions of the system's appearance and interaction in steps five and six, we will proceed to sketch the tangible activity table and develop the screen elements, electronic components, and puzzle game. We have chosen Arduino and Unity as our development tools. On the island, there are coconut trees with coconuts. These balls can be picked up and placed below, where light sensors are installed. When the coconut balls are removed, the light sensors detect the change in light and trigger the appearance of circular beach balls on the screen. In the ocean, there is a triangular sailboat with built-in touch sensors. The sailboat gently caresses the sea breeze, while a triangular ice cream cone appears on the screen. Hidden in the coral reefs are elliptical crabs equipped with sound sensors. When children search for these crabs, slight rustling sounds trigger the appearance of elliptical candies on the screen. In the forest, there are heart-shaped trees equipped with touch sensors and vibration sensors. When touched, the device generates vibrations to mimic the rustling of leaves, and heart-shaped clovers are displayed on the screen. In the city, various buildings contribute to the urban landscape, each adorned with square windows featuring buttons and lights. Simulating the effect of turning the lights on triggers the appearance of square Rubik's cubes on the screen (Fig. 4).

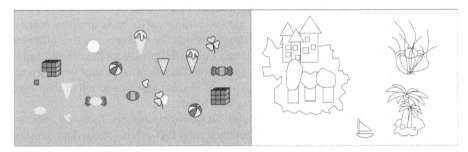

Fig. 4. The left picture shows the game elements in the electronic screen, and the right is the sketch of the tangible operation table

Multisensory Presentation. Based on the interaction methods defined in the sixth step and the sketches drawn in the seventh step, production and development were carried out (Fig. 5).

Fig. 5. Practical effect of interactive system design

6 Discussion

This paper, guided by the multi-sensory design approach, developed a tangible interactive system for children's art education and proposed requirements for a multi-sensory tangible interaction system tailored for 4–6-year-old children. By analyzing existing cases of digital art enlightenment, this study applies multi-sensory tangible interaction to art education. The aim of our study is to stimulate children's curiosity and imagination, integrate traditional teaching with modern technology, promote education towards intelligence and personalization, aid in children's comprehensive development, and lay the foundation for the future sustainable development of society. Through the implementation of the design scheme and exploration of specific steps, this study offers rich learning experiences, guiding children to acquire art knowledge in engaging contexts. In future research, emphasis will be placed on immersive interactive experiences, the organic integration of practical operations and electronic elements, as well as the integration of virtual and real designs. These efforts aim to further enhance the effectiveness of children's art learning and promote the development of their imagination and creativity.

References

1. Burrill, R.R.: Natural biology vs. cultural structures: art and child development in education. Teach. Artist J. **3**(1), 31–40 (2005). https://doi.org/10.1207/s1541180xtaj0301_5
2. Duh, M.: Art appreciation for developing communication skills among preschool children. CEPS J. **6**(1), 71–94 (2016)
3. Barton, G.: Arts-based educational research in the early years. Int. Res. Early Child. Educ. **6**(1), 62–78 (2015)
4. Kazanidis, I., Palaigeorgiou, G., Bazinas, C.: Dynamic interactive number lines for fraction learning in a mixed reality environment. In: 2018 South-Eastern European Design Automation, Computer Engineering, Computer Networks and Society Media Conference (SEEDA_CECNSM), IEEE, 2018, pp. 1–5. Accessed 19 Dec 2023. https://ieeexplore.ieee.org/abstract/document/8544927/

5. Africano, D., Berg, S., Lindbergh, K., Lundholm, P., Nilbrink, F., Persson, A.: Designing tangible interfaces for children's collaboration. In: CHI 2004 Extended Abstracts on Human Factors in Computing Systems, Vienna Austria: ACM, Apr. 2004, pp. 853–868 (2004). https://doi.org/10.1145/985921.985945

6. Zappi, V., McPherson, A.P.: Dimensionality and appropriation in digital musical instrument design, in NIME, Citeseer, 2014, pp. 455–460. Accessed 19 Dec 2023. https://citeseerx.ist.psu.edu/document?repid=rep1&type=pdf&doi=6f21aae6713389a80da2351946fa80970e43b551

7. Kimbell, R., Stables, K.: Researching design learning: Issues and findings from two decades of research and development 2007. Accessed 19 Dec 2023. https://books.google.com/books?hl=zh-CN&lr=&id=aocOFJNuFLEC&oi=fnd&pg=PR9&dq=Researching+design+learning:+Issues+and+findings+from+two+decades+of+research+and+development.&ots=pMmhhfG5lG&sig=9Hz9IXObWS87HJGub3uqUkkTTw4

8. Chu, J.H., Clifton, P., Harley, D., Pavao, J., Mazalek, A.: Mapping Place: Supporting cultural learning through a Lukasa-inspired tangible tabletop museum exhibit. In: Proceedings of the Ninth International Conference on Tangible, Embedded, and Embodied Interaction, Stanford California USA: ACM, Jan. 2015, pp. 261–268 (2015). https://doi.org/10.1145/2677199.2680559

9. Teamlab-futurepark. https://art.team-lab.cn/e/futurepark-cfuturecity/

10. Klemmer, S.R., Li, J., Lin, J., Landay, J.A.: Papier-Mache: toolkit support for tangible input. In: Proceedings of the SIGCHI Conference on Human Factors in Computing Systems, Vienna Austria: ACM, Apr. 2004, pp. 399–406 (2004). https://doi.org/10.1145/985692.985743

11. https://www.peekaworld.com/

12. Ryokai, K., Marti, S., Ishii, H.: 'I/O brush: drawing with everyday objects as ink. In: Proceedings of the SIGCHI Conference on Human Factors in Computing Systems, Vienna Austria: ACM, Apr. 2004, pp. 303–310 (2004). https://doi.org/10.1145/985692.985731

13. Liang, M., Li, Y., Weber, T., Hussmann, H.: Tangible interaction for children's creative learning: a review. In: Creativity and Cognition, Virtual Event Italy: ACM, Jun. 2021, pp. 1–14 (2021). https://doi.org/10.1145/3450741.3465262

14. Kandinsky, W.: Point and line to plane : contribution to the analysis of the pictorial elements (1866–1944)

15. Schifferstein, H.N.J.: Multi-sensory design. In: Proceedings of the Second Conference on Creativity and Innovation in Design, Eindhoven Netherlands: ACM, Oct. 2011, pp. 361–362 (2011). https://doi.org/10.1145/2079216.2079270

16. Csikszentmihalyi, M.: FLOW: The Psychology of Optimal Experience, p. 6 (2000)

Verification of Novel Summarization in Arousing Reading Interests

Hiroya Toyama[1]([✉]), Junjie Shan[2], and Yoko Nishihara[3]

[1] Graduate School of Information Science and Engineering, Ritsumeikan University,
Osaka, Japan
`is0514rv@ed.ritsumei.ac.jp`

[2] Ritsumeikan Global Innovation Research Organization, Ritsumeikan University,
Osaka, Japan
`shan@fc.ritsumei.ac.jp`

[3] College of Information Science and Engineering, Ritsumeikan University,
Osaka, Japan
`nisihara@fc.ritsumei.ac.jp`

Abstract. Young people nowadays spend less time reading books, and their reading comprehension and logical thinking skills are declining. These skills are essential for living in today's information society. On the other hand, polls show that although young people are interested in reading, they usually think that it takes a long time to read a book continuously. The authors considered that if the reading time per book is reduced, readers would read more books and maintain their interest in reading.

One way to shorten reading time is to use summarization. The authors hypothesize that summarizing the text of a novel not only shortens the reading time but also arouses interest in reading. In this paper, The authors implement a novel reading support interface with a summarizing function and test our hypothesis.

The contributions of this paper includes the following two points. (1) the authors implemented a novel reading support interface with a summarizing function and tested the hypothesis. The experimental results show that the implemented interface could arouse the reader's interest in reading a novel while maintaining the reader's comprehension of the novel content. (2) In the validation experiment, the authors created a dataset to measure the comprehension of novels.

Keywords: Effect of summarization · Reading support · Novel

1 Introduction

In recent years, young people have been reading less and less, and the resulting decline in reading comprehension, logical thinking, and emotional capacities has become a social concern [1]. According to a nationwide poll of people aged 16 and older conducted in 2019 [2], 47.3% of respondents answered that they "do not read" any books in a month when asked how many books they read, while 60.4% answered that they "want to increase" their reading volume when asked if they "want to increase" their reading volume. This result suggests that many high school students have interests in reading, but are not able to get involved in reading. In addition, 64.5% of the high school students surveyed by the Ministry of Education, Culture, Sports, Science and Technology (MEXT) answered "I don't have time to read" as the reason for their reluctance. These results indicate that young people believe that reading is a behavior that requires continuity and takes a lot of time. The authors assume that if the time required for each reading could be reduced, readers would have more occasions for reading, which would help them sustain their reading interests.

One way to shorten reading time is to use summarization. The authors argue that if a novel text is summarized, it would not only reduce the amount of time spent on each reading but also allow the reader to access more of the novel's content, which could help to arouse readers' interests. In this paper, the author implement a novel reading support interface with a summarizing function and test the hypothesis.

2 Related Work

Ma et al. [3] proposed a user interface to support reading for readers who read multiple books simultaneously by extracting information on characters and places from the stories and visualizing them in the chronological order in which the characters appear in the story. The proposed user interface is similar to the present study in that it supports users' reading. this study supports users' reading by implementing a summarizing function. This reduces the number of words in a novel and shortens the reading time for each book, thereby stimulating the user's interest and interest in reading.

Lei et al. [4] proposed an interface that allowed users to search the contents and stories of a comic by presenting changes in the frequency of appearance of the components of the comic, such as characters and objects depicted in the comic, while preventing spoilers. The proposed interface is similar to the present study in that it supports users' reading. They assisted users in reading by enabling them to search the contents and stories of comics while preventing users from losing interest due to spoilers. While Ma et al. support user's reading by encouraging them to recall the contents of a story, this study will verify the effect of summarization on user's reading.

3 Implemented User Interface

In this study, the authors implemented a reading support interface with a function to switch between the original text and the summary. Users can use the function to switch between the summary with a reduced number of displayed characters and the novel's original text.

3.1 Interface Overview

The authors implemented a reading support interface which allows users to choose to read the novel's original text or its summary. Figure 1 shows the overview of the implemented user interface. A screen for selecting novel titles will be displayed when a user first launches the interface. After the user selects a novel, the screen will display basic information about the title and the author, followed by sections of the novel divided based on the parts that can be read in about every 10 min. This time is assumed to be a student's commute to school and during breaks, so that the user can read the novel even in his/her spare time. The user can switch between the original text and the summary text while reading each page. Once the user uses the summary function three times, the function will be disabled until the next page. This feature is intended to prevent the user from becoming dependent on the summary function. The bottom right corner of the screen displays the reading completion rate, which increases with each page read. The "Next" button is located in the upper right corner of the screen, while the "Back" button is located in the upper left corner.

The implemented interface uses "Tanteki" as a summarization function that is one of the extractive summarization APIs[1]. One page of the novel text is set as 400 characters. The summary ratio is set to 70%, and each page contain the original text (400 characters) and a summary (280 characters).

In Fig. 1, the user selects the title of the novel. The interface shows the selected title, the author name, and the number of words. The user moves to the content of the novel. The user can select the starting point of reading. By using the "Original" and "Summary" buttons at the bottom of the screen, the user can switch between the original text and the summary text.

4 Evaluation Experiments

The authors conducted experiments to evaluate the hypothesis.

4.1 Experimental Procedures

The details of five novels used in the experiment are shown in Table 1. 14 graduate/undergraduate students were asked to participate in the experiment. The experimental procedures were as follows.

1. The experimenter divided the participants into two groups: Experimental and Control groups. The experimental group uses the implemented interface while the control group uses the other interface that does not have a summarization function.
2. Then the experimenter (1st author) assigns a novel to a participant. The participant reads the novel for 10-min intervals.

---

[1] https://ai-tanteki.com/.

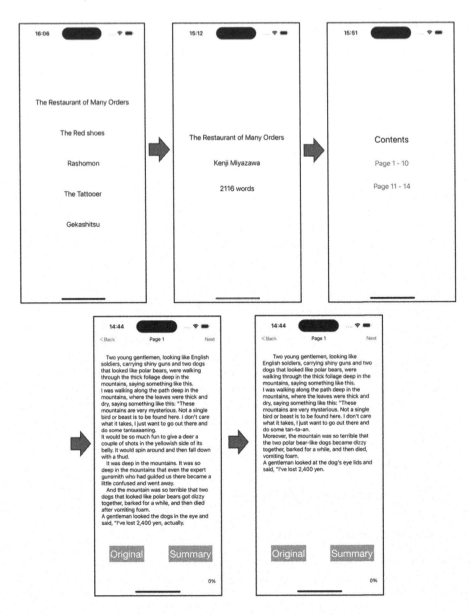

Fig. 1. Implemented User Interface

3. After 10 min of reading, the participant is given quizzes corresponding to the novel contents. The information of the quizzes are shown in Table 2. The quiz examples are shown in Table 3. The questions are six-choice quizzes to check the comprehension of the readings.

4. Repeat steps 2 - 3 for each of the five novels.
5. After the completion of step 4, a questionnaire is given to the participants about their impressions and reading interests.

Table 1. Novels used in verification experiments. Title, author name, and the number of words are described.

Title	Author	The number of words
The Restaurant of Many Orders	Kenji Miyazawa	6,351
The Red shoes	Hans Christian Andersen	7,611
Rashomon	Ryunosuke Akutagawa	6,267
The Tattooer	Junichiro Tanizaki	6,250
Gekashitsu	Kyoka Izumi	8,375

4.2 Evaluation Method

The participants of the experiment were asked to fill out a questionnaire about their reading interest, and the changes in their reading interest were investigated. The authors compared the two groups of participants in terms of changes in reading interest in reading and the percentage of correct answers to the quizzes. The number of questions was from six to nine for each novel, and all questions are six-choice (multiple-choice) questions. Each correct answer is scored $+1$ point and each incorrect answer is scored -1 point. The minimum score for each question was 0, which is not negative. For example, 2 correct answer is and 4 incorrect answers are $+2 - 4 = -2$, but this is not a negative score, so the score is 0 here. The questions were prepared evenly throughout the novel.

Table 2. Number of quizzes for each novel

Title	Number of quizzes
The Restaurant of Many Orders	6
The Red shoes	9
Rashomon	7
The Tattooer	7
Gekashitsu	8

4.3 Experimental Results

Tables 4 show values that indicate changes in interest before and after reading.

Table 3. Quiz samples from "The Restaurant of Many Orders." The underlined option is the correct answer.

Quiz 1	What kind of existence did the dog have for the two young gentlemen?
1	Existence of 2400 yen
2	Existence of 2800 yen
3	Someone who will guide you
4	Existence for hunting
5	Existence like a polar bear
6	Someone who warns of danger
Quiz 2	Which of the following is the correct meaning of "I will never hesitate" ?
1	Do not be afraid
2	Behave
3	No need to worry
4	I don't get paid
5	No need to doubt
6	Please eat as much as you like
Quiz 3	It says, "No matter how the boss writes, it's bad." Who said this?
1	Dog like polar bear
2	Lord of this mountain
3	Owner of blue eyes
4	Mountain bird
5	Rabbit
6	Wildcat
Quiz 4	What is the lesson of this novel?Choose the one that is not appropriate.
1	Horror of nature
2	Value of living things
3	Importance of food
4	Importance of experts
5	Fear of living things
6	Importance of money

A comparison of reading interest between the experimental and control Groups were made. In the experimental and control Groups, it was average 2.85 before reading and average 3.85 after reading, an increase of 1, and in the experimental and control Groups showed average 2 before reading and average 2.42 after reading, an increase of 0.42. The experimental group showed a more significant increase in interest than the control group. This result indicated that the implemented interface could arouse readers' interest in reading novels. The above results indicate that the hypothesis is valid.

Table 5 shows the percentage of correct responses to the quizzes. The averages of the correct rate of quizzes were 48.1% (experimental group) and 48.2% (control group). The percentages were almost equal in both groups. This indicated that the comprehension of the novel's content was similar between reading the original text and its summary.

Table 4. User interest's change in the experimental and control group

	Experimental	Control
Interest before reading	2.85	2
Interest after reading	3.85	2.42
Difference	1.0	0.42

Table 5. Quiz correct rate

	Experimental	Control	Difference
The Restaurant of Many Orders	41.9%	45.7%	3.8%
The Red shoes	54.3%	58.6%	4.3%
Rashomon	40.8%	41.8%	1%
The Tattooer	48.4%	49.4%	1%
Gekashitsu	55.2%	45.7%	9.5%
Average	48.1%	48.2%	0.1%

5   Conclusion

In this paper, the author implemented a reading support interface for novels with a summarization function and verified whether the summarization function can arouse reading interests while maintaining the comprehension of the novel's content. We conducted experiments and found that the summary function could arouse users' reading interest while maintaining their understanding of the novel's content. Future work includes comparing the implemented interface with different summarization ratio and existing summarization systems.

References

1. The Ministry of Education, Japanese language skills required in the future (in Japanese) (2021)
2. The Agency for Cultural Affairs, Summary of the results of the FY 2008 "Public Opinion Survey on the Japanese Language" (in Japanese) (2019)

3. Nishihara, Y., Ma, J., Yamanishi, R.: A support interface for remembering events in novels by visualizing time-series information of characters and their existing places. In: Yamamoto, S., Mori, H. (eds.) HCII 2021. LNCS, vol. 12765, pp. 76–87. Springer, Cham (2021). https://doi.org/10.1007/978-3-030-78321-1_7
4. Lei, K., Nishihara, Y., Yamanishi, R.: Comic Contents Retrieval Support Interface using Speech Frequencies of Characters. In: Yamamoto, S., Mori, H. (eds.) 24th International Conference on Human-Computer Interaction (HCII2022), pp. 33–44 (2022). https://doi.org/10.1007/978-3-031-06509-5_3

STEAM Teaching Research Based on Real and Virtual Technology: A Case Study of 3D Printing Replication and Holographic Interactive Display of Ancient Light-Transmitting Bronze Mirrors

Wei Xiong[1]([⊠]), Liang Hao[2], and Jian Rao[3]

[1] China University of Geosciences, Wuhan 430074, PR China
xiongwei@cug.edu.cn
[2] Southern University of Science and Technology, Shenzhen 518000, PR China
[3] Hubei University of Technology, Wuhan 430074, PR China

Abstract. This study investigates the integration of real and virtual technologies in STEAM (Science, Technology, Engineering, Art, Mathematics) education, specifically in replicating and displaying ancient artifacts. The study presents an example of a Chinese Light-transmitting Bronze Mirror, which belongs to a class of bronze mirrors that reflect light patterns from the back of the mirror onto the wall. The aim is to combine real technologies (e.g. 3D printing) and virtual technologies (e.g. holographic interactivity) into a teaching system. A novel 3D printing method has been developed in the system to replicate the mysterious light-transmitting effect of ancient mirrors, going beyond the traditional teaching of shape-only replication. This method enhances students' comprehension of the correlation between materials, processes, and performance. Additionally, it creatively integrates holographic display with interactive and contemporary optical technologies for artifact exhibition, providing a real-time interactive experience. The outcome is a collection of 3D-printed light-transmitting bronze mirror and a holographic display device that facilitates participatory learning and enhances the appreciation of historical relics. This demonstrates the potential of combining real and virtual technologies in STEAM education and heritage revitalisation.

Keywords: STEAM teaching research · Bronze mirrors · Heritage revitalisation · 3D Printing · Holographic Interactive Display

1 Introduction

The integration of Science, Technology, Engineering, Arts, and Mathematics (STEAM) within educational paradigms not only mirrors the complex interrelations inherent in real-world challenges but also propels forward-thinking in pedagogical methodologies [1]. This study explores the application of a STEAM teaching system to preserve and reinterpret cultural heritage, using the replication and holographic display of ancient

C. Stephanidis et al. (Eds.): HCII 2024, CCIS 2117, pp. 243–250, 2024.
https://doi.org/10.1007/978-3-031-61953-3_27

Chinese translucent bronze mirrors as a case study. This endeavor marries the artisanship of yore with the avant-garde of today, specifically through the avenues of 3D printing and holographic visualization technologies, to deepen the comprehension of historical artifacts while inciting innovation and creative thinking [2].

Ancient Chinese translucent bronze mirrors, celebrated for their intricate designs and enigmatic light-transmitting effect, epitomize the zenith of ancient metallurgy and aesthetic principles [3]. This investigation revisits these cultural treasures through the Light-transmitting Bronze Mirrors of 3D printing, facilitating a tangible interaction with the domains of material science, engineering, and artistic expression, and further, through holographic visualization, it provides a contemporary reimagining of these artifacts [4]. Such an interdisciplinary approach not only forges a continuum between the antiquity and the present but also exemplifies the potential of synthesizing genuine and digital technologies within STEAM teaching system to magnify participatory learning and an appreciation for human ingenuity across epochs.

This inquiry is anchored in the acknowledgment of technology's transformative impact on society and the arts, reflecting the advocacy for the symbiosis of art, science, and technology. This symbiosis is crucial for the evolution of artistic expressions and the conservation of cultural heritage in the contemporary era [5]. The project, dubbed "Looking Back and Moving Forward," delves into the unique interplay of light and shadow intrinsic to Light-transmitting Bronze Mirrors, thereby presenting a novel perspective on traditional Chinese craftsmanship via modern technological mediums. This venture not only aims to rejuvenate a historic art form but also to highlight the seamless integration of ancient skills with contemporary technology, signifying a broader cultural discourse across temporal and spatial dimensions.

Employing STEAM teaching system to recreate and exhibit ancient artifacts in a modern context, this research contributes to a refined understanding of leveraging technological advancements to enrich educational practices, cultural heritage conservation, and artistic innovation. It underscores the educational merit of intertwining hands-on technological applications with the exploration of cultural artifacts, thereby inspiring future generations towards a continuous engagement with innovation, tradition, and creativity. Ultimately, this study stands as a testament to the efficacy of interdisciplinary approaches in education, providing insights into novel pedagogical strategies, practical applications, and the pivotal role of technology in fostering an encompassing and innovative learning milieu [6].

2   Technical Components

The project focuses on using 3D printing for artifact replication, capturing the intricate designs and optical qualities of the mirrors. A specialized printing method replicates the texture and patterns, allowing the mirrors to project light-transmitting effects accurately. Additionally, holographic display technology offers a dynamic way to exhibit the mirrors, providing three-dimensional visuals that enhance viewer engagement and appreciation.

Artifact Replication via 3D Printing. 3D printing transforms object conceptualization and creation, supporting the fabrication of both simple models and intricate, functional items [7]. Within this project's scope, 3D printing is instrumental in duplicating the complex designs and unique optical qualities of the bronze mirrors. The replication commences with an exhaustive analysis of the mirrors' designs, compositions, and manufacturing techniques, guided by historical and metallurgical research. A specialized 3D printing method has been developed to accurately replicate the mirrors' textures and patterns. Adjustments at the micro-scale, based on optical reflection and refraction principles, enable the printed replicas to simulate the mysterious light-transmitting effect of ancient mirrors, creating similar light-transmitting patterns (Fig. 1).

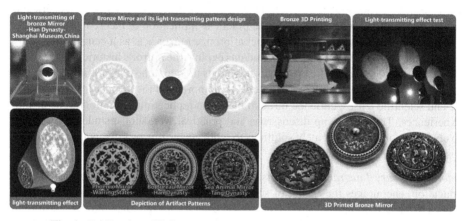

Fig. 1. Replication of light-transmitting bronze mirrors based on 3D printing

Artifact Exhibition Enhancement Through Holographic Interactivity. Holographic display technology marks a significant advancement in artifact exhibition, providing dynamic, three-dimensional visuals that allow viewers to admire objects from multiple perspectives and in varying light conditions [8]. For the ancient bronze mirrors, holography display offers a fresh, engaging method to display their beauty and functionality. The utilized holographic system employs holographic LED fans, real-time vision projection and full-colour ambient lighting to create realistic, interactive holograms, augmenting the appreciation of the mirrors' craftsmanship and the scientific concepts underlying their design (Fig. 2).

HCI for STEAM Education. Incorporating 3D printing and holographic technologies into the STEAM curriculum offers an immersive learning experience [9]. Students delve into the technical facets of artifact replication, covering 3D modeling, material science, and additive manufacturing. They also explore optics and interactive technology through holographic exhibition, gaining insights into ancient innovations' contemporary applications. This hands-on learning approach, supported by real and digital technologies, highlights the importance of interdisciplinary integration in STEAM education, encouraging students to apply scientific and mathematical concepts within creative and artistic frameworks, deepening their appreciation for knowledge interconnectedness and the innovation potential at these junctures.

3 Teaching Methods

Employing case-based learning (CBL) and interdisciplinary integration, this project uses the ancient mirrors as a focal point to encourage practical application of theoretical knowledge [10]. Students engage in hands-on activities, from 3D modeling to holographic display, to replicate and understand the mirrors' historical and scientific significance. This approach fosters collaborative problem-solving and innovation, crucial in STEAM education.

Case-Based Learning (CBL). CBL leverages real-life or hypothetical scenarios to enhance student learning, promoting the practical application of theoretical knowledge [11]. In this project, the ancient translucent bronze mirror acts as a central case study, forming the curriculum's foundation. Students explore the mirror's historical and cultural significance and the scientific principles behind its unique light-transmitting effect. This multidisciplinary approach allows students to comprehend the artifact from both artistic and scientific lenses, enriched through hands-on replication and holographic display experiences. Through group discussions and practical workshops, students collaboratively brainstorm and implement solutions to replicate the mirror's distinctive properties, fostering curiosity and innovation.

Interdisciplinary Integration. Interdisciplinary integration, a cornerstone of STEAM education, encourages the fusion of science, technology, engineering, art, and mathematics to address complex issues. This project exemplifies interdisciplinary learning by merging historical, material science, optics, engineering design, and interactive technology elements. Lesson plans crafted by educators emphasize these disciplines' connections, broadening students' knowledge and showcasing how interdisciplinary collaboration can produce innovative solutions. The project also promotes interdisciplinary integration by involving students in various replication and exhibition aspects, reflecting the diverse expertise contributing to real-world STEAM projects' success [12].

4 Practical Applications

In translating historical craftsmanship into modern technology, students engage in technical practice from conceptualization to execution. Museum exploration serves as the culmination of this process, where students design interactive exhibits. This not only showcases their technical skills but also enhances soft skills like communication and teamwork, as they explain the technology and historical significance to the public.

Technical Practice. The project "Looking Back and Moving Forward" marries technological innovation with historical reverence, extending beyond simple artifact replication. This comprehensive engagement spans from ideation to conceptual realization, exemplifying academic excellence in art, technology, and tradition synthesis. The project begins with an in-depth examination of ancient translucent bronze mirrors, merging aesthetic appreciation with technological application. This phase informs the replicas' functional and aesthetic dimensions, challenging students to blend ancient craftsmanship authenticity with modern technology capabilities. This innovative educational methodology offers an immersive cultural heritage exploration, where students analyze and recreate the artifacts' intricate designs and material properties, bridging historical artisanship with contemporary technological advances.

Museum Exploration. Museum exploration, the project's apex, epitomizes the seamless integration of technical skill and public engagement within a communal context. This endeavor includes exhibition design and public interaction, challenging students to create immersive experiences that effectively communicate the ancient craftsmanship and modern technology interplay to a varied audience [12]. The educational content designed bridges epochs, inviting viewers on a multi-sensory journey through history and technology. As the exhibition opens, it becomes a dynamic interaction stage between students and visitors, fostering a deeper appreciation for the artifacts and the technological achievements in their replication. This engagement nurtures essential soft skills among students, such as communication, teamwork, and public speaking (Fig. 2).

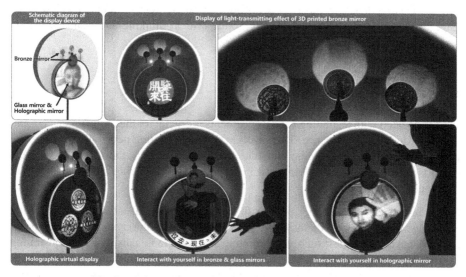

Fig. 2. Holographic display & human-computer interaction

5   Assessment and Feedback

Assessment in this STEAM project focuses on practical skills, creativity, and teamwork, moving beyond traditional exams. Criteria include technical proficiency, innovative problem-solving, and effective collaboration. Continuous feedback throughout the project encourages improvement and supports learning, with evaluations tailored to individual and group contributions.

Performance Assessment. Performance assessment in STEAM education evaluates students' practical skills, creativity, problem-solving capabilities, and collaborative teamwork beyond traditional testing methods. Assessment criteria encompass technical mastery, innovative knowledge application, and effective communication [13]. Technical mastery assessment focuses on students' proficiency with 3D printing and holographic display technologies, including the accurate replication of the bronze mirrors' characteristics and the holographic exhibition's successful implementation. Innovative knowledge application evaluation assesses students' interdisciplinary knowledge application to overcome project challenges, appraising their efforts based on originality and the effective integration of STEAM disciplines concepts. Collaborative teamwork and communication assessment considers students' ability to work effectively in teams and articulate their ideas, including their participation in group discussions and contributions to the project's success.

Continuous Feedback. Continuous feedback is crucial, especially in project-based STEAM education, where students engage in complex, open-ended tasks. Feedback is provided at various project stages, from initial design to the final exhibition, including formative feedback from teachers and peers, reflective feedback through self-evaluation and peer review, and summative feedback to assess final outcomes against established criteria. This feedback fosters a growth mindset, encouraging students to view challenges as learning opportunities and promoting critical thinking and evaluative skills development [14].

6   Technology and Innovation

Staying updated with technological advancements is crucial for the project's success and STEAM education's relevance. This involves not just adopting new tools but fostering a culture of continuous learning and adaptation. Encouraging innovation, the project supports creative problem-solving and iterative design, preparing students for future challenges.

Technology Updates. Keeping pace with rapid technological advancements is vital for STEAM education's vibrancy. The project exemplifies the dynamic integration of cutting-edge technologies, such as 3D printing and holographic displays, demonstrating their potential to transform educational experiences. However, commitment to technology updates involves more than adopting new tools; it encompasses a continuous learning process, adaptation, and application [15]. Educators and students engage in ongoing education to stay informed about technological advancements through workshops, webinars, and professional development courses. As new technologies emerge, the project framework adapts to incorporate these advancements, ensuring the curriculum remains engaging and relevant. This adaptability fosters an environment where interdisciplinary research explores the convergence of technology with art, history, and science, contributing to innovative educational methodologies and resources.

Encouraging Innovation. Innovation is essential to STEAM education, promoting the exploration of new ideas, processes, and solutions. This project creates an environment that values creativity and innovation as fundamental learning components [16]. Through creative problem-solving, students are encouraged to use their knowledge and skills to address complex issues, such as replicating ancient mirrors' intricate designs and optical effects. Collaborative ideation sessions facilitate the exchange of ideas among students, educators, and experts from various fields, highlighting the importance of diverse perspectives in fostering creativity. The design-thinking approach, which involves prototyping and iterative testing, deepens students' understanding of scientific and artistic principles and encourages experimentation and continuous improvement. The project concludes with opportunities for students to showcase their innovative solutions, providing a platform for reflection and discussion, and allowing students to receive feedback on their work's impact (Fig. 3).

Fig. 3. Schematic diagram of STEAM teaching system framework

7   Conclusion and Future Directions

The integration of authentic and digital technologies in STEAM education, as demonstrated by the project on replicating and exhibiting ancient translucent bronze mirrors, marks a significant evolution in educational methodologies. This project showcases the potential of STEAM education to foster an interdisciplinary learning environment, where learners engage in hands-on, project-based learning, developing a deep understanding of the interplay between science, technology, engineering, art, and mathematics. It emphasizes the importance of incorporating cultural and historical perspectives, enhancing students' appreciation for cultural heritage and the technological achievements of ancient civilizations. Looking ahead, the successful integration of authentic and digital technologies opens up new avenues for exploration and innovation in STEAM education, with the potential to broaden the scope of interdisciplinary learning and cultural appreciation. Ensuring the accessibility and inclusivity of STEAM education remains a priority, with further research needed to explore effective strategies for implementation across diverse educational settings. The project on ancient translucent bronze mirrors serves as a compelling example of how STEAM education can bridge the gap between historical and contemporary realms, theoretical knowledge and practical application, and education and innovation, inspiring the next generation to explore the vast expanse of human knowledge and creativity, fostering a future where technology and culture converge in the pursuit of understanding, preservation, and innovation.

Acknowledgments. This research was supported by the National Art Fund's 2023 Art Talent Training Grant Programme "Young Talent Training for Digital Creative Design of Museum".

References

1. Belbase, S., et al.: At the dawn of science, technology, engineering, arts, and mathematics (STEAM) education: prospects, priorities, processes, and problems. Int. J. Math. Educ. Sci. Technol. **53**, 2919–2955 (2022)
2. Katsioloudis, P.J., Jones, M.V.: A comparative analysis of holographic, 3D-Printed, and computer-generated models: implications for engineering technology students' spatial visualization ability. J. Technol. Educ. **29**, 36–53 (2018)
3. Michaelson, C., Portal, J.: Chinese Art in Detail, vol. 3. Harvard University Press (2006)
4. Tam, K.-K. (ed.): Sight as Site in the Digital Age: Art, the Museum, and Representation. Springer Nature Singapore, Singapore (2023)
5. Hosagrahar, J., Soule, J., Girard, L.F., Potts, A.: Cultural heritage, the UN sustainable development goals, and the new urban agenda. BDC. Bollettino Del Centro Calza Bini **16**, 37–54 (2016)
6. Crayton, J.: Designing for immersive technology: integrating art and STEM learning (2015)
7. Malik, U.S., Tissen, L., Vermeeren, A.: 3D reproductions of cultural heritage artifacts: evaluation of significance and experience. Stud. Digital Heritage **5**, 1–29 (2021)
8. Li, Y., Yang, Q., Xiong, J., Yin, K., Wu, S.-T.: 3D displays in augmented and virtual realities with holographic optical elements. Opt. Express **29**, 42696–42712 (2021)
9. Issa, T., Isaias, P.: Usability and Human–Computer Interaction (HCI). In: Issa, T., Isaias, P. (eds.) Sustainable Design: HCI, Usability and Environmental Concerns, pp. 23–40. Springer London, London (2022). https://doi.org/10.1007/978-1-4471-7513-1_2
10. Chen, C.W.J., Lo, K.M.J.: From teacher-designer to student-researcher: a study of attitude change regarding creativity in STEAM education by using Makey Makey as a platform for human-centred design instrument. J. STEM Educ. Res. **2**, 75–91 (2019)
11. Pinto, B.L.: Distinguishing between case based and problem based learning. International J. Kinesiol. High. Educ. **7**, 246–256 (2023)
12. Karnthaworn, N.: Interdisciplinary artists: the collaboration of interdisciplinary artists foster interdisciplinary education (2020)
13. Vicente, F.R., Llinares, A.Z., Sánchez, N.M.: Curriculum analysis and design, implementation, and validation of a STEAM project through educational robotics in primary education. Comput. Appl. Eng. Educ. **29**(1), 160–174 (2021). https://doi.org/10.1002/cae.22373
14. Domenici, V.: STEAM project-based learning activities at the science museum as an effective training for future chemistry teachers. Educ. Sci. **12**, 30 (2022)
15. Huang, Z., et al.: A systematic interdisciplinary engineering and technology model using cutting-edge technologies for STEM education. IEEE Trans. Educ. **64**, 390–397 (2021)
16. Conradty, C., Bogner, F.X.: STEAM teaching professional development works: Effects on students' creativity and motivation. Smart Learn. Environ. **7**, 1–20 (2020)

Research on the Practice of New Media Literacy Education in the Context of Integrated Online Education

Lin Yu and Jingyuan Shi[✉]

School of Film Television and Communication, Xiamen University of Technology, Xiamen, China
shijingyuan0419@163.com

Abstract. Online education has developed rapidly after the new crown pandemic, but along with the development of integrated online education, the new media literacy of primary school students' groups has not been enhanced and improved accordingly, and at the same time, they are looking for a lot of challenges and shortcomings. In this study, we designed a set of experiments to integrate the online media literacy programme into the information technology curriculum of primary school students, so as to verify that the online media literacy programme has a significant effect on improving the new media literacy of primary school students.

Keywords: Primary school student population · New media literacy · Integrated online education

1 Research Background

In 2020, with the new crown epidemic sweeping the world, online education ushered in the large-scale promotion and application of landing, catechism, live class, VR teaching and other convergent online education mode rapidly emerged and widely used, according to the analysis of professional consulting agencies, in 2020, in the field of school education, online education covers nearly 300 million teachers and students users [1]. The popularisation of online education has put forward new challenges to new media literacy education:

The target of media literacy education is lowering in age. With the opening of online classes in schools within the system, a large number of primary school students have flocked to the field of online education other than online English training, the use of multimedia teaching tools has made a radical change in the way of learning, homework and the form of homework, and the "digital divide" is widening. On many educational platforms, the setting of WeChat and QQ identity logins and the opening of a large number of WeChat and QQ groups for course communication have also brought primary school students into prolonged and high-frequency contact with online social media, and the age at which online social interactions take place has moved downward rapidly. The lower

C. Stephanidis et al. (Eds.): HCII 2024, CCIS 2117, pp. 251–258, 2024.
https://doi.org/10.1007/978-3-031-61953-3_28

age of the learning object puts forward new requirements for media literacy education, and the original research on media literacy education with teenagers as the main research object has lagged behind the reality of practice.

The goal of media literacy education has become more positive. As mentioned earlier, the goal of media literacy education, especially for teenagers, is to enhance the audience's ability to identify and use online information or to prevent and control online games and Internet addiction, while in the era of network education, the goal of new media literacy education should be to cultivate the audience's ability to participate in the creation of society by actively using new media tools. The core demand of media literacy has shifted from the past "use" skills to "participation" ability.

Expanding the content of media literacy education. Under the background of online education, the original "protectionist" media literacy education content setting, which mainly aims at "identifying rumours" and "preventing Internet addiction", can no longer adapt to the changes brought about by the new media technology for education. The educational content of media literacy that used to meet the needs of the 1.0 era of traditional media and the Internet must be expanded to include the educational content of the 3.0 era of information production literacy, information consumption literacy, social interaction literacy, social collaboration literacy and social participation literacy. The content of media literacy education beyond "protectionism" needs to be more targeted, systematic and personalised in order to meet the learning needs of younger learners.

Diversification of media literacy education platforms. The flourishing development of online education has brought more abundant platforms and means for the implementation of media literacy education. Compared with the traditional offline education mode of "going to campus", media literacy education can and should be online, and the rapid expansion of the scale of learners, the richness and diversity of teaching methods, and the visible effect of real-time interactive practice have become the accelerator of the development of media literacy education. Exploring the use of multimedia tools in media literacy education can enable educators to increase the sense of immersion, participation and interaction in the process of improving media literacy, which fits the core demand of "participation and sharing" in media literacy education, and helps to promote a new paradigm of media literacy education, so as to achieve the goal of It helps to promote a new paradigm of media literacy education, thus achieving the new goal of media literacy education in the new media society, which is "to educate people through the media, to transform people through the media, to cultivate the elements through the media, and to cultivate virtue through the media".

Low-age learners of online education, mainly targeting primary school students, have outstanding characteristics in new media contact: first, in new media, mobile phone media is the main tool for touching the Internet, and among the various applications of mobile phone media, games and videos are the main content of contact; second, in active media contact behaviours, in addition to the school learning tasks, entertainment is the main motivation, followed by QQ applications as a representative of the social Third, the overall level of network literacy is low, easily influenced by individuals, families, schools, etc., and their new media contact behaviours have a trend of "adultisation".

Through visits and surveys, it is found that there are no special courses and materials on new media literacy education for primary school students, and the most relevant course for primary school students is the "Information Technology" course. The Information Technology course is offered from the third year of primary school. The primary school curriculum centres on the use of computers, teaching basic computer hardware (switching on and off, keyboard input methods, mouse use, etc.), and software, focusing on basic operations such as file management, simple drawing, and editing Word documents.

2 Literature Review

The concept of media literacy was first used in 1933 by the British scholar Leavis et al. in The Cultural Environment: Developing Critical Consciousness, which pointed out that the media could have a negative impact on young people and that there was a need to identify and critique information. It was not until the 1980s that media and information literacy education was gradually developed worldwide, and in 2007, UNESCO issued the Paris Declaration (also known as the 12 Recommendations on Media Education), signalling that media literacy education had become an integral part of civic education for the development of societies around the world, and that there was an urgent need for its widespread promotion and necessary implementation. By now, improving citizens' media literacy and popularising the development of media literacy education have become an important part of the soft power competition among countries.

At present, the concept of "media literacy" has not formed a unified concept in the international arena. In the academic world, western media literacy research has experienced four paradigm changes: protectionism, cultivation of discernment, critical interpretation and participatory culture, and educational theory research mainly focuses on the connotation and essence of media literacy education, development history, development concept and theoretical paradigm, and in terms of the research object, it focuses on the research of media literacy of a specific group.

Domestic research on media literacy education began in 1997 with a paper published by Bu Wei of the Chinese Academy of Social Sciences, "On the Meaning, Content and Methods of Media Education" [2]. After more than twenty years of development, media literacy education research has gone through the stages of importing western media literacy related theories and media literacy education experiences, exploring the theories of "protectionism" as a representative of China's real-world problems, and exploring localised theoretical constructs and practices.

In the 21st century, with the development of new media technology, the study of "new media literacy" has received increasing attention. The Global Framework for Digital Literacy, released by UNESCO in 2018, defines "digital literacy" as the ability to access, manage, understand, integrate, communicate, evaluate, and create information in a safe and compliant manner. The study of new media literacy education has also become a hot research topic.

A search on China Knowledge with the keywords "new media" and "media literacy" yielded 134 papers from 2010 to 2020, of which, in terms of research objects, most research results focus on media literacy education for secondary school and college students. In terms of research objects, most of the research results focus on media literacy education research for young people, mainly for secondary school students and university students, followed by media literacy research for various occupational groups; in terms of research contents, most of the research results refer to western media literacy theories and practice models, and most of the research results are generalised, empty, general and subjective discussions about media literacy in the form of experience. Apart from theoretical studies, there are only a few empirical studies on media literacy. At the same time, most of the studies aim at improving the ability of the audience to screen and use online information in the Internet era. At present, there is no media literacy education research specifically focusing on online education. For example, researcher Shan Jie focuses on the construction of digital literacy index system for junior high school students, with a view to enriching the study of digital literacy assessment index system for junior high school students, and the study provides reference basis for cultivating and enhancing digital literacy of junior high school students [3]. Researcher Zhang Yu explores the cultivation strategy for the improvement of digital literacy of public librarians in China, and builds a three-dimensional ability portrait for the intelligent librarians of smart libraries [4]. Chen Xiaoqi attempts to further improve the digital literacy level of Chinese university students through research and construct a digital literacy evaluation framework applicable to Chinese university students [5].

3   Experiment Design

The purpose of this experiment is to use the children's literacy online education course in the primary school information technology teaching process, whether the primary school students can learn the course content better in the integrated online education environment, as well as to verify whether this method has a better teaching effect. In the experiment, we set up an experimental group and a control group, in the control group the traditional offline teaching method is used for learning, and in the experimental group, some of the courses are integrated with online teaching in the learning process. The syllabus and learning objectives of the two groups of students are the same, and only the differentiation of the teaching method is done. The two groups of experimental subjects after a period of study to carry out academic achievement tests and questionnaires.

3.1   Experimental Participants

A primary school in Xiamen City, Fujian Province, China, 4th grade students were selected for the experiment, and two classes of 30 students each were randomly selected, totalling 60 participants, with Class A as the experimental group and Class B as the control group. The students in the two classes were of the same age, and the ratio of males to females was equal, and there was no major difference in their learning experiences and academic performance.

3.2   Measuring Tools

The measurement of the experimental data consisted of two parts. A measurement was taken before the experiment to ensure that there were no large individual differences between the subjects. A questionnaire was administered to the students at the end of the experiment to measure the experimental data. The content of the questionnaire included the rating of the difficulty of the course, the rating of the concentration of the course, the ability and initiative to obtain information independently, the ability to analyse the information, the ability and initiative to evaluate the information, the ability to disseminate the information, the degree of motivation to use the new media tools for learning, and the degree of the teacher's use of the online course to motivate the students to learn. The questionnaires were set on a scale of 1–5 for each item, and the data were analysed using t-tests (fully called independent samples t-tests) for both tests after the experiment.

3.3   Experimental Process

Class A was set as the experimental group and class B as the control group respectively. The two classes participating in the experiment had a total of 60 students, the students in the two classes had similar performance, the gender ratio of men and women was equal, and the two classes' pre-requisite courses ensured the same, and there were no obvious large individual differences between the two classes. At the beginning of the experiment, the same teacher taught the course "Information Technology" for both groups, and the order of classes in the two classes was exchanged every week to exclude, as far as possible, the different effects of the teacher's motivation on the students.

The two groups maintained the same pace and content in the IT theory and computer practice sections. On this basis, students in the experimental group joined an online course on children's Internet literacy for after-school practice. The teacher then explains the content of network literacy in the classroom in combination with the actual content of the course. After the course was completely finished, questionnaires were administered to the two groups of students separately. The questionnaire data were analysed at the end (Fig. 1).

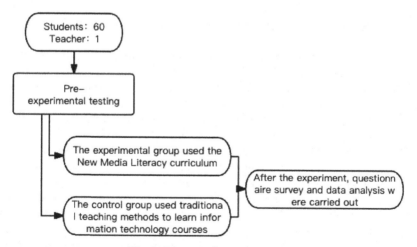

Fig. 1. The experimental process

4 Experimental Results

From the above table, we can see that the t-test (independent samples t-test) was used to study the differences in the degree of students' interest in the course, course concentration scores, ability and initiative to obtain information independently, ability to analyse information, ability and initiative to evaluate information, ability to disseminate information, degree of motivation to use the new media tools for learning, and the degree of the teacher's motivation to motivate students' learning by using the online courses in different ways. From the above table, it can be seen that: the samples of different classes show significant differences in the degree of interest in the course, the score of concentration in the course, the ability and initiative of obtaining information on their own, the ability to analyse information, the ability and initiative of evaluating information, the ability to disseminate information, the degree of motivation to use new media tools for learning, and the degree of the teacher's motivation to use the online course to motivate students to learn. ($p < 0.05$), which means that there are differences in the degree of interest in the course, course concentration score, ability and initiative to obtain information, ability to analyse information, ability and initiative to evaluate information, ability to disseminate information, motivation to use new media tools for learning, and the degree of motivation of teachers to motivate students to learn by using online courses among different classes.

Specific analyses show that: the level of class interest in the course is significant at the 0.05 level ($t = 2.624$, $p = 0.011$), and the difference in comparison shows that the mean of 1.0 (3.10) is significantly higher than the mean of 2.0 (2.40). The different groups showed a 0.01 level of significance ($t = 2.877$, $p = 0.006$) for course concentration scores, as well as specific comparative differences, with the mean of 1.0 (3.30) being significantly higher than the mean of 2.0 (2.60).The ability and initiative of the different groups to obtain information on their own showed a level of significance of 0.01 ($t = 2.828$, $p = 0.006$), as well as specific comparative differences, the mean of 1.0 (3.17), which is significantly higher than the mean of 2.0 (2.53). The ability of the different groups to analyse information showed a 0.05 level of significance ($t = 2.163$, $p = 0.035$), as well as specific comparative differences, with the mean of 1.0 (3.13), being significantly higher than the mean of 2.0 (2.53). The ability and initiative of the different groups for evaluating information showed a 0.01 level of significance ($t = 3.317$, $p = 0.002$), as well as specific comparative differences as shown by the fact that the mean of 1.0 (3.43), will be significantly higher than the mean of 2.0 (2.50). The ability of the different groups to disseminate information is significant at the 0.01 level of significance ($t = 4.810$, $p = 0.000$), as well as the difference in specific comparisons, which shows that the mean of 1.0 (3.20) is significantly higher than the mean of 2.0 (2.10). The level of motivation of the different groups to use new media tools for learning shows a level of significance of 0.05 ($t = 2.199$, $p = 0.033$), as well as a difference in the specific comparisons, which shows that the mean of 1.0 (3.20), is significantly higher than the mean of 2.0 (2.57). The different groups showed 0.01 level of significance ($t = 3.585$, $p = 0.001$) for the degree of teachers' motivation of students using online courses, as well as the difference in specific comparisons, which shows that the mean value of 1.0 (3.13) is significantly higher than the mean value of 2.0 (2.23).

In conclusion, it can be seen that there are significant differences between the samples of different classes in terms of the level of interest in the course, the level of concentration on the course, the ability and initiative to obtain information on their own, the ability to analyse the information, the ability and initiative to evaluate the information, the ability to disseminate the information, the level of motivation to use the new media tools for learning, and the level of teacher's motivation to motivate the students to learn by using the online course (Table 1).

Table 1. Questionnaire data T test results.

	Class (mean ± standard deviation)		t	p
	experimental group($n =$ 30)	control group($n = 30$)		
Course Interest Level	3.10 ± 0.99	2.40 ± 1.07	2.624	0.011*
Course concentration score	3.30 ± 1.12	2.60 ± 0.72	2.877	0.006**
Ability and initiative to obtain information on your own	3.17 ± 1.02	2.53 ± 0.68	2.828	0.006**
Ability to analyse information	3.13 ± 1.28	2.53 ± 0.82	2.163	0.035*
Ability and initiative to evaluate information	3.43 ± 1.25	2.50 ± 0.90	3.317	0.002**
Ability to disseminate information	3.20 ± 1.06	2.10 ± 0.66	4.810	0.000**
Degree of motivation to use new media tools for learning	3.20 ± 1.32	2.57 ± 0.86	2.199	0.033*
Degree to which teachers use online courses to motivate students to learn	3.13 ± 1.11	2.23 ± 0.82	3.585	0.001**

$* p < 0.05 ** p < 0.01$

5   Discussion and Conclusions

After analysing the data after the experiment, we can conclude that adding the online new media literacy course to the Chinese primary school students' information technology course is conducive to the overall improvement of the primary school students' new media literacy, and compared with the traditional information technology teaching mode, the students' interest in the course, course concentration scores, the ability and initiative to obtain information on their own, the ability to analyse information, the ability to evaluate information, and the ability to take the initiative to communicate information, were all significantly different. The students' interest in the course, concentration score, ability and initiative to obtain information, ability and initiative to analyse information, ability and initiative to evaluate information, ability to disseminate information, and motivation to use new media tools for learning were significantly improved compared with the traditional IT teaching mode. It is convenient, fast and low-cost to improve the new media literacy of primary school students, and it will further enrich the comprehensive ability of primary school students and promote their all-round development by cultivating their ability and literacy in acquiring, analysing, applying and disseminating information in advance. The shortcomings lie in the fact that the teaching materials available for the new media literacy enhancement programme are insufficient at present, and the popularity rate among primary school students is low, meanwhile, primary school students' attention is easily diverted by other information, etc., when they use the new media for the media literacy enhancement programme. Network literacy is the extension and development of core literacy in the network environment, network literacy education is an important way to promote the overall development of students, the modernisation of education requires that the development of network literacy education should be constructed to reflect the characteristics of the new era of the network literacy education system, which in turn needs to be achieved through the construction of a subjective, systematic, scientific and constructive network literacy education curriculum system [6]. The improvement of children's media literacy in the future there is still a lot of room for development and improvement.

Funding. This work was supported by The Education Department of Fujian Province Project "Research on the Practice of New Media Literacy Education in the Context of Integrated Online Education" (Funding Number JAS20317).

References

1. AiMedia Report|China K12 Online Education Industry Research Report in the First Half of 2019. https://www.iimedia.cn/c400/65829.html
2. Wei, B.: On the Meaning, content and methods of media education. Mod. Commun. J. Beijing Broadcast. Inst. **01**, 29–33 (1997). https://doi.org/10.19997/j.cnki.xdcb.1997.01.007
3. Shan, J.: Research on the construction and application of digital literacy assessment index system for junior high school students. Northwest Normal Univ. (2023). https://doi.org/10.27410/d.cnki.gxbfu.2023.000246
4. Zhang, Y.: Research on the construction and measurement of digital literacy evaluation system for public librarians. Nanchang Univ. (2023). https://doi.org/10.27232/d.cnki.gnchu.2023.002422
5. Xiaoqi, C.: Research on gender differences in digital literacy of college students in China and its influencing factors. Central China Normal Univ. (2023). https://doi.org/10.27159/d.cnki.ghzsu.2023.001906
6. Chen, M.: Research on the construction of curriculum system of network literacy education for primary school students. Ludong Univ. (2023). https://doi.org/10.27216/d.cnki.gysfc.2023.000295

Design and Evaluation of a Gamified Generative AI Chatbot for Canvas LMS Courses

Ramin Zandvakili[1]($\boxtimes$), De Liu[1], Andy Tao Li[2], Radhika Santhanam[3], and Scott Schanke[4]

[1] Carlson School of Management, University of Minnesota, Minneapolis, MN, USA
{zandv003,deliu}@umn.edu

[2] University of Science and Technology of China, Hefei, Anhui, China

[3] Price College of Business, University of Oklahoma, Norman, OK, USA
Radhika@ou.edu

[4] Lubar College of Business, UW Milwaukee, Milwaukee, WI, USA
schanke@uwm.edu

Abstract. In the post-COVID era, student engagement and performance in traditional courses have declined, presenting significant challenges for educators and institutions. Addressing this issue necessitates innovative tools that enhance student participation and allow for customized instructional support. Notably, students underutilize learning management systems (LMS), highlighting the need for improved interfaces. Generative AI chatbots, known for their adaptability and real-time response capabilities, emerge as pivotal in fostering learning and engagement. Despite their potential, reluctance to adopt chatbots persists among students. Addressing these hurdles, we developed SmartPal, a generative AI chatbot integrated with gamification to bolster learning support. SmartPal capitalizes on psychological gamification theories, offering a personalized, context-aware service by syncing with Canvas LMS. This enables it to provide not just answers but also proactive engagement prompts like reminders and feedback. Incorporating gamification enhances the interactive aspect, motivating students to engage with course content and technology engagingly. Additionally, SmartPal equips instructors with insights into students' progress and engagement, facilitating early identification of and intervention in learning obstacles. Pilot implementations across various undergraduate courses have demonstrated SmartPal's effectiveness in enhancing student engagement and performance.

Keywords: Chatbot · Conversational Agent · Large Language Models (LLMs) · Gamification · Mobile Application

1 Introduction

In contemporary educational landscapes, advanced technological tools and innovations have heralded new prospects for enhancing academic performance. Particularly, the emergence of large language models (LLMs) has unveiled novel

C. Stephanidis et al. (Eds.): HCII 2024, CCIS 2117, pp. 259–264, 2024.
https://doi.org/10.1007/978-3-031-61953-3_29

avenues for deploying them as innovative user interfaces. These interfaces facilitate natural language conversations with students, allowing for the articulation of inquiries and the seamless integration with extant educational systems, such as Learning Management Systems (LMS), to deliver timely and pertinent information to learners.

On the one hand, the advent of LLMs, like ChatGPT, provides new opportunities for designing new user-friendly interfaces that can augment LMS by using the ability to converse with the students in natural language. On the other hand, despite these advancements, prior research indicates a prevalent hesitance among students to engage with conversational agents or chatbots compared to a human counterpart [1]. Gamification strategies have been employed before with notable success to incentivize students and foster greater student engagement [2,3] by adding elements of games to real life [4]. We propose that, in the same way, adding gamification to a conversational agent can alleviate the challenge of students' low engagement with the conversational agent.

Within this context, the current study introduces and evaluates SmartPal, a learning support system that provides students with a chatbot that integrates with and augments the traditional Canvas LMS. This integration allows students to query course-related information through a messaging interface and receive real-time contextual nudges from the chatbot so that they can get information about their own learning and engage in the course. Moreover, SmartPal incorporates gamification elements aimed at motivating student interaction with both the AI chatbot and the LMS course.

2 Design of SmartPal

SmartPal's design is grounded in the principles of psychological gamification theories, incorporating an array of features specifically tailored to assist students. Below, we delve into a more comprehensive exploration of SmartPal's diverse features, elucidating their design and intended support mechanisms for student engagement and learning.

2.1 SmartPal's Features

As illustrated in Fig. 1, SmartPal is positioned to be an intelligent mediator between students, instructors, and the LMS. SmartPal gets information about the course, assignments, submissions, student activities, and grades on Canvas LMS in a timely fashion. To support students, SmartPal provides them with timely reminders, formative feedback, self-reflection opportunities, and actionable recommendations, all through conversations with a chatbot agent. To support instructors' responsive teaching, SmartPal provides reports of student engagement progress and alerts of students who may need additional support.

The design of SmartPal has several key features:

- **Mobile-first**: We take advantage of the mobile app as a powerful delivery mechanism. Compared with traditional website and email-based delivery

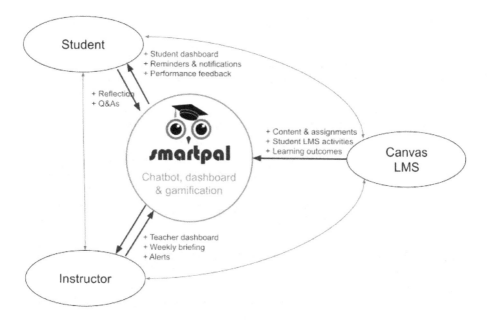

Fig. 1. A Framework for SmartPal

mechanisms, mobile apps have several advantages, including being proactive, ubiquitous, and timely.

- **LMS integration**: The SmartPal app ties in with the LMS system, namely, Canvas, as a crucial source of real-time information. This allows the SmartPal App to be equipped with real-time and accurate information about an ongoing course and provides timely interventions such as reminders, progress reports, performance feedback, and solicitation of reflections.
- **Chatbot-enabled**: We leverage Chatbot technology as a versatile and powerful human-computer interaction tool. Using the latest generative AI technology, the chatbot can provide a natural way for the system to interact with students, delivering context-specific information, nudges, and answers in a natural and easy-to-understand manner.
- **Theory-driven design**: The design of our systems is informed by the gamification literature. The gamification literature informs us of ways to design engaging and meaningful technology systems and motivates students to engage with both LMS and SmartPal using several gamification design elements.
- **Instructor empowerment**: While the app's primary goal is to help students, we also leverage the app to empower the instructors by providing data-driven insights about student progress and engagement and funnel students' needs and feedback in a more timely, effortless manner so that instructors can better identify the learning barriers and take proactive steps to address them.

2.2   Design of the Chatbot

The chatbot embedded in SmartPal leverages the recent Generative Artificial Intelligence (AI) technologies, which makes it more versatile compared to previous generations of chatbots. SmartPal's advanced chatbot is engineered to engage in dialogues with students utilizing natural language, facilitating an interactive learning experience.

SmartPal's chatbot is designed to answer various questions, such as questions related to the syllabus, assignments, grades, course content, and the SmartPal system itself. Since such information is highly specific to the course and often dynamically changing, we cannot rely solely on pre-trained large language models (LLMs). Instead, we leverage Retrieval Augmented Generation (RAG) technology, which enhances the LLM's capability by including pertinent information within the prompt, serving as context for the query. Specifically, we extract course-specific documents such as syllabus, announcements, schedules, course content, and user guides for the chatbot and SmartPal app, store their numerical embedding vectors, and store them into a vector-based database. We organize different documents into different "tools," - such as a tool for the syllabus. For example, students can ask questions about their current grade in the course, ask about the next office hours, or ask the chatbot to explain a concept. With user input to the chatbot, the system first determines which tool is the best match. It then retrieves relevant segments of documents stored in the vector-based database for this tool based on similarity scores. The retrieved documents are then supplied to an LLM (specifically OpenAI's GPT 3.5 language model) as part of the prompt, along with the original question. We prompt the LLM to return text in a form suitable for the chatbot and return it to the user. This way, we ensure the chatbot's answer to the student inquiries is not only pertinent to the course but also fresh. Using this approach, the agent is safeguarded to respond exclusively to relevant inquiries, thereby enhancing the reliability and educational value of student interactions. We have developed the conversational agent using LangChain, a Python framework dedicated to developing LLM applications.

Besides being able to respond to student inquiries and requests, we also empower the agent to proactively inform and nudge users based on LMS events and predefined triggers. These include sending timely reminders to unsubmitted assignments, providing feedback and encouragement, soliciting reflections after students complete an assignment or a quiz, and reminding students of their progress toward their course goals. These interactions are designed to foster a more engaged and reflective learning experience, encouraging students to take an active role in their educational journey.

2.3   Design of Gamification

The app uses gems to keep track of your engagement in the course. Students can collect gems from four types of engagement activities: Canvas pageviews, assignment submissions, chats with the chatbot, and answers to reflection questions.

Students gain levels based on the gems that they have gathered. Each student has an avatar that grows as they progress through levels. Students who gain the highest number of gems are shown on the weakly and overall leaderboards.

3   Evaluation of the Design

We conducted a randomized experiment to evaluate the efficacy of SmartPal. The experiment involved a cohort of over 300 students across several college-level business technology courses. To mitigate concerns that students who self-selected to use the app are systematically different from those who did not use it, we randomly assigned students into two groups: one group received emails that reminded and encouraged them to install the App, whereas the other group did not receive such encouragement emails, though both groups were given the opportunity to install the app and earn extra credits through an initial announcement of the study and the Canvas assignment related to the study. The exogenous encouragement serves as an instrument for the endogenous SmartPal adoption decision, and our subsequent analyses leverage this instrument to obtain a causal estimation of the effects of adopting SmartPal.

The overall adoption rate was 78.59%. Students who received the encouragement emails demonstrated a significantly higher propensity to adopt the app, demonstrating the effectiveness of the encouragement strategy. In our analysis, we use encouragement as an instrument to estimate the causal effect of SmartPal.

The adoption of SmartPal significantly increases student engagement as was observed in on-time submissions of assignments and canvas page-views. We also found evidence of increased academic performance. These preliminary findings underscore the advantages associated with integrating SmartPal into the learning environment.

4   Discussion and Conclusions

This research probed into strategies for designing and deploying a gamified LLM chatbot into an LMS-based learning environment, leveraging mobile technologies for enhanced interaction and real-time information from Canvas for more relevant and timely chatbot conversations. The initial empirical evidence from this study indicates that SmartPal's deployment markedly bolsters student interaction with LMSs and academic achievement, highlighting the efficacy of integrating conversational agents with gamification tactics. The project is poised to yield valuable research insights, emergent digital technologies, foundational design principles, and pedagogical tactics, all of which bear relevance to analogous educational contexts and forthcoming scholarly endeavors.

References

1. Fryer, L.K., Ainley, M., Thompson, A., Gibson, A., Sherlock, Z.: Stimulating and sustaining interest in a language course: an experimental comparison of chatbot and human task partners. Comput. Hum. Behav. **75**, 461–468 (2017)

2. Jansen, R.S., van Leeuwen, A., Janssen, J., Conijn, R., Kester, L.: Supporting learners' self-regulated learning in massive open online courses. Comput. Educ. **146**, 103771 (2020)
3. Leung, A.C.M., Santhanam, R., Kwok, R.C.W., Yue, W.T.: Could gamification designs enhance online learning through personalization? Lessons from a field experiment. Inf. Syst. Res. **34**(1), 27–49 (2023)
4. Liu, D., Santhanam, R., Webster, J.: Toward meaningful engagement: a framework for design and research of gamified information systems. MIS Q. **41**(4), 1011–1034 (2017)

Design Strategies for Children's Science Popularization Books Based on Interactive Narrative

Yue Zhao and Li Ou Yang[✉]

Guangzhou Academy of Fine Arts, Guangzhou, Guangdong, China
Oylee@163.com

Abstract. Under the impetus of the digital wave, Children's Science Popularization Books are gradually transitioning from static dissemination to interactive narrative, signifying an innovative leap in the field of educational communication. This research systematically explores the application of interactive narrative theory in the design of Children's Science Popularization Books, and proposes a complete design framework specifically. This study adopts an integrated research methodology, including literature review, interdisciplinary theoretical analysis, case study, and interview research, delves deeply into the communication situations of interactive narrative, and explores its positive role in promoting children's cognitive development and perceptual cultivation. By conducting meticulous analysis of the narrative modes of Children's Science Popularization Books and combining with Marie-Laure Ryan's tri-element theory of interactive narrative, the study proposes design strategies for Children's Science Popularization Books under Interactive Narrative from the outer, middle, and inner layers respectively. Using a unique cross-disciplinary and cross-media approach that combines the characteristics of children's cognitive development, interactive narrative design and science popularization books, the study offers reference value for the design strategies of future Children's Science Popularization Books, aiming to create a more immersive and interesting reading experience for children.

Keywords: Children's Books · Interactive Narrative · Science Popularization Books · Narrative Design · Design Strategies

1 Introduction

Children's Science Popularization Books represent a multi-faceted cultural medium, imbued with four core qualities: scientificity, interest, artisticity, and educativity [1]. The core purpose of these books is to disseminate scientific knowledge to children, truthfully presenting facts and information about science. The contents of these informational books must be scientific and accurate, demanding not only the correctness of the presented information, but also the simplification and age-appropriate treatment of complex scientific concepts, ensuring that they are both accurate and easily understood by children.

© The Author(s), under exclusive license to Springer Nature Switzerland AG 2024
C. Stephanidis et al. (Eds.): HCII 2024, CCIS 2117, pp. 265–276, 2024.
https://doi.org/10.1007/978-3-031-61953-3_30

In an age overwhelmed with information, traditional print-based books have seen decreasing attractiveness [2]. Emerging digital technologies have led to the adoption of interactive narrative in informational book design, enhancing the reading experience. Immersive interactive reading can strengthen the absorption of scientific knowledge, stimulate children's curiosity, and broaden their learning horizons. This study explores the impact of the design elements of interactive narrative on Children's Science Popularization Books, along with the reading needs of children concerning these books. By applying the theory of interactive narrative, new perspectives can be provided for the design strategies of Children's Science Popularization Books. This can offer innovative ideas for future designs, paving the way for interesting and immersive reading experiences.

2 Theory

2.1 The Cognitive Characteristics of Children

According to the theory of cognitive development proposed by renowned child psychologist Jean Piaget, children aged 3–6 are in the preoperational stage [3]. Their cognitive development is preoperational stage, with their understanding relying more on observation and sensory experience than logical reasoning. Children at this stage show great interest in tangible things, and their rapidly developing physical abilities and neural networks result in enhanced memory, attention, imagination, and creativity.

At the ages of 3–4, children possess a basic level of visual cognition and are sensitive to distinct shapes and musical rhythms. They can express their needs in simple terms, excel at doodling, and exhibit dynamic emotions. They are capable of understanding brief stories, observe images in detail, and comprehend the relationship between text and illustrations. At the ages of 4–5, children's visual and cognitive abilities mature further, enabling them to recognize real-world characters and objects, and are sensitive towards music and simple geometric shapes [4]. They enjoy sketching or assembling objects and are eager to share their internal experiences. At the ages of 5–6, children can summarize the main content of stories and are adept at creating artwork with geometric shapes and manipulating objects according to instructions. They enjoy interacting with others and use descriptive language to express their views. Improvements in emotional management and reading comprehension are also evident at this stage.

2.2 The Characteristics of Interactive Narrative

Interactive narrative integrates traditional narrative with digital media characteristics, providing readers with more opportunities for participation and interaction, while simultaneously bringing possibilities for innovation in the creative industry [5]. Its main features include non-linear narrative, real-time free interaction, and diversified narrative media.

Non-linear narrative breaks the time and space constraints of linear narrative, allowing readers to participate in and create different plots through interaction, enriching users' emotional experience. Real-time free interaction gives the narrative flexibility and dynamism, where user behavior and choices can alter the development and outcome of the narrative, thereby drawing user attention, and enhancing the reading experience. Compared with traditional paper books, interactive narrative offers a wider variety of media choices, including tablets, mobile phones, computers, and AR/VR experiences [6]. This provides narrators with a broader creative space and means of expression, enhancing the readers' reading methods and experiences, immersing them in the story. In the digital age, designer should fully utilize the advantages of diversified narrative media, innovate, and expand narrative forms, injecting new vitality into the development of interactive narrative.

2.3 Interactive Narrative Communication Context

Based on Chatman's narrative communication model, this study reconstructs the interactive narrative context in the design of children's science popularization books [7] (Fig. 1). Through an appropriate narrative structure, disorganized text stories are organized to create a coherent and easy-to-understand narrative context. By integrating different narrative forms such as sound effects, text, images, and interaction, the reading immersion is enhanced and the reading experience is improved. Efforts are made to enhance the visual aesthetics and texture of the illustrations, and carefully design surround sound effects to increase the perceptual appeal of the design. Furthermore, by guiding children's interactive behaviors, taking into account their cognitive abilities, attention, and habitual behaviors, the aim is to provide knowledge while also ensuring interactive fun. The emotional changes of children during the course are taken into account, ensuring they receive scientific knowledge in a relaxed and pleasant environment, thus achieving the goal of combining education with enjoyment.

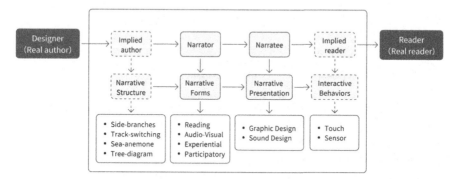

Fig. 1. Interactive narrative communication context of children's science popularization books.

3   Investigative Research

This study adopted the grounded theory proposed by American sociologists Barney Glaser and Anselm L. Strauss to conduct an in-depth analysis of the reading needs of children's science popularization books, aiming to construct theory through systematic collection and analysis of data [8]. Through in-depth interviews and observations, the characteristics and requirements of children's reading process are explored from the children's perspective, and a typical relationship structure is constructed through the induction and abstraction of interview material. Given the instability of children's language expression and thinking, this study used a relatively flexible semi-structured interview method. A question framework was first established, and then appropriate adjustments were made according to the responses of the interviewees. Twenty-two preschool children were selected as interviewees, with an even distribution according to sex, age, and grade. Child-friendly language was used for communication during the interview process.

3.1 Qualitative Research

Open Coding. This is a process of discovering new concepts and categories from raw materials. In the process of analyzing the interview materials in this research, concepts related to interactive children's science popularization reading were extracted word by word, sentence by sentence, and numbered according to the pre-interviewees for subsequent comparison and integration [9]. In order to minimize the influence of personal subjective factors, representative statements from the respondents were used as initial concept labels. Through the open coding process, 20 categories were distilled in total, as shown in Table 1.

Table 1. Open coding process

Original Representative Sentences	Initial Concepts	Categories
I can learn a lot of unknown things	Rich content	Information Acquisition
One time I put an egg in saltwater, it really floated up	Guided with experiments	Association with Reality
I don't quite know how to answer some of the questions posed in the book	Understanding children's cognitive level	Knowledge Verification
After reading the book, I enjoyed watching ants carry food around	Maintain interest beyond the book	Inspiring Thought
I find it hard to keep reading if the text is too long	Text too complex	Concise Text
There was a diagram that showed me where the heart is	Images enhance cognition	Vivid Images
I didn't know it could be opened at first, it took me several times to find out	Unclear operations	Prompt Guidance
I was a little unsure about where to start reading	Confusing information	Clear Structure

(continued)

Table 1. (*continued*)

Original Representative Sentences	Initial Concepts	Categories
There's a book about rainbows, it has a lot of different colors	Colorful and rich pigmentation	Bright Colors
I found out that the illustrations in the book were drawn with crayons	Special textured graphics	Style Presentation
Reading from top to bottom, it's like something ancient	Typography in line with characteristics	Harmonious Composition
There's too much stuff on there, it can get a little tiring to read	Reading obstacles	Details Enhancement
I especially enjoyed playing with the mazes and puzzles within	Games attract children	Fun Games
I wish I could make something like this myself	Space creation for children	Free Creation
Once you've finished the book, you can collect all the badges	Motivational feedback required	Reward Mechanism
If I press the 'lights off' button, everyone would go to sleep	Ability to immerse in scenarios	Plot Involvement
There's an apple falling down, and the tablet will vibrate	Integration with sensory images	Interactive Behavior
There's a book that will make different animal noises when you touch it	Auditory sensory stimulation	Surround Sound Effects
You can go on an adventure with the animals in the book	Plot leading children to explore	Rich Stories
Using the tablet to scan the book, dinosaurs will appear, just like in real life	More immersive form	Extended Reality

Axial Coding. The process of open coding is to discover new concepts and categories from raw sentences, while axial coding further inducts and organizes these, establishing connections between categories [10]. Through axial coding, five core categories were summarized from the scrutiny and arrangement of 20 initial categories, and their connotations were clarified. The process and results of axial coding are shown in Table 2, providing a basis for subsequent theoretical construction.

Selective Coding. Selective coding is the process of establishing associations across core categories, aimed at depicting the overall research phenomenon. By further analyzing and organizing the connections among the five main categories derived from axial coding, typical relationships related to children's demands for interactive science popularization books have been identified, as shown in Table 3. Through encoding and

Table 2. Axial coding process

Primary Categories	Secondary Categories	Implications
Exploring Needs	Information Acquisition	Bountiful popular science knowledge can broaden children's horizons
	Association with Reality	Simple experiments or observations in nature make knowledge more concrete
	Knowledge Verification	Questions and quizzes to check children's comprehension of knowledge
	Inspiring Thought	Continuously engaging children's interest to maintain their exploration of knowledge
Readability Needs	Concise Text	Plain, clear language fits children's cognition for easy comprehension
	Vivid Images	Expressing knowledge in the form of images and diagrams enhances children's impressions
	Prompt Guidance	Prompting children to participate interactively at the right time
	Clear Structure	Properly categorizing information hierarchy for easier reading comprehension for children
Aesthetic Needs	Bright Colors	Children usually prefer higher purity and saturation of colors
	Style Presentation	Enhancing picture texture through forms such as watercolor, colored pencils, collage, crayons, etc
	Harmonious Composition	Emphasizing typography layout, page coordination, enhance the sophistication of the design
	Details Enhancement	Pay attention to details such as font size, line spacing and white space, to improve comfort
Entertainment Needs	Fun Games	Attracting children's attention through games
	Free Creation	Designing open-ended sites to stimulate children's imagination
	Reward Mechanism	Encouraging children to read actively through mechanisms like badges and medals
	Plot Involvement	Engage children in story development to increase autonomy in reading

(continued)

Table 2. (*continued*)

Primary Categories	Secondary Categories	Implications
Experience Needs	Interactive Behavior	Boosting interest through elements such as touch, sliding, haptic feedback etc
	Surround Sound Effects	Enhancing experience by adding matching sound effects, music, and voice-overs to the illustrations
	Rich Stories	Using a multi-level narrative to link knowledge together to stimulate children's curiosity
	Extended Reality	Augmenting children's immersion with extended reality tools such as AR/VR

analyzing these materials, we found that the results basically included the categories previously obtained, and no new category relationship structures were discovered. Therefore, it can be concluded that the model constructed based on grounded theory in this study is theoretically saturated and is of certain universality and applicability.

Table 3. Selective coding process.

Typical Relation Structure	Inherent Meaning of Relation Structure
Exploring Needs → Design Strategies	Exploration and knowledge-seeking are the fundamental needs of children when reading science popularization books, directly influencing the design of these books
Readability Needs → Design Strategies	The content design of science popularization books should be in line with children's cognitive characteristics. The need for easily readable content directly affects the design of these books
Aesthetic Needs → Design Strategies	Visual elements are the first sensory aspects readers encounter when accessing knowledge information. Thus, aesthetic needs influence the design of children's science popularization books
Entertainment Needs → Design Strategies	Presenting knowledge in an interesting manner draws readers' attention. Thus, entertainment needs impact the design of children's science popularization books

(*continued*)

Table 3. (*continued*)

Typical Relation Structure	Inherent Meaning of Relation Structure
Experience Needs → Design Strategies	Rich formatting enhances the immersive experience during the reading process, making experiential needs another factor that influences the design of children's science popularization books

3.2 Result

Based on in-depth research on child users, this study constructed a design need model for children's science popularization books under interactive narrative (Fig. 2). This includes the exploratory need that encourages children's desire for knowledge; readability need that presents scientific content in a concise, understandable manner; aesthetic need that nurtures children's sense of beauty; entertainment need that prevents reading fatigue with humor; experiential need that provides an immersive reading experience; and preference need that takes into consideration reading habits and other factors.

Fig. 2. The Reading Needs Model

4 Design Strategies

Interactive narrative enhances traditional narrative forms with characteristics like non-linearity and spatiality, and is mainly characterized by interactivity and immersion, realizing user story participation and control. The theoretical core includes three levels: an outer layer centered on plot, focusing on story attractiveness and cohesion; a middle layer centered on immersion, inducing user emotional resonance and engagement; an inner layer centered on interactivity, focusing on natural human-computer interaction. These three levels together shape the characteristics and attractiveness of interactive narrative. Combining this theory, design elements, and analysis of children's reading needs, this study proposes an interactive narrative design strategy model for children's science popularization books (Fig. 3).

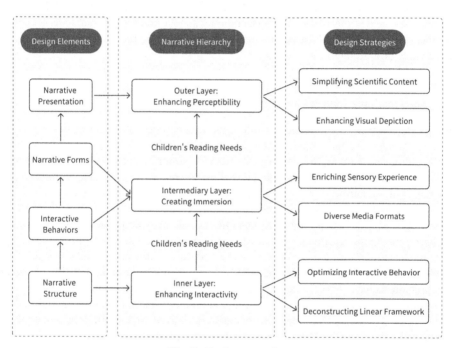

Fig. 3. Design strategies

4.1 Outer Layer: Enhancing Perceptibility

Simplifying Scientific Content. Firstly, it is premised on the curiosity and explorative desires of children, choosing closely related scientific themes such as environmental protection and scientific inventions, and concretizing abstract concepts to ensure accurate transmission of scientific knowledge. Secondly, complex scientific concepts are expressed in understandable language to reduce cognitive difficulty and enhance understanding. Thirdly, it involves designing science popularization content that caters to different age groups and interests considering age and individual differences. Lastly, children's science popularization books should act as propagators of scientific knowledge and spirit, demonstrating the value and impact of science through knowledge conveyance, and guiding children to treat and use scientific knowledge carefully and correctly.

Enhancing Visual Depiction. The aesthetic ability of children gradually develops with age, in which children's science popularization books play a vital role in auxiliary education. Designing children's science popularization books requires consideration of visual axis, color, visual style, and other elements to foster children's aesthetic perception capability. The visual axis guides readers to delve deeply into scientific knowledge by adjusting various parameters, thereby conveying different emotions and atmospheres. Colors, as critical tools for transmitting emotional information, can be applied to create an abundance of visual effects and emotional experiences. The design of visual styles emphasizes the flexible use of painting techniques and the creation of atmospheric scenes. It aims to attract children's attention and resonance, guiding them into a colorful world of science through interactive narrative.

4.2 Intermediary Layer: Creating Immersion

Enriching Sensory Experience. Children's science popularization books based on interactive narrative have made significant attempts in innovating text and form, with the key innovation being the sensory experience combining audio and visual elements. By offering reading patterns that integrate illustrations, audio, and video, children can interact with scientific content from a multi-sensory perspective, thereby enhancing their audio-visual cognitive abilities. For example, the "Little Newton Kindergarten" uses mobile Internet teaching models and QR codes to provide video expansions for the children, enhancing its educational and entertainment value. However, during the design process, it is imperative to avoid redundant and confused information and to consider the ability of children to absorb information to prevent distractions and confusion. Another example, the science book "Listen, What's That Sound", integrates visual, auditory and tactile experiences, enhancing the reading experience. The integration of multimedia provides a rich reading experience in an innovative way, demonstrating the potential for new development in Children's Science Popularization Books.

Diverse Media Formats. In the design of Children's Science Popularization Books, the introduction of Augmented Reality (AR) and Virtual Reality (VR) technologies can connect the real and virtual worlds and bring new interactive experiences. AR integrates virtual elements into the real environment, such as turning animals, plants, buildings, and other elements in the book into three-dimensional virtual models, enhancing the depth of observation and learning. VR creates a virtual environment through specific devices, allowing readers to freely explore and experience, such as playing different roles in the virtual scene and experiencing different cultures. Utilizing digital technologies to provide a variety of interactive experiences, such as interacting through sound, gestures, and games, increases the interest and participation in reading.

4.3 Inner Layer: Enhancing Interactivity

Optimizing Interactive Behavior. The creative and fun elements are designed to satisfy children's entertainment needs, integrating life-like story plots and game tasks, introducing forms like virtual experiments, to stimulate children's curiosity and fulfill their desire for exploration, while nurturing creativity, cooperation awareness, and problem-solving skills. Optimizing interactive behaviors for children of different age groups and cognitive levels, participation in reading is guided through the use of interactive elements such as touching and clicking, stimulating a desire for scientific exploration and creativity. This kind of design is beneficial in optimizing the process of children's reading, enhancing the reading effect, and cultivating interest and understanding in science.

Deconstructing Linear Framework. The interactive narrative of Children's Science Popularization Books is exemplified by its non-linear narrative characteristics, where the order of the story is determined by the reader's choices, enhancing the appeal of the story and highlighting its themes. The conventional narrative chronology can be disrupted, using techniques like "time reversion" for instance, adding a diverse temporal dimension to the story and enriching its connotations. Children's Science Popularization Books with interactive narrative traits focus on the conveyance of scientific knowledge. Their structure and order can aid content organization and expression methods. These include a structure guided by the exploration of scientific questions and the use of scientific stories, both of which are effective in attracting children's attention, enhancing their reading interest, and improving their scientific literacy.

5 Conclusion

This study explores the application of interactive narratives in Children's Science Popularization Books, concluding with three main findings: firstly, it constructs an interactive narrative communication scenario, providing a theoretical framework for children's reading situations and interactive processes; secondly, it delves into children's interactive reading needs, identifying six primary requirements; thirdly, based on interactive narrative theory, it puts forward design strategies for Children's Science Popularization Books, emphasizing the design process that starts from enhancing the outer layer of perception, then building a sense of immersion in the middle layer, and finally increasing the interactivity in the inner layer. This research offers a new perspective on the design of Children's Science Popularization Books, which can help to boost children's reading interest and experience, effectively absorbing scientific knowledge.

This project is one of the research outcomes of the Guangzhou Academy of Fine Arts project "Cultural Elements and Creative Design Education" (Project number 6040122027SFJD).

Acknowledgments. The project originates from Guangdong Province's First-ClassCourse"Fundamentals of Design (Three-Dimensional Space) (Project Number: 6040324137)". The project is the interim results of the ideo- logical and political demonstration course "Fundamentals of Design (Three-Dimensional Space)" at Guangzhou Academy of Fine Arts in 2021 (Project Number: 6040321061); and Guangzhou Academy of Fine Arts Graduate Program "Cultural Elements and Creative Design Education" (Project Number: 6040122027SFJD).

References

1. Liu, W.: Major features of best-selling contemporary chinese original children's popular science books: based on the analysis of the 2021 Kaijuan book best selling list. Sci. Writing Rev. **2**(02), 24–30 (2022)
2. Wang, X., Wang, H.: Innovation in the publishing and operation of science popularization audiobook products. China Publ. J. **20**(4), 56–59 (2022)
3. Hu, Y., He, N.: Educational Psychology: An Integrated View of Theory and Practice, 1st edn. East China Normal University Press, Shanghai (2009)
4. Ministry of Education of the People's Republic of China: Learning and Development Guide for 3–6 Year Olds. http://www.moe.gov.cn/. Accessed 5 Mar 2024
5. Koenitz, H., Ferri, G., Haahr, M., et al.: Interactive digital narrative. History, Theory and Practice (2015)
6. Li, Y.: The strategy of interactive digital narrative in thematic publication. Sci. Technol. Publ. **11**(7), 93–99 (2018)
7. Chatman, S.: Story and Discourse: Narrative Structure in Fiction and Film, 1st edn. Cornell University Press Ithaca (1978)
8. Corbin, J., Strauss, A.: Basics of Qualitative Research: Techniques and Procedures for Developing Grounded Theory, 4th edn. Sage publications (2014)
9. Deng, W., Yang, Y.: Research on the design strategy of children's smart dollhouses based on grounded theory and PCA. Furniture Interior Des. **30**(08), 118–123 (2023)
10. Ni, C., Li, W.: Deduction of theory of narratology in cultural and creative design of intangible cultural heritage. Packag. Eng. **44**(12), 368–377 (2023)

HCI in Games

Picky Monster: Examining the Effects of Visual Reinforcements Through Gamified Avatars and Personalized Goal Setting on Reducing Sugar Consumption

Yun-Hsuan Chou[(✉)] [iD], Yu-Chen Wang [iD], Amanda J. Castellanos [iD],
Hadar Natanson [iD], and Pei-Yi Patricia Kuo [iD]

National Tsing Hua University, Hsinchu 300044, Taiwan
amber.chou@iss.nthu.edu.tw

Abstract. High sugar consumption is a known risk factor for various diseases. While technological solutions for food decision-making and diet control have shown promise in maintaining user engagement and adherence to health goals, there is a lack of research on adapting visual reinforcement mechanisms and personalized daily consumption goals to reduce sugar intake. Our study aims to improve snacking behavior through positive and negative visual reinforcement. We created *Picky Monster*, a mobile app to track and gamify sugar intake to raise awareness and promote healthier habits. Personalized daily sugar goal is based on one's physiological data, visually represented by a four-stage monster avatar. In a two-week field study involving 15 students with snacking habits, we evaluated *Picky Monster*'s effectiveness. Findings revealed that visual cues of gamified avatars helped decrease people's sugar intake and improved their health literacy. Participants reduced sugar intake and expressed heightened awareness. The number of participants who indicated to prioritize total sugar as a purchasing factor has doubled post-study. Although negative visual reinforcement did not yield expected results, design implications are provided. This research advances technology-driven interventions for healthier eating and suggests integrating positive and negative visual cues for promoting sugar reduction during snacking through gamified avatars.

1 Introduction

Sugar is present in our daily life, even disguising itself in seemingly healthy foods like cereals, natural juices, and yogurt. Research has found that excessive consumption of sugar leads to health risks, including obesity, cardiovascular disease, metabolic syndrome, and type 2 diabetes [13]. Despite efforts made by governments and organizations to regulate sugar intake, discrepancies exist in defining "free," "added," and "total" sugars. For instance, while the World Health Organization (WHO) recommends reducing free sugar intake [24], the U.S. Food and Drug Administration (FDA) mandates labeling added sugars [3]. Currently, there is limited research on the implications of sugar classifications [15].

Although people's awareness toward the adverse effects has grown, many remain struggling to manage intake due to challenges such as understanding Nutrition Facts labels [2, 9, 10], lack of knowledge [14, 18, 22], inadequate tools, and withdrawal symptoms [23]. Our research explores mechanisms to improve snack purchasing behavior and promote healthy choices. Through the Picky Monster mobile app, we aim to raise awareness by visually demonstrating sugar's impacts on the avatar's appearance. By creating a bond between users and digital avatars, we accelerate the depiction of sugar's effects and fostering attentiveness to snacking habits. Our goal is to empower users to understand the consequences of overconsuming sugar. The illustrations of avatars encourage users to be more aware of their snacking habit, reinforce the adoption of healthier choices, and reduces sugar consumption. We aim to investigate the following research question: How do the visual representation of people's sugar intake amount through gamified avatars and the personalized daily maximum sugar consumption goal influence their snacking habits?

Distinguishing our work from prior similar studies, our contributions include: (1) illustrating the consequences of sugar intake, fostering awareness and encouraging mindful dietary decisions through emphasizing the appearances of digital avatars; (2) providing both negative and positive feedback of consuming sugar instead of solely emphasizing adverse outcomes, which might lead to negative emotions and hinder users from achieving their goals; and (3) focusing exclusively on total sugars therefore eliminating confusion when attempting to analyze nutritional facts.

2 Related Work

2.1 Facts About Sugar

Although reading the Nutrition Facts labels on packaged foods allows for a quick understanding of sugar content, studies have shown that less than one-third of U.S. young adults read this data, often focusing only on calorie intake [4]. While all sugars consumed end up as monosaccharide carbohydrates, they do not affect us equally or lead to the same diseases [6, 7]. Consumers often feel confused and unsure about how to properly manage their sugar intake due to three main reasons. First, sugar intake recommendation standards vary between organizations and countries [5]. Second, many countries do not distinguish between added sugar and total sugar on Nutrition Facts labels [11, 23]. Lastly, there is a debate on whether tracking both added and total sugars instead of only total sugars is more effective or beneficial for health [15]. Considering these factors, *Picky Monster* focuses on displaying total sugars specifically, avoiding technicalities and confusion associated with Nutrition Facts labels.

2.2 Negative Effects of Excessive Sugar

For decades, high sugar consumption has been a significant concern, with health organizations and researchers focusing on its harmful effects on human body. Excessive sugar intake is associated with chronic inflammation, autoimmune diseases, hypertension, coronary heart disease, obesity, and tooth decay [13]. Furthermore, it negatively impacts physical appearance by accelerating skin aging through a process called gly-cation. Sugars bond with proteins, leading to the formation of advanced glycosylation end products (AGEs), which affect collagen fibers' cross-linking. This results in various skin issues such as decreased elasticity, dehydration, thinning, dark spots, stiffness, and wrinkles [16, 19, 21].

2.3 Existing Gamified Technological Solutions to Food Decision Making

Existing gamified technological solutions to food decision making in Human-Computer Interaction (HCI) offer innovative approaches to promoting healthier eating behaviors. The *Pirate Bri's Grocery Adventure (PBGA)* app [1] enhances food literacy by pro-viding nutrition information and engaging challenges during grocery shopping (avatar dogs became sad when consumers chose to buy unhealthy grocery). *SnackBreaker* [20] provides nutrition information for healthier snack choices through a mobile game (users chose between two snacks offered to learn about healthy information). *Monster Appetite* [9] explores the impact using visual cues to encourage healthier snack choices through gamified avatars by providing negative reinforcement (monsters became uglier when unhealthy snacks were chosen during an online game). These studies showcase tech-nology's potential to positively impact food decisions. However, there is limited prior work on combining negative and positive reinforcements via gamified avatars to promote healthier snacking habits.

3 Methods

Figure 1 shows our four-step study procedure. We recruited study participants via social media channels. Our inclusion criteria are: students age between 18 and 30 years old who have snacking habits A total of 16 students were recruited. They were consented before study participation. However, data from one participant was removed due to invalid responses, resulting in a total of 15 valid participants for the study.

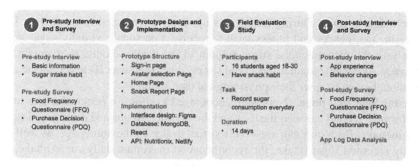

Fig. 1. Overview of Study Procedure

Participants were interviewed in the pre-study stage to collect information regard-ing their physical conditions, snack consumption patterns, attitudes and perceptions of sugar intake, as well as past sugar reduction attempts. We adapted the Food Frequency Questionnaire (FFQ) [8] and Purchase Decision Questionnaire (PDQ) [9] for our pre- and post-study surveys. FFQ determined the frequency and types of snacks our participants consumed during a week. The design of FFQ could vary depending on the differences in ethnicity, socioeconomic status, cultural background, and research topic [12]. We modified the original FFQ by removing items that were not snacks and by changing the recording duration from one week to two weeks in order to comply with our two-week study. Regarding PDQ, it identified the primary factors that influenced participants' snack purchase habits.

Our web-based mobile application was designed using Figma and programmed in React, including the MongoDB shared servers for database hosting and serverless functions for communication. Monster images were stored on Google Drive, and notifications were sent via the LINE application. Nutritional information was provided through the Nutritionix[1] API. Usability of our application was evaluated through a pilot study and subsequent refinements were made based on the user feedback collected.

We conducted a two-week field study to assess the effects of *Picky Monster* on users' snacking behavior and reactions to avatar appearances. In the post-study stage, participants were interviewed to discuss their experiences with *Picky Monster* and sugar reduction attempts, resulting in 30 h of interview data. We conducted thematic analysis to analyze qualitative interview data, and used SPSS to analyze survey data (results of FFQ and PDQ) including a paired t-test to assess changes after the study.

4 Design of Picky Monster

4.1 Picky Monster Pages

Picky Monster prototype was designed as a web-based mobile app and offered users the following functions: (1) reporting snacks consumed (2) searching for sugar amounts of non-labeled foods, and (3) following a personalized monster avatar which visualized how sugar affects human body. Participants are expected to switch easily among the pages, as shown in Fig. 2.

- **First sign-in page.** During initial sign-up, users were asked to input their height, weight, age, gender and fitness level to receive a personalized daily sugar amount. We save the recommended sugar amount in the database only, to maintain user's privacy. At the next login, users could simply enter their user ID to access the system without having to enter their physiological data again.
- **Avatar Selection page.** Users were encouraged to choose a personal avatar to assist in forming a bond between the user and the monster. Requested during sign-up only.
- **Homepage.** Each user can view their virtual avatar on the homepage, as well as the daily recorded sugar intake, the recommended maximum daily sugar intake, and a chart showing their sugar intake for the past five days.
- **Snack report page.** User can report a snack by searching it in the database, manually writing the sugar amount, or looking through the history list and re-reporting a snack (help users record their favorite foods quickly).

---

[1] https://www.nutritionix.com/.

Fig. 2. Screenshots of the *Picky Monster* Prototype

4.2 Daily Personal Recommended Sugar Intake

During sign-up, the system asks the user for its' weight, height, age, gender and how many workouts they partake in a week to calculate their personalized daily sugar amount. The amount is calculated by first calculating users' Basal Metabolic Rate (BMR) using Mifflin-St Jeor Eq. [17], where C is constant based on the users' gender, as shown in the following.

$$BMR = (10 \times weight\ in\ kg) + (6.25 \times height\ in\ cm)$$
$$- (5 \times age\ in\ years) + C$$

We then determine the "Total daily energy expenditure (TDEE)" using the calculated BMR and a multiplier reflecting the user's weekly workout amount, on a scale of 1.2 to 1.9. To conclude the process, we calculate 10% of the overall result - following the World Health Organization (WHO) instructions, suggesting sugar should constitute 10% of a person's daily calorie intake [24]. The last stage is converting the results from kcal to gram.

4.3 Four Monster Stages

To show the effects of sugar intake on the human body, we created four types of monsters, each has four stages (Fig. 3), resulting in 16 variations of monster avatars. The alterations of the monsters' traits are made to symbolize both positive and negative impacts of sugar consumption - the stage A monster is considered to be the cutest while the stage D monster is considered least attractive.

The initial character users are presented with is stage B, showing the monster before any excessive positive or negative changes which will be revealed with time. Each day at 5 AM (Taiwan time) the system compares the consumed sugar amount during the last 24 h versus the recommended amount, and chooses what monster stage to present to each user. Daily reminders are also sent via LINE to non-reporting users. The system allows reporting snacks with zero-gram sugar consumed, in order to not confuse with lack of reporting or inactivity.

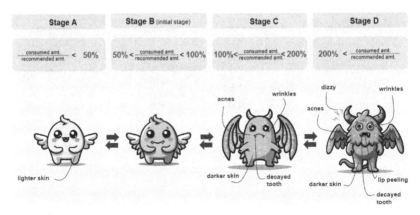

Fig. 3. Example of a four-stage monster avatar and their growth rates

5   Results

The data was collected through both qualitative and quantitative analysis. Qualitative analysis included pre- and post-study interviews. During the pre-study interviews, we gathered information on participants' snacking habits, sugar consumption, and purchasing preferences. For the post-study interviews, we collected data on changes in sugar consumption, attitudes towards reducing sugar, and the app experience. Quantitative analysis included the pre- and post- study surveys and app log. By analyzing the pre- and post- FFQ and PDQ surveys, we could determine whether there was a decrease in the frequency of snack consumption and a change in the stage of purchase decision-making. Data was also retrieved from the app log to understand the changes in monsters and the percentage of each of the four stages.

5.1   Results from Pre- and Post-study Interviews

The pre-study interviews helped us uncover participants' snack habits and awareness of sugar consumption. It revealed that 13 participants (P2, P3, P4, P7, P8, P9, P10, P11, P12, P13, P14, P15, P16) lacked awareness regarding their daily sugar intake and only three participants tried to control the amount of sugar they consumed (P2, P8, P12).

After the two-week study, 75% of the participants reduced sugar intake using various strategies. They became more aware of monitoring Nutrition Facts labels (*"I prioritized low-sugar options for sweets and snacks. At 7–11, I found out the soy milk that I usually picked had over 20 g of sugar, exceeding half of my daily limit. I switched to the unsweetened version to control my sugar intake."-P3*), and manually searched the information online (*"The breakfast shop milk tea did not have a Nutrition Facts label. However, I found out that 300cc of it contained 28g of sugar after researching it online."-P4*). Some participants reported that the daily recording task helped them to be more aware of their eating habits and eat snacks with less sugar (*"I felt that having to fill out this information every day kept me be constantly mindful of my sugar intake. It made me become more cautious about snacks with sugar."-P2*). Furthermore, the specified personalized daily maximum sugar intake gave them a goal to work toward *("Knowing my daily maximum sugar is 33 g was crucial. Initially, I thought I could consume 50 g a day, so I had to eat no more than 33 g from now on."-P3)*. Nine participants (P2, P4, P5, P8, P9, P10, P11, P12, P13) learned about the negative impact of sugar on appearance *("Lately, I got some acne, so I had been wondering if it's related to consuming too much sugar."-P4)*, motivating them to cut the sugar intake.

Moreover, regarding the effects of visual cues on sugar reduction, a third of the participants noted significant effects from the monster's visual changes on their motives and behaviors after the study *("I noticed the monster reached the third stage once and I knew I had consumed too much. The next day, I reduced my sugar intake, I was being reminded."-P4)*. They expressed intentions to modify dietary habits according to the monster's condition *("There was a feeling of alertness. On that day, I resolved to eat less and prevented the situation from getting worse."-P3)*. However, some participants (P3, P7, P9, P10, P16) pointed out that they could not thoroughly discern the pathological features on monsters due to its small size, such as pimples, wrinkles, dark skin, and decayed teeth. This could potentially lower the degree of changes made by participants *("I felt the changes in the four stages were not very noticeable. Even when the monster became ugly, I still found it cute and would not feel any alertness."-P7)*.

In terms of the app experience, participants praised the simple and intuitive design of the interface and functions, the attractiveness of the monster avatars *("Having a cute mascot as an icon prevented me from getting ugly and motivated me to use the app."-P8)*, and the statistical charts that clearly visualized the amount of sugar intake *("Histograms were very helpful, it was alarming to see that one day was low and the next was high, and changes in the graph could be stressful and inhibit one's sugar intake."-P6)*.

However, participants suggested that the app could be improved by enlarging the monsters' pathological features *("I do not think the monster's facial features are obvious, they should be enlarged."-P10)*, and enhancing their characteristics with interactive elements *("I hoped the monsters could be more interactive, to increase the connection between them and myself."-P8)*. In addition, participants expressed the need to be able to modify prior historical records *("I accidentally filled in the wrong number one day, but I could not change it by myself. Hoping the modification function was available."-P9)*.

5.2 Results from the Pre- and Post-study Surveys

The Food Frequency Questionnaire (FFQ) was used to evaluate the frequency and types of snacks consumed by participants. The questionnaire consisted of seven main categories of snacks, including dietary snacks, candy and chocolate, bakery desserts, and sweetened beverages. Participants reported their snack intake frequency using a scale ranging from 'never' to 'always', with corresponding values of 1 to 5. For the FFQ analysis, no significant differences were found between pre- and post-test scores ($M = 2.00$, $SD = 8.992$, $t = 0.861$, $p = 0.404$). However, ten participants decreased sugar intake during the study (P2, P3, P4, P6, P8, P9, P11, P12, P14, P15), reflecting in changes of the mean FFQ.

We chose the Purchase Decision Questionnaire (PDQ) to examine the factors that affected snack purchase decisions. Participants ranked the three primary factors that influenced their snack choices from a list of eight factors, including flavor, package, total calories, total sugar, ingredients, convenience of purchase, convenience of consumption, and other health concerns. Prioritizing sugar as the top concern earned three points, the second priority earned two points, the third priority earned one point, and not considering sugar in the top three considerations earned zero point. As for the PDQ analysis, there was also no significant differences between pre- and post-test scores ($M = -0.600$, $SD = 1.404$, $t = -1.655$, $p = 0.120$). Yet, more participants prioritized sugar in their purchasing decisions, increasing from four participants prior to study participation (P3, P7, P10, P15) to nine participants after study participation (P1, P2, P4, P5, P7, P8, P11, P13, P15).

5.3 App Log Data

The Stage A monster (Fig. 3), the cutest version of the four stages, appeared frequently-112 days for all users together. This meant that participants maintained a consumption level of less than 50% of their personalized daily recommended sugar intake for most of the study period. However, this did not mean that the participants did not consume any sugar. In fact, participants consumed small amounts of sugar for 100 days.

6 Discussion

6.1 Reduced Sugar Intake

During the 14-day experiment, participants exhibited a tendency to reduce their sugar intake. Strategies like cutting back on snack frequency and portion size, as well as opting for lower-sugar alternatives were mentioned in post-study interviews. Furthermore, two-thirds of participants reported a decrease in snack intake frequency, as indicated by responses collected through the FFQ. However, quantitative results from FFQ did not show statistically significant differences. Based on researcher's observation, this discrepancy could be attributed to recall bias as five participants (P8, P10, P11, P14, P15) faced challenges recalling snack intake over the prior two weeks, making participants provide rough estimates in the pre-study FFQ. Participants attributed their reduced sugar intake to specific features of the *Picky Monster*. First, the daily recording of sugar intake fostered self-observation. Second, the personalized maximum daily sugar intake amount provided clear and measurable goal for self-discipline. Third, the visual changes in the monster avatar served as a practical educational tool, illustrating the consequences of excessive sugar consumption or the benefits of moderation. The results of our study align with previous studies indicating that simply delivering nutritional information may yield only moderate impact on individuals' choices [2, 10]. Targeted interventions, such as addressing health risks or reminding people of positive social norms, can be more effective in encouraging individuals to adopt healthier behaviors [14, 22].

6.2 Enhanced Awareness to Sugar

The pre-study interview uncovered an initial lack of awareness among our participants regarding their sugar intake. However, they became more vigilant as they discovered hidden sugars in snacks by examining Nutrition Facts labels and searching sugar content online during the study. This enabled them to learn the amounts of sugar in their frequently eaten snacks. Once they had the basic concept in mind, their increased awareness led to greater ability to recognize snacking patterns and excessive sugar intake, as shown in the post-study interviews.

6.3 Improved Health Literacy

Picky Monster educated participants by illustrating the risks of excessive sugar consumption through the monster avatar. This influenced participants' snack choices and reasons for selection, as evidenced by the PDQ results. The number of participants prioritizing sugar as a top-three factor in snack purchases more than doubled, increasing from four to nine. Increased health literacy led to reconsideration of dietary habits, promoting informed decision-making for better health. Contrary to previous studies that used only negative visual reinforcement [9], our study introduced both negative and positive visual reinforcement. This was praised by our participants during the post-study interviews, stating that maintaining the avatar's healthiest state (stage A) positively motivated them to reduce their sugar intake.

7 Limitations

Our study has four primary limitations. First, the study would benefit from a larger sample size over a longer study length. Second, some participants we recruited had a snacking habit, yet the snacks consumed did not have high amounts of sugar. For future work, we plan to examine how our results would differ from a study focusing particularly on participants who consume snacks containing high amounts of sugar. Third, another limitation involved the potential estimation error of sugar consumption. To calculate and estimate sugars for non-labeled snacks, we imported the Nutritionix database, which mainly contained items commonly found in the United States and lacked the types of snacks available in the region where this study was conducted. This could lead to discrepancies in estimation when participants reported similar snacks instead of the exact snacks consumed. Lastly, we found some visual cues of monster avatars were too small to be recognized due to limited mobile phone screen size (e.g., tooth decay and pimples). Future iteration of *Picky Monster* will address this issue.

8 Conclusion and Future Work

In conclusion, our study investigates the impact of visual cues and gamified avatars on reducing sugar intake. Our research findings suggested positive effects on people's snacking habits, such as building a habit of checking Nutrition Facts labels and establishing a daily sugar intake maximum goal. Additionally, participants learned about the negative effects of sugar consumption on appearance. This research contributes to the emerging field of technology-driven interventions for healthier eating behaviors. Future work involves expanding the sample size and study duration to gain a more comprehensive understanding of the effects over time and across diverse demographics. Moreover, we plan to improve the design of *Picky Monster* to make the negative visual cues more salient, and include more interactive features.

Acknowledgement. We thank our study participants for their participation and feedback. This work was partially supported by the National Science and Technology Council in Taiwan (grant 112-2221-E-007-083).

References

1. Bomfim, M.C.C., Kirkpatrick, S.I., Nacke, L.E., Wallace, J.R.: Food literacy while shopping: motivating informed food purchasing behaviour with a situated gameful app. In: Proceedings of the 2020 CHI Conference on Human Factors in Computing Systems (2020)
2. Elbel, B., Kersh, R., Brescoll, V.L. and Dixon, L.B.: Calorie labeling and food choices: a first look at the effects on low-income people in New York city. Health affairs **28**(6), w1110–w1121 (2009)
3. Changes to the Nutrition Facts Label (2022). The United States Food and Drug Administration. https://www.fda.gov/food/food-labeling-nutrition/changes-nutrition-facts-label. Accessed 28 October 2022
4. Christoph, M.J., Larson, N., Laska, M.N., Neumark-Sztainer, D.: Nutrition facts: who is using them, what are they using, and how does it relate to dietary intake? J. Acad. Nutr. Diet. **118**(2), 217–228 (2018)
5. Erickson, J., Slavin, J.: Total, added, and free sugars: are restrictive guidelines science-based or achievable? Nutrients **7**(4), 2866–2878 (2015)
6. Holesh, J.E., Aslam, S., Martin, A.: Physiology, Carbohydrates. StatPearls Publishing, Treasure Island (FL) (2023)
7. Huang, C., Liang, Z., Ma, J., Hu, D., Yao, F., Qin, P.: Total sugar, added sugar, fructose, and sucrose intake and all-cause, cardiovascular, and cancer mortality: a systematic review and dose-response meta-analysis of prospective cohort studies. Nutrition **111**, 112032 (2023). https://doi.org/10.1016/j.nut.2023.112032
8. Chen, H.J., Huang, M.C.: Design consideration and validity evaluation of food-frequency questionnaires. Taiwan J. Diet. **12**(1),1–12 (2020)
9. Hwang, M.L., Mamykina, L.: Monster appetite: effects of subversive framing on nutritional choices in a digital game environment. In: Proceedings of the 2017 CHI Conference on Human Factors in Computing Systems (2017)
10. Kozup, J.C., Creyer, E.H., Burton, S.: Making healthful food choices: the influence of health claims and nutrition information on consumers' evaluations of packaged food products and restaurant menu items. J.Mark. **67** (2), 19–34 (2003)
11. Louie, J.C.Y., Tapsell, L.C.: Association between intake of total vs added sugar on diet quality: a systematic review. Nutr. Rev. **73**(12), 837–857 (2015)
12. Lu, Z.H.: A Study of the Correlation Between Stress Index and Added Sugar Food Intake among Students in Providence University (2020). https://hdl.handle.net/11296/4rg45w
13. Ma, X., Nan, F., Liang, H., Shu, P., et al.: Excessive intake of sugar: An accomplice of inflammation. Front. Immunol. **13**, 988481 (2022)
14. Wakefield, M.A., Loken, B., Hornik, R.C.: Use of mass media campaigns to change health behaviour. Lancet **376**(9748) 1261–1271 (2010)
15. Mela, D.J., Woolner, E.M.: Perspective: total, added, or free? What kind of sugars should we be talking about? Adv. Nutr. **9**(2), 63–69 (2018)
16. Melnik, B.C.: Linking diet to acne metabolomics, inflammation, and comedogenesis: an update. Clin. Cosmet. Investig. Dermatol. (2015). https://doi.org/10.2147/CCID.S69135
17. Mifflin, M.D., St Jeor, S.T., Hill, L.A., Scott, B.J., et al.: A new predictive equation for resting energy expenditure in healthy individuals. Am. J. Clin. Nutr. **51**(2), 241–247 (1990)

18. Olszewski, P.K., Wood, E.L., Klockars, A., Levine, A.S.: Excessive consumption of sugar: an insatiable drive for reward. Curr. Nutr. Rep. **8**(2), 120–128 (2019)

19. Pageon, H.: Reaction of glycation and human skin: the effects on the skin and its components, reconstructed skin as a model. Pathol. Biol. **58**(3) (2010). https://doi.org/10.1016/j.patbio. 2009.09.009

20. Park, J., Koo, B.C., Cho, J., Bae, B.C.: SnackBreaker: A game promoting healthy choice of snack foods. In: Proceedings of the 2015 Annual Symposium on Computer-Human Interaction in Play (2015)

21. Passeron, T., Krutmann, J., Andersen, M.L., Katta, R., Zouboulis, C.C.: Clinical and biological impact of the exposome on the skin. J. Eur. Acad. Dermatol. Venereol. (2020). https://doi. org/10.1111/jdv.16614

22. Dumanovsky, T., Huang, C.Y., Bassett, M.T. and Silver, L.D.: Consumer awareness of fast-food calorie information in New York City after implementation of a menu labeling regulation. Am. J. Public Health **100**(12) 2520–2525 (2010)

23. Tierney, M., Gallagher, A.M., Giotis, E.S., Pentieva, K.: An online survey on consumer knowledge and understanding of added sugars. Nutrients **9**(1), 37 (2017). https://doi.org/10. 3390/nu9010037

24. Yan, R.R., Chan, C.B., Louie, J.C.Y.: Current WHO recommendation to reduce free sugar intake from all sources to below 10% of daily energy intake for supporting overall health is not well supported by available evidence. Am. J. Clin. Nutr.Nutr. **116**(1), 15–39 (2022)

Application of Digital Game-Based Learning in Popular Science Education: A Case Study on Taiwan Butterfly Ecology Conservation

Wen Huei Chou and Bing Shuan Chuang[✉]

National Yunlin University of Science and Technology, 123 University Road, Section 3, Douliou, Yunlin 64002, Taiwan, R.O.C.

v35004icky@gmail.com

Abstract. In recent years, the butterfly population in Taiwan has significantly declined due to human-induced environmental development. As an optimal indicator of insect ecology, butterflies exhibit strong connectivity with the environment, highlighting the escalating environmental issues in Taiwan. Education can effectively address butterfly ecological concerns from the grassroots level upwards. Gamification leverages games to enhance students' self-learning motivation and effectiveness, offering particular assistance to environmental education's advocated sense of connection. However, educational games with poor content quality fail to engage students. Drawing upon existing entertainment games, this study integrates diverse gameplay with butterfly knowledge and environmental science education principles to develop a digital butterfly-themed puzzle game targeting Taiwanese students aged 9–12. With a gameplay duration of approximately forty minutes, the game primarily elucidates knowledge of the four stages of butterfly development, shaping a comprehensive butterfly knowledge framework. Within the puzzle-solving gameplay framework, various game types deepen the learning process, while employing storytelling to underscore the importance of butterfly conservation to the environment, prompting cognitive and behavioral changes among children.

Keywords: Butterfly Ecology · Digital Game-based Learning · Educational Games

1 Introduction

Once renowned as the "butterfly kingdom," Taiwan has seen a sharp decline in the butterfly population owing to human factors. As an easy-to-monitor type of insect for environmental observation, butterflies can serve as critical subjects for studying the baseline threats to the most diverse group of animals on the planet, i.e., approximately 5.5 million species of insects [14]. Environmental education aims to solve environmental issues, particularly focusing on raising student awareness, imparting knowledge, changing attitudes, helping obtain relevant skills, and boosting participation [6] to increase

C. Stephanidis et al. (Eds.): HCII 2024, CCIS 2117, pp. 290–300, 2024.
https://doi.org/10.1007/978-3-031-61953-3_32

environmentally friendly behaviors. Considering students are exposed to digital technology at an earlier age, modern education faces technological and social development challenges. Moreover, the demands on school education are also changing, being no longer limited to general abilities, such as reading and writing, and instead expanding to a series of specific "21st-century skills," such as creativity, critical thinking, cooperation, and other basic skills. Game-based learning is one of the most appealing approaches to acquiring these skills [5, 11].

Raising public awareness of butterfly-related knowledge is crucial for the environment, and game-based learning is a comprehensive, diverse, and engaging method. However, many existing educational games are monotonous and dull, making it challenging to draw students' attention to improve learning outcomes [11]. Game designers and educators must collaborate on the design to ensure an ideal alignment between game content and learning objectives [2]. This study attempted to translate butterfly knowledge into the format of digital game-based learning by designing a digital butterfly knowledge puzzle game in collaboration with experts in the field, targeting middle-grade Taiwanese students (aged 9–12). With popular science and environmental education at its core, the game focuses on puzzle-solving and integrates various game genres referencing recreational games. The four stages of butterfly knowledge are compiled into a coherent system to enhance children's butterfly knowledge, environmental awareness, and connection to nature, as well as motivate their interaction with the environment.

2 Literature Review

This chapter explores three main areas related to the research topic: butterfly ecology education, game-based learning, and principles for interface design for children. The current research status and background were clarified and compiled into research design principles to support the subsequent game development and design.

2.1 Butterfly Ecology Education

Butterflies—widely distributed worldwide, with the highest species diversity found in tropical regions—are highly dependent on the environment, with species richness and abundance increasing as the proportion of these factors rises with factors such as flower density and surrounding habitat [3]. Taiwan was once renowned as a "butterfly kingdom" for its abundance of butterflies. However, extensive human development has shrunk their habitats, causing a significant decrease in the butterfly population—a synopsis of the environmental issues in Taiwan. Studies have shown that improving the connection with nature and developing environmental knowledge through education can effectively increase ecological behaviors [8]. Popular science, also known as pop sci, targets the general public and disseminates scientific knowledge through various media channels in an easily understandable manner, allowing the public to acquire a better understanding of what scientists are focusing on and providing people with better skills to evaluate science [10].

2.2 Game-Based Learning

With the widespread availability of technology and the internet, the new generation has become more reliant on them [1]. Game design and gameplay require players to be familiar with media and technology as well as possess the skills of creativity and critical thinking. Gaming is considered an effective learning method with the potential to promote the development of students' 21st-century skills [11]. Krath's systematic review integrates gamification, serious games, and learning theories in game-based learning to propose ten principles, including goal setting, immediate feedback, sociability, adaptive content, user-friendly experience, multiple choices, and guidance [4]. The success of game-based learning is highly related to game design. Educational games require collaboration between designers and educators. If educational game development only involved educators, the result would lack appeal or become monotonous, whereas if it only involved game developers, educational games would fail to apply learning theories effectively [15]. Recreational games provide a highly realistic environment for creating a sense of immersion and can serve as a successful design model for digital game-based learning [11]. Referencing existing puzzle games for entertainment purposes can contribute to the diversity of educational content displayed in educational games and be attractive to the digitally raised generation of today's media era.

2.3 Interface Design for Children

According to the cognitive load theory, humans have strict limitations on processing novel and domain-specific secondary information. Different age groups experience different cognitive loads, with the load on the elderly and children often being higher [12]. Games for children should be challenging with the proper level of difficulty, being careful not to be frustrating and boring. Children's interaction with applications may be influenced by factors including game experience and consistency between game content and developmental level [7]. Tahir & Arif (2014) proposed a measurement model for children's interface design principles consisting of 17 items, including input and output, cognitive load, multimedia application, customization, screen design, screen frame, learning potential, feedback, operation, guidance, assistance, error messages, interactivity, effort, time requirements, encouragement, and readability [13]. When designing interfaces, these elements should be considered carefully, and adaptive content should target the different intended audiences to maximize the effect of game-based learning.

2.4 Brief Summary

The principles proposed in the above literature review for various domains can be summarized into three aspects: game content, game design, and interface. (1) Game content should evoke a connection with nature, change perceptions, and deliver information in a simple and easy-to-understand manner while maintaining accuracy. (2) Game design should provide clear goals, immediate feedback, and usability, considering theories on learning and game design. (3) The interface should adapt to the cognitive load of different age groups. As this study focuses on design for children, the design should adhere to the principles of interface design for children and provide clear guidelines and assistance.

3   Research Methods

This study mainly consisted of two stages: game design and expert interviews. In the game design stage, three main principles corresponding to game content, game design, and interface were compiled from the literature. The research team collaborated with experts to revise game and popular science scripts to further examine the connection between game content, game design, and interface. Regarding the usability for children, the game was continuously optimized through the design iteration method. The second phase focused on expert interviews. Survey questions were designed based on game-based learning principles, with interviews with field experts conducted for effectiveness assessment. After the survey, the interviews were analyzed to optimize the game based on the suggestions, which resulted in the final version.

3.1   Game Design

The game design process can be divided into four main stages: background research, script writing, design implementation, and internal and external testing. The following paragraphs describe each stage. During the background research stage, studies and issues related to the three main aspects—including studying and gathering Taiwanese butterfly-related information and research on previous studies about popular science game-based learning integration—were collected and studied based on the overall research objectives. In addition, types of games suitable for translation and integration into popular science were collected to analyze the similarities in game content and understand the practical applications of games in learning.

The script writing stage focused on "game content design." The interactive puzzle game was adopted as the main structure for game script writing, with previous research on butterflies mentioned above integrated into the script. The game structure comprised four levels corresponding to the four stages of complete metamorphosis of butterflies, in the order of "egg and life cycle," "larva," "pupa," and "adult." Environmental conservation content was introduced to emphasize the connection between butterflies and the environment. The background story was designed based on the experiences of Taiwanese children, i.e., a form that would resonate with them and guide their gameplay.

Game levels were designed according to the game-based learning principle model (consisting of challenge, response, and feedback) [9]. In addition, the game difficulty was gradually increased from easy to difficult to familiarize and guide the players with the operations. The levels were built based on static and dynamic tasks. The former included multiple-choice and memory quizzes, with the children asked to select the correct choice based on their knowledge. The latter included limited-time tasks, character interactions, and interactive tasks to create tension through different game types and restrictions. Game timing and factors contributing to the level of adjustment or failure were included to adjust to the game pace, helping achieve a balance between static and dynamic elements.

During the design implementation stage, game art and other assets were created, with a hand-drawn picture book style to reflect the themes of "adventure," "childhood memories," and "partnership" in this popular science puzzle game. The color was mainly warm tones, with transitions between warm and cool tones based on the atmosphere. Scenes in each of the four main levels had their own color palette to distinguish between levels, following the colorful, clear, and captivating principle. The characters were simple, cute, and memorable. Popular science icons closely mimicked the real images to retain their distinct features, as shown in Fig. 1.

Example of warm tone   Example of cool tone

Fig. 1. Examples of Characters and Scenes

The interface art style was centered around the theme of a "journal" (Fig. 2), showcasing unity between the story and the art. The interface maintained a simple and easy-to-read layout based on interface design principles for children. The operation was simple and intuitive, with pop-up messages indicating available levels and exploration venues to ensure sufficient guidance for users.

Fig. 2. Interface Example

During the internal and external testing stage, the first version of the game was tested multiple times by internal and external personnel. After testing, screen issues were reported and documented in a list for planners and programmers to modify and optimize. The main modifications during this process included adjusting the guidance level of the interface and interaction usability, adding dialogue cues and guides, and fine-tuning the difficulty of some levels to make the game easier to operate. Moreover, programming errors encountered during testing were fixed to complete the second testing version.

3.2 Level Design Results

The finalized game consisted of four major levels: "egg," "larva," "pupa," and "adult," representing the complete metamorphosis stages of butterflies. With character narratives as the core of the game, students were gradually guided to reach the end. Each level comprised three to four sub-tasks, where students explored scenes, absorbed knowledge, and undertook challenges at that level. A brief overview of the content of each level is provided below. Figure 3 shows examples of images from each level.

Fig. 3. Examples of Screens from Each Level

The Level 1 popular science theme is "Eggs and Life Cycle," with the narrative topic "Study Room Secret Chamber." The goal is to collect journal puzzle pieces. For instance, in the "Identifying the Eggs from Different Families" memory game, students flip two identical-looking wooden blocks printed with egg images. If they flip blocks with eggs from different families, the blocks automatically turn back. Memory games can deepen their impression of eggs from different families. Once they collect journal puzzle pieces by completing various object-related tasks, they can finish the journal puzzle and clear the level. The journal serves as a key plot device in the game to guide the students to grasp the storyline and complete the game journey.

The Level 2 popular science theme is "Larvae," with the narrative topic "Picture Book Adventure." This level covers the stories of the adventures experienced by the protagonists in the picture book. Character interaction is introduced at this level to increase richness. For example, in the "Conditions for Growing Butterfly Plants" task, students help the butterfly garden owner replant butterfly plants, checking the correct options to plant in the most suitable environmental conditions.

The Level 3 popular science theme is "Pupa," with the narrative topic "Book Maze." Each of the four rooms contains different knowledge and puzzles, with increasing scene exploration difficulty. The primary task at this level is "Creating an Overwintering Environment for Butterflies." Students need to search the rooms back and forth to clear the level. They have to collect props to complete the winter environment for butterflies, change the seasons by setting the clock in the room, and pick the correct options in each season to create the right winter environment and obtain the challenge props for the final level.

The Level 4 popular science theme is "Adult Butterfly," which relates to the concept of butterfly conservation, with the narrative topic "Garden Outside the Window." Players solve puzzles and collect props to create a butterfly habitat. For this level, students need to complete three picture frame tasks to collect the props, whereby props collected in the scene and through tasks play crucial roles in rebuilding the habitat—once again emphasizing the primary spirit of the game, i.e., the connection between butterflies and the environment. After completing the fourth level, the entire game comes to an end. Table 1 shows a brief description of each level.

Table 1. Summary of the four levels

Level	Prop/Event	How to play	Popular science connection
Level 1	Red and blue grid box	Click on different tiles to flip the wooden blocks with matching eggs according to memory	Strengthen impressions of eggs from different families
	Butterfly cube box	Click on wooden blocks to switch between different plants and match butterflies with host plants	Common butterfly host plants in Taiwan
	Plant model	Put eggs in the correct places for laying eggs according to the hints	Places for butterflies to lay eggs
Level 2	Butterfly garden commission	Choose the correct planting condition according to the hints	Growing conditions for plants that attract butterflies
	Street vendor	Catch a certain number of young leaves within a time limit	Favorite plant parts for larva
	Old door	Click on the handle to change the patterned door blocks to tackle predators at different stages	Butterfly predators at different stages
	Repel parasitic wasps	Paint the right color combination BUBU according to the hints	Larva defense strategies
Level 3	Room 1	After obtaining the patterned blocks, match them with the corresponding specimen blocks	Matching different stages of common butterflies in Taiwan
	Room 2	Click on the clock to change the season and choose the correct options during each season, following hints to clear the level	Creating an overwintering environment for Graphium sarpedon

(continued)

Table 1. (*continued*)

Level	Prop/Event	How to play	Popular science connection
	Room 3	Choose the leaf color for hiding to avoid predator challenges	Defense strategies during the pupal stage
	Room 4	Press the button according to the four butterfly metamorphosis stages to beat the level	Complete metamorphosis
	Boss Challenge	Press and hold on to the parasitic wasp to fill up the pesticide green bar and eliminate parasitic wasps	Non-natural ways to protect pupae
Level 4	Glass cover	Use props to build a habitat suitable for butterflies after meeting the conditions	Rebuilding butterfly habitats
	Double butterfly frame	Keep taping the screen to prevent the male butterfly from falling and dodging obstacles on the way to the end	Peak butterfly mating behavior
	Poster frame	Provide different butterflies with corresponding nectar plants	Matching common butterflies and nectar plants
	City frame	Click on the cubes to connect the water sources to complete the waterway	The importance of water sources to butterflies and the environment

3.3   Design of Expert Interview Questions

After internal and external testing, the game was handed to experts for a trial play with follow-up interviews. The interviews were conducted in a semi-structured format, lasting approximately 60 min each. Two experts were interviewed, including a butterfly ecology specialist and the director of an ecology elementary school. During the interview, they could freely express their opinions on the provided topics. The designer served as the interviewer and kept a record during the process. The dimensions of the questions were structured around game-based learning principles— consisting of aspects such as self-directed learning, guidance, sense of achievement, and game pace (effect of diverse game types)—to evaluate learning outcomes and game design effectiveness. Table 2 displays the interview questions.

Table 2. Interview Questions

Dimension of the Question	Question
Learning interest and motivation	From your perspective as a teacher, which aspects of the game design help stimulate children's interest in learning about butterflies?
Self-directed learning	Based on your professional experience, which game levels or steps do you think align with the spirit of using gameplay to enhance the effectiveness of students' knowledge absorption and self-directed learning?
Guides	In the game design, we tried guiding students step by step through storytelling, providing visual cues to complete each level. In your opinion, which parts of the game do you think are well-designed? What can be improved?
Hints	Do you think the flow and progress of the levels is easy for the students to understand? For example, do the dialogue hints after completing the level, arrow guides, or game failed screen successfully guide the players to the next step and help them understand their current goals?
Sense of rewards and achievement	The item-collecting elements and goalposts—such as collecting pieces of the journal, finding missing parts of the story, or locating BUBU—aim to provide students with a sense of achievement as they continue to complete the levels until they finish the game. How effective is this aspect?
Game pace	There are many different types of levels in this game. At each level and order of gameplay experience, the students adjust their pace and emotions. For example, time-limited levels can make players nervous and focused, whereas exploration and puzzle-solving levels slow down the pace to encourage players to think. Are there any levels that you believe children would find impressive and emotionally engaging?

4 Research Results

Analysis of the sorted interviews showed recurrent content, including guidance, integration of knowledge and gaming, and steps of grasping the information. (1) The experts reported that some parts of the game lacked guidance, which can lead to children losing track of their objectives. (2) The experts generally agreed on the effectiveness of the game, through which students can effectively acquire knowledge on butterflies. The game successfully integrated environmental conservation concepts. Game props and level rewards provided a sense of achievement at each stage to retain the freshness of the gameplay. (3) Knowledge absorption should include the three steps of reading the text, gameplay, and feedback to confirm successful knowledge acquisition. Some content required additional guidance or feedback. In addition, the experts also provided suggestions for game modifications, including revisions to the popular science text, readability, and difficulty of the levels.

After the interview, modifications were made based on expert recommendations. (1) Game guidance: adding clearer instructions (clearer cues for the mistakes made at that level, positioning of popular science text) and improving existing hints. (2) Adjusting some overly challenging levels and lowering requirements for clearing the level. (3) Moving popular science pages and game text to the top of the default first page, as well as adjusting the resolution to ensure that the users would intuitively read downwards. (4) Adding a save function for students to pause midway if unable to finish the game during class time. (5) Correcting errors in the popular science content. The other parts were reviewed to ensure compliance with the design principles, with additional plot and game clues added to the final version.

5 Conclusion and Recommendations

This study collected and organized design principles through a literature review and case studies. After expert interviews and multiple trials, a puzzle game with diverse gameplay and knowledge integration was developed, serving as a reference for future applications of diverse gameplay in environmental and popular science education games. The study emphasizes the complete metamorphosis of butterflies through four main levels. At each level, popular science knowledge was packaged into various gameplay types to regulate the player's emotions and highlight the importance of connection to the environment. The storyline packages a complete butterfly knowledge system into the game. However, despite multiple rounds of testing and revision, the game still has limitations and flaws, such as the need for clearer instructions and content discarded due to game length constraints. Continuous optimization is required to create a better version of the game. In the future, a second revised version will be examined in expert interviews to optimize the game, evaluate its effectiveness, summarize game design principles to impart environmental cognition, and improve knowledge of popular science.

References

1. Akçayır, M., Dündar, H., Akçayır, G.: What makes you a digital native? Is it enough to be born after 1980? Comput. Hum. Behav. **60**, 435–440 (2016). https://doi.org/10.1016/j.chb.2016.02.089
2. Clark, D.B., Tanner-smith, E.E., Killingsworth, S.S.: Digital games, design, and learning: a systematic review and meta-analysis. Rev. Educ. Res. **86**(1), 79–122 (2016). https://doi.org/10.3102/0034654315582065
3. Habel, J.C., Ulrich, W., Biburger, N., Seibold, S., Schmitt, T.: Agricultural intensification drives butterfly decline. Insect Conversation Divers. **12**(4), 289–295 (2019). https://doi.org/10.1111/icad.12343
4. Krath, J., Schürmann, L., Korflesch, H.F. o. von.: Revealing the theoretical basis of gamification: a systematic review and analysis of theory in research on gamification, serious games and game-based learning. Comput. Hum. Behav. **125**, 106963 (2021).https://doi.org/10.1016/j.chb.2021.106963

5. Liu, Z., Shaikh, Z., Gazizova, F.: Retracted article: using the concept of game-based learning in education. Int. J. Emerg. Technol. Learn. **15**(14), 53–64 (2020). https://www.learntechlib.org/p/217589/

6. Michelsen, G., Fischer, D.: Sustainability and Education. In: Hauff, M.V., Kuhnke, C. (Eds.), Sustainable Development Policy: A European Perspective. Routledge, London (2017)

7. Neumann, M.M., Neumann, D.L.: Touch screen tablets and emergent literacy. Early Childhood Educ. J. **42**, 231–239 (2014). https://doi.org/10.1007/s10643-013-0608-3

8. Otto, S., Pensini, P.: Nature-based environmental education of children: environmental knowledge and connectedness to nature, together, are related to ecological behaviour. Glob. Environ. Chang. **47**, 88–94 (2017). https://doi.org/10.1016/j.gloenvcha.2017.09.009

9. Plass, J.L., Homer, B.D., Kinder, C.K.: Foundations of game-based learning. Educ. Psychol. **50**(4), 258–283 (2015). https://doi.org/10.1080/00461520.2015.1122533

10. Peters, H.P.: Gap between science and media revisited: scientists as public communicators. Sci. Sci. Commun. **110**, 14102–14109 (2013). https://doi.org/10.1073/pnas.1212745110

11. Qian, M., Clark, K.R.: Game-based learning and 21st century skills: a review of recent research. Comput. Hum. Behav. **63**, 50–58 (2016). https://doi.org/10.1016/j.chb.2016.05.023

12. Sweller, J.: Cognitive load theory and educational technology. Educ. Tech. Res. Dev. **68**, 1–16 (2020). https://doi.org/10.1007/s11423-019-09701-3

13. Tahir, R., Arif, F.: A measurement model based on usability metrics for mobile learning user interface for children. Int. J. E-Learning Educ. Technol. Digital Media (IJEETDM) **1**(1), 16–31 (2014)

14. Wepprich, T., Adrion, J.R., Ries, L., Wiedmann, J., Haddad, N.M.: Butterfly abundance declines over 20 years of systematic monitoring in Ohio, USA. PLoS ONE **14**(7), e0216270 (2019). https://doi.org/10.1371/journal.pone.0216270

15. Zahari, A.S., Rahim, L.A., Nurhadi, N.A., Aslam, M.: A domain-specific modelling language for adventure educational games and flow theory. Adv. Sci. Eng. Inf. Technol. **10**(3), 999–1007 (2020)

CheMate: Anthropomorphic-cues-Mediated Experiential Learning Game Using Generative AI

Fengsen Gao, Ke Fang, and Wai Kin Chan[✉]

Tsinghua Shenzhen International Graduate School, Tsinghua University, Shenzhen, China
gfs22@mails.tsinghua.edu.cn, {fang.ke,chanw}@sz.tsinghua.edu.cn

Abstract. Anthropomorphic design cues (ADCs) refer to giving non-human objects human-like characteristics, widely used in human-computer interaction (HCI) and education. However, the current interactive modes of anthropomorphized knowledge roles (KRs) are relatively monotonous, with insufficient educational content integration, which may weaken user interaction and learning experiences. In this paper, we propose the Anthropomorphic-cues-Mediated Experiential Learning Game (AMELG) framework and implement a chemistry puzzle game called CheMate. In the framework, ADCs serve as intermediary signs, and KRs engage in interactions, providing feedback on player's actions. Subsequently, players reflectively observe the experiential process, associate abstract conceptualization with existing knowledge, understand new knowledge conveyed through ADCs, actively apply the knowledge, and thereby better memorize, understand, and master it. In the game, atoms KRs with different personalities can gather into molecules. These KRs are driven by large language models (LLMs) for dialogues. First, players talk with various KRs, accumulate intimacy, and gain the ability to move them. Then, players engage in searching, reasoning, and chemical reactions. The game dramatizes scenarios of chemical reactions. Players improve conditions or mediate through KR dialogues to drive the reactions. We set each reaction as a process of atoms' growth and provide the player with a retrospective review of it. A pilot study was conducted to validate the effectiveness of the framework, indicating its potential to enhance interactive experiences and learning outcomes. The article briefly summarizes and analyzes effective ADCs design methods in the game, and provides insights into the HCI modes of ADCs and their integration with educational content.

Keywords: Anthropomorphic Design Cues · Interactive Experiences · Education · Game Design

1 Introduction

Anthropomorphic design cues (ADCs) are crucial and profound design strategies in the field of human-computer interaction (HCI) [1]. Attributing human characteristics such as psychological, behavioral, and social traits to non-human objects, satisfies users' need for social interaction and enhances user experience, may having a positive impact on building relationships [1–3]. Subjects like cells, chemical elements, and microscopic particles often pose learning challenges for many students because these concepts are intangible and abstract, leading to a lack of confidence [4]. Moreover, being at the micro level, these concepts lack direct relevance to students' life experiences, making them not only difficult to grasp but also causing students to underestimate their value in learning [4]. Research indicates that anthropomorphizing concepts into knowledge roles (KRs) can enhance students' ability to grasp abstract concepts [5]. Therefore, research on ADCs in education holds significant importance.

Compared to traditional textbook learning, educational games have been proven to be an effective learning environment [6]. However, in existing works, ADCs of knowledge content are mainly presented through media such as text, images, and animations, with low interactivity. Even in games that utilize ADCs, gameplay primarily revolves around activities like card games or matching [7], with relatively limited interaction modes. The gameplay mechanics of educational games and the interaction methods with KRs lack deep integration with the knowledge content. This could weaken the player's experience of interacting with KRs during learning, diminish learning motivation, and consequently hinder the establishment of a profound emotional connection between players and KRs.

Therefore, in this paper, to address the aforementioned issues, we propose the Anthropomorphic-cues-Mediated Experiential Learning Game (AMELG) framework. This framework anthropomorphizes target knowledge points into KRs, using ADCs as intermediary signs between knowledge content and players, integrating experiential learning theory [8] and the model of game-based learning [9]. As an example of the framework, we have designed and developed a chemistry education game called Che-Mate. In this framework, players interact with KRs, forming the concrete experience. For instance, players can use tools to heat up or electrolyze the anthropomorphic water molecules. Subsequently, players receive feedback, and with the support of ADCs, they reflectively observe their previous concrete experiences. For example, when heating, the water molecules become more excited, dance around, and move faster. During electrolysis, the oxygen and hydrogen atoms within the water molecule separate. Oxygen atoms become friends with other oxygen atoms, gathering together to play at the anode; while hydrogen atoms gather at the cathode. Players then connect their experiences with existing knowledge through abstract conceptualization processes, understanding the new knowledge conveyed through ADCs. For example, players learn that molecules move more vigorously when heated, electrolysis of water produces hydrogen and oxygen gases, and they differentiate between physical changes (heating) and chemical changes (electrolysis). Finally, players apply their knowledge actively, conducting experiments to better grasp the concepts. For example, when sodium atoms are needed in the scenario, players first go to the beach to obtain the sodium chloride KRs, then heat them to melt them, and finally electrolyze them to obtain sodium atoms. This introduces new gameplay challenges and experiences, initiating a new cycle of the game loop.

To better iterate the game, we conducted a pilot study to prepare for subsequent large-scale empirical research. Preliminary experimental results indicate that the framework shows promising potential in terms of usability, gameplay experience, and learning outcomes. Our research proposes a novel framework for incorporating ADCs into experiential learning games and summarizes and analyzes potential ADC strategies in educational games, thus providing new HCI research directions.

2   The AMELG Framework

Drawing from semiotic mediation theory [10], the learning process can be understood as students reacting to stimuli of knowledge content. ADCs can serve as semiotic tools to mediate this process. Under the mediation of ADCs, in order to enhance students' interactive experiences during learning, emphasize the intimacy brought by KRs to players, and guide game design, the experiential learning model is introduced into the learning process mediated by ADCs, resulting in the AMELG framework (see Fig. 1). The AMELG framework consists of 3 layers: the ADCs Layer, the Experiential Learning Layer, and the Game Interaction Layer.

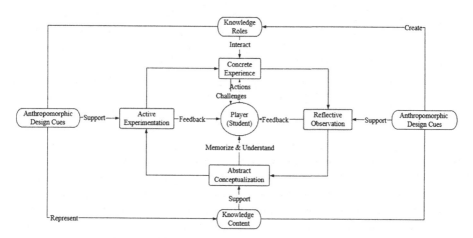

Fig. 1. The AMELG framework.

In the ADCs Layer, target knowledge points are extracted from the knowledge content, and KRs are obtained through ADCs. These KRs engage in interactions reflecting the knowledge content. Typically, the target knowledge points should represent the active agents in knowledge activities or processes. For example, in chemistry, target knowledge points could include sodium, water, sodium hydroxide, and other reactants and products; in biology knowledge, target knowledge points might encompass various types of cells or the cooperative organelles within cells. Designing ADCs for target knowledge points involves both external features such as appearance, dialogue, and behavior, and internal features such as personality, emotions, and thoughts.

In the Experiential Learning Layer and the Game Interaction Layer, players' concrete experiences stem from their interactions with KRs on one hand, and their responses to challenges within the game on the other. Subsequently, players receive feedback, allowing them to reflectively observe their previous experiences with the support of ADCs. Then, through abstract conceptualization processes, players connect their experiences with existing knowledge, understanding the new knowledge conveyed through ADCs. For example, when heating water molecules in the game, the hydrogen and oxygen atoms within the water molecule characters may accelerate their running and jumping, exhibiting larger actions. In reality, players already know that larger actions indicate more intense motion, so they connect the two, understanding that heating intensifies molecular motion. Finally, players apply this knowledge through active experimentation to better grasp the concepts. This leads to the emergence of new game challenges and experiences, thus initiating the next learning cycle.

3   Game Design and Implementation

3.1   Game Design

The initial version of the game CheMate, formerly known as Chemical Life, focused on the design of personality, emotions, and action cues in educational games. An academic paper based on it was published at the 2023 IEEE Conference on Games (CoG) [11]. In Chemical Life, each atom was represented by a humanoid game character (using KR alternately). Players interacted with these KRs, explored scenes to collect and gather them, and synthesized target substances to advance through the current level.

Building upon this setup and core gameplay mechanics, CheMate, integrating the experiential learning model, aimed to enhance the interactive experience brought by ADCs in educational games. Additionally, in terms of gameplay, CheMate expanded upon Chemical Life by introducing new features such as game bullet comments (a common feature in live streaming where real-time comments float across the screen like bullets, also called danmaku), knowledge character profiles and intimacy levels, and knowledge character diaries, aiming to create more innovative and meaningful educational gameplay experiences related to ADCs. These gameplay elements will be further explained below. In terms of KR representation, updated generative models, richer skeletal animations, and more distinct external features were utilized. Moreover, for the game scenes, laboratory scenes received visual updates, and beach and volcano scenes were added as new gameplay environments.

The game is set in the microscopic world of molecules and atoms, where each atom is represented as a humanoid character. Atoms can combine to form molecules in accordance with chemical principles. For example, oxygen is light blue in its solid and liquid states, so the image of an oxygen atom is that of a little girl wearing blue clothes. An oxygen molecule consists of two oxygen atom sisters connected by two lines, symbolizing the chemical bond between the two oxygen atoms (see Fig. 2). Sodium metal is silver-white, so the image of a sodium atom is that of a little boy wearing silver-white clothes. Hydrogen atoms are small in size, so the character image of hydrogen atoms is small and cute. In terms of personality traits, oxygen molecules actively participate in chemical reactions, reflecting an outgoing personality, which in turn influences their dialogue and behavior as external humanized traits. The game is targeted at learners of basic chemistry, hence the visual style of the game primarily features cartoons and low-polygon graphics.

The game is a third-person puzzle-solving game. To complete a level, players need to synthesize a specific substance. Achieving this requires exploring different scenes,

Fig. 2. The Player avatar, oxygen molecule, sodium atoms, and hydrogen molecule.

finding reactant KRs, and then gradually synthesizing them through multiple rounds of reactions. We use UI to provide hints for the sub-reaction process (see Fig. 2), ensuring players don't get stuck during gameplay. However, the hints we provide are just one possible synthesis path; players can still use other paths to carry out chemical reactions and progress through the levels. Currently, CheMate offers three scenes: laboratory, beach, and volcano. Players control an avatar to explore the scenes in the game and encounter KR molecules and atoms. We've created character profiles for specific atom and molecular characters, which include their microscopic properties like molecular structure, as well as macroscopic properties of corresponding substances, such as color, smell, and uses. Players gather information through observing and talking with KRs (see Fig. 3a). Each time they complete a piece of information in a character profile, their intimacy with that character increases (see Fig. 3b). When intimacy is full (see Fig. 3c), players gain the ability to move the KR.

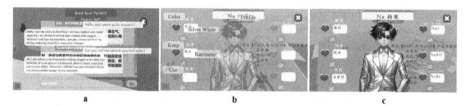

        a   b   c

Fig. 3. The player (a) talks with sodium atom KR, (b) fills in the sodium atom character profile, and (c) accumulates intimacy.

In the laboratory, there are two Workbenches (see Fig. 4a and b). One allows electrolysis and heating operations (Workbench 2), while the other is set to accommodate all reactions (Workbench 1). Some atoms and molecules are prepared in the laboratory beforehand, but to progress through the levels, players also need to obtain more reactants from the beach and volcano. For example, there's only one sodium atom available in the laboratory. Following the law of conservation of mass, a single sodium atom can't react with oxygen (at least four are needed) or with water (at least two are needed). Players need to go to the beach scene to acquire sodium chloride, learning about chemical processes like sea salt purification along the way. Afterward, they bring the sodium chloride back to the laboratory, remove the water from Workbench 2, heat the sodium chloride to its molten state, and then electrolyze the molten sodium chloride to obtain sodium atoms. In the volcano scene, players will also learn about relevant metals, non-metals, and their compounds (see Fig. 4d).

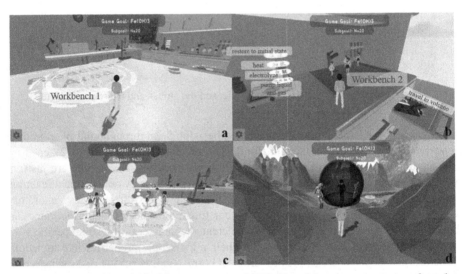

Fig. 4. The (a) Workbench1 in laboratory scene, (b) Workbench2, volcano scene transfer point, (c) chemical reaction, and (d) player moving sodium chloride in volcano scene.

Players move KRs to the reaction area, and when the number and types of KRs meet the requirements of the chemical equation, the conditions for the reaction are met. In CheMate, to highlight the partnership between players and KRs, players sometimes need to participate in the reactions as well. For example, sodium metal slowly oxidizes in the air. Therefore, unlike oxygen atoms that eagerly react, sodium atoms may have psychological resistance to the reaction because they don't want to lose their freedom by combining with oxygen atoms, and they fear that their strong reducing nature may pose a danger to other KRs in the reaction. At this point, players need to persuade and reassure the sodium atoms, telling them that the oxidation of sodium in the air is a mild process that won't cause harm and will make the sodium atoms feel more stable emotionally, to advance the entire reaction.

Inspired by live streaming, we introduced the bullet comments mechanism into the game for the first time. In live streaming, bullet comments are a means of viewer interaction, providing viewers with a sense of companionship and belonging from other viewers. This aligns closely with the experience goals CheMate aims to create, fostering feelings of social interaction, companionship, and belonging between players and

KRs. Additionally, bullet comments are effective in providing prompts and warming the atmosphere. Therefore, we introduced the bullet comments mechanism into the game, categorizing game bullet comments into three types: those from KRs, operation prompts, and key information. We differentiated them using different text colors, background colors, and varying speeds of motion. Operation prompts and key information are presented in more noticeable colors and move slower to ensure they are easily noticed by players. For example, when a player sees sodium behaving normally in kerosene but shows fear when moved out because there's oxygen nearby, it triggers bullet screens like "[Key Information] Sodium reacts with oxygen to produce sodium oxide," "[Operation Tips] Try moving the positions of sodium and oxygen to see how sodium's reaction changes!" "Oxygen molecule: Why is the sodium atom acting so scared near me? Does he not want to react with me?" (see Fig. 5).

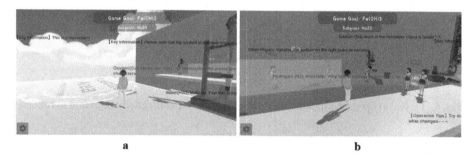

Fig. 5. The (a) bullet comments at the beginning of the game and (b) bullet comments at the kerosene.

Finally, when players achieve the ultimate goal, they can obtain character diaries (see Fig. 6). These diaries provide insights into the reactions that occurred with the characters in that level, symbolizing the characters' growth. With this design, we aim to deepen the emotional connection between players and KRs, make players aware of the positive impact they have on the characters, and provide a systematic review of the reactions and characteristics of various substances that occurred in the level to enhance knowledge retention. The content of character dialogues, bullet screens, and character diaries all utilize generative AI technology, controlled through Prompt Engineering to ensure consistency, accuracy, and appropriate variations in the content.

3.2 Implementation

We implemented the CheMate game in Unity 3D, and the game runs on the PC platform. We pre-designed the characteristics of each KR and used large language models (LLMs) to generate character dialogues in the game based on these designs. We continuously maintain a shared memory module for all KRs to enable the AI to understand the current situation. Some UI art assets, such as the image of the sodium atom in the character profile, are generated by AI.

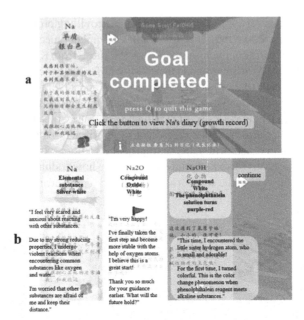

Fig. 6. Player (a) opens the sodium atom's character diary and (b) clicks the button to continue.

4 Assessment

To better iterate game development and preliminarily validate the framework's effectiveness, we invited 6 participants for a pilot study to experience the first level of CheMate. Both before and after playing the game, participants underwent a chemistry knowledge quiz through a questionnaire. Additionally, we employed the System Usability Scale (SUS) [12] to assess game usability and conducted enjoyment surveys using the In-game Game Experience Questionnaire (GEQ) [13]. Three participants were randomly selected for semi-structured interviews, which were recorded with their consent and transcribed for further analysis.

Based on the pilot study, the SUS total score is 81.67, indicating that the game's usability exceeds "Good" and comes near to "Excellent", with a grade of A on a percentile scale, surpassing approximately 90–95% of products [12]. This suggests the usability of the AMELG framework and the game. We selected the dimensions of Sensory and Imaginative Immersion (Q1, Q3), Flow (Q4, Q8), Tension (Q5, Q7), Challenge (Q10, Q11), Negative Affect (Q2, Q6), and Positive Affect (Q9, Q12) from the In-game GEQ for comparative analysis of the gaming experience. The results of the knowledge test and the In-game GEQ scale are shown in Fig. 7. The results indicate that the AMELG framework and its game can enhance players' learning outcomes and promote their gaming experience.

Based on the results of the semi-structured interviews, we found that the advantage of bullet comments lies in their ability to guide player actions, making players feel the gaze of KRs, thereby increasing the sense of purpose and companionship in player actions. Character profiles are a clever form of assessment in the game, allowing players'

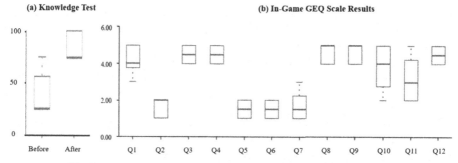

Fig. 7. The (a) knowledge test results and (b) In-game GEQ Results.

knowledge mastery to be tested at any time during gameplay without creating resistance as in exams. Character diaries require players to click to gradually reveal content, creating a sense of accomplishment as players witness memories unfolding step by step. This also helps players retain knowledge acquired in the game that may be forgotten after playing for some time.

5   Discussion and Future Work

The results of the pilot study indicate that the AMELG framework and the CheMate game have good usability, promoting positive interactive experiences between players and KRs. This interaction forms an essential foundation for strengthening the emotional connection between players and knowledge. New gameplay features such as bullet comments and character diaries have played a positive role in the above results. Therefore, we summarize and propose some potentially effective methods for designing educational game ADCs.

Firstly, providing retrospective content can deepen memory while enhancing the sense of companionship that the growth of KRs brings to players, akin to the core experience of simulation games. Secondly, allow player actions to influence game levels and create interdependence between KRs and players. For example, players can cause items on a table to drop to the ground through an explosion reaction, and then use these dropped items to jump to another platform. This enhances the player's sense of achievement. Moreover, players receive assistance from KRs, which adds a higher value to the learning content. Lastly, knowledge can be conveyed through the narration and performance of KRs. This conversational approach reduces the pressure on players to acquire knowledge, making the learning process more active and natural.

However, we found that sometimes players may overlook bullet comment content when focusing on completing a goal. This is likely because players' attention is primarily on their own controlled avatars, driven by tasks, leading them to unconsciously prioritize efficiency over carefully reading bullet comments. Additionally, poorly timed bullet comments can obstruct players' views and create a sense of confusion, resulting in a negative gaming experience. Therefore, in the subsequent development of the game, we will introduce a bullet comment review feature to allow players to revisit missed bullet comment information. We will optimize the timing, playback speed, and text length of bullet comments. For example, we will display bullet comments when players are exploring scenes, feeling lost, or stuck, rather than during moments when players are intensely focused on completing objectives.

Based on our observations during the experiment, players tend to read character diaries quickly and superficially. This might be because the content of the character diaries is a recap of the game, and players already have a grasp of it after playing. Additionally, after completing game objectives, there is a lack of incentive for players to read character diaries. Therefore, in future work, character diaries will be presented in a combination of hand-drawn sketches and text, utilizing generative AI to adapt character diaries to both character personalities and game plot development.

Furthermore, our game currently has some shortcomings. For example, in terms of storytelling, there is a lack of background setup and meaningful descriptions for synthesizing substances. We will make improvements in subsequent updates. Alongside enhancing the narrative, we will introduce various chemical instruments into the scenes as reaction tools instead of relying solely on simple lab workbenches, and so forth. There are also some limitations to the study, such as the small number of participants, making it difficult to draw quantitative statistical conclusions. In the future, we will invite more participants to conduct empirical research on the new version.

6   Conclusion

In this paper, we present the Anthropomorphic-cues-Mediated Experiential Learning Game (AMELG) framework, enriching the interaction modes between users and anthropomorphic KRs in educational games. This framework tightly integrates gameplay with knowledge content, enhancing user interaction experience and building the emotional connection between users and knowledge. We have implemented a chemistry education game called CheMate as an example of this framework. In the game, innovative features such as interactions with anthropomorphic KRs, game bullet comments, KR profiles and intimacy levels, and KR diaries are utilized to achieve the experiential objectives of the framework. By incorporating generative AI into the game to drive dialogue, bullet comments, and other text-based content, KRs become more vivid and realistic, while also significantly mitigating negative feelings arising from repetitive content generation. We conducted a pilot study to optimize our demo, and preliminary results indicate that the AMELG framework and CheMate game exhibit good usability, providing players with a sense of warmth, companionship, growth, and a positive gaming experience with learning outcomes. Therefore, they have the potential to foster a strong emotional connection between players and knowledge. Finally, we summarize effective design methods for educational games mediated by ADCs, such as "providing retrospective content" "KRs cooperating with players and influencing game maps through player actions", and "KRs serving as storytellers of knowledge." Our research contributes novel design and research directions for the use of ADCs in educational games.

Acknowledgments. This research was funded by the NetDragon Websoft Holdings Limited (Grant No. 20239680164), the Fujian Tianquan Education Technology Co., Ltd (Grant No. 5926116), and the Guangdong Pearl River Plan (Grant No. 2019QN01X890).

References

1. Araujo, T.: Living up to the chatbot hype: the influence of anthropomorphic design cues and communicative agency framing on conversational agent and company perceptions. Comput. Hum. Behav. **85**, 183–189 (2018)
2. Rhim, J., Kwak, M., Gong, Y., Gweon, G.: Application of humanization to survey chatbots: change in chatbot perception, interaction experience, and survey data quality. Comput. Hum. Behav. **126**, 107034 (2022)
3. Sheehan, B., Jin, H.S., Gottlieb, U.R.: Customer service chatbots: anthropomorphism and adoption. J. Bus. Res. **115**, 14–24 (2020)
4. Mokiwa, H.O.: Reflections on teaching periodic table concepts: a case study of selected schools in South Africa. Eurasia J. Math. Sci. Technol. Educ. **13**, 1563–1573 (2017)
5. Türkoguz, S., Ercan, I.: Effect of visual anthropomorphic stories on students' understanding of the particulate nature of matter and anthropomorphic discourse. Chem. Educ. Res. Pract. **23**, 206–225 (2022)
6. Vogel, J.J., Vogel, D.S., Cannon-Bowers, J.A., Bowers, C.A., Muse, K., Wright, M.F.: Computer gaming and interactive simulations for learning: a meta-analysis. J. Educ. Comput. Res. **34**, 229–243 (2006)
7. Zuo, T., Birk, M.V., Spek, E.V.D., Hu, J.: The effect of fantasy on learning and recall of declarative knowledge in AR game-based learning. Entertain. Comput. **46**, 100563 (2023)
8. Kolb, D.A., Boyatzis, R.E., Mainemelis, C.: Experiential learning theory: previous research and new directions. Perspectives on thinking, learning, and cognitive styles, pp. 227–247. Routledge (2014)
9. Plass, J.L., Homer, B.D., Kinzer, C.K.: Foundations of game-based learning. Educ. Psychol. **50**, 258–283 (2015)
10. Vygotsky, L.S., Cole, M.: Mind in Society: Development of Higher Psychological Processes. Harvard University Press (1978)
11. Gao, F., Fang, K., Chan, W.K.V.: Chemical life: knowledge-based personality, emotion and action cues in educational games. In: 2023 IEEE Conference on Games (CoG), pp. 1–3. IEEE (2023)
12. Sauro, J.: Measuring usability with the system usability scale (SUS) (2011)
13. IJsselsteijn, W.A., De Kort, Y.A., Poels, K.: The game experience questionnaire. (2013)

A Streamlined Game Logic and Locomotion Authoring System for VR Escape Rooms

Gerick Jeremiah Niño N. Go$^{(\boxtimes)}$, Jed Laszlo O. Jocson ,
and Eric Cesar E. Vidal Jr.

Ateneo de Manila University, 1108 Quezon City, Metro Manila, Philippines
{gjgo,jljocson,evidal}@ateneo.edu

Abstract. This study explores an authoring system for game logic and locomotion for virtual-reality escape rooms (VRER). This paper presents a preliminary interface that allows novice game developers to create virtual rooms connected through teleporters and a lock-and-key system that allows for linking these rooms together, providing users the ability to prototype their own VRER games.

Keywords: Authoring Tools · Virtual Reality · Escape Rooms · Immersion and occlusion · Tactile and haptic interaction · Training education and tutoring · locomotion · game logic

1 Introduction

In its early years of popularization, the usual idea of an Escape Room (ER) was to unlock the exit to a room, with the key obtainable only by solving a series of puzzles. However, in recent years, this concept has evolved into multiple different styles, not necessarily involving a locked room. This has led to the current characterization of an escape room as simply a big puzzle composed of smaller puzzles within a room setting. [6] Escape rooms have seen moderate success in education, due in part to recent attempts at formalizing escape room design elements to target learning goals, such as the Star model [7].

More recently, Virtual Reality (VR) technology such as headsets and motion controllers can render a virtual escape room, which opens possibilities that are not possible with physical rooms (such as vastly decreased setup time, and simulation of fantastical, magical, and/or dangerous environments). The use of VR in education has generally led to positive results in learning, motivation, enjoyment, and knowledge retention [4]. Furthermore, VR blurs the line between virtual and physical space by creating a closely related environment in the latter [2]; this allows for the creation of self-contained learning environments that closely resemble their counterpart real-world locations but prevents or limits dangers to the personal safety of users or to valuable properties.

VR adventure games that center around an escape-room design are sometimes referred to as Virtual Reality Escape Rooms (VRER); these are relatively new, and there have been some studies that explore its uses and effects as an alternative form of

C. Stephanidis et al. (Eds.): HCII 2024, CCIS 2117, pp. 312–320, 2024.
https://doi.org/10.1007/978-3-031-61953-3_34

learning. For example, a study on biology education that uses escape rooms to teach students in which the respondents of the study show an increase in knowledge acquisition due to the active learning approach of the medium. [3].

Although there is emerging research on using VRER systems as a tool for the design of serious games, there is still a present lack of accessibility to creators and educators wishing to develop VRER experiences. This may stem from the relative difficulty of developing VR content, despite a surge of interest in human-computer interaction research involving general VR modalities. Ashanti et al. [1] discusses several barriers in creating VR experiences, including but not limited to: (1) the difficulty of finding a starting point in development, (2) finding learning resources, and (3) the lack of concrete guidelines or documentation.

Thus, our study aims to cover the gaps in creating VR experiences for escape room games. A preliminary framework has been designed, which is intended as a platform to support several upcoming VRER educational applications.

At its core, our VRER framework features an authoring tool that shall allow for fast prototyping of navigation between multiple escape room levels. Currently, this subsystem facilitates the modeling of existing real-world locations via the use of 360-degree camera captures. Furthermore, an event subsystem is also currently being developed to allow authors to specify game logic conditions depending on player actions (e.g., what happens when a player uses a key on a lock); this subsystem currently works independently of the navigation modeling. The design of the aforementioned navigation and event authoring subsystems shall be explored in the next section, followed by a section discussing their intended uses and integration within our overall VRER framework; we also discuss future upcoming work on the said framework.

2 Authoring System Design

The authoring tool of our VRER framework is a PC application written in Godot 4; while the actual produced games will require the use of a VR headset, the authoring is accomplished without the use of a headset. The intention of the tool is to allow novice game designers and developers to design VRER experiences with minimal coding knowledge. Currently, there are two main subsystems that are implemented in the tool: (1) locomotion, and (2) event management, each of which shall be discussed in the following two subsections.

2.1 Locomotion

Teleportation has become the de facto locomotion method for many VR experiences as it is simple to implement, easy to grasp for the player, and does not require mapping real-world movement to the virtual space, among other reasons. [5] Previous evaluations of VR locomotion methods [10] have found that teleportation is preferred by users over other methods as it induces less motion sickness than other methods; as such, our authoring tool focuses on this locomotion technique (although another method, arm-cycling, is currently still being evaluated for future work).

The output of the locomotion authoring tool shall let players interact with triggers that teleport them to other locations in the world. The locomotion authoring tool uses a simple workflow, requiring no coding experience from the user. The workflow is detailed as follows:

Nodes and Connections. The locomotion system allows the user to place nodes in which players can enter. These nodes require 360-degree captures of real-world locations to function as intended (although future versions of the system will also consider the modeling of fully-virtual locations, as well as mixed real and virtual locations). These nodes can then be connected to each other as shown in Fig. 1; the connections indicate which nodes the player can teleport to from any given node.

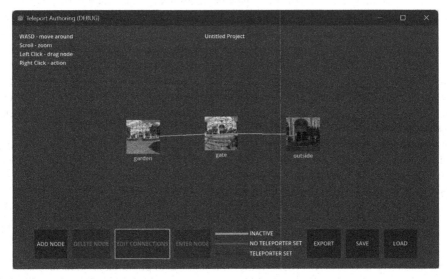

Fig. 1. Nodes connected to each other by lines

Now, these connections only show which nodes are connected to which. To allow the player to teleport from one node to another, the user must add triggers, called teleporters, that, when interacted with, will transport the player to the node attached to the teleporter.

The authoring tool shows connections that have no corresponding teleporter by highlighting these connections in red, as shown in Fig. 2. To place the triggers that ultimately teleport the player to a different node, the user must enter the node, which brings them to the 360-degree view (see Fig. 3).

Placing Teleporters. Inside the node, the user may pick the connection for which they would like to place a teleporter. The user places the teleporter by using the WASD keys to move the teleporter marker horizontally and vertically, and the scroll wheel for moving it nearer or farther from the camera.

Once the user places a teleporter, it will show as a gray disc (Fig. 4). The user may also delete already placed teleporters through the left sidebar. Once the user is satisfied with the placement of the teleporters, they can then exit the node. They will then see

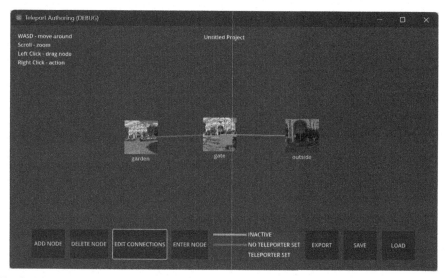

Fig. 2. Node "gate" has two connections (nodes "garden" and "outside") that have no teleporters

Fig. 3. Placing a teleporter for the "garden" connection inside node "gate"

that the previously red connections are now blue, indicating that these connections now have teleporters attached to them (Fig. 5).

Saving, Loading, and Exporting. The user can then export their progress, which will convert the required data for the nodes and teleporters to work into JSON files. These JSON files can then be used in separate projects that require the use of these nodes and

Fig. 4. A teleporter is placed and shown as a gray disc, just above the steps

teleporters. The user may also save their progress in the authoring tool and load it in another time.

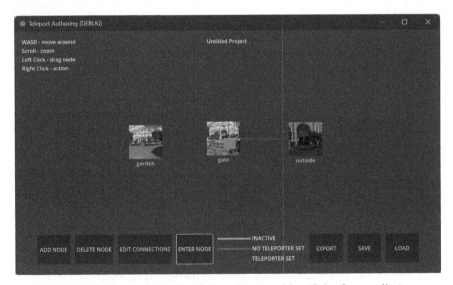

Fig. 5. The connections of node "gate" are now blue (Color figure online)

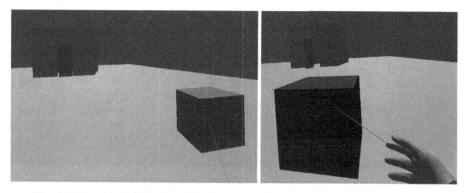

Fig. 6. The color lock that is locked (left), and unlocked (right) (Color figure online)

2.2 Game Logic

The game logic subsystem focuses on a lock-and-key system that makes use of locks and keys to set conditions for events to occur. The current implementation of the system is able to color-code the locks according to their current state, and position the lock and room objects.

Lock Types. The color lock changes color to red when locked and green when unlocked. This is done by casting a ray and triggering the switch that sends a signal to the door to open. (Fig. 6).

The position lock activates when a dedicated object is on top of the detection area. The current implementation of the system only opens connected doors within the world. (Fig. 7).

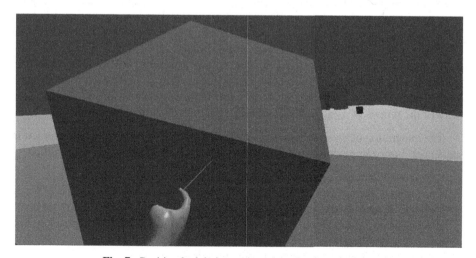

Fig. 7. Position lock being activated on the detection area

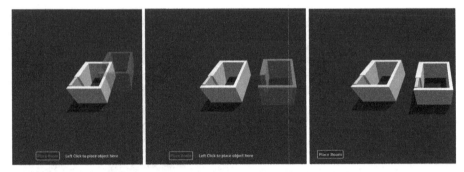

Fig. 8. Room placement sequence from left to right: (1) overlapping rooms, (2) room is placeable in the world, and (3) room is placed (Color figure online)

Room Placement. Rooms can be placed on the scene by the "Place Room" button. It brings the user to an interface wherein rooms can be placed in the game world. Figure 8 shows placement of the room. Overlapping rooms are not allowed to be placed, as indicated by a red color. When the room is placeable, it changes the color to green. The user can then left-click to place the room in the world.

3 Discussion and Future Work

The two subsystems currently exist independent of one another. In the final authoring tool, these shall be combined in one interface to allow users to create VR experiences with minimal coding experience, and will also interface with two other existing subsystems:

- An inventory management subsystem [8], which allows a player to hold key objects in their possession to transport them to other rooms. The inventory system is fully customizable depending on the type of escape room experience that is desired by the developer (e.g., cabinet style, wrist-attached, etc.).
- An object interaction subsystem [9], which allows a player to use inventory objects to realistically interact with objects or features that are present in the current room, such as twisting, levering, and hitting. An example of this would be using a screwdriver to twist the screws of a panel, which may, in turn, unlock a different room.

The integration of these subsystems shall allow an author to specify rich interaction sequences. For example, overlapping puzzles such as the following can be specified:

1. Picking up a hammer and placing it in the inventory system.
2. Navigating to the next room, which contains a cabinet with breakable glass.
3. Using the hammer (with a hitting action) on the breakable glass to open up a "virtual" adjacent room, which would contain additional interactable objects (e.g., a key to a drawer that can be placed in the inventory)
4. Navigating to a fourth room, which contains a drawer.
5. Using the inventory key (with a twisting action) on the drawer (and so on…)

Additional subsystems will also handle finer-grained event sequencing, such as implementing interrupt events for scripted sequences (which can be used to add, for example, voice-over narration or quick-time interactions), as well as a semaphore-based system that can enhance escape rooms with multiple participants to facilitate both direct and indirect communication [11] while preventing conflicting actions between players.

This overall framework shall be used to produce a full educational VRER game that explores a historical museum in the province of Quezon, Philippines. The specific requirements of this VRER game has led to the design decisions of the aforementioned locomotion and game logic subsystems—in particular, the use of 360-degree capture images of the real museum to model the virtual museum. The goal of the said VRER game is to engage visitors of the museum to learn more about the individual historical artifacts housed in the museum (without risking damage to the said artifacts), as well as provide fun logic puzzles to enhance the user's experience and promote learning retention. An upcoming study on the effectiveness of the VRER game shall involve a hands-on user test, which will also solicit insights on the viability of the above-described navigation and game logic subsystems for creating future escape-room games.

Acknowledgement. This research is part of a larger ongoing project of the Ateneo Virtual Augmented and Mixed Reality (VAMR) with grants provided by DOST-PCIEERD (through their Grants-In-Aid program, project no. 11169), Accenture Philippines, and Ateneo de Manila University.

References

1. Ashtari, N., Bunt, A., McGrenere, J., Nebeling, M., Chilana, P.K.: Creating augmented and virtual reality applications: current practices, challenges, and opportunities. In: Proceedings of the 2020 CHI Conference on Human Factors in Computing Systems (2020)
2. Chen, Y.J., Hu Y.L., Wu, B.: Impact of 360°VR on Pre-Service Teachers' Empathy——Taking Educational Equity as an example. In: Proceedings of the 31st International Conference on Computers in Education, pp. 250 (2023)
3. Christopoulos, A., Mystakidis, S., Cachafeiro, E., Laakso, M.J.: Escaping the cell: virtual reality escape rooms in biology education. In: Behaviour & Information Technology, vol. 42, no. 9, pp.1434–1451 (2022)
4. Padne, D.: Enacting biomolecular interactions in VR: impact on student conceptual understanding in biochemistry. In: Proceedings of the 31st International Conference on Computers in Education, pp. 317 (2023)
5. Prithul, A., Adhanom, I.B., Folmer, E.: Teleportation in virtual reality; a mini-review. Front. Virtual Reality **2**, 730792 (2021)
6. Spira, D., "What's a Room Escape?", Room Escape Artist. https://roomescapeartist.com/2015/06/18/whats-a-room-escape/. Accessed 04 Mar 2024
7. Botturi, L., Babazadeh, M.: Designing educational escape rooms: validating the Star Model. Int. J. Serious Games **7**, 41–57 (2020)
8. Ko, K.K.L., Restoles, D.M.D., Vidal, E.C.E.: A multimodal virtual reality inventory system. Lect. Notes Comput. Sci. **14058**, 82–100 (2023)
9. Lee, J.D.L., Restoles, D.M.D., Vidal, E.C.E.: A virtual reality object interaction system with complex hand interactions. Lect. Notes Comput. Sci. **14058**, 122–134 (2023)

10. Coomer, N., Bullard, S., Clinton, W., Williams-Sanders, B.: Evaluating the effects of four VR locomotion methods: joystick, arm-cycling, point-tugging, and teleporting. In: Proceedings of the 15th ACM Symposium on Applied Perception, pp. 1–8. Association for Computing Machinery, New York, NY, USA (2018)
11. Ioannou, A., Lemonari, M., Liarokapis, F., Aristidou, A.: Collaborative VR: Solving Riddles in the Concept of Escape Rooms. The Eurographics Association (2023)

Make NPC More Realistic: Design and Practice of a Hybrid Stealth Game NPC AI Framework Based on OODA Theory

Zhiyue Lin[1], Zetao Zhang[2], Xing Sun[1], and Hai-Tao Zheng[3(✉)]

[1] Tsinghua Shenzhen International Graduate School, Shenzhen 518055, China
lin-zy22@mails.tsinghua.edu.cn, sunxking@sz.tsinghua.edu.cn
[2] Yunnan Daily Press Group, Kunming 650000, China
zzt@yndaily.com
[3] Shenzhen International Graduate School, Tsinghua University, Shenzhen 518055, China
zheng.haitao@sz.tsinghua.edu.cn

Abstract. Stealth game is a game genre that mainly focus on avoiding the enemy's detection, in which the intelligent behavior of NPC is crucial to create an excellent player experience. This requires not only vivid and diverse NPC appearance, actions, and dialogue, but also real and credible interactions in game. However, to develop a stealth game NPC AI system is difficult, and it often shows some shortcomings in terms of diversity, autonomy, and emotionality.

This paper introduces a hybrid NPC AI framework for stealth games based on OODA (Observe-Orient-Decide-Act) theory. Unlike the Observe-Decide-Act cycle used by most stealth games, our framework incorporates an "Orient" element, enhancing NPC believability in narrative and gameplay by emphasizing unique character traits.

Our framework consists of four layers. The Observe layer integrates visual and auditory perception at the sensory level, generates distinct stimuli events for customized stimulus-response relationships. The Orient layer incorporates emotional, factional, identity, and reaction pattern for personalized decision-making. The decision layer supports dynamic environment triggers and scripted events. The Action layer interacts with the game world, and it also adds vivid dialogue, voice, and animation to enhance player immersion.

The designed framework is implemented in a third-person, dual-protagonist, action-stealth game developed under Unreal Engine. Players control one protagonist and command the other, navigating dangerous levels filled with menacing enemies to silently approach and eliminate targets.

This paper plans to use comparative experiments and questionnaires to validate the effectiveness of this framework in enhancing player experience.

Keywords: Artificial Intelligence · Stealth Games · NPC

1 Introduction

Stealth games are a game genre that primarily involves the playstyle of evading enemy detection, encouraging players to act without being noticed by enemies in order to achieve game objectives. Social stealth games represent a novel gameplay style within the stealth genre, involving the utilization of blend in crowds, disguises, and other tactics to conceal one's threatening identity from enemies [1]. NPCs play an important role in stealth games, with their behaviors and reactions directly impacting players' gaming experience. In stealth game design, the core enjoyment for players lies in navigating levels with high freedom and creativity, and the more realistic NPCs behave, the greater the player's immersion grows [2, 3]. Therefore, designing a NPC AI system that balances playability and realism is crucial for enhancing the immersion and challenge of the game.

However, the current NPC AI in stealth games faces many shortcomings, one of which is that NPCs behave in a way that seems lack of intelligence, thus damaging players' gaming experience. The lack of realism in NPCs is mainly manifested in three aspects of behavior: autonomy, diversity, and emotionality. Autonomy refers to NPCs being able to spontaneously choose actions, diversity means NPCs have different ways of achieving the same goal, and emotionality indicates involving emotional factors in NPCs' decisions and behaviors. Therefore, addressing the lack of autonomy, diversity, and emotionality in NPC behavior can effectively enhance the playability of stealth games.

The OODA (Observe-Orient-Decide-Act) theory is a strategic decision making theory proposed by John Boyd in 2006 [4]. He believed that an individual's decision-making process consists of a closed-loop cycle of four states: Observe, Orient, Decide, and Act. Among these, the Orient state is the most crucial part of the decision-making process, as it involves an individual's distinctive traits, such as experience, culture, and identity. The OODA theory is similar to the SOAR (State, Operator And Result) decision process used in most stealth game NPC AI systems [5], but shows difference by adding the unique Orient state, which heavily relies on personal attributes. This state can incorporate factors such as NPC's unique behavior, identity, and emotions to enhance the intelligence level both in decision-making criteria. Therefore, the OODA theory has the potential to address the issue of low intelligence in NPCs.

To enhance the playability and realism of stealth game NPCs, we propose a hybrid NPC AI framework based on the OODA theory, utilizing multiple decision-making methods suitable for social stealth game NPC AI system. We have also developed a third-person stealth game based on this framework to validate its effectiveness in enhancing NPC intelligence. The results indicate that the hybrid NPC AI framework can effectively increase NPC intelligence level, leading to better player enjoyment and increased immersion during gameplay.

2   Framework Design

To enhance the playability and realism of NPC AI, we propose a hybrid NPC AI framework for stealth games. This framework consists of decision processes and decision methods, where the decision process is based on the OODA loop theory, and the decision methods utilize a hybrid approach including state machines, behavior trees, and rule-based methods. The decision process comprises four interconnected closed-loop states, each serving as a layer, incorporating various decision methods at each layer to enhance autonomy, diversity, and emotionality, as shown in Fig. 1. Each NPC decision will go through these four states, all of which aim to closely simulate human cognition in the real world.

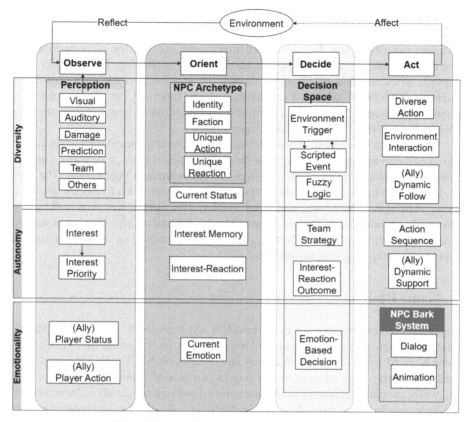

Fig. 1. The hybrid stealth game NPC AI framework.

In the Observe layer, the most critical aspect is the perception system, which determines the information NPCs can percept from the external environment. There is a diversity of perceptual system types, with each NPC possessing independent visual, auditory, damage, and other sensory perceptions. Each time a sensory information is perceived, it will be transformed into an interest event [6], and then passed to the Orient layer. NPCs can also perceive the conditions of teammates and their actions, and can make decisions based on emotions, such as showing sympathy towards injured teammates or spite towards enemies.

The Orient layer represents a significant departure from the SOAR framework, constituting the primary innovation of this study. In this layer, a repository of archetype information is maintained for each NPC, encompassing details such as their identity, affiliation, occupation, distinct behaviors, and specific responses to various stimuli. Additionally, it retains the NPC's current state information, including their emotional state, level of perceived threat, ongoing tasks, and recollection of past events. Upon receiving the interest event from the Observe layer, the Orient layer will go through the NPC archetype information to determine suitable responses based on the NPC's current state. If appropriate responses are identified, they are then passed to the decision layer.

In the Decide layer, NPCs process the responses obtained from the orientation layer to determine the final actions to be executed. This layer supports both script-based decisions written by game designers and dynamic reactions based on outer environment. The decision layer can also engage in team collaboration planning. For example, when multiple NPCs are handling the same interest, the decision layer can allocate different tasks to each NPC to achieve a cooperative action. Emotions can also influence the results of decisions. For example, a calm NPC will use its hands to gently open the door, while an angry NPC will kick the door open [7].

The Act layer is where to execute actions and influencing the external environment. This layer executes the output actions from the decision layer, and it also supports various audio-visual expressions and dynamic environmental interactions. The NPC Bark System in the Act layer enables NPCs to convey their own information to players through dialogue, animations, and other medias. This system has been validated to effectively provide playability and enhance player immersion [2, 8]. Combined with the Orient layer of this framework, NPCs can express content that is more characteristic of their own prototypes and richer in emotions.

3   Game Design

To validate the effectiveness of the hybrid NPC AI framework, we have developed a third-person action-stealth game under Unreal Engine, incorporating the hybrid stealth game NPC AI framework in both enemy and companion NPCs within the game. The stealth gameplay style adopted in this project is a mix of planner and predator style [9], where the player character can hunt enemies down or strategically influence enemy behavior and decisions through various disturbances. By defining the gameplay style, we can maximize the presentation of the characteristics of this NPC AI framework in gameplay, enhance player experience, and make the results more significant.

In the game, players will play the roles of two skilled mercenaries, there mission is to assassinate high value targets. They need to evade numerous enemies, find the optimal routes, approach and assassinate targets, then extract to a safe place. Players can only control one protagonist at a time, with the other protagonist serving as a friendly support. The player-controlled protagonist can issue commands to the friendly ally for execution and can switch control between the two characters at any time. While evading numerous enemies, players also need to strategize cooperation with their friendly ally, contemplating tactics to overcome the challenges presented in the game.

3.1   Enemy AI Design

The enemy AI design in this game is based on the hybrid NPC AI framework proposed in this paper, drawing inspiration from conventional stealth game enemy AI designs [3]. A hybrid decision-making approach is employed utilizing a combination of state machines, behavior trees, and rule-based methods. The enemies consist of aggressive NPCs capable of posing threat to the player character, as well as non-aggressive civilian NPCs who can alert aggressive NPCs of the player's presence.

Fig. 2. a) The four alert states of enemies. b) Both enemies receive a noise interest, only one of them will go to investigate. c) Companion AI in Dynamic Follow state and Standby state (executing synchronized shooting command).

In Precept layer, enemies utilize visual perception from their eyes, auditory perception within a certain radius, damage perception, and touch perception. Upon receiving perceptual information, enemies abstract this information into an interest event and transmit it to the orientation layer. For instance, if an enemy's eyes perceive the player character, the enemy converts this perception into an interest event of "detecting enemy intrusion", as shown in Fig. 2a. The benefit of this mechanism is the ability to handle perceptual information more flexibly, and to extend other perceptions with ease, such as team perception which can be implemented by auditory perception and a "team communication" interest.

In Orient layer, the enemy NPCs archetype incorporates personalized elements such as alert states, ranks, factions, interest-reaction relationship libraries, and memory of current status. Enemies have four basic alert states: neutral, investigate, search, and combat, which represent the level of threat perceived by an enemy. Civilian NPCs will have an additional fleeing state. Depending on the alert state, their behaviors and reactions to interests vary. For example, enemies in an engage state will prioritize investigating gunfire interest and ignore other interests. Additionally, ranks also influence enemy behavior. For instance, upon hearing a noise, enemies of higher ranks within the same faction may instruct lower-ranked enemies to investigate.

In Decide layer, enemy NPCs employ a decision-making approach utilizing a hybrid decision-making method. The four alert states are represented by four state machines, each contains a behavior tree to compute actions, while interest-reaction relationships control the selector nodes of the behavior trees. To achieve a more controllable enemy behavior, the behavior trees employ a hierarchical concept of goal, strategy, and action to calculate the final output action [5].

In Act layer, enemy NPCs execute action nodes provided by the decision layer. The content of these action nodes can be classified into two kinds, modify the environment and altering their own states, such as moving to a certain location within the scene or changing their current alert level. Additionally, these nodes can invoke the NPC Bark System to convey the NPC's current state to the player through actions such as playing animations or voice lines, thereby showing a certain level of human intelligence to the player and enhancing gameplay immersion. For example, when enemies hear a noise, they will first express confusion, then start communicating who should go check it out, as illustrated in Fig. 2b.

3.2 Companion AI Design

The NPC AI framework developed in this project is also suitable for designing companion NPC AI for players. Unlike the cooperative NPC AI among enemies, the friendly AI prioritizes the player's gameplay experience and may deviate from the principles of realism when necessary [10].

The decision-making process of friendly AI primarily involves a state machine and interest-reaction relationships. Companion NPCs operate within two states: dynamic follow and standby, as illustrated in Fig. 2c. During dynamic follow, companion NPCs maintain an appropriate distance from the player character, mirroring their actions. For instance, they adopt a crouched stance when the player character sneaks, or provide assistance during combat encounters. Upon receiving player commands, friendly NPCs transition to the standby state, where they autonomously execute the given instructions. Command functionalities for companions in our game encompass moving to specified locations, synchronized shooting, and interaction with designated objects. Additionally, the integration of NPC Bark System is slated to enhance players' emotional engagement with companion NPCs.

4 Result and Analysis

4.1 Result

The NPCs utilizing the hybrid NPC AI framework in this project exhibit a high level of intelligence, demonstrating autonomy, diversity, and emotionality throughout the game, creating a high level of immersion and replayability.

In a combat scenario, the player character enters the enemy's field of view, then the enemy character's alert level gradually increases until reaching its maximum value, triggering a combat state. Enemies will then equip weapons to confront the player and call nearby allies to join the battle. When the player exits the field of view, enemies will enter search state, focusing their search near the player's last seen location and emphasizing searching behind cover. Meanwhile, the player's companion NPC will actively evade enemies. If enemies continue to search without finding the player, they will abandon the search and return to a neutral state, returning to their patrol path from where they are interrupted. Players can also manipulate enemy behavior through their own actions for strategic gameplay. For instance, players can throw a coin to create a distraction, making enemies to investigate the source of the noise and leave their position. When multiple enemies are present, the closest one will investigate, while others remain in place until the investigation is finished, after which they return to normal patrol status together.

4.2 Analysis

The hybrid NPC framework utilized in this project not only achieves a playable and immersive NPC AI system through a simple framework design, but also supports designers to develop their own NPC systems effectively. In combat scenario, enemies perceive the player character through visual perception and generate an interest to transfer to the Orient layer. Subsequently, upon reaching a full increase in alertness, the Decide layer generates an action that will turn to combat state. Following this, enemies initiate a special reinforcement interest by emitting auditory stimuli, and nearby enemies receive this interest, leading them to engage in combat. Similarly, in strategic gameplay, the sound of a coin initiates a "suspicious noise" interest, which is perceived by multiple enemies. A cooperation manager system then sends investigate and standby reactions to different enemies, resulting in one conducting an investigation while others observe. By utilizing this framework, developers can easily create their own NPC AI system by designing layered decision models and write corresponding interest-reaction relationships to achieve vivid NPC behaviors.

5   Conclusions and Future Work

In this study, we proposed a hybrid NPC AI framework based on the OODA theory aimed at enhancing the realism of NPCs and player experience in stealth games. The decision-making process of this framework consists of four layers: observe, orient, decide, and act. By emphasizing unique character traits and personalized decisions within the Orient layer, the credibility of NPCs in narrative and gameplay is enhanced. We implemented this framework in a third-person action stealth game, designing both predator and planner gameplay style, utilizing a combination of techniques including state machines, behavior trees, and rule-based reactions to support. Players can experience increased replayability and immersion due to the heightened intelligence level of NPCs. In summary, this paper proposes a novel NPC AI framework suitable for stealth games, offering new insights and methods for the design and implementation of NPC AI in stealth games.

Certain limitations exist within the current study. Concerning framework design, the algorithm for retrieving suitable reactions to specific interests from a custom interest-reaction relationship library is excessively intricate, necessitating future optimization to facilitate a more adaptable design workflow. Additionally, in the Decide layer, the decision of updating or switching states still requires meticulous debugging by designers. In future work, we intend to conduct further experimental validations, encompassing testing across varied game scenarios and with diverse player groups, to verify the applicability and effectiveness of the framework. Moreover, with the emergence of new AI technologies such as large language models, we aspire to explore their practical application within this framework and in the design of stealth games.

References

1. Peel, J.: Inside the revival of social stealth games. https://www.gamesradar.com/inside-the-revival-of-social-stealth-games/. Accessed 14 Oct 2023
2. Enezi, W.A., Verbrugge, C.: Investigating the influence of behaviors and dialogs on player enjoyment in stealth games. Proc. AAAI Conf. Artif. Intell. Interact. Digital Entertainment **19**, 166–174 (2023)
3. Stealth Game Design. https://www.gamedeveloper.com/design/stealth-game-design. Accessed 08 Mar 2024
4. Fusano, A., Sato, H., Namatame, A.: Study of multi-agent based combat simulation for grouped OODA Loop. In: SICE Annual Conference 2011, pp. 131–136 (2011)
5. Lent, M., Laird, J.: Developing an artificial intelligence engine (2023)
6. Miles, B.: How to Catch a Ninja: NPC Awareness in a 2D Stealth Platformer. Game AI Pro: Collected Wisdom of Game AI Professionals. 413 (2013)
7. Orkin, J.: Three States and a Plan: The A.I. of F.E.A.R. GDC (2006)
8. Redding, P.: Aarf! Arrf Arf Arf: Talking to the Player with Barks. In: Lecture, Game Developer's Conference 2009 (2009)
9. The Three Philosophies of Stealth Game Design. https://www.gamedeveloper.com/design/the-three-philosophies-of-stealth-game-design. Accessed 08 Mar 2024
10. Dyckhoff, M.: Ellie: Buddy AI in The Last of Us. In: Game AI Pro 360: Guide to Character Behavior, pp. 25–36. CRC Press (2019)

A Study of Ethics Education Game Design Based on a Reflective Framework

Guozhang Ma, Ping Li[✉], Ke Fang, Yueer Mao, and Chu Zhang

Tsinghua University, Beijing, China
{mgz22,mye21,chu-zhan22}@mails.tsinghua.edu.cn,
liping.thu@hotmail.com, fang.ke@sz.tsinghua.edu.cn

Abstract. This study focuses on the design of ethical education games, aiming to enhance players' ethical awareness and critical thinking abilities through a reflective framework. The research surveys and identifies the necessity of ethical education, highlighting various societal issues stemming from a lack of effective ethical education. It also delves into the role of educational games in ethical education, emphasizing their potential in improving moral reasoning and empathy. The current state of research on ethical education games, both domestically and internationally, has also been analyzed in this study.

Building on this background, the study proposes several innovative points: the integration of a reflective learning framework specifically tailored for game-based education, enabling more effective ethical education through the gaming medium. Based on pedagogical principles, this study develops a reflective gaming framework for game design, which includes learning objectives of the game, player developmental stages, the design of reflective activities, provision of multi-dimensional feedback, and the use of interactive and adaptive learning elements. Additionally, the use of AIGC technology to create emergent interactive episodes aids in establishing emotional connections and effectively fosters deep reflection on moral and ethical issues among players. The aim of this study is to address the deficiencies in mechanisms, narratives, and moral education in existing ethical education games by utilizing a reflective framework from educational theory to design ethical education games.

Keywords: Ethical Educational Game · Reflective learning · wicked problems · AIGC

1 Problem Statement

In recent years, with the rapid development of society and continuous advancement in technology, the importance of ethical education has increasingly come to the forefront. In a diverse societal environment, people face various ethical decision-making challenges. These challenges involve not only personal moral choices but are also closely related to the overall harmonious development of society. Society faces numerous problems due to the lack of effective ethical

C. Stephanidis et al. (Eds.): HCII 2024, CCIS 2117, pp. 329–336, 2024.
https://doi.org/10.1007/978-3-031-61953-3_36

education [1], including but not limited to the absence of professional ethics, academic dishonesty, and a weak sense of social responsibility. The presence of these issues severely hinders the healthy development of society and the comprehensive growth of individuals. Against this backdrop, ethical education games, as an emerging educational method, can guide players in moral reasoning and critical thinking [2,3].

The role of educational games in ethical education cannot be overlooked. By simulating real or fictional ethical dilemmas, games not only provide an interactive way of learning but also stimulate players' interest and participation in learning. Players assume various roles in the game, facing complex ethical decisions; they need to consider the consequences of various decisions. This process helps develop players' moral judgment and sense of responsibility. Compared to traditional classroom learning, this method is more intuitive and effective, allowing players to gain a deeper understanding and reflection on ethical issues while enjoying the fun of the game.

Based on existing research [4], this study proposes a new theoretical framework for reflective learning, designing a game named "Desert Island Survivor" as an educational tool for ethical education. The game aims to cultivate players' moral education, role responsibility, and ethical responsibility. It introduces a trolley problem scenario, placing players in a wicked problems [5], enhancing their sense of immersion and facing them with moral choices. Additionally, the game employs AIGC technology to create emergent interactive episodes, facilitating the establishment of emotional connections. Moreover, this study conducted experiments to test the game and verified its preliminary effects through interviews. This represents a new attempt and exploration in using games for ethical education.

2   Reflective Design Principles

Currently, ethical education games face issues with insufficient reflectiveness and immersion, which prevent the educational function of ethical games from being fully realized [6]. Boyd et al. [4,7,8] believe that increasing reflectiveness can be achieved through the following points:

1. Design reflective activities. Create game scenarios and decision points that encourage ethical and moral decision-making, stimulating reflection and discussion.
2. Provide multidimensional feedback. Design game outcomes to display the consequences of decisions and pose guiding questions.
3. Utilize interactive elements. The game should adjust its difficulty and complexity based on the player's performance and progress.

To enhance the reflective impact of ethical education games, we have designed a reflective game framework.

1. To address the issue of insufficient reflectiveness, we have constructed a wicked problems within the game, a scenario without a standard answer. Such wicked problems are crucial for ethical reflection, presenting significant challenges in moral decision-making. The characteristics of these wicked problems [5] make them important and complex subjects for discussion in ethical education, testing the problem solver's creativity, critical thinking, and moral judgment abilities.
2. To address the issue of insufficient immersion in ethical games, we use AIGC for the creative rendering of narratives around wicked problems. Simultaneously, we draw on methods proposed by Jerrett et al. to foster empathy [9], thereby enhancing players' sense of engagement and immersion.
3. Finally, it's necessary to assess the levels of reflection experienced by players after the game ends to validate the effectiveness of the game. For this purpose, we employ the "Levels of Reflection" framework proposed by Elisa D. Mekler et al. [8], which categorizes the effects of players' reflections into several levels (Table 1):

Table 1. Levels of Reflection.

Injury level	Resource consumption
R0	Non-reflective description
R1	Reflective description
R2	Dialogical reflection
R3	Transformative reflection
R4	Critical reflection

This approach allows for a more comprehensive understanding of the depth of players' thoughts on their gaming experience (Fig. 1).

3   Game Design

Based on the theory of reflective learning, we have designed an ethical education game. The purpose of this game is to cultivate players' moral education, role responsibility, and ethical responsibility. Our game requires only one player to participate. The game setting is on a deserted island. In the game, the story background is set as follows: an airplane encounters a flight accident. The game's player(protagonist) is the pilot of this airplane, a veteran. The plane crash-lands on this deserted island. All the passengers on the plane, including the game's player, total four people. Apart from the player, the remaining three individuals have sustained injuries of varying degrees. One NPC character has sustained the most severe injuries (we have named this game NPC as A1), while the other two game characters have sustained varying degrees of minor injuries (we have

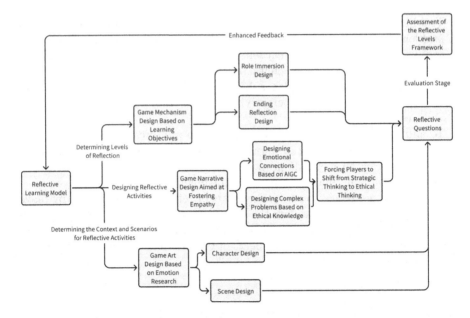

Fig. 1. The reflective framework proposed in this study.

named these two game NPCs as B1 and B2). Now, all four characters, including the player, face the threat of death due to a lack of medical care, food, and water sources. As the pilot, a veteran, and the only able-bodied character, the player is the only one capable of leading the remaining three injured NPCs, who lack wilderness survival skills, to survive on the deserted island and wait for rescue.

The game lacks a save mechanism, and the profiles of the 3 game NPC characters are generated by the ChatGPT 3.5 model. Throughout the game, the player needs to lead the other 3 NPCs to survive until they encounter a passing ship. The arrival time of the ship is set to be random, between 3 to 5 days. Each NPC consumes a certain amount of resources, and for simplification, we have set two resource consumption states for NPCs (Table 2):

Table 2. The amount of resources consumed by different damage levels.

Injury level	Resource consumption
Minor injury	1 resource
Severe injury	2 resources

To simulate a real and harsh survival environment, we start the game with 8 numbers of resources. An NPC that loses their life can be used as 3 resources (This setting is inspired by the real historical case of "R v Dudley and Stephens," based on descriptions in Dudley's diary). The player must use their moral reasoning to progress the game until rescue arrives.

At the end of the game's story, we will expand the narrative and reveal to the player the stories of the surviving NPCs as well as those of the lost NPCs. Afterwards, the game will present the player with different ethical choices from various standpoints in text form and encourage them to try again. If the player wishes to attempt different survival strategies, a new round of the game will begin. In this new round, besides the character controlled by the player, the remaining three NPC characters will be regenerated through the ChatGPT 3.5 model (Fig. 2).

Fig. 2. The group of images displays the game running screen on the left side and a photo of the experimenter experiencing the game on the right side.

Throughout the entire game design process, we adhered to the key principles of the reflective learning framework and integrated elements that promote empathy. Application of the Reflective Framework:

Introducing Wicked Problems. Players are faced with a wicked problem that has no standard answer. Engaging in this, players will take responsibility for their decisions, prompting them to reflect on the correctness of their decision-making.

Enhancing Immersion. The AI-generated characters are unique, players need to take measures carefully. Additionally, using AIGC to extend the stories of NPC characters after they are rescued, as well as the stories of NPC characters who have passed away, encourages players to contemplate the consequences of their decisions.

4 Verification

To examine the effects of applying the reflective learning framework to the game, as well as the learning outcomes of players after playing the game, we conducted semi-structured interviews with participants who took part in the game test. Initially, we recruited 6 testers to participate in the test, with their ages ranging from 19 to 25 years (median age 24), all of whom had received a high school education or higher and were well-educated. In the following article, these 6 testers will be referred to as P1 P6.

Before the game started, we introduced the participants to the interactive mode of the game and informed them that the experiences of the game characters were generated by AI-generated text. After that, the game test could begin.

4.1 Result

After completing all experiments, we recorded all interviews through semi-structured interviews, and then transcribed the interviewees' voices into written form. The interviews focused mainly on players' levels of reflection, empathetic states, and game experience. From the summary, we identified the common game experiences of most players:

1. Induced Reflective Thinking. P2 said, "Seeing the outcomes of others at the end of the game made me feel that the person who was sacrificed should have been hopeful about the future, wanting to live on and have their own life. But with my choice, all of that was gone."

2. Strategic Thinking Shifted to Ethical Thinking. P1 mentioned, "I didn't care much about the severity of the injuries, what mattered more was considering whether they deserved others to sacrifice for them." P3 added, "Maybe drawing lots would be better than me choosing; that way, I wouldn't feel the moral pressure."

3. Established Emotional Resonance with NPC Characters. P3 mentioned, "In the rounds I played, I was deeply impressed by a character named Zhang Qin. Her backstory of flying to North America to visit her parents moved me, so even though she was severely injured, I always kept her till the end." Meanwhile, P5 shared, "When faced with the situation of having to choose one character to abandon, I would weigh each person's background according to my criteria because I resonated with some characters' family relationships."

4. Limitations in Gameplay. Several players pointed out that there is substantial room for improvement in the game framework, suggesting that the survival process should incorporate many aspects where players can exert their initiative. P6 mentioned, "I thought that during the wait for the rescue ship, we should have been able to collect berries in the wild to satisfy our hunger, which would have given me more options."

4.2   Analysis

According to the "Levels of Reflection" framework proposed by Elisa D. Mekler et al., it can be observed that after the game experience, most players were able to reach Level R3 - Transformative reflection: players re-examine their experiences with the aim of changing behavior, gaining new insights, or reconsidering personal assumptions. This indicates that characters and stories generated by AIGC creating emotional resonance and enhancing immersion are effective in inducing reflective thinking and can also enhance the overall game experience.

However, feedback for Level R4 - Critical Reflection was lacking. The speculated reason might relate to the significant potential for enhancing the game experience. According to Result 4, P3 feedback stated, "In the end of the stories, the AI-generated stories attribute the characters' ending to the environment rather than my choices, which greatly reduced my sense of guilt"; Player P2 mentioned, "Every character is good and also very tragic, which didn't open up my space for choice," "The lack of variables in the game process made me wish to get everything done on the first day." These feedbacks suggest that during the game development process, the AI's prompts still have room for improvement. Enhancing game content and richness can deepen players' reflective understanding.

5   Conclusion

In this study, based on the reflective ethical education framework we proposed, we designed an ethical education game "Desert Island Survivor", aimed at cultivating players' moral responsibility, making players accountable for their actions, and inducing reflection. Our game design followed the principles of increasing reflectiveness, promoting immersion, and examining levels of reflection, aiming to challenge players' moral principles through tough ethical wicked problems. Through experiments and interviews, this study verified the effectiveness of the game in promoting players' moral reasoning and critical thinking. The wicked problems and moral decisions faced by the players in the game not only stimulated their thinking but also triggered deep emotional resonance, thus achieving the intended educational objectives.

However, our study also has certain limitations. Firstly, although AIGC technology provided rich storylines and character settings for the game, the quality and diversity of AI-generated content still need further optimization. The wicked problems and plot settings in the game need to be more refined and diverse to promote higher levels of reflection among players. Moreover, this study mainly focused on the immediate educational effects of the game, and the long-term impact on players' moral development has not been explored in depth.

Moving forward, our research will assess the lasting impact of ethical education games on players' moral cognition and behavior through long-term follow-up surveys. At the same time, it will explore the specific contributions of different design elements in the game, such as game mechanics, storylines, character design, etc., to educational effects, to guide the optimization and innovation of future ethical education games.

References

1. Prensky, M.: Digital game-based learning. McGraw-Hill, New York (2001)
2. Kickmeier-Rust, M.D., Mattheiss, E., Steiner, C., Albert, D.: A psycho-pedagogical framework for multi-adaptive educational games. Int. J. Game-Based Learn. IJGBL **1**(1), 45–58 (2011). https://doi.org/10.4018/ijgbl.2011010104
3. Noemí, P.-M., Máximo, S.H.: Educational games for learning. Univers. J. Educ. Res. **2**(3), 230–238 (2014). https://doi.org/10.13189/ujer.2014.020305
4. Boyd, E.M., Fales, A.W.: Reflective learning: key to learning from experience. J. Humanist. Psychol. **23**(2), 99–117 (1983). https://doi.org/10.1177/0022167883232011
5. Bosman, F.G.: There is no solution!: 'Wicked Problems' digital games. Games Cult. **14**(5), 543–559 (2019). https://doi.org/10.1177/1555412017716603
6. Sicart, M.: Moral dilemmas in computer games. Des. Issues **29**(3), 28–37 (2013). https://doi.org/10.1162/DESI_a_00219
7. Ryan, M., Ryan, M.: Theorising a model for teaching and assessing reflective learning in higher education. High. Educ. Res. Dev. **32**(2), 244–257 (2013). https://doi.org/10.1080/07294360.2012.661704
8. Mekler, E.D., Iacovides, I., Bopp, J.A.: A game that makes you question...': Exploring the role of reflection for the player experience. In: Proceedings of the 2018 Annual Symposium on Computer-Human Interaction in Play, Melbourne VIC Australia: ACM, pp. 315–327 (2018). https://doi.org/10.1145/3242671.3242691
9. Jerrett, A., Howell, P., Dansey, N.: Developing an empathy spectrum for games. Games Cult. **16**(6), 635–659 (2021). https://doi.org/10.1177/1555412020954019

Peadom: An Endogenous Educational Game to Learn Hybridization and the Framework to Guide It

Yueer Mao(ID), Ping Li(✉)(ID), Yuan Zeng(ID), and Zhiyue Huang(ID)

Tsinghua Shenzhen International Graduate School, Shenzhen, SZ 518055, China
mye21@mails.tsinghua.edu.cn, liping.thu@hotmail.com

Abstract. In recent years, advanced techniques and proficient design skills have led to the rise of many educational games. Among these, games for science learning hold a significant place. However, many games designed for science education suffer from rigid implementation and poor playability, failing to stimulate players' interest and resulting in a limited educational impact. To address this, we propose the Endogenous Educational Games Design (EEGD) Framework. This framework guides designers in creating games around specific science themes, drawing on Ian Bogost's Persuasive Games theory and subsequent research. The gameplay of educational games should naturally evolve from the chosen theme, providing players with an engaging virtual environment to explore, learn, and understand the given knowledge. We developed a game called Peadom based on this framework. This hybridization-learning game allows players to control a pea hero living on a remote island, trying to understand the chaos in Peadom by hybridizing with other peas, having conversations, and solving puzzles. Through this game, players can enjoy the gameplay while learning about genes, hybridization, and other genetic knowledge. They will also understand the importance of gene diversity for biological species and reflect on gene-related scenarios in everyday life.

Keywords: Educational games · Game-based learning · Endogenous games

1 Introduction

Science educational games, a form of informal education, have garnered much attention from in recent years. However, most games designed for science education have issues such as knowledge cramming, a disconnection between gameplay and content, and poor playability, which make it challenging to stimulate players' interest. Simultaneously, many science educational games focus on conveying fragmented knowledge rather than establishing a systematic understanding of the subject and introducing the social values behind the knowledge. The integration of playful and educational nature, the improvement of science educational games' quality, and the enhancement of players' learning outcomes are still problems to be solved.

In his book Persuasive Games, Ian Bogost argued that games have the potential to convey information to players during the gameplay process, especially systematic knowledge, and spread opinions to players [2]. He also introduced the concept of "procedural rhetoric" as the core mechanism of game persuasion. Therefore, based on the outcomes of game persuasive research, we combined our own practice and proposed an Endogenous Educational Game Design (EEGD) Framework. We analyzed how procedural rhetoric works in endogenous educational games and built a design guide for science educational games accordingly. We hope it can help designers generate gameplay and content from the educational theme, and produce endogenous educational games that allow players to learn systematically.

In addition, based on the above EEGD framework, we designed a genetic education game, Peadom, intending to help players understand genes, hybrids, and other genetic knowledge. We aim for players to grasp the significance of gene diversity and reflect on some genetic-related social phenomena (such as discrimination) while enjoying the game. Our subsequent pilot study preliminarily verified its utility.

2   Previous Research

Traditional educational game designs often rely on gamification techniques, using methods like rewards to motivate players. However, this often results in disjointed gameplay and mechanics.

As research in educational games advances, endogenous educational games have gained attention for their superior educational outcomes. As Habgood's empirical studies suggest, these games skillfully integrate educational content with core game mechanics, thereby embedding learning objectives within the gaming experience [4]. This not only enhances learners' engagement and motivation, but also promotes active, contextual learning, making education more effective and enjoyable.

Despite these advantages, there are few outstanding endogenous educational games in the market. This is because endogenous design, which involves extracting thematic elements from content and transforming them into gameplay, is more challenging and requires greater effort. As a result, many educational game designers prefer non-endogenous designs. Furthermore, despite the proven educational effectiveness of endogenous games, the underlying mechanisms are rarely discussed. This leads to a lack of frameworks guiding their production.

3   Related Theories

Education aims to impart knowledge, skills, foster values, and encourage critical thinking. Simultaneously, rhetoric is the art of conveying opinions or assertions. In essence, education is a rhetorical process, with rhetoric serving its purpose.

In his book Persuasive Games, Bogost introduced "procedural rhetoric", a core mechanism through which games achieve their persuasive functions. Its arguments are made not through the construction of words or images, but through the authorship of rules of behavior, the construction of dynamic models [3]. These rules get implemented through programming, which is the fundamental part of video games. Players learn and understand a system's operation by exploring a "possibility space" constructed by a set of rules during gameplay.

From 1980s, with the recognition of Piaget's cognitive development theory and Vygotsky's sociocultural theory, constructivism became the mainstream learning theory. It views learning as an active knowledge construction process, not passive information reception. According to constructivist views, learners construct knowledge and understanding through interaction with their environment. In endogenous educational games, the gameplay mechanics stem from the educational theme itself, making the constructed "possibility space" an interactive environment. The process of playing and exploring within this "possibility space" aligns with the construction process as described by constructivism, explaining why gameplay and exploration can enhance learning outcomes.

Furthermore, the idea of games' persuasive potential through procedural rhetoric can fit within broader game production frameworks. The widely recognized MDA (Mechanics, Dynamics, Aesthetics) framework [5], comprising mechanics, dynamics, and aesthetics, aligns with the rules, possibility space, and persuasive effects in procedural rhetoric. In other words, procedural rhetoric can be seen as an aspect of the MDA theory in persuasive games. This association makes a game design framework based on procedural rhetoric practically viable for guiding the production of endogenous educational games.

4   EEGD Framework

Based on theories above, we suggest the EEGD (Endogenous Educational Games Design) framework. It consists of two parts: the construction of procedural rhetoric and the process of procedural rhetoric. In the process of procedural rhetoric, the expression of educational content begins from the designer's side, relying on the game rules set by the designer, building its potential space, and through the player's gameplay, persuasive achievements in both education and entertainment are formed at the player's end. The construction of procedural rhetoric, on the other hand, starts from the player's end, starting with the educational content that needs to be conveyed, establishing the design goal of the game, constructing the system and content design of the game according to it, and finally going to the specific logic implementation of the game (Fig. 1).

4.1   Setting Goals

In the construction phase, establishing design goals begins with the game's educational theme. Each discipline encompasses a vast array of knowledge, yet the

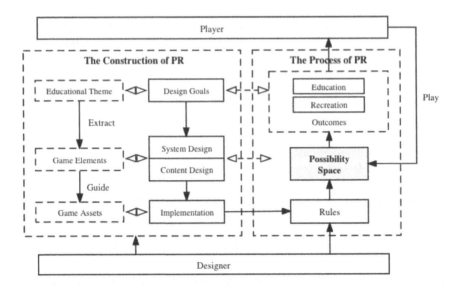

Fig. 1. The EEGD Framework

content of a game is limited. At this stage, designers need to define the educational content the game will focus on and understand it thoroughly. After that, designers should have a clear understanding of which aspects of the discipline is the most crucial, thereby establishing clear design goals.

4.2 Elements Extraction

After establishing clear design goals, the next step is system design. In previous frameworks for endogenous educational game design, scholars focused on detailing the design process to assist designers, offering less advice on how to extract game elements from educational themes to construct system gameplay [1]. Indeed, in the game design process, the step of core gameplay design often relies on "borrowing" or the Eureka moment, but based on the experience summarized from game development, we attempt to provide methods to help designers extract game elements from educational themes here.

In writing, there's "The 5Ws" guideline, which can also be used in game design to help designers develop their concepts. Who, What, Where and When are used to establish the game's subject, objectives, environment and time scale, forming the main framework of game mechanics, while How and Why are used to establish the connections between variables and narrative driving forces, forming the main framework of game narrative. When extracting these elements from educational themes, we offer the following guides:

Who: Extract the game's 3C from classic figures in the disciplinary field.
What: Establish the game's objectives through reasonable behaviors of the subject in the disciplinary field.

Where: Determine the game's setting by considering common scenes in the disciplinary field.

When: Determine the game's time scale based on the time scale fitting the disciplinary field.

How: Find connections between variables and elements from real systems in the disciplinary field.

Why: Find values relevant to the disciplinary field as the narrative driving force of the game.

The methods above serve as a reference for educational game creators to extract elements from educational themes. However, for the creation of endogenous educational games, it's not necessary to adhere strictly to them. During the design phase, designers should apply these guides flexibly to maintain the game's quality and uniqueness.

4.3   Implementation

During the implementation phase, the game enters formal development. The developers create game assets based on the design from the previous phase. This ensures that the intended design is perceptible to players. Also, the system rules of the discipline in the real world can serve as references for data structures and algorithms, assisting developers in logic programming.

5   Game Design

Based on the EEGD framework, we selected hybridization-a significant aspect of genetics-as our core gameplay mechanism. Genetics is a branch of biology that studies the inheritance and variation of organisms. It not only deepens our understanding of life but also provides tools for addressing challenges in human health, agriculture, and biodiversity. Hybridization is a breeding method integral to genetics and is widely used in reality. It inherently includes elements of challenge and strategy, making it suitable for adaptation into a game system. Hence, our game aims to help players understand the process of hybridization and its underlying significance.

5.1   System Design

In the game system design, we identified the main elements using the 5W method. In the game, players assume the role of a pea on a secluded island. They hybridize with other peas to explore more areas and communicate with different NPCs, thereby uncovering the secrets of Peadom. We further elaborated on the game design, focusing on gameplay and narrative aspects. As hybridization and dialogue form the primary interactions between the protagonist and the game, the game system primarily comprises a crossbreeding system and a dialogue system.

Hybridization System. The hybridization system in our game is based on real-world hybridization rules. In schools, teachers use words, graphics, and Punnett squares to explain these rules, detailing how parents produce gametes and how these combine to form the offspring's genotype. The Punnett squares, represented through mathematical symbols, offer multiple probabilities of hybridization outcomes, assisting learners in quickly calculating the results. However, this method can be abstract. Our game aims to offer players a more tangible experience (Fig. 2).

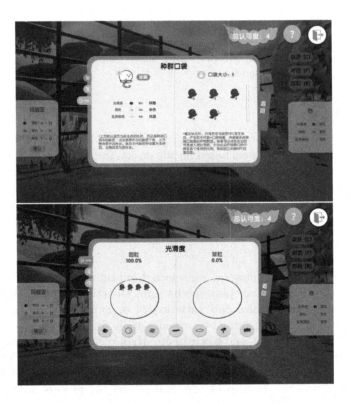

Fig. 2. Hybridization System in Peadom

In our game, both the protagonist and NPC peas possess their genotypes, which influence their traits. In reality, traits are observable, while genes are hidden hereditary factors playing a decisive role. Thus, in the game, players observe NPC pea traits and deduce the genotype by noting the impact of hybridization results. This way, they can better hybridize to achieve desired traits. This forms the basis of our hybridization system.

To stimulate player understanding and exploration of the hybridization system, we've structured the game as an open world. Players don't have a fixed exploration order; they interact based on their interest in traits and NPCs.

With this design, we've created a possibility space for pea hybridization within the game, grounded in real-world principles. Here, players can set their objectives (hypothesize), act freely (verify), and increase their comprehensive understanding of hybridization (conclude).

Dialogue System. In the role-playing game Peadom, the dialogue system is a crucial part of the gameplay. The game world contains eight NPCs, each with three approval levels. Players must decipher each NPC's genotype to increase their approval, unlocking more dialogue. This dialogue includes information about genetics, NPC backstories, and the Peadom world background (Fig. 3).

Fig. 3. Dialogue System in Peadom

Dialogue is tied to Peadom's history and NPC relationships. To understand the game world and advance the plot, players need to correctly guess NPC genotypes, improving NPC acceptance. To achieve this, players must conduct in-game hybridization experiments. This intertwining of the hybridization and dialogue systems ensures a strong connection between gameplay and content.

NPCs' hybridization preferences are revealed through dialogue. Instead of merely providing descriptions, the game integrates these preferences with NPC personalities, creating a logical connection and maintaining the game's integrity. To succeed, players should closely monitor dialogue while hybridizing, enhancing the uptake of knowledge conveyed through conversation.

5.2   Content Design

Storyline. The game unfolds on a secluded island inhabited by a group of peas known as Peadom. Initially, the peas coexisted harmoniously until an exotic pea was dropped by a large bird a month ago, sparking the emergence of various new traits within Peadom.

The reign of Peadom is held by the UnderMattress pea family. UnderMattress the First, known from the fairy tale The Princess and the Pea, landed on this island and became its ruler. The UnderMattress family, through inbreeding, has retained the original traits of the island's peas, which are seen as noble symbols. However, the emergence of numerous new traits among the common peas led to division and hostility, as peas began to attack each other over these differences.

Tensions reached a peak with the appearance of Snow White, a royal pea with a distinct white flower trait, unlike the other purple-flowered royal members. In contrast to UnderMattress the 108th, who practices "racial segregation," the common white-flowered peas rallied behind Snow White, inciting an unprecedented upheaval in Peadom.

Character Design. The protagonist is a pea that drifted ashore from the island's coast and was taken back to the underground cavern by an elder named Mendel. To unravel the mysteries surrounding themselves and the secrets of Peadom, the protagonist needs to explore the island. The game has eight NPCs so far, each with a personality setting related to their traits and genotypes, and dialogue based on this. The relationships between NPCs and the confrontation between forces unfold with the player's dialogue in the game.

Level Design. The game's levels are integrated with the narrative, mostly through subtle guidance to stimulate players' curiosity, driving their behavior in the game. We divided the island into four areas: plain, lake, highlands, and lowlands, further dividing the plain into five smaller areas: the garden, mine, three sprout area, municipal square, and mountain road. Each area has its Landmark combined with the narrative dialogue text to attract players' attention, subtly guiding players in the game.

In the specific layout of levels, we first used 2D design to list the locations and connectivity of NPCs in the game, forming an abstract level, then built the level prototype in Unreal Engine 5 to verify its playability, and finally used art assets to beautify the scene, ensuring the level's practicality and aesthetics, maintaining the game's quality, and conveying the expected educational effect to players.

6   Pilot Study

To assess the feasibility of Peadom and the EEGD framework, we carried out an pilot study. We enlisted 21 participants with different backgrounds. Among them, 38.1% of the participants are female and 61.9% are male. 71.4% of the participants have a high school level of genetics study, 19.0% have a college level or above, and 9.5% have less than high school level. All participants have experience with video games (Fig. 4).

All players were asked to play the game for a minimum of twenty minutes. After playing, we use the GEQ (Game Experience Questionaire) [6] to evaluate players' experience. To better understand How and Why the game works, we also conducted interviews with 2 players based on following questions:

Fig. 4. Playing session

Q1: What is your interest in genetics? Why?
Q2: How do you think in Peadom? How is this different from other ways of learning?
Q3: How do you form short-term goals in the Peadom?

7   Result and Analysis

Figure 5 shows the GEQ statistical results, indicating that the dimensions of competence, immersion, flow, and positive emotions scored well. The flow score is slightly lower, which might be due to the game's challenges being either too easy or too hard for players of different learning abilities and levels. The game's challenge dimension has a median score of 2.0, which is average. However, the box body is skewed upwards, suggesting that the game presents moderately high challenges for most players, requiring significant effort to succeed. The scores for tension and negative emotions are low, meaning players remain relatively calm during the game. This calmness allows them to absorb and apply knowledge effectively. Furthermore, they encounter fewer frustrating situations and can maintain a positive emotional state throughout the game.

In interviews conducted with participants after the game, we recorded their answer to the questions listed above and concluded them accordingly:

- P1 is very interested in genetics, finding it captivating because *"there are many practical parts, so I can operate in reality."* However, due to his boarding school environment, he didn't get the chance to conduct pea hybridization experiments personally. He believes *"Peadom provide a chance to conduct hybridization experiments in a more efficient way."* P2 also expressed interest in genetics, but he did not get good grades. He states, *"Some concepts of genetics are very abstract and confusing."* and *"This game simplifies many concepts in genetics, making them more intuitive and easier to understand."*

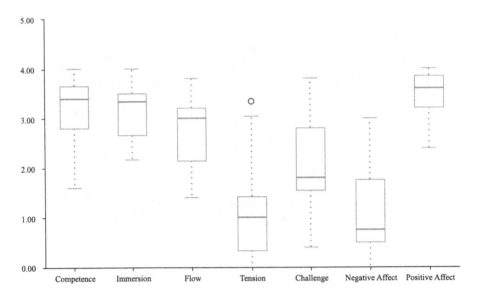

Fig. 5. The statistical results of GEQ

- Unlike other forms of learning, Peadom provides them with a space to try. P1 states, *"I am not afraid of making mistakes in the game, and I have enough time and opportunities to verify my ideas."* But in the classroom, *"Wrong answers bring greater psychological burden."* P2 believes, *"The characters and stories in the game will attract me to continue playing. In the game, any of my actions will get immediate feedback, and the results of hybridization will also be presented immediately, which strengthens my motivation to explore."*
- In the early stages of the game, participants went through a short period of confusion. P2 said, *"In the first five minutes, I didn't know what I was supposed to do, just keep understanding traits and the UI panel."* However, as the game advanced, P2 noted he *"gradually understood the gameplay and noticed the genotype changes after hybridization. By applying this method and conducting multiple hybridizations with NPCs in the game, I was able to determine their genotypes one by one."* And stated that *"I was indeed attracted by this game during the play."*

In summary, 1) by providing players with a space for free hybridization, and making abstract concepts concrete, Peadom plays a noticeable role in helping players understand the process of hybridization. 2) The game's content design stimulates the curiosity of players, thereby enhancing their initiative to continue learning in the game. 3) The game is quite challenging for some players and at the beginning of gameplay. This might be because the open-world design leads to some players getting lost, which can be resolved in future by improving the tutorial and level guidance.

8   Conclusion

This research explores the design and practice of endogenous educational games, emphasizing the importance of closely integrating educational content with game mechanics to enhance learners' engagement and motivation. It also points out the challenges such design methods face in practice. To address these gaps, we proposed the EEGD framework to guide the design of educational games and demonstrated how to extract elements from educational themes and proceed with design through the example of a genetics-learning game Peadom. The pilot study suggests that Peadom effectively enhances players' understanding of genetics, engaging them through challenges and narrative-driven exploration. Despite identifying areas for improvement, such as initial player guidance, the study underscores the potential of Peadom and the EEGD framework.

References

1. Athavale, S., Dalvi, G.: ENDOGEN: Framework for Designing Endogenous Educational Games (2020)
2. Bogost, I.: Persuasive Games: The Expressive Power of Videogames. MIT Press, Cambridge, MA (2007)
3. Bogost, I.: The rhetoric of video games. In: John, D., Catherine, T. (eds.) MacArthur Foundation Series on Digital Media and Learning, pp. 117–139 (2007). https://doi.org/10.1162/dmal.9780262693646.117
4. Habgood, J., Ainsworth, S., Benford, S.: Endogenous fantasy and learning in digital games. Simul. Gaming **36**, 483–498 (2005)
5. Hunicke, R., LeBlanc, M., Zubek, R.: MDA: A Formal Approach to Game Design and Game Research
6. IJsselsteijn, W., de Kort, Y., Poels, K.: The Game Experience Questionnaire. Technische Universiteit Eindhoven, Eindhoven (2013)

Ourhotel: A Two-Player Cooperative Game Designed for Young Couples in Long-Distance Relationships

Xiaoke Pu[1], Ruoxin You[2], and Wei Huang[1(✉)]

[1] Tsinghua University, Haidian District, Beijing 100084, People's Republic of China
huangw@sz.tsinghua.edu.cn
[2] University College London, Gower St, London WC1E 6BT, UK

Abstract. Emotional maintenance poses a significant challenge in long-distance relationships (LDRs). Previous works exhibit high repetitiveness in user experiences and lack consideration for real-life, long-term use. Recognizing the enduring nature of multiplayer games, couples in LDRs have adopted some of the prominent large multiplayer games to fulfill their needs for sustaining emotional connections. However, existing game designs fall short of aligning perfectly with the requirements of long-term relationships. This paper introduces Ourhotel, a game designed for young couples in LDRs. We scrutinized existing games embraced by long-term distance relationship couples, and identified six factors that significantly impact their experience. Building upon these insights, we designed a two-player cooperative simulation management game, incorporating material collection, manufacturing building and arrangement, manufacturing growth, multi-finality narration and two-player interaction. We conducted two rounds of usability tests utilizing paper prototypes and an interactive demo to evaluate the user experience. The results demonstrate that during the game, the frequency and the length of communication were boosted. Players provided positive feedback on the topics introduced by the game, expressing enjoyment of the manufacturing growth mechanism.

Keywords: Game design · Long-distance relationships (LDRs) · Cooperative simulation management game

1 Introduction

Long-Distance Relationship (LDR), characterized by the geographical separation of partners, has become more prevalent due to the rising trends in job-related and educational mobility [1]. In contrast to couples living together, individuals in LDRs face limitations in their ability to connect. The absence of face-to-face communication, in-person interaction, and shared experiences poses challenges to effective communication, hindering prompt conflict resolution and hastening the emergence of strains in romantic relationships, ultimately leading to their dissolution.

Presently, individuals in LDRs employ various technological means to maintain connection. Couples utilize methods such as phone calls, video chats, text messages, instant

C. Stephanidis et al. (Eds.): HCII 2024, CCIS 2117, pp. 348–358, 2024.
https://doi.org/10.1007/978-3-031-61953-3_38

messaging, and emails to sustain their LDRs. These technologies support information exchange in LDRs. However, the communication needed in intimate relationships is not limited to information exchange [2], as various communication and interactions are needed to build and maintain relations [3]. A survey on LDRs among college students research (2019) [4] shows that emotional connection is important for LDRs. However, traditional technologies used in LDRs overlooked the crucial aspect of subtle emotional communication within intimate relationships.

Digital games have emerged as promising tools for fostering connection in LDRs, offering flexibility, engaging gameplay, and collaborative experiences. However, the addictive nature and challenging designs of commercial games can strain relationships. Besides, synchronous engagement requirements limit accessibility for those with differing schedules in LDRs.

To address these limitations, we designed Ourhotel, a game specifically crafted for individuals in LDRs' daily lives. We aimed to facilitate emotional communication for people in LDRs while avoiding the shortcomings typically associated with games, including addiction and excessive challenge. Our research questions are:

1. How can games be designed to meet the communication needs of individuals in LDRs?
2. How will a game for LDRs function in the daily lives of those involved in LDRs?

2 Related Work

2.1 Design for Long-Distance Relationships

Research in the field of Long-Distance Relationships (LDRs) encompasses a broad array of topics, including communication methods, relationship satisfaction, trust issues, and strategies for maintaining relationships.

Laura Stafford delved into how couples in LDRs utilize various communication modalities to sustain their relationships [5]. Further expanding on this theme, L. Crystal Jiang and Jeffrey T. Hancock's investigation examined the influence of geographical separation on the selection of communication methods and the level of intimacy in relationships, revealing a propensity among partners in LDRs to engage in communication that is rich in emotional content [6].

The significance of love and a sense of connection with significant others cannot be overstated, playing a critical role in individuals' satisfaction with life and overall happiness. The notion of "relatedness" is integral to several psychological theories on human needs. Maslow's hierarchy posits "belongingness and love" as one of the essential human needs. Similarly, Epstein's Cognitive-Experiential Self-Theory includes relatedness among its four fundamental needs, while Ryan and Deci's contemporary Self-Determination Theory places it within the top three essential needs for humans [7]. Sheldon et al. [8] conceptually define relatedness as the experience of regular, intimate interactions with caring individuals, contrasting with feelings of loneliness and neglect.

For individuals in LDRs, emotional needs focus on sustaining and forging a sense of connectedness during periods of separation, essentially manifesting a tangible perception of "love" without the benefit of direct, face-to-face communication. Through an analysis of 143 published products (encompassing both design concepts and technologies), Hassenzahl identified six key strategies for fostering connectedness: awareness, expressivity, physicalness, gift giving, joint action, and memories [9]. These strategies serve as the foundation for an experience-oriented approach to design, emphasizing the importance of cultivating a deep sense of relatedness, even in the absence of physical proximity.

2.2 Products and Games for Individuals in LDRs

Current works for individuals in LDRs include industrial products, traditional interactive media, and some commercial games adapted and utilized by the LDRs.

Physical products demonstrate their distinctive advantages through tangible interaction. Prior research has explored simulated tactile experiences such as hand-holding facilitated by Frebble (2013) [10] and simulated kissing experiences enabled by Kissenger (2012) [11]. However, most industrial products targeting LDRs offer a one-size-fits-all solution, providing the same software and hardware to every user. This approach may not appeal to all users or meet their individual needs.

Traditional interactive media encompass online communication tools, social platforms, and specialized intimate mobile applications like Couple (2012) [12] designed for the LDR community. However, shortcomings in emotional communication design led to a lack of sustained stimulation for users in traditional interactive media. Unlike commercial games, traditional interactive media struggle to maintain high user engagement, with users losing interest in emotionally evocative yet less relevant products to their daily lives after an initial trial.

Games, on the other hand, have been repeatedly highlighted for their accessibility, engaging playability, and capacity to foster cooperative communication experiences Nevertheless, the inherently addictive nature of commercial games poses a risk of excessive time investment, and many such games overlook the asynchronous interaction patterns typical among LDRs participants. Additionally, the gameplay challenges present in some commercial games might inadvertently exacerbate communication conflicts within LDRs communities, rather than fostering harmony and connection.

This nuanced understanding of the current product landscape for LDRs underscores the necessity for a more customized, emotionally resonant approach in designing solutions that truly cater to the distinctive needs and dynamics of long-distance relationships.

2.3 Theoretical Foundation for Game Design in LDRs Field

The Mechanics-Dynamics-Aesthetics (MDA) framework presents a methodology for both analyzing and designing games, initially proposed by Robin Hunicke, Marc LeBlanc, and Robert Zubek in 2004[13]. This framework breaks down a game into three interconnected components: Mechanics, the rules and base components of the game; Dynamics, the run-time behavior of the mechanics acting on player inputs and each other's outputs; and Aesthetics, the emotional responses evoked in the player. Together, these elements form the foundation of a player's gaming experience. By adjusting the game's mechanics, designers can influence its dynamics, which in turn can affect the player's aesthetic experience. Furthermore, an understanding of the player's aesthetic experience provides valuable feedback for designers to refine the game's mechanics and dynamics, highlighting a continuous loop of interaction between game design and player engagement. This research incorporates Hassenzahl's six design strategies as a foundational guide, reverse-engineering the mechanics and dynamics that inform the comprehensive design of a game.

3 Game Design

3.1 The Combination of MDA Theory and Hassenzahl's Six Strategies

Based on MDA Theory and Hassenzahl's Six Strategies, we concluded potential mechanics and dynamics for our game design. (See Table 1).

Table 1. The combination of MDA theory and Hassenzahl's six strategies.

Design strategies	Experience/ Aesthetics	Mechanics	Dynamics
Awareness	Sense of connection	Environment editing	Edit and choose environment
Expressivity	Self-expression/Emotional transmission	Composable module/ Customized Interaction	Use communication languages
Physicalness	Sense of security	Simulated physical interaction	Design Actions and contact parts/Create private spaces
Gift Giving	Thoughtfulness/Shared symbolism	Props making and giving	Make and give things
Joint Action	Sense of dependency and creativity/ Surprise of the unknown	Shared space/Cooperation	Collaborate and manufacture/Select strategies
Memories	sense of ritual, commemorative value, uniqueness, and tangibility	Saving and invoking	Document and review

3.2 Game Framework Design

Our game proposed following systems to meet our design goals:

Real-time Interaction System: This system is designed to simulate physical interaction, aiming to evoke feelings of intimacy and realism within the player experience. It offers extensive customization options and flexibility, allowing players to tailor their interactions to their preferences.

Asynchronous Interaction System: Tailored for players in different time zones or with varying schedules, this system supports both direct and indirect forms of interaction. Direct interactions include, but are not limited to, message exchanges and the gifting of virtual items. Indirect interactions occur when actions taken by one player have a consequential impact on the gameplay or experience of another player, fostering a connectedness even in absence.

Cooperative Gameplay System for Collection, Cultivation, or Survival: This component includes both compulsory and optional elements designed to cater to diverse player skill levels. The compulsory elements are crafted to ensure inclusivity, minimizing potential conflicts by accommodating players with varying abilities. Conversely, the optional elements are structured to highlight and leverage the strengths of more adept players, promoting a gameplay experience rooted in mutual dependence, respect, and a shared sense of community.

Memorialization System: This system underscores the importance of items and temporal milestones with sentimental value, offering players the opportunity to create and customize memorabilia within the game. It serves to deepen the player's engagement with the game world by enabling the preservation and celebration of significant moments and achievements.

3.3   Game Detailed Design

We decided to develop an idle simulation game:

Based on user research findings, most users prefer idle simulation games. They express concerns that overly complex game mechanics could lead to friction in cooperative play. Users desire a relaxing and mutually supportive experience during cooperative gameplay. Thus, we have decided to develop an idle simulation game characterized by its casual content, strong sense of cooperation, and effective use of fragmented time.

Most simulation game themes are drawn from everyday life, allowing players to understand the gameplay with minimal guidance. We have chosen "hotel management" as the game's thematic focus. Hotels accommodate the gameplay of building mechanics and provide a setting for introducing traveler NPCs (Non-Player Characters). The concept of a "couple running a store" is imbued with real-life emotional nuance, and store management is a familiar theme for players.

To ensure the game's playability, we tapped into the LDRs' longing for the concept of "home", introducing the idea of "room growth" and designing an innovative gameplay feature: house development. This gameplay combines house construction and development in a semi-idle manner. After constructing a house, it will grow on its own, with its growth affected by player interaction. Interaction factors influencing this growth include the player's login time and duration of play.

The gameplay of simulation management games is based on a cycle of resource management and numerical systems. In "Ourhotel", the core loop of the game is illustrated in Fig. 1. Players repeatedly engage in this loop throughout the gameplay to advance the development of the inn and unfold the narrative.

Additionally, we have refined other gameplay elements. These elements not only enrich the game content but also provide players with avenues for resource acquisition

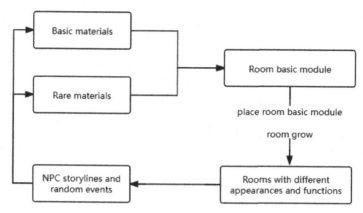

Fig. 1. Resources cycle system in "Ourhotel".

and playable duration. Integrating all design strategies into a single work represents the greatest advantage of using games as design vehicles. Below is a mapping of all gameplay mechanics and various impact strategies in "Ourhotel" (Fig. 2).

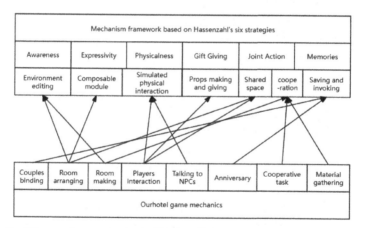

Fig. 2. All gameplay mechanics in "Ourhotel" designed with the MDA framework.

3.4 Paper Prototype Test

Before the official development of the game, we conducted paper prototype testing:

The paper prototype for "Ourhotel" utilized the collaborative platform Figma to enable simultaneous operation by researchers and participants. The prototype included the game's core mechanics: material collection, room crafting, construction, and growth. The provision of materials, the success of room crafting, the development of rooms, and NPCs dialogues were all simulated manually.

Throughout the gameplay, players demonstrated a solid understanding of the game mechanics. Following an initial tutorial, participants spontaneously engaged in material collection, room crafting, and layout construction. The testing phase revealed that players had a good grasp of and receptiveness towards the game mechanics, showing particular interest in the combined building and cultivation gameplay. Players expressed approval of the idle cultivation mechanic, noting that its lightweight nature was particularly well-suited for players new to gaming, allowing them to quickly grasp the gameplay while minimizing the game's time demands. Both groups suggested that more visually appealing art would enhance the game's attractiveness. One group of players suggested introducing more narrative conflicts, pointing out a need for deeper emotional communication topics within the current narrative framework (Fig. 3).

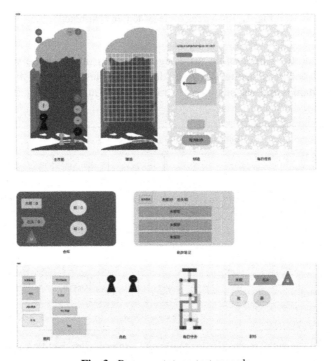

Fig. 3. Paper prototype test records.

3.5   Second Iteration

Based on player feedback, we iterated on the game, including the selection of the art style, modifications to the cooperative segment mechanics, optimization of interaction methods, and narrative improvements. We completed the game using the Unity engine.

Art Design: We designed a complete game interface and UI, making the game style warm and adorable.

Cooperative Gameplay Mechanic: The current cooperative gameplay mechanics were too difficult for players, leading to communication disputes among them. So, we removed the punishment mechanism and time limits from the cooperative gameplay, allowing players to easily complete the cooperative content.

Interaction Optimization: The user interface's color scheme was standardized, with dynamic effects and sound cues added to enhance player guidance.

Narrative Enhancement: We added game plots and set ending branches to increase the design of dramatic plots.

Figure 4 shows the final version of the game, including online collection crafting, building, player interaction, NPC dialogues, and more.

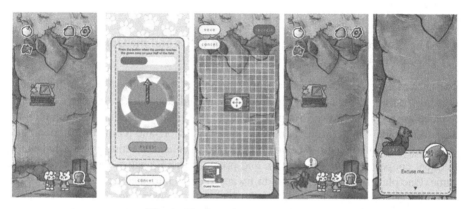

Fig. 4. Final Version of "Ourhotel".

4 Method

We conducted experiments with seven couples (6 males, 8 females, aged 23 to 29) in LDRs. This study employed a within-subjects design. Participants were asked to use "Ourhotel" for three days. Participants were required to record their interactions with their partners during the period. After the gameplay concluded, all participants were subjected to semi-structured interviews, which were then transcribed and coded for further analysis.

5 Results

During the user testing phase, we collected data on changes in the quality of intimate relationships and communication, as well as qualitative conclusions from interviews. The following sections present the themes distilled from the qualitative data.

5.1 Playing "Ourhotel" Positively Influences Communication in LDRs

The data indicates an increase in communication frequency and an improvement in the quality of communication during the game-playing periods, with some discussions directly related to the game content. Three groups mentioned that, over the three days of playing the game, they became accustomed to allocating time daily to engage with the game and communicate beyond its content. One participant from a cross-border relationship stated, "It provided us with a goal that motivated us to synchronize our schedules daily, which we wouldn't have done without such a (collecting) target due to significant time differences." Another group noted that during gameplay, they used specific abbreviated terms to coordinate their gaming actions: "I would send a single word through WeChat to remind him to collect resources timely, enabling us to construct enough rooms for our hotel."

5.2 The Link Between Gaming Behavior in LDRs and the Quality of Intimate Relationships

Two groups experienced noticeable improvements in the quality of their intimate relationships during the gameplay, including increased dependency on each other and reduced anxiety. These two groups exhibited more positive gaming behaviors among the seven, evident in login frequency, resource collection, and room construction numbers. Hence, positive gaming behavior may lead to enhanced intimacy, as it represents frequent cooperative communication and provides more positive feedback within the game. One player commented, "I didn't want to delve into specific resource collection strategies, but I was eager to see the results of our room construction. This led to a natural division of labor: I decided on the room arrangement and what rooms we needed, and he fulfilled those needs while I frequently reminded him it was time to progress to the next gameplay step."

5.3 "Ourhotel" Appeals to LDR Users for Long-Term Play

Interviews revealed that all seven groups expressed a desire to continue playing "Ourhotel" to maintain their long-distance emotional connection. They appreciated the light, mobile, casual game format for accommodating asynchronous communication between distant partners, finding it suitable for integrating interaction into the gaps of daily work. One group mentioned, "Compared to messaging apps, this method leaves clearer records. We can see the results of our collaboration at any time, instead of having to sift through extensive chat histories when we want to recall something. This is a key reason for our interest in long-term gameplay." A participant with no interest in simulation management games noted, "I prefer more thrilling games and am usually not interested in this type of gameplay. However, it doesn't consume much of my time and is simple enough for my girlfriend to understand, so playing it doesn't lead to arguments. That's why I'm willing to keep playing."

6 Discussion and Conclusion

Through designing and testing the game "Ourhotel" we explored how to craft games to meet the specific emotional needs of LDRs. By integrating the MDA framework and Hassenzahl's six strategies, we successfully developed a game design that facilitates emotional communication and interaction among LDRs users.

"Ourhotel" not only provides a new medium for communication but also has a positive effect on enhancing the emotional connection within the LDRs. Player feedback indicates that the game meets their needs for emotional exchange, increasing the frequency and quality of communication, especially in strengthening shared experiences and goal-oriented communication. Furthermore, there is a clear correlation between players' positive gaming behavior and the improvement of relationship intimacy, highlighting the potential value of such games in supporting the maintenance of their relationships.

From the design and experimental results of "Ourhotel" we deduce that the following mechanisms are effective for designing emotional communication games for LDRs: 1. Easy cooperative mechanics; 2. Resource acquisition mechanisms that require little time; 3. Customizable interaction mechanisms; 4. Spaces that can be modified together. Additionally, we found that future LDRs games might need to continually provide content updates to ensure players' sustained interest in playing.

Although the design and experimental results of "Ourhotel" are encouraging, this study has some limitations. Firstly, the relatively small sample size may affect the generalizability and extendibility of the results. Secondly, the long-term effects and ongoing appeal of the game require further investigation. Future research could explore different types and styles of game design based on this research framework to meet the diverse needs of LDRs.

References

1. Neustaedter, C., Saul, G.: Intimacy in long-distance relationships over video chat. In: Proceedings of the SIGCHI Conference on Human Factors in Computing Systems (2012)
2. Quintanilha, M.S.: Buddywall: a tangible user interface for wireless remote communication. In: CHI 2008 Extended Abstracts on Human Factors in Computing Systems, pp. 3711–3716 (2008)
3. Rooney, V.: Maintaining intimacy at a distance: an exploration of human–computer interaction's approach to mediating intimacy. Behav. Inf. Technol. **33**(9), 882–891 (2014)
4. Youth.cn. https://edu.youth.cn/jyzx/jyxw/201902/t20190213_11868189.htm
5. Stafford, L.: Maintaining Long-distance and Cross-residential Relationships. Routledge (2004)
6. Crystal, J.L., Hancock, J.T.: Absencemakes the communication grow fonder: geographic separation, interpersonal media, and intimacy in dating relationships. J. Commun. **63**(3), 556–577 (2013)
7. Ryan, R.M., Deci, E.L.: Intrinsic and extrinsic motivations: classic definitions and new directions. Contemp. Educ. Psychol. **25**(1), 54–67 (2000)
8. Sheldon, K.M., et al.: What is satisfying about satisfying events? Testing 10 candidate psychological needs. J. Pers. Soc. Psychol. **80**(2), 325 (2001)
9. Hassenzahl, M., et al.: All you need is love: current strategies of mediating intimate relationships through technology. ACM Trans. Comput.-Hum. Interact. (TOCHI) **19**(4), 1–19 (2012)

10. Toet, A., et al.: Reach out and touch somebody's virtual hand: affectively connected through mediated touch. In: 2013 Humaine Association Conference on Affective Computing and Intelligent Interaction. IEEE (2013)
11. Samani, H.A., et al.: Kissenger: design of a kiss transmission device. In: Proceedings of the Designing Interactive Systems Conference (2012)
12. McVeigh-Schultz, J., Baym, N.K.: Thinking of you: vernacular affordance in the context of the microsocial relationship app, couple. Soc. Media+ Soc. 1(2), 2056305115604649 (2015)
13. Hunicke, R., LeBlanc, M., Zubek, R.: MDA: a formal approach to game design and game research. In: Proceedings of the AAAI Workshop on Challenges in Game AI, vol. 4, no. 1 (2004)

Research into the Development of Game Assets by Independent Artists for a Valve's Workshop Game Dota 2

Nicolas C. Romeiro(✉) [ID], André Salomão [ID], Flávio Andaló,
Letícia Maria Fraporti Zanini [ID], Fabíola Borges, Jacob Neto,
and Milton Luiz Horn Vieira [ID]

DesignLab, Universidade Federal de Santa Catarina, Florianópolis, SC, Brazil
nicolas.romeiro@ufsc.br

Abstract. The goal of this article is to assess and demonstrate the process of independent creators when developing an asset for a game supported by the Workshop Tool created by Valve. At the research lab DesignLab there are projects working with undergraduate students to research both games and animation academic field, including but not limited to game design, serious games, 3D rendering in real-time with a game engine, and brand study. The following study project proposed to research the process by developing an asset set for the character Meepo, a character that is part of the Dota 2 popular game. The development process will at first create the concept arts (Pre-production), followed by the modeling process, skin and texture (Production). The increase of venue available in digital games, while also the emergence of new methods of monetization for the independent artist creates the necessity of research in this area of development, not only to prepare students for the market but also to create more knowledge for the academic environment.

Keywords: Workshop · Game Assets · Asset Development

1 Introduction

The game industry is showing constant growth surpassing even long-established industries like music and cinema combined [2]. The development of an online platform for games sales is one of the innovations made to sell games, allowing not only the reduction in cost due to lack of physical copies [8] but also allowed the change in the relationship between the consumer and the developer, since these online platforms can work like a social media [9].

In 2003 the North American company Valve Corporation launched their online platform to sell digital games called Steam [12]. Nowadays Steam has roughly 120 million monthly active users, with roughly 62 million using it daily [10]. 2011 saw the launching of the Workshop Tool by Valve on Steam, allowing developers to have independent creators create assets and/or content for

C. Stephanidis et al. (Eds.): HCII 2024, CCIS 2117, pp. 359–369, 2024.
https://doi.org/10.1007/978-3-031-61953-3_39

their games [3]. By 2014 this tool had generated according to Alden Kroll, a UI Designer at Valve, roughly 57 million dollars for independent creators that worked on only three games, Team Fortress 2, Dota 2, and Counter-Strike: Global Offensive [1].

At the research lab DesignLab they have had projects working with undergraduate students to research both games and animation academic field, including but not limited to game design, serious games, 3D rendering in real-time with a game engine, and brand study [7]. Undergraduate students show interest in the work-flow for independent 3D artists' works in the marketplace, they were looking to prepare themselves for life after university by studying how this process works, therefore that allowed us to work with two undergraduate students to assess and demonstrate the process of independent creators when developing an asset for a game supported by the Workshop Tool created by Valve. it was decided to study the entire process by developing an asset set for the character Meepo, a character that is part of the Dota 2 popular game, and that doesn't have as many submissions as other more popular characters have.

Therefore, the goal of this article is to assess and demonstrate the process of independent creators when developing an asset for a game supported by the Workshop Tool created by Valve. For this, it was decided to study the entire process by developing an asset set for the character Meepo, a character that is part of the Dota 2 popular game, and that doesn't have as many submissions as other more popular characters have.

2 Procedures

The development of 3D production requires multiple computer graphics software, phases and in different ways, being all dependent on what is being proposed (Fonseca, 2018). The development of a game is, usually, separated into three phases, preproduction, production, and post-production, with the creation of an asset encompassing generally all phases of development [4].

According to Ciszek [4], the process of creation starts with the exploration of ideas, prototypes, and documentation that works as guidelines, establishing all the requirements and basis for the production phase. Following the generation of ideas, a phase focused on the production of visual pieces, called concept arts, is necessary to establish ideas like design, color, illumination, and composition [6].

The next step is to create 3D surfaces of the visual arts created in the previous step, beginning the modeling phase of production, which can be done by two different methods, polygonal modeling, by modifying faces to shape the object or digital sculpture, which simulate the process of traditional sculpture [11].

Assets developed in this phase will have to go through the process of Skinning, allowing it to adjust and animate according to the character's Meepo in-game animations [11].

The last two steps are about developing the asset's textures, by creating their UV map, allowing the independent artist to 'paint' over the 3D object in a 2D image, and then wrapping it to give the asset color, material, and details [5].

Therefore, our development process will at first create the concept arts (Preproduction), followed by the modeling process, skin and texture (Production).

3   Development

Alongside the standard procedures utilized in the development of a game asset, Valve has set several guidelines for the asset to be accepted and possibly inserted into the game, these will be evaluated and discussed alongside the creation of the set in this chapter.

3.1   Concept Art

One of the guidelines set by Valve is regarding the concept design for each character the community wishes to create. There are a few rules that are mandatory and must be followed for the asset to be accepted in the game. Regarding the concept art, the artist must follow the idea that the character's silhouette should be clear and visible at first glance, the color scheme should be either complementary, analogous, or semi-complementary, finally the greyscale should go from light (top of the model) to darker (bottom of the model). All of these should result in an idea that has visual balance.

It was chosen to start with the simple assets first to understand better in practice what those guidelines meant, by designing the accessories weapon, mask, and the backpack in this order.

The general idea is that Meepo is a scavenger, with this theme in mind we decided to expand it by creating the narrative purpose of what if he needed to scavenge in radioactive trash. Following this theme, we decided to explore it with his weapon, a destroyed and/or very used shovel that would work as his weapon Fig 1.

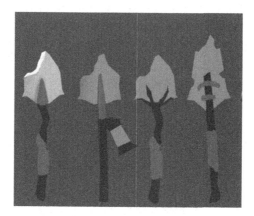

Fig. 1. Shovel concept art

Due to how simple it looked and not very radioactive during the development, another iteration for the weapon was a crowbar, something he could use to scavenger and could last the test of time. The crowbar was also inspired by another game owned by Valve, Half-Life.

The last accessory to be designed was his backpack, again due to the nature of the chosen theme, a simple backpack wasn't cut for such a toxic environment, so something more along the lines of being sturdy, but still able to carry stuff in it was necessary. It was decided something close to a barrel would fit this description. Due to technical limitations, the design of the barrel ended up going back and forth between the concept and development phase going through several iterations. Figure. 2 shows a few examples of what the idea behind it was.

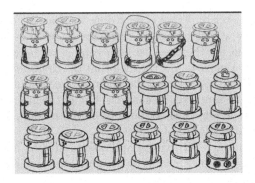

Fig. 2. Backpack/Barrel concept arts

His mask's design would not only dictate its design, but also his clothing, once the theme of going to the toxic environment was set, the standard Meepo's design gear isn't suited for it, as shown by changing his weapon and backpack design, but his clothing also doesn't protect him from those environments, so the moment we decided a protective mask was necessary, the same was applied to the design of his new clothing assets Fig. 3.

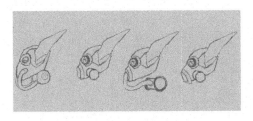

Fig. 3. Mask concept arts

Therefore, with the mask design set, and the idea of his clothing also covering his entire body to protect him from toxic environments, Fig. 4 shows the final concept of the assets to be developed.

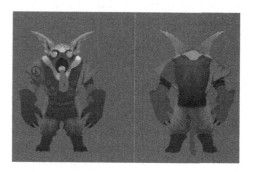

Fig. 4. Clothing concept art

3.2   3D Modeling and Skin

The modeling process had to go through a few iterations due to Valve's guideline being updated mid-development, allowing the artist to have more wiggle room with the number of polygons the final models could have.

According to the new Valve's guideline, the limit for the headpiece would be 3000 triangles, 2500 for the shoulders, 1500 for the arms, 3000 regarding the back, 2500 in the weapon, and last 1000 for the tail, which was, in general, the double of triangles allowed compared to before (Dota2b).

The first object to be modeled was the gloves for the arms. Using the poly-by-poly method of modeling, it was decided to use quads on most of the mesh

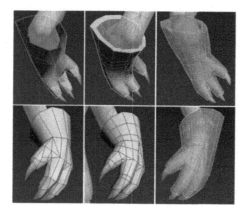

Fig. 5. Gloves modeling process

but at places like between the fingers with a couple of triangles. The decision was made because the gloves would need to deform following the animation's movement of the arm without both meshes merging, creating an artifact that would affect the aesthetic result Fig. 5.

The following asset developed was the back piece, during early development this was one of the assets that were more troublesome to create due to the heavy limitation of triangles it could have. Due to how the character Meepo is and where the piece is located, need to cover the shoulder, part of the arms, and part of the body, having a low count of polygons would make it very difficult for the mesh to properly deform during the character's animation, causing several artifacts like the mesh not having enough information to stretch, causing it to merge with the main body for example. Even after the increase in polygons count in the new guideline set by Valve, the difficulty was still present, but the new polygons allowed the model to have specific loops in the mesh focused on fixing the deformation that caused the character's animation Fig. 6.

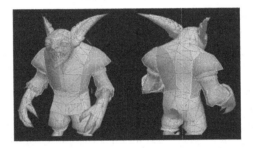

Fig. 6. Clothing modeling process

Alongside the same issue of needing more polygons to fix the asset deformation during animation, there existed a necessity to have more polygons closer to the elbow to cover the area properly. The solution to this problem was to hide the fact that the area had a complete tissue and make the gloves a bit larger to cover up the lack of a finished mesh. Aesthetic wise the result doesn't show the small trick done to hide the issues, but performance-wise was necessary to do them so the asset could stay confined to Valve's guidelines Fig. 7.

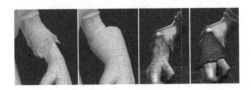

Fig. 7. Gloves and Clothing modeling process

The first accessory design was the weapon, which originally was a generic shovel worn out by time and use, but due to the nature of the character's design, it didn't look like it fit the design, so it was changed to be a crowbar, more in line with the design choice of Meepo being a scavenger needing to access more places than just cave-ins for rewards Fig. 8.

Fig. 8. Weapon modeling process

The second accessory modeled was the barrel he would carry around as his backpack. The initial concept demonstrated to be too simple and not in line with the rest of the assets, due to that, a few iterations were made to its model to bring its design more in line with its purpose Fig. 9.

Fig. 9. Barrel modeling process

The barrel started as a model with 1300 polygons, but with the increase in details and smoothing of the edges, the final high-poly version of it had around 1900 polygons. The increase in polygons made mid-development by Valve allowed the barrel to have extra details that wouldn't have been possible. Following the modeling process, it was necessary to connect it to the character's skin through a single bone, which demanded development time to check which bone would influence the barrel movement during animation and by how much.

The shoulder strap was the main issue in this last process since any mispositioned or value set during the skinning process would result in it invading the original Meepo's model or detaching from it, so multiple tests with the character's animation were required to find the proper balance Fig. 10.

Fig. 10. Barrel with Meepo's orginal model

The last piece of the set, the mask also started with a different design and ended up going through the iteration process to find the ideal aesthetic matching both the original concept and the number of polygons permitted Fig. 11.

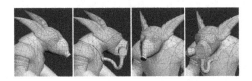

Fig. 11. Mask Modeling process

3.3   Texture

Following the guidelines set by Valve, it was decided to follow an analogous color scheme due to the original Meepo's model already having as basis brown, working with complementary colors or triadic color scheme wouldn't bring the desired outcome.

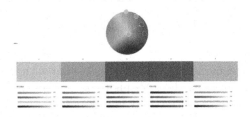

Fig. 12. Used Color scheme(Colour Figure Online)

The main issue with the current color scheme in Fig. 12 was the difficulty adapting the toxic garbage effect it should have on the newly created assets due to the main color for it being green, which is not in the color scheme. So, to not deviate much from the set color scheme, we changed the green for a mixture between

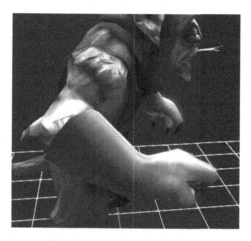

Fig. 13. The Colour scheme was applied to the glove's model

yellow and brown color types, it would signify something that has been through toxic environments but not as glaring as green would Fig. 13.

The following assets created encountered similar issues to the gloves and similar solutions were applied to them. The only other issue regarding texture that showed up in development was the difficulty in reaching the requirement of the greyscale in different parts of the model due to how the illumination works inside the game Fig. 14.

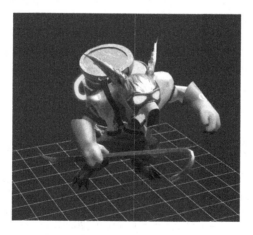

Fig. 14. Final Model with texture applied

4 Conclusions

Nowadays more often students are willing to work on gaming projects that simulate a real work pipeline or propels them to be more prepared to work in the current market status. Therefore, this article proposed to study the development process of what two independent artists would have to go through to work in this specific case with the Steam's Workshop, a system made for the independent artist to publish their works in a different variety of games inside Steam's library. The developed project was made by two undergraduate students that due to their familiarity with the game decided to work on Meepo's 3D character model in the game called DoTA2.

Even though the students worked the entirety of this process with teachers as advi-sors, they demonstrated some difficulty at the beginning having to work with very little guidance, with most being from the default guidelines given by Steam and being their bosses. Even though there was a clear goal, the decisions along the way would challenge the undergraduate student's knowledge, the results being that the pre-production of this project had a huge variety of ideas, but not a clear choice is cho-sen. The clarity of their work would begin to shape only during production when their ideas were executed, they could see the good and the flaws, giving them better guide-lines of what they could, should, and would do in new iterations of their models.

The increase of venue available in digital games, while also the emergence of new methods of monetization for the independent artist creates the necessity of research in this area of development, not only to prepare students for the market but also to create more knowledge for the academic environment. Therefore, this type of study is important not only to help the teachers prepare new students for the current layout of the market, by being able to pinpoint more clearly wherein the decision-making process the students are having troubles with but to also prepare the students them-selves of the future decisions they might have to make to find their own space in the market.

References

1. A, K.: Content creators earn over $50m through steam workshop, can now earn money in more games (2021). https://steamcommunity.com/games/SteamWorkshop/announcements/detail/154581565731694927
2. Ashraf, Z., Goodwin, M., Loffler, T.: Growth in the video gaming market: the changing state of play (2020). https://www.occstrategy.com/br/insights/insight/id/5924/growth-in-the-video-gaming-market-the-changing-state-of-play
3. Bui, T.: Embracing User Generated Content (2021). http://media.steampowered.com/apps/steamdevdays/slides/ugc.pdf
4. Ciszek, P.: 3D production pipeline in game development (2012)
5. Gomes Sarmento Da Fonseca, A.: 3D modeling pipeline for games: work methods for low poly models with hand painted textures (2018)
6. Rässa, J.: Concept art creation methodologies: visual development of rock boy (2018)

7. Salomão, A., Andaló, F., Vieira, M.L.H.: How popular game engine is helping improving academic research: the designlab case. In: Ahram, T.Z. (ed.) AHFE 2018. AISC, vol. 795, pp. 416–424. Springer, Cham (2019). https://doi.org/10.1007/978-3-319-94619-1_42
8. Simpriano, M.A.A.: Criação de recursos visuais para o jogo eletrônico dota 2 (2015)
9. Soares, N.: O steam e a produção de conteúdo pelos jogadores
10. Steamworks: Steam 2020 year in review (2021). https://steamcommunity.com/groups/steamworks/announcements/detail/2961646623386540827
11. Terävä, T.: Workflows for creating 3D game characters (2017)
12. Thorhauge, A.M.: The steam platform economy: capitalising from player-driven economies on the internet. In: AoIR Selected Papers of Internet Research (2020)

The Effects of Enriched Narratives on Presence and Motion Sickness in Game-Guiding

Chian Shing Wang and Cheng-Jhe Lin[✉]

National Taiwan University of Science and Technology, Taipei 106335, Taiwan
Robert_cjlin@mail.ntust.edu.tw

Abstract. In recent years, the game-streaming industry has become increasingly popular, and diverse styles of game-streaming have emerged. "Game-guiding" stands out as a genre in the game-streaming industry that strongly emphasizes on providing viewers with a feeling of high presence and a satisfying watching experience. However, motion sickness is still a potential risk. Previous studies have suggested mixed results regarding the correlation between presence and motion sickness, and presence could be enhanced by enriched narratives that described not only the progress of the game but also the details in the game environment. It is assumed that the enriched narratives may also be used to enhance the presence and reduce motion sickness of the viewers in the game-guiding context. This study investigated the effects of the enriched narratives and game experience on the feeling of presence in the game-guiding context. Fifteen participants with various game experiences were recruited to watch a horrific game-guiding video (Fig. 1) and subjectively report their feelings of presence and motion thickness through a Presence Questionnaire (PQ) and a Simulator Sickness Questionnaire (SSQ). Their heart rate and electrical dermal activity were measured simultaneously with response time to visual and auditory probes in the video to indicate their attention level. While objective evidence was not found, subjective reports showed that the enriched narratives significantly increased presence scores related to sensory factors in PQ and reduced the nausea scores in SSQ. The implications of the results for the game-guiding are discussed.

Keywords: Game-guiding · Presence · Motion Sicness

1 Introduction

1.1 Game-Streaming and Game-Guiding

Game-streaming is a process of sharing one's gameplay experience through real-time broadcasting or pre-recorded videos [1]. The game-streaming industry is getting more and more popular due to the increasing need of people for online entertainment during the COVID-19 pandemic, which later gave rise to online streaming platforms. A new group of the audience was then entitled "cloud players" in that they did not play games but watched the game-streaming hosts (streamers) play instead.

C. Stephanidis et al. (Eds.): HCII 2024, CCIS 2117, pp. 370–376, 2024.
https://doi.org/10.1007/978-3-031-61953-3_40

At the early stage of the game-streaming industry, its style was similar to that of sports broadcasts. Later the content of the game and the technique used in the gameplay were emphasized in broadcasting games of a competitive nature. However, as the scene of the game becomes more delicate and the online streaming platforms become more accessible to streamers of different styles, the emphasis gradually turns from the professionalism of the streamer as a game player to the charisma of the streamer and the experience of watching the story of the game unfold. In such a "Game-guiding" process, the streamer needs to provide the audience with a better sense of immersion and presence in the game. So, narration becomes an important tool to facilitate the audience's understanding of the content of the game without having to play the game by themselves.

However, as the audience watched the game-guiding, they could suffer from motion sickness which caused nausea, vomiting, blurred vision, loss of sense of direction, and other discomfort. The motion sickness originated from conflicts between visual stimuli and vestibular senses of body motions. In game-guiding, such conflicts are expected to be worse in that the audience no longer imagines themselves as active game players but rather as passive viewers, and the lesser feelings of involvement in gameplay activities, the more conflicts generated from the discrepancy between the real physical movements sensed and the "imaginary" gameplay activities implied by visual cues.

1.2 Presence and Motion Sickness

Presence was described as a believable feeling of oneself being somewhere when in fact it is not. Previous studies have suggested mixed results regarding the correlation between presence and motion sickness, and it is not clear about their causal relationship. One previous study [2] has shown that they are negatively correlated and suggested that the presence might have driven one's attention away from their discomfort and mitigated motion sickness. However, the opposite could be also true in that the lesser the motion sickness, the more cognitive capacity would be reserved for the audience to feel the presence.

Nevertheless, the presence and the motion sickness were proven to be correlated and researchers have been interested in knowing how to enhance the presence because it was considered a positive factor to user experience. Some techniques have been proposed to enhance the presence in gameplay such as increasing freedom of control, minimizing distractions that drive players' attention to the real world, providing visual fidelity, and using enriched narrative in context. Among those techniques, providing enriched narratives seemed to be the most relevant one because it was feasible for the streamer to implement in game-guiding.

A previous study [3] has investigated the effect of enriched narratives on the presence and motion sickness. In the experiment, two kinds of narratives, enriched narrative context and minimal narrative context, were provided to the subjects BEFORE their play. The enriched narrative context, which included more adjectives and details to the scene of the game, was 49 s long, while the minimal was 28 s. The subjects then played a VR exploration game for 7 min. The results showed that the presence and motion sickness scores measured by questionnaires were indeed negatively correlated if the enriched narrative context was provided. Such a negative correlation, however, was not significant when minimal narrative context was provided. Furthermore, the enriched narrative context significantly increased the presence score but did not significantly decrease the motion sickness. Such intriguing results indicate the necessity for further study.

1.3 The Current Study Goals

The current study aims to investigate the effects of enriched narratives on presence and motion sickness in game-guiding. It is assumed that the enriched narratives should significantly increase the presence scores and reduce the motion sickness scores measured by a Presence Questionnaire (PQ) and a Simulator Sickness Questionnaire (SSQ), respectively. The current study also wanted to find out if the game-playing experience and the design of the provision of the enriched narratives, namely the timing and the duration, will affect the effectiveness of the enriched narratives. It is suspected that the non-gamers who were not experienced in game-playing and not tested in the previous study will be more susceptible to the enriched narratives, and providing the enriched narratives during the game instead of before the game for a longer time will be more effective in terms of enhancing the presence and mitigating the motion sickness. Finally, the study would like to clarify whether the negative correlation would also be present in game-guiding.

2 Methodology

2.1 Participants

Fifteen participants were recruited for the study and they were categorized into two groups: 7 gamers and 8 non-gamers. The criterion to be classified as gamers is that they have played games for more than 10 h per week on average in the past 6 months. In contrast, the non-gamers played games for less than four hours. However, they must all have played first-person viewpoint games and experienced motion sickness during play. In addition, they must have not played the game used ("Devotion" developed by Red Candle Games, Taiwan) in the experiment, to guarantee their identical familiarity with the game. Finally, they must not feel reluctant to horrific puzzle games as it is the nature of the game "Devotion."

2.2 Experimental Tasks

The participants were required to watch two sessions of pre-recorded game-guiding videos, one with the enriched narratives and the other with the minimal ones. They were instructed to pay attention to details in the videos and to notice random visual and auditory prompts that appeared in the videos for them to respond. The priority was to remember the details in the videos as they would be tested by a questionnaire but they also had to respond to the prompts by pressing any key on the keyboard as soon as possible. Their heart rates (HRs) and Galvin Skin Responses (GSRs) were collected during the game-guiding sessions by a biofeedback system (FlexComp with/ BioGraph Infiniti Software developed by Thought Technology, Canada) and later used as quantitative evidence for stress. After the game-guiding sessions, they reported subjective presence and motion sickness by the Presence Questionnaire (PQ) and the Simulator Sickness Questionnaire (SSQ), respectively. The experimental setting is shown in Fig. 1.

Fig. 1. The experimental setting (right: game-guiding; left: response measurement)

2.3 Experimental Design and Data Collection Procedure

The independent variables of the experiment were the provision of the narratives (within subjects) and the gameplay experience (between subjects). The enriched and minimal narratives were provided during the two game-guiding on different days to avoid excessive fatigue due to the length of the videos (62 min on average). The sequence of enriched and minimal narratives was balanced to cancel possible order effects. Before the experiment, the participants were pre-tested for their baseline response time to visual and auditory prompts so that the differences between the baseline and response time measured in the session could reflect the change in their attentive levels. For the HRs and GSRs, only data associated with selective highlights in the middle 40 min of the sessions were extracted.

3   Results

3.1 The Effect of the Enriched Narratives on Presence

The analysis of variance (ANOVA) showed that the enriched narratives significantly increased the presence score in the sensory factor (SF) dimension of PQ (*F-value* = *4.88; P-value* = *0.044*). No other main factor or interaction, including the game-play experience, was found to significantly affect PQ scores in any dimension. The main effect plot of the enriched narratives on the SF score of PQ is shown in (Fig. 2).

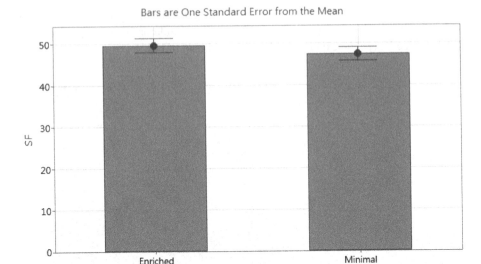

Bars are One Standard Error from the Mean

Fig. 2. The main effect plot of the enriched narratives on the SF score of PQ

3.2 The Effect of the Enriched Narratives on Motion Sickness

The analysis of variance (ANOVA) showed that the enriched narratives significantly reduced the nausea score of SSQ (*F-value = 7.93; P-value = 0.015*). From a grouped effect plot (see Fig. 3) it seemed that the gamers were less affected by nausea if the enriched narratives were provided, but a further stratified analysis demonstrated the inference was untrue. No other main factor or interaction was found to significantly affect either weighted scores in different dimensions or total scores of SSQ.

3.3 Correlations Between Presence and Motion Sickness

The correlation was found to be mildly positive (*Pearson correlation coefficient r = 0.527; P-value = 0.003*) between the total scores of PQ and SSQ. A further stratified analysis revealed that the mildly positive correlation maintained significance when the minimal narratives were provided (*r = 0.556; P-value = 0.003*) but not the case for enriched narratives (*r = 0.556; P-value = 0.226*).

3.4 Response Time, Performance and Physiological Indices

No significant effect was found for response time to random prompts present. The participants' performance in terms of accuracy in answering details in videos was satisfactory (*90.3 ± 10.5%*). The physiological indices (HRs and GSRs) were not significantly affected by the types of narratives of the gameplay experience of the participants.

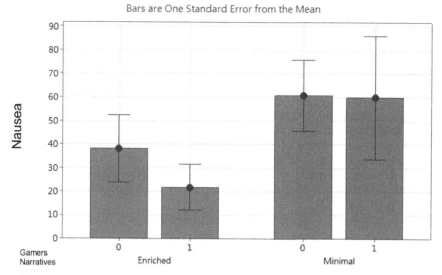

Fig. 3. The grouped effect plot of the enriched narratives on the nausea score of SSQ

4   Conclusion and Discussion

The current study partially proved that the enriched narratives could be used to increase the presence associated with sensory factors and decrease nausea of motion sickness. The reason why the control, distraction, and realism factors were not significantly affected may be that those factors were not manipulated by the enriched narratives. The nausea was the only dimension where a significant reduction was observed for the enriched narratives because it helped the participants focus and avoid difficulty in concentrating, a major phenomenon resulting from nausea. The negative correlation between the presence and the motion sickness, however, was not found despite the simultaneous presence of the increasing sensory score in PQ and the decreasing nausea score in SSQ.

The assumption that non-gamers were more susceptible to the manipulation of the narratives was not proven but there was an observable difference in their responses to the enriched narratives, i.e. the gamers were more sensitive. A possible explanation for the failure of the difference to reach statistical significance is that the game-guiding sessions were relatively long and the post-hoc questionnaires were not able to capture the dynamics of the presence and the motion sickness, resulting in a rather saturated reflection after lengthy exposure to the manipulation. The physiological indices were supposed to compensate for this limitation but unfortunately, the significance was not found either. The insignificant fluctuation in response time also supported the notion that the participants' attention was not affected. The result implied that the enriched narratives might have affected the subjective presence and the motion sickness through mechanisms other than altering and directing attention.

The current results encourage streamers to optimize their narratives by adding more details related to the scene and the plots of the game that enhance their perception of the design features of the scenes and help focus on the progression of the plots. The motion sickness still threatens user experience in game-guiding and future studies should continue on investigating other possible techniques to reduce its potential risks.

References

1. Tammy Lin, J.-H., Bowman, N., Lin, S.-F., Chen, Y.-S.: Setting the digital stage: defining game streaming as an entertainment experience. Entertainment Comput. **31**, 100309 (2019). https://doi.org/10.1016/j.entcom.2019.100309
2. Weech, S., Kenny, S., Barnett-Cowan, M.: Presence and cybersickness in virtual reality are negatively related: a review. Front. Psychol. **10**, 158 (2019)
3. Weech, S., Kenny, S., Lenizky, M., Barnett-Cowan, M.: Narrative and gaming experience interact to affect presence and cybersickness in virtual reality. Int. J. Hum. Comput. Stud.Comput. Stud. **138**, 102398 (2020)

An Educational Simulation Game Framework and Practice Based on Complex Adaptive Systems Theory: For Fostering Systems Thinking

Chu Zhang, Ping Li[✉], Ke Fang, Yueer Mao, and Guozhang Ma

Tsinghua Shenzhen International Graduate School, Shenzhen 518055, China
chu-zhan22@mails.tsinghua.edu.cn, liping.thu@hotmail.com

Abstract. *Background:* In an era where complex systems, including economies, ecosystems, and social networks, play a pivotal role, a systems thinking approach is crucial for comprehending their intricate characteristics and dynamics. Educational games, emerging as a novel pedagogical medium, inherently hold the potential to simulate and portray these multifaceted systems. Nevertheless, existing simulation games frequently suffer from a lack of adaptability in complex systems, a deficient representation of network structures and an absence of efficient trial-and-error mechanisms, thereby constraining their educational efficacy.
Framework: Grounded in the Complex Adaptive Systems (CAS) theory and the Complexity Learning theory, this study introduces the "World-Network-Gameplay" framework tailored for CAS simulation games. The core concept is threefold: (World) The adaptability of system arises from the simple agent's adaptive rules: genetic algorithms and imitation mechanisms. (Network) The system's network structure should be hierarchically presented to players, (Gameplay) Players should construct the system in person, balance influencing factors and perform rapid simulations to validate outcomes.
Game Practice: We developed an educational simulation game demo based on the WNG framework. Players assume the role of God, tasked with founding a primitive society on an island and guiding its evolution to enable human survival through successive disasters. In the game, players will observe the system's evolution from simplicity to complexity, and cultivate systems thinking by comprehending and intervening in the system's adaptability.
Verification: We did a pilot study including questionnaire surveys and semi-structured interviews, and verified the educational efficacy of the game framework.

Keywords: Educational Game · Systems Thinking · Complex Adaptive System · Self-Adaptability

1 Introduction

From the complex cellular interactions within organisms to the ever-changing global climate patterns and dynamic social network connections, all fall within the realm of complex systems. Understanding complexity is intimately linked to each individual.

© The Author(s), under exclusive license to Springer Nature Switzerland AG 2024
C. Stephanidis et al. (Eds.): HCII 2024, CCIS 2117, pp. 377–387, 2024.
https://doi.org/10.1007/978-3-031-61953-3_41

However, due to nonlinearities and emergent properties in complex systems, their internal structures and links remain elusive, and their behaviors defy reductionist understanding [1].

Systems thinking, a cognitive approach that emerged with the complexity revolution, advocates for a holistic, dynamic, and continuous problem-solving methodology [2]. This mindset emphasizes understanding the connections between elements, data trends, and time delays, capturing driving factors to discern the essence of complex systems. Developing systems thinking is essential for addressing challenges in our complex world.

In conventional education, systems thinking is often overlooked. However, games naturally possess the potential to describe and explain complex systems, offering clear structural visualization, comprehensive information, low-cost trial-and-error, and effective simulation. Extensive case studies and research [3, 4] have demonstrated games' potential in facilitating the understanding of complexity and enhancing cognitive skills.

Yet, existing complexity simulation games often underperform educationally. This underperformance is partly due to their lack of focus on educating about complexity and systems thinking. They generally exhibit the following problems:

- P1: Insufficient Adaptability in Complex Systems. Often, the lack of adaptability in complex systems within games stems from non-scientific modeling methods. This paper utilizes improved classical modeling approaches to develop a truly adaptive game system.
- P2: Unclear Network Structure Representation. A common issue in simulation games is an excessive focus on gameplay rather than element relationships, sometimes even intentionally concealing these relationships. Effective educational games should present system structural information across multiple dimensions and hierarchical levels.
- P3: Limited Verification Methods for Players. This refers to the inability of players to swiftly assess the impact of their decisions on complex systems, thereby hindering reflection and strategic adjustment. The paper introduces targeted gameplay strategies that have demonstrated positive results.

Conclusively, this paper develops a game design framework, based on existing research, and presents a sandbox simulation game designed under this framework as a practical example, aiming to enhance the educational effectiveness of complexity simulation games.

2 Framework and Method

The World-Network-Gameplay (WNG) framework is divided into three modules, addressing the generation, presentation, and learning of complexity in simulation games, and responds to the three issues outlined in the introduction (Fig. 1).

2.1 World: Establishing Virtual Complex Systems

The construction of complex systems forms the fundamental basis of complexity simulation games. To address P1, "Insufficient Adaptability in Complex Systems," this

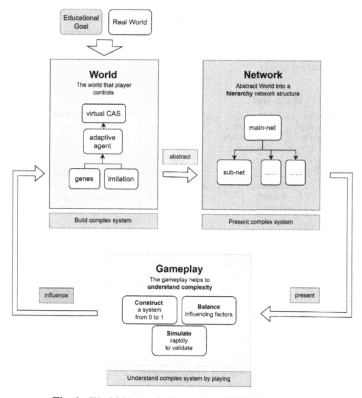

Fig. 1. World-Network-Gameplay (WNG) framework

framework utilizes Holland's Complex Adaptive Systems (CAS) theory and the ECHO [5] model. It constructs virtual complex systems within the game, referred to as "World".

Adaptive Agent. Within CAS theory, complexity arises from the interactions of adaptive agents [5]. These agents operate based on simple logic and can adjust their strategies based on feedback, embodying "adaptability." in this paper, the adaptability of agents primarily derives from two mechanisms: Genetic algorithms and imitation.

Imitation Mechanism. The imitation dynamics posit that individuals within a system emulate successful behaviors observed in their vicinity [6]. This explains the propagation of behaviors across a group and the formation of social norms and cultural trends. In the game context, "imitation" effectively simulates individuals' bounded rationality and group behaviors, enhancing the adaptability of the echo model at the micro-group level.

2.2 Network: Extracting Complex Relationships

In alignment with John D. Sterman's Complexity Learning theory [7], learning through the system's feedback structure diagrams is an effective approach. Addressing P2, developers should extract the complex relationships among elements in the World and present them to players in the form of network diagrams, termed as *Network*. The *Network* should be hierarchical, with a main network (*Main-Net*) encompassing multiple subnetworks (*Sub-Net*), or multi-dimensional, illustrating connections between elements across various levels (Fig. 2).

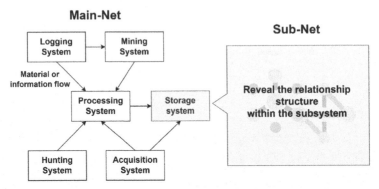

Fig. 2. A kind of hierarchical *Network*

The hierarchical and multi-dimensional design aligns with cognitive psychology and HCI principles, enhancing learning efficiency [8].

2.3 Gameplay: Learning Complex Mechanisms

In response to Question 3 (Q3), developers should incorporate the following core gameplay elements to assist players in understanding complexity and fostering systems thinking.

Balance. To regulate and predict a system, it's essential to keenly identify and balance the major influencing factors. Thus, discovering and balancing several interconnected elements must be a central aspect of the gameplay.

Construct. Both Complexity Learning Theory and Constructivist Learning Theory [9] assert that the best way to understand a system is to participate in its construction. Simulation games make this feasible, allowing players to actively build and engage with the system.

Rapid Simulation. Games should provide means for players to swiftly validate their decisions. In Sterman's learning cycle [7] for understanding complexity, trial and error, and decision adjustment are crucial. Virtual complex systems offer a natural environment for low-cost experimentation and are a potent advantage of learning through gaming.

3   Game Design

We developed a complex system sandbox simulation game using the Unity game engine, titled "Genesis Land." Players assume the role of a deity, personally **creating, observing,** and **controlling** a primitive societal complex system. The game's disaster mechanics ultimately **assess** the adaptability of the system created by the player.

The game's design closely follows the WNG framework, detailed as follows:

3.1 World

World. In the game, the virtual complex system *World* comprises four types of terrain (grasslands, forests, beaches, and mountains), with each geographical environment fostering distinct civilizations (Fig. 3).

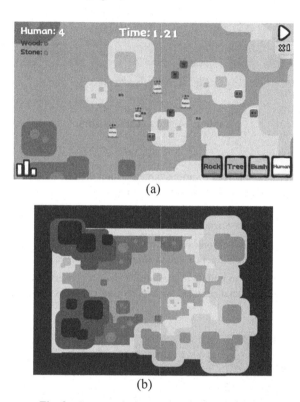

(a)

(b)

Fig. 3. Game main interface and map overview

Agent. The humans in the game are *Adaptive Agents*, following a perception-decision behavior logic, gradually altering their behavioral rules through interactions with their environment (Fig. 4).

Disaster. Disasters serve as a means to assess the system's adaptability. Every game year, a random disaster will strike the island. If the system has good adaptability, it can either remain stable during the disaster or recover after severe damage (Fig. 5).

3.2 Network

Players can access the Network Map (*Network*) and Data Statistics Chart (*Stats*) at any time. The Network Map reveals the relationships among various elements in the system,

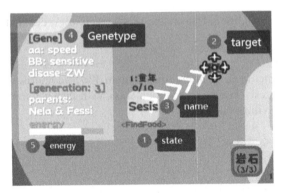

Fig. 4. Adaptive Agent

Table 1. Agent's characteristics.

Characteristics	Meaning
Perception	Agents can perceive various targets within their field of vision, including dangers, food, work, and social interactions
Behavior	Agents possess a weighted behavior tree: Escape Death Threat > Foraging > Production > Socialization
Genetics	Agents inherit chromosomes from parents, including alleles controlling perception-intelligence, speed-strength, and genetic diseases
Imitation	Agents tend to imitate "successful" behaviors observed within their visual range and social network, with an indicator to assess the success of a behavior

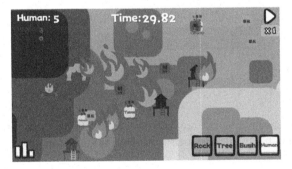

Fig. 5. Disaster: Forest Fire

while the Data Statistics Chart displays the genetic and age information of all humans, aiding in making long-term decisions (Fig. 6).

Table 2. Disasters and effects

Type	Effect
Volcanic Eruption	Burns trees and houses, enriches soil fertility
Tsunami	Destroys coastal houses and facilities, brings an abundance of water resources
Forest Fire	Burns trees and houses, enriches soil fertility
Plague	Individuals without specific resistance will die upon infection
Drought	Prolonged cessation of rainfall
Flood	Prolonged heavy rainfall

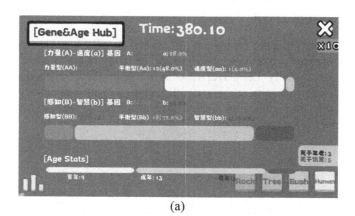

(a)

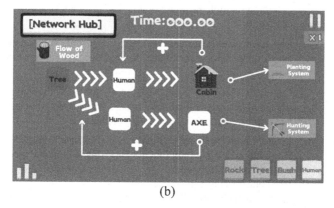

(b)

Fig. 6. Network and *Stats*

3.3 Gameplay

Construct: Hands-On System Building. Players place characters, trees, berry bushes, and other objects on a blank canvas. These elements interact based on predefined rules, generating fascinating chemical reactions, gradually evolving into a primitive societal system. (Fig. 7).

Fig. 7. Items that the player can place

Balance: Controlling Influential Factors. In the autonomous functioning of the primitive society, **diversity**, **redundancy**, and **modularity** collectively affect the system's **adaptability**.

Players' actions influence the system's characteristics. For instance, rapidly placing many bushes increases redundancy but invades the living space of other plants, detrimental to species diversity. The player's goal is to balance these three influential factors optimally, enhancing the system's overall adaptability to withstand disasters.

In this game, the influential factors are measured through a combination of quantitative and qualitative methods.

Table 3. Influencing factors and evaluation criteria

Influential Factor	Meaning	Evaluation Criteria
Diversity	Variety of elements in the system, providing multiple response options to challenges	Measure using Shannon diversity index
Redundancy	Repetition level of similar elements, ensuring operational continuity during partial system failure	Quantify by individual count and segmented scoring
Modularity	Degree to which components can be separated and recombined, limiting harm spread and risk	Assessed qualitatively through distribution of habitats and storage
Adaptability	Includes robustness and resilience **Robustness**: Maintaining functionality under minor disturbances **Resilience**: Recovering or reaching a new equilibrium after major impacts	Evaluate through key variable fluctuation and recovery time post-impact

Sim: Rapid Simulation. Players can set the initial state and strategic policies of the island, allowing the computer to manage specific decisions for swift system evolution. Rapid simulation enables players to quickly validate and compare the outcomes of different decisions.

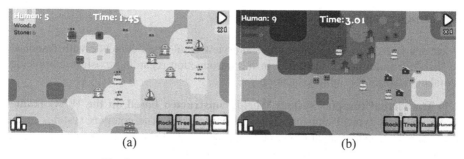

(a)   (b)

Fig. 8. Sim results for different development strategies

4 Pilot Study

To evaluate the educational impact of our game, its framework's effectiveness, and to guide future formal experiments, we conducted a pilot study. Four participants, aged 17–23 (M = 21, SD = 2.82), were recruited from a community of friends. The group consisted of 25% male and 75% female participants, with educational backgrounds of one high school, one undergraduate, and two master's students. They were curious about complexity but not specialized in system science or experienced in related learning, offering considerable representativeness.

The participants first completed a questionnaire on systems thinking knowledge, followed by a 30–40-min gameplay session, and then answered the questionnaire again. The pre- and post-game questionnaire results showed a significant improvement in their understanding of complex systems. Additionally, we conducted a semi-structured interview lasting about 20 min, focusing on key data.

Key questions and some responses from the interview are as follows:

1 **Resilience and Robustness of *World* Post-Impact.**
"The system's adaptability was vivid and impressive in the post-disaster reconstruction process.", "Felt stronger trauma in disasters with monoculture crops.", "Some disasters posed no threat to more developed human communities."

2 **Effectiveness of *Network* and *Stats* in Understanding System Structure and Monitoring Value Fluctuations.**
"The Network revealed connections I hadn't noticed, like the impact of population and overharvesting on tree regeneration.", "Noticed changes in genetic distribution when humans migrated.", "Wish the Network map was more dynamic, reflecting real-time numbers for each connection."

3 **Player Experience and Feedback on Sim Functionality:**
"Sim feature quickly showed results.", "Sim didn't have the custodial strategy I expected.", "Outcomes of custodianship often showed little change."

4 **Player Awareness of Complexity System Properties like Diversity, Redundancy, and Modularity:**
"Noticed diversity in habitats and resources; developing just one type of terrain isn't enough to unlock new technologies.", "Less diversity in species.", "The role of modularity became clear during forest fires; dense settlements and storage led to significant losses."

5   Conclusion

After analyzing the questionnaire and interview results, we conclude with responses to the three main issues identified in the introduction regarding existing complexity simulation games for public education.

C1) The virtual complex system World, constructed based on the WNG framework, exhibits typical characteristics of complexity. The complex systems in the game exhibit typical adaptability under impact, manifested as resilience or robustness. Players gain insight into the process and reasons behind adaptability, as well as the factors influencing it. The disaster system needs adjustment to generate targeted disasters based on human development levels, such as introducing plagues in tightly connected human communities or plant diseases when there's heavy reliance on a specific crop, posing significant challenges.

C2) The multi-dimensional Network graph has improved the clarity of network structure representation, yet the implementation of a multi-tiered Network still requires further exploration. The *multi-dimensional Network* not only shows resource flow but also reveals previously unnoticed connections, aiding players in understanding complex system structures and decision-making. The design of a *multi-dimensional Network* is successful in this regard. Future research should continue to explore methods for implementing a layered dynamic Network.

C3) Gameplay elements like Sim significantly offer players rapid trial-and-error opportunities, though there are areas that need enhancement. *Constructs*, *Sim*, and *Balance* achieve their purposes to an extent. However, *Sim* gameplay has shortcomings, such as limited custodial strategies and poor outcomes from ineffective strategies. *Balance* gameplay also requires clearer feedback on decision consequences.

References

1. Mitchell, M.: Complexity A Guided Tour. Oxford University PressNew York, NY (2009). https://doi.org/10.1093/oso/9780195124415.001.0001
2. Meadows, D.H.: Thinking in systems: a primer. chelsea green publishing, p. 240 (2008)
3. Pfeilstetter, R.: Gamificación en la enseñanza de teorías antropológicas. Crítica, aprendizaje y el videojuego Civilization. Disparidades. Revista de Antropología **75**(2), 016 (2020). https://doi.org/10.3989/dra.2020.016
4. Squire, K.: Civilization III and whole-class play in high school social studies. Civilization. 34, (**1**) (2010)
5. Holland, J.H.: Hidden Order: How Adaptation Builds Complexity. Addison Wesley (1995)
6. Arbib, M.A.: The mirror system, imitation, and the evolution of language. (2002). https://doi.org/10.7551/mitpress/3676.003.0011
7. Sterman, J.D.: Learning in and about complex systems. Syst. Dyn. Rev. **10**, 291–330 (1994). https://doi.org/10.1002/sdr.4260100214

8. Djamasbi, S., Siegel, M., Tullis, T.: Visual hierarchy and viewing behavior: an eye track-ing study. In: Jacko, J.A. (ed.) Human-Computer Interaction. Design and Development Approaches: 14th International Conference, HCI International 2011, Orlando, FL, USA, July 9-14, 2011, Proceedings, Part I, pp. 331–340. Springer Berlin Heidelberg, Berlin, Heidelberg (2011). https://doi.org/10.1007/978-3-642-21602-2_36
9. Kriz, W.C.: A systemic-constructivist approach to the facilitation and debriefing of simulations and games. Simul. Gaming **41**, 663–680 (2010). https://doi.org/10.1177/1046878108319867

Design and Application of Family Intergenerational Social Game Based on Proxemics Play Framework

Yueming Zhou and Wei Huang[✉]

Tsinghua University, Beijing, China
huangw@sz.tsinghua.edu.cn

Abstract. Recent technological advancements have widened the generational divide, impacting intergenerational communication within family leisure activities. While video games hold potential for fostering intergenerational interaction through engaging content, common social games often present high entry barriers and overlook key design elements that facilitate both verbal and non-verbal communication during play.

Proxemics play integrates proxemic principles into game design, leveraging interpersonal distance to enrich co-located social game experiences. This study synthesizes insights from intergenerational social games and proxemics literature, offering a design framework for integrating proxemics into game mechanics. Employing this framework, the study created a co-located motion-sensing game, *Three-body Dream Interpretation*, using Unity and Kinect, followed by a trial to assess its impact on intergenerational gaming interactions.

This research enables game developers to consciously integrate interpersonal distance as a design material in social experience design, providing a better intergenerational social gaming experience and fostering the domain of intergenerational social games.

Keywords: Proxemics Play · Intergenerational Play · Social Game

1 Introduction

Recent shifts towards smaller family units have seen a decline in traditional familial interactions, marked by reduced intergenerational communication, particularly among post-90s and post-95s generations, challenging the conventional family culture [21,22]. Concurrently, the rise in mobile internet users to 1.047 billion by June 2022 [1] illustrates technology's significant influence on family leisure dynamics, transitioning from physically shared experiences to virtual engagements. This technological immersion has fostered a "phubbing" culture, detracting from active familial interactions [22].

Notwithstanding, "family-friendly games" have emerged as potent mediums for revitalizing family bonds through shared digital leisure, with 61% of players acknowledging video games as a conduit for family connection, and 77% of parents engaging in gaming with their children [4]. These statistics underscore the

C. Stephanidis et al. (Eds.): HCII 2024, CCIS 2117, pp. 388–398, 2024.
https://doi.org/10.1007/978-3-031-61953-3_42

potential of digital games to facilitate meaningful emotional exchanges among family members.

Given the demographic trends towards an aging population and the increasing digitization of media, this study aims to examine the potential of digital games in enhancing family leisure by promoting physical interaction and inclusivity across generations. An empirical investigation was conducted, developing a game designed for proximal play to assess its impact on intergenerational social gaming experiences.

2 Related Work

2.1 Sociality in Games

Granic et al. emphasize direct inter-player interactions as crucial for social games [5], while Kaye discusses "alone together" scenarios in multiplayer environments, suggesting a need for a classification system focused on co-presence and interdependence [3,11]. Mueller advocates for physical interactions to innovate social gaming experiences [15]. The GX framework by Dennis et al. details how game design and player relationships shape experiences [10]. Rocha et al. [20] and Harris et al. [7] highlight design strategies that foster cooperation and enhance connection, pointing to the critical role of interaction and communication in deepening social engagement in games.

2.2 The Impact of Proxemics on Social Experience

Proxemics, a concept that first appeared in anthropology in the 1960s, is mostly used to study human relationships. In the past decade, it has gained attention in the field of human-computer interaction and has been used to study the relationship between people and devices, explaining how interactive devices are more deeply connected with what we are operating, how we operate, and environmental factors. Marquardt and Greenberg applied five proxemic dimensions (interpersonal distance, body orientation, movement, identity recognition, location) to the design of biologically ubiquitous computing interactions in small indoor spaces, mediating interactions between entities in ubiquitous environments in a way that is more in line with human cognition [13].

Muller et al. advocate incorporating proxemic principles in game design to enhance digital gaming experiences, offering a framework for designers to foster player affinity and engagement [14]. They propose strategies to: 1. Challenge proxemic norms by leveraging the game's "magic circle" to create safe spaces for interaction, thus liberating players from conventional social boundaries [8]. 2. Enhance awareness of proxemic zones, facilitating immersive experiences and emotional connections through spatial awareness. 3. Encourage physical movement and exploration of proxemic spaces to evoke emotional responses. 4. Blur the lines between personal and intimate zones, adapting to players' cultural contexts [6], and designing systems that dynamically respond to interpersonal distances, thereby focusing on the nuances of human relationships [13].

2.3   Intergenerational Social Games

Research demonstrates that intergenerational social games foster relational intimacy within families, enhancing life quality across generations [18]. Os Pe's
studies reveal that such gaming facilitates social connections, with both young
and elderly participants valuing video games as a medium for relationship building and engagement [16,17]. Elderly players enjoy the informal interaction and
shared experiences with younger family members, while the youth prioritize
relationship maintenance and shared discussions within the comfortable gaming environment [17].

Teresa et al. highlight the importance of considering target and space-related
interactions in intergenerational game design, suggesting that games using physical space can enhance closeness and interaction between generations. Khoo &
Cheok argue for cooperative over competitive formats in intergenerational games,
accommodating the elderly's typically less competitive nature [12].

Rasmus et al. created a location-based mobile game rooted in proxemics play
to enhance family engagement in parks. By challenging conventional proxemic
norms with humorous movements, they significantly improved family groups'
shared emotional experiences. Intergenerational game design tends to favor the
use of tangible objects, communication tech, and physical spaces. Yet, proxemics
play's potential in game design is still largely untapped, with a focus mainly on
integrating it into real-world activities.

3   Methods

3.1   Proxemics Play Design Framework Based on MDA

This paper explores the domain of proxemics play within game design, building upon the foundational design knowledge established by our predecessors. By
integrating the four lenses of embodied interaction as proposed by Mueller et al.
[15] with the Mechanics, Dynamics, and Aesthetics elements of the MDA game
design framework [9], we aim to elucidate the utilization of proxemic elements
as vital design materials. Specifically, we examine the role of interpersonal distance in enhancing players' social experiences through game interdependence.
Following the theoretical framework's derivation, the paper proceeds to validate
its applicability through the development and analysis of an intergenerational
social game, titled "*Three-body Dream Interpretation*," inspired by the proxemics
play design framework. The subsequent sections will detail the implementation
process of this game (Fig. 1).

3.2   Game Design and Development

Game Interaction Design. To accommodate players of varying technological
proficiency in intergenerational social games, simplifying interaction mechanics
reduces learning barriers and improves user experience. The game's interaction
design, rooted in proxemic elements and enactive knowledge, utilizes physical

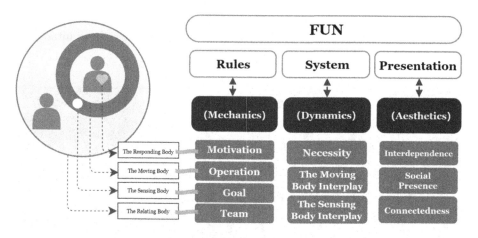

Fig. 1. Proxemics play design framework based on MDA

and gestural inputs. Enactive knowledge, a concept introduced by psychologist Bruner, is understanding gained through physical actions, applied here to intuitive game controls. This approach enables less tech-savvy players to use natural movements instead of complex button commands, employing right-hand positioning for distance recognition and left-hand up gestures for confirmatory actions (Fig. 2).

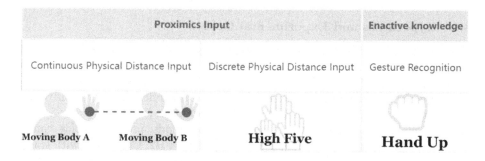

Fig. 2. Interaction Design

Game Mechanic Design. This cooperative game encourages physical interaction and non-verbal communication among players, exemplified by the "Three in a Row" mechanic where players physically activate game progression by jointly touching an object, thus enhancing engagement through positive feedback and intimate activities.

Core mechanics also feature music and image decryption tasks that require players to solve puzzles based on auditory cues and collaboratively manipulate objects to form specific shapes, deepening the cooperative experience.

The game's essential sequence involves alternating between Music Decryption, Image Decryption, and "Three in a Row," creating a continuous interactive cycle (Fig. 3).

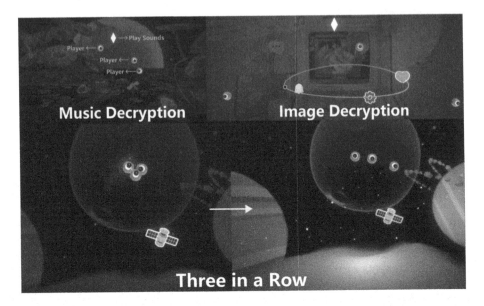

Fig. 3. Core Gameplay Mechanics of *Three-body Dream Interpretation*

3.3   Hypotheses and Experimental Goals

his study aims to evaluate the impact of introducing proxemics play on the intergenerational social game experience. Referring to previous studies, this study hypothesizes that the introduction of proxemics play can have a positive impact on intergenerational social experiences, verbal communication, and non-verbal communication among players. The specific hypotheses are:

H1: Compared with traditional interaction methods, proxemics play games can bring a better intergenerational social experience. H2: Compared with traditional interaction methods, proxemic interaction games as family leisure activities can promote verbal and non-verbal communication among family members.

3.4   Participants

This research enlisted core family units of university students, initially assessing family backgrounds via surveys to inform a controlled family leisure study. Criteria for participation included families with children aged 18 to 30, ensuring all three members were in good physical and mental health, without significant sensory impairments or physical disabilities. Selected families, informed about the study through an invitation letter detailing experimental procedures, comprised 24 households (72 individuals) from Mianyang, Sichuan Province, China.

3.5   Experimental Materials

This study uses "*Three-body Dream Interpretation*" as the game experimental prop. To control proxemic interaction as a variable, the game development process also incorporates the Xbox controller as the interaction method for the controller game group. This approach aims to minimize the variance in experimental outcomes due to changes in game content (Fig. 4).

Fig. 4. The controller game group(left) the proxemic game group(right)

3.6   Experiment Design

Randomized Controlled Trials (RCT) are used to collect and evaluate experimental data. The experimental environment is the living room of each family, ensuring that subjects are familiar with the setting of the experiment. Before the experiment begins, the experimental content and data collection are explained again, and the video recording of the subjects' gameplay process is started after obtaining their agreement. The activity content of the controller game group is to play intergenerational social games with the Xbox controller as the interaction device in a natural state for about 30 min; the activity content of the proxemic game group is to play intergenerational social games using proxemics as the interaction method in a natural state for about 30 min. During the activity, a camera with a frontal perspective is used for video recording, recording the interaction process of the subjects during leisure activities. The controller game group and the proxemic game group simultaneously record the game screen (Fig. 5).

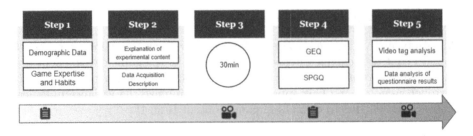

Fig. 5. Overview of the study procedure, showing the sequence of gaming sessions and the applied questionnaires

3.7   Measurements

The Social Presence in Gaming Questionnaire (SPGQ), utilizing a 5-point Likert scale, evaluates players' perception of social presence in gaming environments.

For assessing verbal and non-verbal communication, this study employs video recording and observational techniques, recognized for their efficacy in analyzing digital game-induced social interactions [23]. These methods afford researchers the capability to generate, store, and replicate comprehensive data on intricate social dynamics, facilitating longitudinal analyses. Specifically, the study investigates family intergenerational engagement through the analytical examination of game screen and family activity recordings, categorizing behaviors based on established verbal and non-verbal communication metrics [2], such as dialogue, collective laughter, and eye contact. The classification of these elements is detailed in the corresponding table.

The study analyzed verbal and non-verbal player interactions from 24 video recordings, using dual cameras and ELAN software for synchronized annotation [19]. Initial coding based on an event sampling-derived intergenerational interaction framework [23] was refined through repeated video evaluations. The comprehensive coding schema, presented in Table 1, categorizes interactions into verbal (task-related, general, and assistance communication) and non-verbal (laughter, eye contact, and physical touch) behaviors, with examples provided for efficient analysis.

4   Results

4.1   Social Presence Analysis

Data underwent reliability and normality assessments, with Q-Q plots indicating approximate normal distribution, warranting the use of an independent sample t-test for group comparisons.

An independent sample t-test revealed significant differences between controller (N = 36, mean = 3.9500, SD = .36839) and proxemic game groups (N = 36, mean = 4.3056, SD = .52696). Levene's test confirmed variance homogeneity (F = 8.090, p = .006), validating the t-test's applicability. The t-test highlighted

Table 1. Category system for the observation of family social interaction behaviors.

Category		Definition	Anchor examplesa
Verbal communication	Game-related communication	Conversations that are directly related to the activity, such as discussions about the process and outcome of the game, as well as strategies and ways to work together.	"Win!" "That's interesting!"
	General biography	Players share exchanges related to personal experiences, life stories, and more.	"I used to hear it all the time when I was a kid." "I've played games with young people before and they think I'm the same age."
	Help seeking	Players actively seek help related to the technical operation of the game or ask questions about the game content.	"How do I get this one?" "What to do with this?"
	Help giving	Players answer or help solve collaborators' questions related to technology and game content.	"Come here! You move to the right!"
Nonverbal communication	Laughing together	Players laugh together, including laughing as well as smiling during verbal exchanges.	–
	Eye contact	Players look at each other.	–
	Body contact	Players touch each other's bodies, such as slaps on the back as well as arm touches	–

a significant disparity in mean scores between groups (t = −3.318, df = 70, p = .001), with the proxemic game group outperforming the controller group, evidencing the proxemics play's effectiveness.

4.2   Verbal and Non-verbal Interaction Analysis

In this study, intergenerational communication behaviors were coded from video data, analyzing both verbal and non-verbal interactions concurrently. Differences in video lengths were normalized by calculating the proportion of each behavior's duration to the total. Initial analyses confirmed data normality via Shapiro-Wilk tests and Q-Q plots, allowing for subsequent variance analysis and independent sample t-tests on communication behavior ratios.

Significant differences were found, notably in biographical communication (t = −2.229, df = 22, p = .036) and physical contact (t = −13.694, df = 22, p < .001), highlighting enhanced non-verbal communication through proxemics play. These findings indicate an increase in non-verbal behaviors such as laughter and eye contact, with biographical communication also rising, though overall verbal interactions remained statistically unchanged between groups (Table 2).

Table 2. Independent Samples t-Test Results for Verbal and Non-verbal Communication Among Different Groups.

Category		Experimental conditions (mean ± standard deviation)		t	df	p
		Joystick Gaming Group	Proxemics Play Group			
Verbal communication	Game-related communication	0.205± 0.037	0.234±0.059	−1.406	22	0.174
	General biography	0.018± 0.010	0.031±0.018	−2.229	17.121	0.039
	Help seeking	0.062± 0.015	0.060±0.012	0.234	22	0.817
	Help giving	0.101± 0.026	0.096±0.019	0.467	22	0.645
	Verbal communication overall	0.385± 0.057	0.421±0.057	−1.563	22	0.132
Nonverbal communication	Laughing together	0.106± 0.032	0.149±0.062	−2.118	22	0.046
	Eye contact	0.010± 0.006	0.016±0.008	−2.089	22	0.048
	Body contact	0.013± 0.006	0.112±0.024	−13.694	12.526	0.000
	Nonverbal communication overall	0.129± 0.036	0.277±0.072	−6.340	22	0.000

4.3   Hypotheses Test Result

H1 posits that proxemics play enhances intergenerational social experiences beyond traditional methods, a claim supported by social presence analyses. Data indicate an 8.86.

H2 suggests proxemic interactions in family leisure activities boost verbal and non-verbal communication among family members, confirmed through video analysis. Proxemics play significantly increases physical contact and shared laughter, with non-verbal communication time in proxemics play groups rising by 114.73.

These findings validate the effectiveness of proxemics play as a framework for designing intergenerational social games, which positively impact game sociality, and non-verbal communication, demonstrating the viability and potential of proxemics play in enhancing intergenerational social interactions.

5   Discussion and Conclusion

This study explores enhancing family bonds and intergenerational communication via family-oriented games, leveraging proxemics as a novel design approach. It introduces a proxemics play framework, grounded in MDA theory and proxemic principles, to develop a proxemic-based intergenerational social game. The implementation and subsequent user evaluations confirmed the framework's efficacy in fostering game-related sociality and non-verbal interactions among family members.

The investigation targets three-person core family units, achieving theoretical and practical insights. Yet, its focus on university students' families limits its applicability across diverse family configurations, marking an area for future exploration. Notably, the study's experimental design, while controlling for major variables, does not encompass all possible influences on the leisure experience, such as game mechanics, audio-visual elements, and participant preferences. Future research could address these gaps, broadening the understanding and application of proxemics play in family leisure contexts.

References

1. Statistical report on internet development in China, Tech. rep., China Internet Network Information Center (CNNIC) (2022)
2. Argyle, M.: Non-verbal communication in human social interaction. Nonverbal Commun. **2**(1) (1972)
3. Ducheneaut, N., Yee, N., Nickell, E., Moore, R.J.: "Alone together?" exploring the social dynamics of massively multiplayer online games. In: Proceedings of the SIGCHI Conference on Human Factors in Computing Systems, pp. 407–416 (2006)
4. Entertainment Software Association (ESA): 2022 essential facts about the video game industry (2022). https://www.theesa.com/resource/2022-essential-facts-about-the-video-game-industry/. Accessed 1 Nov 2022
5. Granic, I., Lobel, A., Engels, R.C.: The benefits of playing video games. Am. Psychol. **69**(1), 66 (2014)
6. Hall, E.T.: The Hidden Dimension, vol. 20. Anchor Books, New York (1969)
7. Harris, J., Hancock, M.: To asymmetry and beyond! improving social connectedness by increasing designed interdependence in cooperative play. In: Proceedings of the 2019 CHI Conference on Human Factors in Computing Systems, pp. 1–12 (2019)
8. Huizinga, J., Iudens, H.: A Study of the Play Element in Culture. Beacon, Boston (1955)
9. Hunicke, R., LeBlanc, M., Zubek, R., et al.: MDA: a formal approach to game design and game research. In: Proceedings of the AAAI Workshop on Challenges in Game AI. vol. 4, p. 1722. San Jose, CA (2004)

10. Kappen, D.L., Gregory, J., Stepchenko, D., Wehbe, R.R., Nacke, L.E.: Exploring social interaction in co-located multiplayer games. In: CHI 2013 Extended Abstracts on Human Factors in Computing Systems, pp. 1119–1124 (2013)
11. Kaye, L.K.: Understanding the "social" nature of digital games. Entertainment Comput. **38**, 100420 (2021)
12. Khoo, E.T., Merritt, T., Cheok, A.D.: Designing physical and social intergenerational family entertainment. Interact. Comput. **21**(1–2), 76–87 (2009)
13. Marquardt, N., Greenberg, S.: Informing the design of proxemic interactions. IEEE Pervasive Comput. **11**(2), 14–23 (2012)
14. Mueller, F., et al.: Proxemics play: understanding proxemics for designing digital play experiences. In: Proceedings of the 2014 Conference on Designing Interactive Systems, pp. 533–542 (2014)
15. Mueller, F., Gibbs, M.R., Vetere, F., Edge, D.: Designing for bodily interplay in social exertion games. ACM Trans. Comput. Hum. Interact. **24**(3), 1–41 (2017)
16. Osmanovic, S., Pecchioni, L.: Beyond entertainment: motivations and outcomes of video game playing by older adults and their younger family members. Games Cult. **11**(1–2), 130–149 (2016)
17. Osmanovic, S., Pecchioni, L.: Family matters: the role of intergenerational gameplay in successful aging. In: Zhou, J., Salvendy, G. (eds.) ITAP 2016. LNCS, vol. 9755, pp. 352–363. Springer, Cham (2016). https://doi.org/10.1007/978-3-319-39949-2_34
18. Pecchioni, L.L., Osmanovic, S.: Play it again, grandma: effect of intergenerational video gaming on family closeness. In: Zhou, J., Salvendy, G. (eds.) ITAP 2018. LNCS, vol. 10926, pp. 518–531. Springer, Cham (2018). https://doi.org/10.1007/978-3-319-92034-4_39
19. Rack, O., Zahn, C., Mateescu, M.: Coding and counting-frequency analysis for group interaction. In: The Cambridge Handbook of Group Interaction Analysis (2018)
20. Rocha, J.B., Mascarenhas, S., Prada, R.: Game mechanics for cooperative games. ZON Digit. Games **2008**, 72–80 (2008)
21. Shi, J.q.: Independence and Dependence: Intergenerational Relationships of Urban Families in Transitional China. Social Sciences Academic Press, China (2015)
22. Xiao, M.: China family closeness index report, Tech. rep. (2020)
23. Zahn, C., Leisner, D., Niederhauser, M., Roos, A.L., Iseli, T., Soldati, M., et al.: Effects of game mode in multiplayer video games on intergenerational social interaction: randomized field study. JMIR Formative Res. **6**(2), e29179 (2022)

Author Index

A

Aich, Swagatalaxmi   203
Ait Mou, Younss   3
Al Marri, Saeed Mohd H. M.   3
Al-Absi, Hamada R. H.   3
Amaluisa-Rendón, Paulina Magally   66
Amaral, Ângelo   54
Andaló, Flávio   359
Azevedo, Roger   9

B

Berdejo, Javier   75
Blanchard, Nathaniel   203
Bolaños-Pasquel, Mónica   20
Borges, Fabíola   359
Bradford, Mariah   203
Brown, Michael   9

C

Capello, Sophia   9
Castellanos, Amanda J.   279
Chan, Wai Kin   301
Chandan Sashank, Gadepalli   29
Chen, Zhen   135
Chiu, Jen-I   39
Chou, Wen Huei   290
Chou, Yun-Hsuan   279
Chuang, Bing Shuan   290
Cóndor-Herrera, Omar   20
Crawford, Chris   123
Crum, Sibel   48

D

Daoud, Amina   3
de Carvalho Amaral, Carolina   54
Dinh, Anh   75
Dovhalevska, Alina   114

E

Elene Bataliotti, Soellyn   54
Espinosa-Pinos, Carlos Alberto   66

F

Fang, Ke   301, 329, 377
Fernando, Owen Noel Newton   29

G

Gao, Fengsen   301
Garcia, Andrew   75
Go, Gerick Jeremiah Niño N.   312
Guo, Ying   192

H

Hao, Liang   243
Hassan, Jaffer   75
Huang, Wei   348, 388
Huang, Zhiyue   337

J

Jadán-Guerrero, Janio   86
Jocson, Jed Laszlo O.   312
John, Tina   95

K

Kang, NaYeon   103
Kim, Jung Hyup   103
Kim, Soojung   109
Kojić, Tanja   114
Kou, Xiaojing   48
Krishnaswamy, Nikhil   203
Kuo, Pei-Yi Patricia   279
Kurati, Sakyarshi   75
Kurup, Devi G.   3

L

Lee, Chei Sian   143, 156
Lee, Yun Gil   109
Lewis, Myles   123

Li, Andy Tao   259
Li, Belle   48
Li, Ping   329, 337, 377
Li, Qiang   135
Lim, Kok Khiang   143, 156
Lin, Cheng-Jhe   370
Lin, Lin   225
Lin, Zhiyue   321
Ling, Jie   180, 192
Liu, De   259
Liu, Jinrong   192
Liu, Yaxin   169
Llinas, Andrea   9

M
Ma, Guozhang   329, 377
Mao, Yueer   329, 337, 377
Marcayata-Fajardo, Clemencia   20
Margondai, Ancuta   9
Méndez, Elena   86
Miyagi, Mamiko   176
Möller, Anna Lena   95
Möller, Sebastian   114
Motoyama, Aoiko   176

N
Naderi, Evan   9
Nakatoh, Tetsuya   176
Natanson, Hadar   279
Neto, Jacob   359
Nie, Xiaomei   169, 214
Nishihara, Yoko   235

O
Ou Yang, Li   180, 192, 265

P
Patel, Milouni   9
Pu, Xiaoke   348

R
Ramos-Galarza, Carlos   20
Rao, Jian   243
Rodríguez-Ortiz, Noemi Viviana   66
Romeiro, Nicolas C.   359

S
Salomão, André   359
Santhanam, Radhika   259

Schanke, Scott   259
Schneider, Jens   3
Seefried, Ethan   203
Shan, Junjie   235
Shastri, Dvijesh   75
Shi, Chufan   214
Shi, Jingyuan   251
Shoemaker, Katherine A.   75
Shui, Bo   214
Siebert, Caspian   203
Sun, Xing   321
Sun, Yuwen   225

T
Tamayo-Narvaez, Karla   86
Tan, Zong Wei   29
Toyama, Hiroya   235
Tsuei, Mengping   39

U
Ukegawa, Ayana   176

V
Valenzuela, María   86
Vergari, Maurizio   114
Vidal Jr., Eric Cesar E.   312
Vieira, Milton Luiz Horn   359
Voigt-Antons, Jan-Niklas   114

W
Wang, Chian Shing   370
Wang, Yu-Chen   279
Wiedbusch, Megan   9
Wu, Tianqi   135
Wu, Zhiyong   169

X
Xiong, Wei   243

Y
Yang, Yujiu   214
You, Ruoxin   348
Yu, Lin   251

Z
Zaghouani, Wajdi   3
Zandvakili, Ramin   259
Zanini, Letícia Maria Fraporti   359
Zeng, Yuan   337

Zhang, Chu   329, 377
Zhang, Zetao   321
Zhao, Yue   265

Zheng, Hai-Tao   321
Zhou, Yueming   388
Zhuang, Yunyi   180

Printed in the United States
by Baker & Taylor Publisher Services